Information Security Management Handbook

Sixth Edition

VOLUME 2

Information Security Management Handbook

Sixth Edition

VOLUME 2

Edited by

Harold F. Tipton, CISSP · Micki Krause, CISSP

CRC Press
Taylor & Francis Group
Boca Raton London New York

CRC Press is an imprint of the
Taylor & Francis Group, an informa business

AN AUERBACH BOOK

CRC Press
Taylor & Francis Group
6000 Broken Sound Parkway NWSuite 300
Boca Raton, FL 33487-2742

First issued in paperback 2019

© 2008 by Taylor & Francis Group, LLC
CRC Press is an imprint of Taylor & Francis Group, an Informa business

No claim to original U.S. Government works

ISBN-13: 978-1-4200-6708-8 (hbk)
ISBN-13: 978-0-367-38766-2 (pbk)

Library of Congress Cataloging-in-Publication Data

Tipton, Harold F.
    Information security management handbook / Harold F. Tipton, Micki Krause. -- 6th ed.
        p. cm. ((ISC) 2 Press ; 27)
    Includes bibliographical references and index.
    ISBN 1-4200-6708-7
    1. Computer security--Management--Handbooks, manuals, etc. 2. Data protection--Handbooks, manuals, etc. I. Krause, Micki. II. Title.

QA76.9.A25154165 2006
005.8--dc22   2006048504

Visit the Taylor & Francis Web site at
http://www.taylorandfrancis.com

and the CRC Press Web site at
http://www.crcpress.com

Contents

DOMAIN 1: INFORMATION SECURITY AND RISK MANAGEMENT
Security Management Concepts and Principles

Policies, Standards, Procedures, and Guidelines

Risk Management

DOMAIN 2: ACCESS CONTROL
Access Control Techniques

Access Control Administration

Methods of Attack

DOMAIN 3: CRYPTOGRAPHY

DOMAIN 4: PHYSICAL SECURITY
Elements of Physical Security

DOMAIN 5: SECURITY ARCHITECTURE AND DESIGN
Principles of Computer and Network Organizations, Architectures, and Designs

DOMAIN 6: TELECOMMUNICATIONS AND NETWORK SECURITY
Communications and Network Security

Internet, Intranet, and Extranet Security

Network Attacks and Countermeasures

DOMAIN 7: APPLICATION SECURITY
Application Issues

DOMAIN 8: LEGAL, REGULATIONS, COMPLIANCE, AND INVESTIGATION
Information Law

Incident Handling

Preface

Traditionally, the preface for this handbook focuses on the evolving landscape of the security profession, highlighting industry trends such as the burgeoning impact of privacy laws and regulations, emerging technologies that challenge de facto security, or any of the other various and sundry topics *du jour*. This time, we shift the focus.

Information security is an interesting, many times frustrating discipline to institutionalize. The commonly accepted triad—people, process, technology—trips easily off the tongue. However, breaking down the threesome into its subcomponents gives one pause. Information security truly is a complex composite of many fields of study, including sociology, psychology, anthropology, virology, criminology, cryptology, etiology, and technology.

Thus, we give tribute here to those who willingly choose to slay the dragons, oftentimes finding themselves tilting at windmills instead.

Further, and importantly, we want to give tribute to, and underscore the contributions of, our authors.

We can only speculate on what compels an individual to take keyboard in hand in an effort to share information and experiences that will benefit others. And yet, year after year, we have a select community of practitioners and professionals who give their all for the good of the industry.

This volume of the handbook is no exception. The topics featured encompass a broad spectrum of areas, ranging from the fundamentals of access control, malicious software, and network security to more esoteric, but equally important, organizational culture and governance framework discussions. All of the chapters share a common property—they contain gems of information that afford the readers a leg up in their individual efforts to instill adequate and appropriate levels of security within their organizations.

To our readers, Don Quixotes that you are, we wish you good luck and good reading.

And to our authors, we sincerely thank you for your valuable and valued contributions.

Hal Tipton
Micki Krause

Editors

Harold F. Tipton, currently an independent consultant and past president of the (ISC)², was director of computer security for Rockwell International Corporation for about 15 years. He initiated the Rockwell computer and data security program in 1977 and then continued to administer, develop, enhance, and expand the program to accommodate the control needs produced by technological advances until his retirement from Rockwell in 1994.

He has been a member of the ISSA since 1982, was president of the Los Angeles chapter in 1984, and was president of the national organization of ISSA (1987–1989). He was added to the ISSA Hall of Fame and the ISSA Honor Role in 2000.

He was a member of the National Institute for Standards and Technology, Computer and Telecommunications Security Council, and National Research Council Secure Systems Study Committee (for the National Academy of Science).

He has a B.S. in engineering from the U.S. Naval Academy, an M.A. in personnel administration from George Washington University, and a certificate in computer science from the University of California at Irvine. He is a CISSP®, an Information System Security Architecture Professional (ISSAP®), and an Information System Security Management Professional.

He has published several papers on information security issues with Auerbach Publishers (*Handbook of Information Security Management, Data Security Management,* and *Information Security Journal*); National Academy of Sciences (*Computers at Risk*); Data Pro Reports; Elsevier; and ISSA *Access* magazine.

He has been a speaker at all the major information security conferences, including Computer Security Institute, the ISSA Annual Working Conference, the Computer Security Workshop, MIS conferences, AIS Security for Space Operations, DOE Computer Security Conference, National Computer Security Conference, IIA Security Conference, EDPAA, UCCEL Security & Audit Users Conference, and Industrial Security Awareness Conference.

He has conducted/participated in information security seminars for (ISC)², Frost & Sullivan, UCI, CSULB, System Exchange seminars, and the Institute for International Research. He participated in the Ernst & Young video "Protecting Information Assets." He is currently serving as editor of the Auerbach *Handbook of Information Security* publications. He received the Computer Security Institute Lifetime Achievement Award in 1994 and the (ISC)² Hal Tipton Award in 2001.

Micki Krause, M.B.A., CISSP, has held positions in the information security profession for the past 20 years. She is currently the chief information security officer at Pacific Life Insurance Company in Newport Beach, California, where she is accountable for directing the information protection and security program for the enterprise. Pacific Life is the 15th largest life insurance company in the nation and provides life and health insurance products, individual annuities, mutual funds, group employee benefits, and a variety of investment products and services.

Krause was named one of the 25 most influential women in the field of information security by industry peers and *Information Security* magazine as part of their recognition of Women of Vision in the information technology (IT) security field and received the Harold F. Tipton Award in recognition of sustained career excellence and outstanding contributions to the profession.

Micki has held several leadership roles in industry-influential groups including the Information Systems Security Information (ISSA) and the International Information Systems Security Certification Consortium (ISC)$^{2®}$ and is a passionate advocate for professional security leadership.

She is a reputed speaker, published author, and coeditor of the *Information Security Management Handbook* series.

Contributors

Dean R. Bushmiller has had fun for the past 20 years learning and teaching everything he can in technology and security. His consulting experience in accounting systems, inventory control, migrations, and patch management has breathed life into his 12 years in the classroom. Dean is a courseware developer who specializes in CISSP and patch management. He is a member of (ISC)^2, the Information Systems Audit and Control Association (ISACA), and the Center for Internet Security. He is proud to be a recipient of both the DISA/FSO and the Air Force 92IOS mission coins. Very little of this would have been possible without Helaine— a partner, friend, and wife.

Tom Carlson is a certified ISO 27001 auditor and a recognized expert on information security standards and programs. His background spans diverse environments, including national security, academia, private enterprise, and Antarctic research, encompassing design, development, deployment, operations, and knowledge transfer. Throughout his career, Tom has worked with multiple government agencies on a variety of mission critical projects, as well as security solutions for the private sector. His area of expertise is in information security management systems and risk management. Tom holds a BS in electrical engineering as well as various education and industry certifications.

Glenn J. Cater has over 14 years experience in IT covering information security, software development, and IT management. Glenn currently holds the position of director of IT risk consulting at Aon Consulting. In this role, Glenn supports Aon's electronic discovery services, high-tech investigations, and IT security consulting practices. Glenn joined Aon from Lucent Technologies, where he held management positions in Lucent's internal IT security team and Lucent Worldwide Services consulting group. Before joining Lucent, Glenn had begun his career as a software engineer at British Aerospace working on military systems.

Jeff Davis, CISSP, CISM, has been working in the information security area for the past 15 years. He is currently a senior manager for IT global security operations at Alcatel–Lucent. He is responsible for IT security architecture as well as operations of network intrusion detection and prevention, security compliance, and threat evaluation. He also consults on risk assessment and security governance and has worked with Bell Labs on evaluating and implementing new security initiatives. He holds a bachelor's degree in electrical engineering and a master's degree in computer science from Stevens Institute of Technology.

Scott Erkonen is principal and director of client relationships for Hot Skills, Inc. He is the U.S. International Representative to ISO JTC1/SC27 INCITS CS/1 Cyber Security. He successfully led one of the first ISO 27001 certifications in the U.S.

Todd Fitzgerald, CISSP, CISA, CISM, serves as a Medicare systems security officer for National Government Services, LLC (NGS), Milwaukee, Wisconsin, which is the nation's largest processor of Medicare claims and a subsidiary of WellPoint, Inc., the nation's largest health insurer.

Todd was named as a finalist for the 2005 Midwest Information Security Executive (ISE) of the Year Award, nominee for the national award, and judge for the 2006 central region awards and has moderated several ISE Executive Roundtables in 2006. Todd is the co-author of *CISO Leadership: Essential Principles for Success*, and has authored articles on information security for *The 2007 Official (ISC)² Guide to the CISSP Exam, Information Security Magazine, The Information Security Handbook, The HIPAA Program Reference Book, Managing an Information Security and Privacy Awareness and Training Program*, and several other security-related publications. Todd is also a member of the editorial board for *(ISC)² Journal, Information Systems Security Magazine*, and the Darkreading.com security publication and is frequently called upon to present at international, national, and local conferences. Todd serves on the board of directors for the Health Insurance Portability and Accountability Act (HIPAA) Collaborative of Wisconsin and is an active leader, participant, and presenter in multiple industry associations such as ISSA, Blue Cross Blue Shield Information Security Advisory Group, CMS/Gartner Security Best Practices Group, Workgroup for Electronic Data Interchange, ISACA, Executive Alliance Information Security Executive Roundtables, and others.

Todd has 28 years of IT experience, including 20 years of management. Prior to joining NGS, Todd held various broad-based senior IT management positions for Fortune 500 organizations such as American Airlines, IMS Health, Zeneca (subsidiary of AstraZeneca Pharmaceuticals), and Syngenta as well as prior positions with Blue Cross Blue Shield of Wisconsin.

Todd holds a BS in business administration from the University of Wisconsin at LaCrosse and an MBA with highest honors from Oklahoma State University.

Robby S. Fussell, MS, CISSP, GSEC, CCSE, NSA IAM, is an information security/assurance manager for AT&T Government Solutions. Robby has been working in the IT/Security field for the past 13 years and has authored numerous topics in the security realm. His career has taken him through the areas of security in both the public and private sectors. Robby is currently completing his PhD in the area of cascading failures within scale-free networks.

Nick Halvorson is recognized for his expertise in information security, risk assessment, and management consulting. Currently, Nick is a senior consultant for Hotskills, Inc., specializing in information security and management consulting.

His experience includes the development of risk management strategies, process implementation, and security management solutions. His efforts have led directly to the creation of several information security management systems and formal certification under ISO 27001:2005.

Nick holds a bachelor of science in computer information systems from Dakota State University, Madison. His professional certifications include CISSP and ISO 27001 Certified Lead Auditor among others. He is considered an expert in ISO 17799, ISO 27001, and various other technical disciplines. He currently resides in South Dakota.

Sasan Hamidi, PhD, CISSP, CISA, CISM, has been involved with information security for the past 20 years. He is currently the chief information security officer for Interval International, Inc., the leading global timeshare exchange company, where he is also involved with electronic privacy matters. Prior to joining Interval, Sasan was the director of enterprise architecture and security at General Electric Power Systems and senior project manager for IBM Network Security Services, where he was involved with the overall security assessment of IBM's global networks.

Sasan's area of interest and research is steganography, emergence, chaos, and complexity as they apply to network security. It is on these topics that he regularly speaks and has published several articles.

Paul A. Henry, MCP+I, MCSE, CCSA, CCSE, CFSA, CFSO, CISSP, CISM, CISA, ISSAP, CIFI, is one of the world's foremost global information security experts, with more than 20 years of experience managing security initiatives for Global 2000 enterprises and government organizations worldwide.

At Secure Computing®, Henry plays a key strategic role in launching new products and retooling existing product lines. In his role as vice president of technology evangelism, Henry also advises and consults on some of the world's most challenging and high-risk information security projects, including the National Banking System in Saudi Arabia; the U.S. Department of Defense's Satellite Data Project; and both government and telecommunications projects throughout Japan.

Henry is frequently cited by major and trade print publications as an expert on both technical security topics and general security trends and serves as an expert commentator for network broadcast outlets such as NBC and CNBC. In addition, Henry regularly authors thought leadership articles on technical security issues, and his expertise and insight help shape the editorial direction of key security publications such as the *Information Security Management Handbook,* for which he is a regular contributor.

Paul serves as a featured and keynote speaker at network security seminars and conferences worldwide, delivering presentations on diverse topics including network access control, cybercrime, distributed denial-of-service attack risk mitigation, firewall architectures, computer and network forensics, enterprise security architectures, and managed security services.

Rebecca Herold, CIPP, CISSP, CISA, CISM, FLMI, is an information privacy, security and compliance consultant, author, and instructor with her own company since mid-2004, Rebecca Herold, LLC. She has over 16 years of privacy and information security experience, and assists organizations in various industries throughout the world with all aspects of their information privacy, security, and regulatory compliance programs. Rebecca was instrumental in building the information security and privacy program while at Principal Financial Group, which was recognized as the 1998 CSI Information Security Program of the Year. In October 2007, Rebecca was named one of the "Best Privacy Advisers" in two of the three categories by *Computerworld* magazine. Rebecca was also named one of the "Top 59 Influencers in IT Security" for 2007 by *IT Security* magazine. Rebecca is an adjunct professor for the Norwich University master of science in information assurance program.

Rebecca has authored or coauthored many books and is currently authoring her eleventh. Some of them include *The Privacy Papers* (Auerbach, 2001), *The Practical Guide to HIPAA Privacy and Security Compliance* (Auerbach, 2003), *Managing an Information Security and Privacy Awareness and Training Program* (Auerbach, 2005), the *Privacy Management Toolkit* (Information Shield, 2006), and coauthored *Say What You Do* (2007). Rebecca is the editor and primary contributing author for *Protecting Information*, which is a quarterly security and privacy awareness multimedia publication by Information Shield. She has also authored chapters for dozens of books along with over 100 other published articles. She has been writing a monthly information privacy column for the CSI *Alert* newsletter since 2001, and regularly contributes articles to other publications as well. Rebecca has a BS in math and computer science and an MA in computer science and education.

George J. Jahchan graduated in 1980 as an electrical engineer from McGill University in Montreal, Canada. He has been in various personal-computer-related positions for over 25 years, of which six related to gateway security and three were as a security officer in a university. He currently works as a senior security and enterprise systems management consultant in the Levant, North Africa, and Pakistan with CA. He holds CISA, CISM, and BS7799-2 Lead Auditor certifications.

Kenneth J. Knapp is an assistant professor of management at the U.S. Air Force Academy. He received his PhD in 2005 from Auburn University, Auburn, Alabama. His research focuses on topics related to information security effectiveness and has been published in numerous outlets including *Information Systems Management, Information Systems Security, Communications of the AIS, Information Management & Computer Security, International Journal of Information Security and Privacy, Journal of Digital Forensics, Security, and Law,* as well as the 2007 edition of the *Information Security Management Handbook* edited by Tipton and Krause.

Franjo Majstor holds an electrical engineering degree from the Faculty of Electrical Engineering and Computing, University of Zagreb, Croatia, and a master of science degree from the Department of Computer Sciences, Faculty of Science, University of Leuven, Belgium. He started his career in the IT industry in 1989 at Iskra Computers and NIL Ltd. in Slovenia. He was with Cisco Systems, Inc., in Belgium from 1995 to 2004, and Fortinet, Inc., until 2005; since 2006 he has been with CipherOptics, Inc.

As EMEA senior technical director at CipherOptics, Inc., he is responsible for driving to market the latest generation of data-protection solutions. Previously, as technical director at Fortinet, Inc., he was responsible for security products and solutions based on the modern perimeter security architecture, whereas at Cisco Systems, Inc., he was recognized as a trusted advisor throughout the EMEA for the leading security projects. He achieved a CCIE certification from Cisco Systems, Inc., in 1995 and CISSP certification from (ISC)² in 2000. Franjo is also an external CISSP instructor at the (ISC)² international vendor neutral nonprofit organization for certification of information security professionals and is a mentor and recognized lecturer of an ICT Audit and Security postgraduate study joint program between ULB, UCL, and Solvay Business School in Brussels, Belgium.

As a recognized security professional, Franjo is also a frequent speaker at worldwide conferences on network security topics. Most relevant so far were NetSec (New Orleans, 2001), IPSec Summit and IPv6 Global Summit (Paris, 2002), ISSE (Vienna, 2003), IEEE (Bonn, 2003), RSA Security (Paris, 2002; Amsterdam, 2003; Barcelona, 2004; San Francisco, 2005; San Jose, 2006; Nice, 2006), and IDC (London, 2004; Prague, 2005). For the RSA Security 2005 conference, he was invited as an independent judge for the Perimeter Defense Track paper selections.

George G. McBride, CISSP, CISM, is a senior manager in the Enterprise Risk Services group at Deloitte & Touche, LLP, in New York City and has worked in the network security industry for more than 14 years. Before joining Deloitte, George was with Aon Consulting, Lucent Technologies, and Global Integrity. George has focused on the financial and telecommunications industry and has supported risk management, secure network architecture development, technology risk assessments, and more. He has spoken at MIS, RSA, (ISC)², and other conferences worldwide on a wide variety of topics such as penetration testing, risk assessments, Voice-over-IP and telephony security, and mobile data security. He has contributed to *The Black Book on Corporate Security* and *Securing IP Converged Networks,* hosted several Webcasts, and contributed to several editions of the *Information Security Management Handbook.*

R. Scott McCoy, CPP, CISSP, CBCP, is the chief security officer for Alliant Techsystems. He has 23 years of security experience, starting as an Army explosive ordnance disposal technician. He also has 12 years of security management experience in five critical infrastructures.

David McPhee is an information security manager for a financial services provider in Milwaukee, Wisconsin. He has over 18 years experience in the information security profession, with an extensive background in such diverse security issues as risk assessment and management, security policy development, security architecture, infrastructure and perimeter security design, outsource relationship security, business continuity, and information technology auditing. David began his career in Canada, as a senior security analyst for eight years with the Atlantic Lottery Corporation, in Moncton, New Brunswick. He moved to the United States in 1998, working as a firewall consultant in St. Louis, Missouri. He joined his current employer in 1998 as a senior UNIX security analyst. Since 2000, he has held a management role within information security, and is currently managing the infrastructure support team.

R. Franklin Morris, Jr., is an assistant professor of management information systems at The Citadel in Charleston, South Carolina. He received his PhD in management information systems from Auburn University, Auburn, Alabama. He holds an MBA from Georgia Southern University and a bachelor of science in aerospace engineering from Georgia Institute of Technology. Morris has more than 20 years of experience working in private industry and has published his work in *Communications of the AIS*.

Ralph Spencer Poore is chief scientist and principal for Innové Labs LP. He has over 30 years of information technology experience with emphasis on high-assurance systems, applied cryptography, financial and fusion intelligence, information forensic investigations, cyber-terrorism, transnational border data flows, information assurance, audit and control, and enabling technologies. He was cited for his major contribution to the *Guideline for Information Valuation* and for his service as president of (ISC)². Poore is an inventor, author, and frequent speaker on topics ranging from privacy in electronic commerce to transnational border data flows. Poore worked closely with the GLBA, HIPAA, and Sarbanes–Oxley rollouts for a Fortune 400 company.

Poore is a Certified Fraud Examiner, Certified Information Systems Auditor, CISSP, Qualified Security Assessor, and is certified in Homeland Security-Level III.

Sean M. Price, CISA, CISSP, is an independent information security consultant residing in Northern Virginia. He provides security consulting and architecture services to commercial and government entities. Price has more than 12 years of information security experience, which consists of system security administration, user information assurance training, policy and procedure development, security plan development, security testing and evaluation, and security architect activities. His academic background includes a bachelor's degree in accounting and business, a master's degree in information systems, and he is currently pursuing doctoral studies in computer information systems. He has previously contributed to the *Information Security Management Handbook*, the *Official (ISC)² Guide to the CISSP CBK*, and the IEEE *Computer* magazine. His areas of interest in security research include access control, information flow, insider threat, and machine learning.

Edward Ray is president of NetSec Design & Consulting, Inc., which specializes in computer, data, and network security and secure network design. Specific areas of expertise include implementation of defense in-depth layered security solutions utilizing Cisco, Juniper, Tipping Point, Windows, UNIX, Linux, Free/OpenBSD, Novell, and Mac-based hardware and software; PKI/Kerberos/LDAP implementation on Windows 2003/XP/Linux; intrusion detection and analysis; wired and wireless penetration testing and vulnerability analysis; HIPAA security and privacy rule implementation; and wired and wireless PC & network security design (802.11 a/b/g/i). Ray has an MS in electrical engineering from the University of California at Los Angeles (1997) and a BS in electrical engineering from Rutgers University (1990) and holds the CISSP, GCIA, GCIH, and MCSE professional certifications.

Marcus K. Rogers, PhD, CISSP, CCCI, is the head of the Cyber Forensics Program in the Department of Computer and Information Technology at Purdue University. He is a professor and a research faculty member at the Center for Education and Research in Information Assurance and Security. Dr. Rogers was a senior instructor for (ISC)², the international body that certifies information system security professionals (CISSP), is a member of the quality assurance board for (ISC)²'s SCCP designation, and is international chair of the Law, Compliance, and Investigation Domain of the Common Body of Knowledge Committee. He is a former police detective who worked in the area of fraud and computer crime investigations. Dr. Rogers is the editor-in-chief of the *Journal of Digital Forensic Practice* and sits on the editorial board for several other professional journals. He is also a member of various national and international committees focusing on digital forensic science and digital evidence. Dr. Rogers is the author of numerous book chapters and journal publications in the fields of digital forensics and applied psychological analysis. His research interests include applied cyber-forensics, psychological digital crime scene analysis, and cyber-terrorism.

Ben Rothke, CISSP, CISM, is a New York City–based senior security consultant with BT INS and has over 15 years of industry experience in information systems security and privacy.

His areas of expertise are in risk management and mitigation, public key infrastructure (PKI), security and privacy regulatory issues, design and implementation of systems security, encryption, cryptography, and security policy development. Prior to joining INS, Ben was with AXA, Baltimore Technologies, Ernst & Young, and Citicorp and has provided security solutions to many Fortune 500 companies.

Ben is the author of *Computer Security: 20 Things Every Employee Should Know* (McGraw-Hill) and a contributing author to *Network Security: The Complete Reference* (Osborne), and *The Handbook of Information Security Management* (Auerbach). He writes a monthly security book review for *Security Management* and is a former columnist for *Information Security, Unix Review,* and *Solutions Integrator* magazines.

Ben is also a frequent speaker at industry conferences such as the Computer Security Institute (CSI), RSA, MISTI, NetSec, and ISACA and is a CISSP and Certified Information Security Manager (CISM). He is a member of HTCIA, ISSA, ISACA, ASIS, CSI, and InfraGard.

Don Saracco, Ed.D., joined MLC & Associates, Inc., in 1997 with over 25 years experience in human resource and organizational development in manufacturing, health care, and government organizations as a manager and consultant. His background includes the design and delivery of corporate education and training as well as executive coaching, facilitation of organizational change, and process improvement. In addition, he has served as an adjunct faculty member for a state university and a private business school.

Don served for several years as a faculty member of the Business Recovery Managers Symposium presented by the MIS Institute. His speaking credits include Business Continuity Planning and Y2K Preparedness workshops for the International Quality & Productivity Center in Atlanta, Georgia; Orlando, Florida; and Las Vegas, Nevada; and the 4th International Conference on Corporate Earthquake Programs in Shizuoka, Japan, as well as the annual *Contingency Planning and Management Magazine* Conference and Exposition. In addition, Don has presented papers at national and international conferences sponsored by the International Society for Performance Improvement, the Association for Quality and Participation, RIMS, and Continuity Insights. He has also worked as an adjunct faculty member in graduate business programs at two accredited universities.

Derek Schatz, CISSP, is currently the lead security architect for network systems at Boeing Commercial Airplanes. He has been in information security for over 10 years in both enterprise and consulting roles, including a stint in the Big 5. He has spoken at a number of conferences besides teaching information security. He holds a bachelor's degree in economics from the University of California at Irvine.

Craig A. Schiller CISSP-ISSMP, ISSAP serves as chief information security officer of Portland State University and as the president of Hawkeye Security Training, LLC.

He has worked in the computer industry for the past 27 years. For 17 of those years, he worked as an information security professional.

Craig is the primary author of *Botnets: The Killer Web App*, which is the first book published on the subject of botnets. He is known and respected in the security industry as the primary author of the first publicly distributed version of the GSSP, now known as the Generally Accepted Information Security Principles. He has published 12 chapters in various security books, including several previous editions of the *Information Security Management Handbook*.

Craig is a volunteer police reserve specialist for the Hillsboro Police Department. He is the organizer of volunteers for their Police to Business Program.

Craig led the development of the NASA Mission Operations AIS Security Engineering team and founded NASA's Technology for Information Security conference. He is a cofounder of two ISSA chapters.

E. Eugene Schultz, PhD, CISM, CISSP, is the chief technology officer and chief information security officer at High Tower Software, a company that develops security event management software. He is the author/coauthor of five books: the first on UNIX security, the second on Internet security, the third on Windows NT/2000 security, the fourth on incident response, and the latest on intrusion detection and prevention. He has also published over 110 papers. Dr. Schultz is the editor-in-chief of *Computers and Security* and is an associate editor of *Network Security* and the *Information Security Bulletin*. He is also a member of the editorial board for the *SANS NewsBites*, a weekly information security-related news update, and is on the technical advisory board of two companies. He has been professor of computer science at various universities and is retired from the University of California at Berkeley. He has received the NASA Technical Excellence Award, the Department of Energy Excellence Award, the ISSA Professional Achievement and Honor Roll Awards, the ISACA John Kuyers Best Speaker/Best Conference Contributor Award, the Vanguard Conference Top Gun Award (for best presenter) twice, the Vanguard Chairman's Award, and the National Information Systems Security Conference Best Paper Award. Additionally, Eugene has been elected to the ISSA Hall of Fame. While at Lawrence Livermore National Laboratory he founded and managed the U.S. Department of Energy's Computer Incident Advisory Capability. He is also one of the founders of the Forum of Incident Response and Security Teams. Dr. Schultz has provided expert testimony before committees within the U.S. Senate and House of Representatives on various security-related issues and has served as an expert witness in legal cases.

Robert M. Slade is an information security and management consultant from North Vancouver, British Columbia, Canada.

His initial research into computer viral programs developed into the writing and reviewing of security books and eventually into conducting review seminars for CISSP candidates. He also promotes the Community Security Education project, attempting to promote security awareness for the general public as a means of reducing overall information security threats.

Samantha Thomas is the CSO at a $290-billion financial regulatory organization in the United States. Thomas is a founding board member of the University of California at Davis Network Security Certification Program, and she has developed curricula for universities, institutes, and private industries. She is a regularly requested international keynote and think tank facilitator. Thomas has been a featured speaker in five European Union countries, South Africa, Australia, Mexico, and Papua New Guinea. Her writings, interviews, and quotations are published in international newspapers, magazines, and books. Thomas creates and provides "online safety" for K–8 children, parents, and school administrators. She is a U.S. Executive Alliance Information Security Executive of the Year (Western Region) nominee.

Guy Vancollie is the MD EMEA for CipherOptics, leading provider of data protection solutions. Prior to joining CipherOptics, Guy was the CMO for Ubizen and an evangelist in the emerging space of managed security services. Earlier in his career, he managed both U.S. field marketing and international marketing for RSA Security, was director of EMEA marketing for AltaVista Internet Software, and held several positions with Digital Equipment Corp.

Vancollie has spoken on Internet and security topics at conferences such as IT Asia and CommunicAsia, EEMA, and IMC, as well as Gartner Sector 5, Infosecurity Europe, and the RSA Conference.

Vancollie earned an MS degree in electrical engineering *magna cum laude* from the State University of Ghent in Belgium, a degree in management from the Vlerick School of Management, and an MBA from the MIT Sloan School.

INFORMATION SECURITY AND RISK MANAGEMENT

Security Management Concepts and Principles

Chapter 1

Integrated Threat Management

George G. McBride

Contents

Integrated threat management (ITM) is the evolution of stand-alone security products into a single, unified solution that is generally cheaper and easier to implement and maintain. Combine a single console for management, updates, reports, and metrics, and you will wonder why you do not have one at home too. This chapter will introduce what an ITM solution is, the benefits and drawbacks of the solution, what to look for, and how to select a solution. Finally, the chapter will wrap up with some lessons learned to help avoid some of the common pitfalls and gaps in a typical ITM solution.

Introduction

One cannot read an information security magazine or attend a trade show without hearing about ITM. Within the same magazine or across the aisle, the next vendor may be advertising "unified threat management" or even perhaps "universal threat management." What these are, what the benefits to an organization are, what to look for when evaluating solutions, and lessons learned are discussed in this chapter. Even if you have no intention today of deploying an integrated or unified solution, this chapter provides you with a solid background to understand thoroughly and leverage this emerging technology in the future.

Integrated, unified, and universal threat management all have much the same implementations and goals; their names are different only because they were chosen by different vendors. For the sake of consistency within this chapter, we will choose to use the phrase "integrated threat management."

To start, let us examine the definition of ITM and what it brings to the enterprise. First, ITM is focused on threats that may affect an organization. A threat is defined as some entity that may be capable of attacking or affecting the organization's infrastructure. When used in a quantitative manner, the threat component also includes likelihood and impact considerations as well. Perhaps it is a malicious payload carried via Hypertext Transfer Protocol or via e-mail, or perhaps it is a "0-day" virus not yet seen by an antivirus software manufacturer. It may be a phishing site and the accompanying e-mails inviting users to visit the site to verify their account information or it may be a polymorphic worm whose purpose is to evade firewalls while continuously morphing its signature as it attacks the next target.

An ITM platform should, by definition, protect an enterprise against all of these threats and provide a platform to monitor and manage the ITM. To address these threats, the platform may include the following functions:

■ An intrusion detection system (IDS) or an intrusion prevention system (IPS)
■ Antivirus solution
■ Antispyware solution
■ Unsolicited commercial e-mail filtering
■ Content filtering that includes e-mail and instant messenger content management
■ Uniform resource locator (URL) filtering, which may include serving as a Web cache proxy
■ Firewalls
■ Virtual private network (VPN) connectivity

It is important to note that in the absence of a defined standard for ITM, almost any product with an integrated (unified) combination of functions listed here can and likely has been called an ITM solution. Fortunately, if you follow the steps identified under "Evaluating an ITM Solution," you will learn how to identify and include the components that are important and relevant to your ITM requirements.

What Is an ITM?

The ITM platform is an extension to the information security life cycle within a typical organization. As you may recall, a number of organizations typically started with very rudimentary (compared to today's standards) IDS capabilities that complemented an existing firewall solution at the perimeter. Some number of IDS personnel actively monitored a number of consoles for anomalies and reacted accordingly based on the alarms produced by the consoles. As the technology matured, a more effective and valuable event correlation function developed that allowed us to see longer term, more sophisticated and professional style attacks. Somewhat concurrent with the advancements in event correlation came IPSs, which allowed connections that either the user or the system determined to be a threat to the system's environment to be actively shut down. The ITM platform is the next stage of evolution, by which one can monitor and manage not only firewall and IDS data, but all security appliances.

It is important to note the similarities, as well as the functional differences, between an ITM program and an effective enterprise risk management (ERM) program, which are different, but complementary, programs. Recall that the function to calculate risk can be defined as

$$\text{Risk (asset)} = \frac{T \bullet V}{C}$$

where T is the threat, V the vulnerability, and C the control or safeguard employed to protect the asset. The asset need not be a single system, but can be a collection of systems grouped by function (such as the Human Resources systems or all e-mail servers), by physical or logical location (such as New Jersey or systems in the corporate demilitarized zone), or even by system administrators or groups of users.

An ERM program is a continuously measured enterprisewide view of the risks affecting an organization. A properly implemented ERM program identifies and measures the risks from perspectives such as financial, operational, reputational, and strategy. One of the most dynamic aspects of enterprise risk is the operational component, as it includes the logical and physical security risks of an organization. Having an effective ITM program provides a component of the many inputs required to support a successful ERM program. Although it is quite possible to have a successful ERM program without an ITM program, it significantly simplifies the collection and management of data to support one aspect of the program.

Returning to the ITM discussion, the platform as such does not require that all components be manufactured by the same company, but rather the components have their life-cycle activities consolidated. These activities include the following:

- Implementation and deployment
- Management
- Reporting
- Maintenance
- Updates

Rarely does a single manufacturer produce a best-in-class product in each area that it attempts. As we will see, an ITM solution may include components from several manufacturers utilizing a completely separate third-party integration tool or it may include using the management of several components to serve as its integrated solution. Alternatively, an organization may choose to develop its own integrated solution, relying on the framework of the individual components to satisfy its needs.

As has been presented here, an ITM solution typically integrates several IT security components within the infrastructure. Consider the simplified network diagram shown in Figure 1.1, which highlights the IT security components of a typical organization.

There are equally viable architectures that could support an ITM program. In this situation, the firewall, VPN, antispyware, antivirus software, and IDS solution are individual solutions and are managed individually. One typical solution is shown in Figure 1.2.

As a typical ITM solution, the functions identified in the traditional solution in Figure 1.2 are combined into a single, integrated solution. It is quite possible, and in fact quite likely, that a typical ITM architecture may include two ITM devices to support high availability and load-balancing requirements. The primary components of an ITM solution are the management functions, the individual engines, event data, and configuration data of the ITM solution.

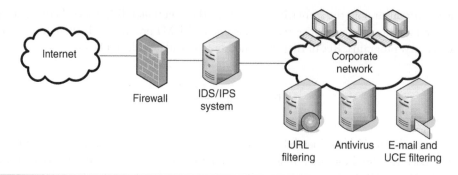

Figure 1.1 Traditional IT security components.

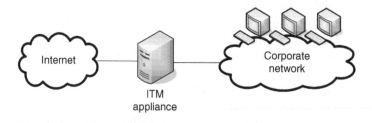

Figure 1.2 Typical ITM solution.

The management of an ITM solution is one of the most critical functions of the solution, as IT support personnel will need to manage and maintain the system. The ITM management functions should be a cohesive and tightly integrated module that includes the following:

■ A dashboard that clearly shows the overall operating efficiency, critical events, and ITM functions that require attention and action and can be customized to the individual conducting the monitoring
■ The ability to run queries that may be predefined by the vendor or ad hoc queries defined by the organization
■ The ability to throttle traffic or reallocate processing capability to prioritize traffic or functions
■ The ability to assign and manage user accounts and roles and responsibilities
■ The ability to support multiple concurrent sessions to manage and monitor the device and events

The maintenance and update functions within the management component should focus on the maintenance of the ITM platform, including interfaces to the database backups, restoration, and repair. This is quite important and should also include provisions for archiving of data, and more importantly, an effective method of recalling and viewing the archived data. For example, if we need to recall the data from four months ago that has been archived to tape and stored off-site, a valuable feature of the ITM platform would be the identification of which particular tapes we need to recall and then an easy way to view the data once it has been recalled.

The core of an ITM solution is the processing engines that do the work. The antivirus engine, the firewall engine, and perhaps the reporting engine are the foundation of the solution and are utilized by the management function to provide an integrated solution. Whether the engines are single or multiple processors, shared or independent, commercial or proprietary; the customer is typically concerned about making sure that his or her requirements are satisfied during regular and peak periods.

One of the most useful and desirable benefits of an integrated solution is the correlation of the data collected and analyzed across the engines. Consider an innocent-looking e-mail message that would typically pass through an antivirus server. If the message has an HTML-based attachment that includes a Trojan or other malicious payload, an integrated solution can utilize a combination of antivirus, antispyware, unsolicited commercial e-mail filtering, and other security engines to detect the blended threat and block it from entering the network.

As part of the correlation functionality of an ITM, the management console can typically identify threats across a wider range of types of attacks, which can result in a more efficient response and can also look at the destination of more than one type of attack (such as firewall and antivirus messages) to develop an appropriate response to ensure that the organization's assets are appropriately protected.

In both examples, it is the combination of data from multiple sources that allows the analysis of aggregated data typically not detectable from a single vantage point. It is important to note, however, that most ITM solutions focus on the active protection of the organization rather than serving as a complete security event management (SEM) system. For those organizations, the adoption of a more robust SEM solution that takes input from the ITM may be preferable, as its core strength is the correlation and analysis of the data.

There is typically a database engine that focuses on maintaining the events that are detected and generated by the ITM solution. Depending on user preferences stored in the configuration database, an almost unlimited combination of events may be logged, stored, or analyzed. Some examples include

- Packets dropped by the firewall
- VPN users that were successfully authenticated and connected to the intranet
- Messages sent via e-mail that contained a predefined pattern and were logged in accordance with the requirements
- Sources of unsolicited commercial e-mail messages

The database may be a proprietary solution that can be accessed only through interfaces provided by the vendor or may not be directly accessible at all. Some vendors utilize commercially available databases on separate systems for scalability and flexibility issues that also may come with or without appropriate interfaces and may or may not require additional tuning and maintenance.

The engines and management console typically rely on a configuration database that maintains user preferences, user accounts and roles and responsibilities, and other system configuration information. This is the information that maintains the current state (and sometimes past state for rollback) of the system. Depending on the level of integration by the vendor, the ITM solution may provide a unified console to manage the configuration information but may utilize one or more databases to store the information.

It should be extensible. An ITM platform should include functions to support the implementation and deployment of additional components. For example, the inclusion of data and metrics from the desktop antivirus solution should not require a complete rewrite of the code, but perhaps an incremental additional licensing cost. A well-designed ITM console should provide a documented and supported interface to devices and other platforms and be capable of accepting, correlating, and analyzing the data that they provide.

The extensibility of the ITM solution should not be exclusive to the front-end or "input" side, but should also include the back-end or "output" side. Many organizations may utilize the ITM solution and the built-in tools to generate alerts to appropriate persons that will conduct further investigations or obtain additional data. Some organizations may wish to use the ITM solution as an input to their dispatching or trouble ticket system. Depending on the organization's requirements, how and what the ITM solution produces may need to be evaluated and be part of the decision-making criteria.

One of the most important functions of an ITM platform from a senior management perspective will be the development of metrics and reports that highlight the overall effectiveness (or ineffectiveness) of the ITM platform. Typical metrics include the following:

- New threats identified
- Total threats encountered
- Effectiveness of managing new threats
- Trouble tickets generated
- Trouble tickets closed
- Coffees consumed while troubleshooting the ITM appliance

Well, OK, the last one was thrown in as a joke, but it should be realized that although metrics are important to the ITM platform and the organization, one should not get carried away in creating numbers for the sake of creating numbers. Metrics and reports should be generated to identify areas of the ITM program that need improvement or require some additional action to support, to measure progress, and, very important, to measure compliance to existing corporate policies and regulations.

An effective ITM solution is more than just the box and some tools to manage it. Although a separate IT security program focused on the ITM solution may not be necessary (but quite helpful), integration of the ITM solution into the existing security program is necessary. An effective program should address the following areas:

- Responsibilities of the various roles required to support and monitor the solution.
- Appropriate training and required qualifications for the various roles.
- How the system is updated (including testing) with patches, datafile updates, operating system updates, etc.
- Processes to request, review, approve, and implement changes, such as firewall rule changes and content monitoring criteria.
- All required policies, practices, standards, and procedures to support and monitor the solution. It is very important that the implementation of an ITM solution include a review or creation of a policy so that associates know what activities are monitored and logged.
- What system parameters and characteristics are monitored and included in the metrics and reports. How the metrics and reporting data are used to drive efficiency and effectiveness into the ITM solution should be addressed.
- How reports and alerts are reacted to, managed, and ultimately closed after being resolved. The ITM program should address the interface, if any is required, between the ITM solution and any system used to facilitate a response to a threat that is detected.

This is not an inclusive list of the components of an ITM solution but serves as a foundation to develop a program that can grow and adapt as necessary. Finally, the program also serves to help drive and support IT governance by ensuring that the ITM program (including all required documentation, monitoring, reaction to events, etc.) is fully operational and receiving the required support by upper management.

The ITM program should also include an IT security assessment of the implementation to measure the compliance with industry best practices and organizational policies. The assessment should review the ITM appliance or infrastructure to identify any vulnerabilities introduced, it should review the rules implemented within the ITM, and it should validate that the rules are being properly evaluated and processed by the ITM device. Finally, as part of the ITM program, assessments and audits of the ITM infrastructure should be scheduled on a regular basis.

Pros and Cons of an ITM Solution

There are a number of benefits to the deployment and implementation of a successful ITM program. Those benefits include consolidation, which typically drives cost and complexity, ease of management, and integrated reporting. The benefits of an ITM solution are not without a few drawbacks, which may include a lack of flexibility and potential performance issues if not scaled properly.

One of the most obvious and visible benefits of an ITM solution, and one of the most prevalent arguments made by ITM vendors, is the consolidation of a number of components and functions into a single, unified solution. Combining multiple functions into a single solution, and potentially a single appliance, will likely provide initial and ongoing cost savings.

Initial "capital" costs of an ITM solution are traditionally less than the costs of the individual components that comprise the ITM solution. Costs associated with vendor negotiations and licensing can be reduced from five or six vendors to a single ITM vendor. Additionally, the price of the appliance is typically substantially less than the sum of the components, through economies of scale and the use of common hardware and software. Likewise, the maintenance costs of a single appliance or solution are generally less than those of the separate components, which increases cost savings continuously over the product's life.

In the future, when the company needs another function provided by the ITM solution, it can be as simple as generating a purchase order and installing a license key that was received via e-mail. That alone often saves weeks of time and quite a bit of money for the organization. Although new policies and inputs may be needed, rearchitecting the network and lengthy vendor evaluation and negotiations will likely not be needed.

An often overlooked factor in cost savings is the cost to house the components in the data center. Just like traditional real estate costs, some organizations bill back data center costs to the business. Consider the significant reduction in costs, moving from several boxes consuming rack space to a single unit with comparable functions. Additionally, overall power consumption will be reduced, as will the cooling costs, two important factors today in data center costs. To a data center that is already at maximum capacity with existing equipment, being able to retrofit several devices to a single solution or the addition of a single box that previously would have needed half of a rack is a tremendous advantage. Adding an additional equipment rack or maintaining equipment in multiple locations adds additional costs, complexity, and overhead.

Having a single console to manage will reduce the amount of time required to maintain and manage the infrastructure. Although it is imperative to ensure that all components are regularly updated with any appropriate signatures such as antivirus and antispyware data files, equally important are the updates at the system level. Maintaining the operating system and application updates on one system will require less time and money than maintaining the updates on several systems.

Consider the benefits of deploying an ITM solution at each branch office or location when the equipment, maintenance, and management costs are multiplied across the organization. Additionally, whether conducting an audit or an assessment at one location or each of the branch offices, having one console to measure compliance and conduct audits and assessments will be tremendously useful and beneficial to the organization.

A unified console to manage the ITM components also requires less training and shorter timeframes for employees to learn and understand. Many ITM solutions also provide for granular user-account provisioning (including roles and responsibilities) that allows individuals to have access to maintaining or monitoring their respective components. Depending on the configuration of the ITM infrastructure, logging and alerting may be "unified" as well or at least provide for a consistent and uniform notification process that can be easily integrated into an SEM architecture. Likewise, the management of the ITM infrastructure from a single console allows an administrator to view all aspects and parameters of the system without needing to hop from system to system. The benefits of an integrated ITM reporting system can help with metrics, troubleshooting, return on investment studies and compliance, audits, and assessments (as noted earlier).

Some organizations consider the lack of flexibility of an ITM solution to be a significant drawback. For example, consider the ITM solutions that are available today. Although most vendors often do not attempt to develop their own solutions for all ITM functions, they partner or form alliances to deliver that integrated solution. If you are an organization moving toward an ITM infrastructure, are you willing to use the antivirus software that the vendor has chosen versus the one that you have or want to have? What about the firewall or the VPN connectivity solution? Although you do not have to license and use all of the components offered within an ITM solution, the cost savings, management, and benefits of an integrated solution may outweigh the inconveniences. It is unlikely that each component of the ITM will have been voted "best in class," but it is likely that the overall benefits of a well-integrated solution have that vote.

Some organizations are concerned with performance issues with available ITM solutions and feel that a single appliance cannot efficiently handle all functions without significant trade-offs. Just like any other solution, corresponding requirements need to be developed individually for each function. Once those requirements are developed, ITM solutions can be evaluated. Design and architecture of the ITM solution can be evaluated. Questions such as whether specific functions are sandboxed and managed to ensure that the required memory and processing power are provided should be answered. Having a significant peak in messages with large attachments that need to be scanned should not cause the firewall to block traffic or, worse yet, allow traffic to pass without the defined screening.

Although many of the ITM solutions today are appliances, there are some software-only platforms that operate on top of hardware and operating system platforms provided by the user. Although the vendor typically provides the specifications of those systems, it may or may not define security requirements to help ensure that the platform itself is secure. Customers should understand that if a system is an appliance, they may be prohibited by licensing or may not even have access to perform security updates to the core operating system.

Evaluating an ITM Solution

One of the most important aspects of the ITM life cycle is the development of the evaluation criteria so that the available products can be reviewed and assessed against standard criteria. With more than a single person conducting the assessment process, this is critical to help ensure a consistent approach to the process. This section will discuss the development of selection criteria, scoring of solutions, and selection of the product.

The development of the selection criteria should be based on what is expected from each of the individual components as well as what the requirements are from the consolidated reporting, management, and maintenance functions. First, develop a list of the functions that are critical to being part of the ITM solution. Although firewall, VPN, and antivirus are the most common functions of an ITM solution, other functions discussed in the introduction may be considered mandatory or optional to the organization. It is important to note that many vendors market their ITM products to small to medium business enterprises. These are the organizations that may not have extensive and complex firewall, content monitoring, logging, etc., requirements. For those firms that require complex rules, have extremely heavy bandwidth requirements, or have very specific needs, an ITM solution may not fit their needs. Following the process provided here should help determine the answer for you.

Once those components are identified, individual requirements should be developed and labeled as mandatory or optional. For example, consider the firewall component and ask whether you have or expect to have Voice-over-IP (VoIP) traffic passing through your firewall. If so, Session Initiation Protocol application inspection capabilities may be a requirement to support the VoIP traffic and may be heavily weighted as such. If VoIP traffic requirements are still under review, it may be considered mandatory, with a lighter weighting according to the relative importance to the organization, or even labeled as optional.

Once the individual components have been identified and their respective requirements defined, the requirements of the unified solution should be identified and weighted. Requirements in these areas typically include

- Ability to define user roles and responsibilities that meet the organization's security needs
- Reports and metrics that support compliance, auditing, and any required return on investment information
- Extensibility and ease of access to the database engine to extract custom reports or feed to any other system
- Appliance and component updates including datafiles (such as antivirus or antispyware) and system-level updates including ease of installation, frequency of updates, and reliability of updates
- Space, size, power, and cooling requirements for integration into the data center
- The vendor road map: with appropriate consideration, the product road map including additional features and integration opportunities
- Ability to add increased capacity such as storage and bandwidth processing through systems in parallel or upgrades
- Ability to support the device, such as on-site support, 24/7 telephone service, and same-day or next-day replacement options
- Correlation features that allow one to look at data across a longer time range by threat, by asset, by physical location, etc.

Criteria	Vendor A	Vendor B	Vendor C	Vendor D	Vendor E	Vendor F	Vendor G	Vendor H	Vendor I
High availability	✓		✓		✓	✓			✓
Customizable URL filtering	✓	✓		✓					✓
FW supports 100 MB/s	✓		✓		✓		✓	✓	
SSL VPN		✓			✓				✓
FW supports VoIP	✓	✓		✓		✓		✓	
Accepts alerts from other devices			✓			✓			✓

Figure 1.3 Sample evaluation table.

When all of the requirements have been considered, a table should be developed that includes all of the requirements and their respective weighting that can be utilized to evaluate the products. A sample table is shown in Figure 1.3.

In addition to the myriad of technology-based evaluation criteria, the ITM manufacturer should also be evaluated. Moving toward an ITM solution is a difficult choice. Although the risk of going out of business may be marginal, it is a risk, as is perhaps the greater risk of a product line being dropped as a result of an acquisition or merger. When you are putting the protection of your entire infrastructure into the hands of a single organization, the company itself should be evaluated. Is the vendor venture capital financed, public, or private? What is the direction of the company? What is the reputation of the company in the industry? Is the ITM solution the main focus of the company or just a small part? Although there may not be a wrong or right answer to any of these questions, understanding the company is part of the informed decision-making process.

Many organizations follow a two-phased approach to evaluate solutions. In any event, it is important to understand and follow the product or solution evaluation methodology for your organization. The first phase is a non-technology-based review, which may consist of discussions with vendors, reading of white papers, reading of independent evaluations, and discussions with peer and industry groups. Rather than evaluating 20 or 30 ITM solutions that may satisfy your requirements, the first phase is intended to narrow the list down to a smaller, manageable list of vendors that require a more thorough evaluation. By eliminating solutions that do not meet your requirements up front, the selection pool is reduced. Solutions that marginally meet your requirements or have additional benefits and features should be noted and marked for further evaluation.

The second phase is one of further discussions with vendors and a further review of white papers, product specification sheets, and manuals and documentation. For those systems that make the short list (typically two to three systems), a "try before you buy" program may exist that allows you to implement the product in an environment that you maintain. Some organizations may have a test lab in which products are evaluated, some may choose to run the ITM solution under evaluation in parallel with preexisting solutions, and some may wish to evaluate the ITM solution operating in lieu of the preexisting solutions. The merits of each solution are varied, but the reader is warned not to test an unproven security solution in a production environment as the sole line of defense.

Conclusion and Lessons Learned

The selection, implementation, and maintenance of an ITM solution should follow the life cycle of any other IT security product deployed within an organization's infrastructure. However, given that any ITM solution typically encompasses several critical security and control components of an organization, any mistake is often amplified due to its criticality and function. Make an error on the selection of an ITM solution and five different components may not perform as expected. Realize the difficulty of developing a business case to implement an ITM solution and then realize how difficult it will be to develop a business case to implement a second, better performing, ITM solution.

To avoid these errors, during the selection phase, you must define your selection criteria accurately. It makes no difference whether an ITM solution has the best e-mail filtering if that is not nearly as important as having a firewall that serves as a VoIP gateway. Many organizations have suffered because they decided to move toward a solution that offered great and wonderful features and functionality in areas that were not part of their mandatory requirements and were perhaps actually lacking in those areas that were part of their requirements.

The development of an effective program including the ITM solution is imperative to ensure that it is properly used, monitored, and reacted to. Too many companies focus on the IT aspects of a deployment and fail to include any of the requisite training, awareness, documentation, and integration into the existing infrastructure. Without a program that addresses those areas, an organization will, at best, not fully utilize the solution. At worst, the security posture of the organization will be significantly reduced below an acceptable level if alerts are missed, personnel are not trained, parameters are not properly configured, etc.

In addition, organizations habitually neglect to plan for growth in terms of size and bandwidth within their network. Many of the ITM solutions are geared toward small- to medium-sized businesses and have plenty of room to grow and add capacity as the organization grows. However, many organizations fail to plan far enough into the future and at some point the chosen ITM solution may no longer scale to support the business needs. Be sure to look far enough into the future and be sure that the solution meets your needs today and tomorrow.

The ITM market continues to grow in terms of both number of features within each solution and number of vendors that are marketing solutions. Whether it is a single appliance or an integrated solution and whether it is from one vendor or many, you will find that there are both extremely stellar and extremely inferior products available. Understanding what your requirements are and evaluating the available products to find a viable and effective solution that meets your requirement are half of the solution. Developing and implementing a robust ITM program that supports, governs, and sustains the ITM infrastructure completes the solution and serves as the remaining foundation to a successful ITM implementation that helps reduce risk posture, saves costs, and increases management and insight into the threats affecting the organization.

Chapter 2

Understanding Information Security Management Systems

Tom Carlson

Contents

What Is an Information Security Management System?

Definitions

Information security: Preservation of confidentiality, integrity, and availability of information.
Management system: Coordinated activities to direct and control an organization.
Information security management system (ISMS): Coordinated activities to direct and control the preservation of confidentiality, integrity, and availability of information.

History and Background

The current process-based approach to management systems is derived from the work of W. Edwards Deming and the world of Total Quality Management (TQM). His holistic and process-based approach to the manufacturing sector was initially ignored but eventually embraced after the rapid rise in quality of Japanese products in the 1960s. Although initially viewed as relevant only to a production-line environment, the concepts of TQM have since been successfully applied to many other environments.

Concept

ISMS is an example of applying the management system conceptual model to the discipline of information security. Unique attributes to this instance of a management system include the following:

- Risk management applied to information and based upon metrics of confidentiality, integrity, and availability
- TQM applied to information security processes and based upon metrics of efficiency and effectiveness

- A monitoring and reporting model based upon abstraction layers that filter and aggregate operational details for management presentation
- A structured approach toward integrating people, process, and technology to furnish enterprise information security services
- An extensible framework from which to manage information security compliance

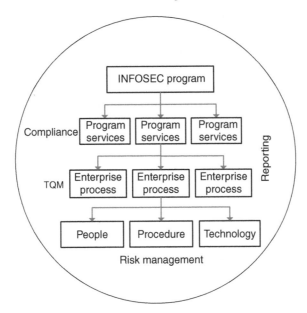

Why Is an ISMS Beneficial?

On the surface, ISMS may appear to be a paperwork exercise. Although this may be true, the benefit of ISMS far outweighs the resultant documentation. Of equal or greater value is the resultant thought processes, awareness, and informed-choice decision making.

Defensible

The structure inherent to an ISMS shows clear direction and authorization. Executive management direction is linked to operational detail. Details are derived from documented informed-choice decision making. Measuring and monitoring ensure reasonable awareness of the information security environment. This documented due diligence provides a defensible posture.

A standards-based ISMS allows extra defensibility through third-party validation such as certification to the ISO27001 information security management standard. This defensibility works whether one is a consumer or a source of information. Choosing to do business with an externally validated partner is a defensible decision.

Differentiator

An ISMS may serve as a market differentiator, as well as enhancing perception and image. Marketing your information services to external information-sharing partners or clients requires a degree of confidence from all parties. The extra effort of information security certification makes their decision defensible.

Business Enabler

An ISMS may serve as an umbrella to cover several regulatory components simultaneously. Most relevant regulations deal with very specific data types such as health or financial information. Controls deployed for one regulation, and managed by an overarching or blanket ISMS, typically meet the requirements of multiple regulations simultaneously. Most legal regulations also require demonstrable management of information security, something inherent in an ISMS. The potential legal and regulatory cost savings of an overarching ISMS are obvious.

An ISMS allows for, and generally is based upon, risk. Risk analysis and risk rating may serve as a fundamental justification for the selection and deployment of controls that populate the ISMS. A risk-based ISMS, such as required by the ISO27001 standard, allows for business to accept risk based upon informed-choice decision making. This ability to accept risk enables businesses to react to their environment, not someone else's interpretation of their environment.

A standards-based ISMS offers the basis for enhanced interoperability with information trading partners. The ISMS framework eases interfacing and is extensible to absorb future expansion or change. Standardized terminology facilitates communication.

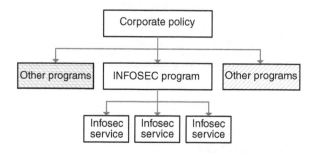

Structure

An ISMS brings structure to the Information Security Program. With clear direction and authorization, roles are understood. Defined functions or services allow derivation of tasks that can be delegated. Metrics can be collected and analyzed, producing feedback for "continuous process improvement."

In many situations, creation of an ISMS inspires and spawns complementary management systems in other disciplines such as human resources, physical security, business continuity, and more. The framework and management system principles transcend disciplines and tend to enhance multidisciplinary interoperation.

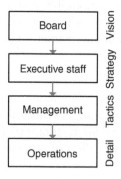

Who Participates in an ISMS?

An ISMS transcends an organization from the board room to the data center. There are typically three organizational layers with four very distinct audiences.

Board

The board of directors typically provides the organizational vision and guiding principles in response to managing risk on multiple fronts, from regulatory compliance to fiduciary responsibility. The board of directors participates in the ISMS through empowerment. This empowerment or authorization is a strategic control in response to risks such as regulatory noncompliance and fiduciary irresponsibility.

Executive Staff

Senior executives are the typical owners of programs that would be managed by a management system. Management systems enhance an organization's horizontal and vertical integration and visibility. Senior executives participate in the ISMS through definition and provision of services to the enterprise by the program, such as incident management.

Management

Directors manage the tactics required to provide the program services. In a process-based ISMS, program services are provided by a collection of complementary and integrated processes. Directors participate in the ISMS through the definition, execution, and ongoing improvement of these relevant information security processes, such as contain, eradicate, restore.

Operations

Managers implement the program on an operational level. The ISMS will generate standardized methodologies and requirements, codified in organizational process and standards. Managers participate in the ISMS through integration of people, procedure, and technology in response to these organizational directives.

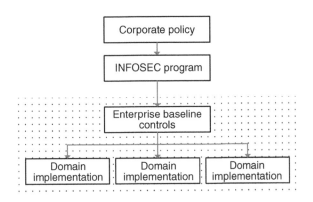

Where Does an ISMS Live?

An ISMS lives within an organization from the board room to the production floor, each strata addressing a different need.

Enterprise

At the enterprise level the ISMS lives in the form of a minimum enterprise information security baseline created in direct response to the enterprise information security risk addressed by upper management. The enterprise information security baseline typically consists of enterprise information security standards, processes, and roles or responsibilities. Risk acceptance for nonconformance to the information security baseline has enterprisewide information security significance.

Information Security Domains

At the operational level, an ISMS lives in multiple places and instances, based upon functional areas, or information security domains. A typical information security domain may be a data center, office area, or reception area, each with a unique security profile. Information security domains serve as the basis for enterprise information security baseline implementation. Each domain is autonomous in how it tailors the enterprise information security baseline requirements to its unique environment.

How Is an ISMS Built?

An ISMS is typically risk based and process oriented. There may be multiple layers of abstraction to accommodate the distinct audiences whose concerns must be addressed. The ISO27001 standard recommends a Plan, Do, Check, Act process-based approach defined as

> *Plan*. Establish the ISMS
> > Understand the environment
> > Assess enterprise risk
> > Charter Information Security Program
> > Assess program risk
> *Do*. Implement and operate the ISMS
> > Create enterprise information security baseline
> > Create domain-specific implementations
> *Check*. Monitor and review the ISMS
> > Assess operational risk
> *Act*. Maintain and improve the ISMS
> > Measure and monitor

Understand the Environment

The structure and the content of the ISMS must take into account the management environment to be successful. Organizational considerations will influence the ISMS framework. Cultural sensitivities may change usage of terminology. Regulatory requirements will certainly influence approach, contents, and packaging.

Assess Enterprise Risk

Enterprise risk is usually assessed and addressed through upper management directives such as corporate policies. The assessment of high-level enterprise risk, such as regulatory compliance and fiduciary responsibility, is inherently understood and intuitively addressed. Upper management directives serve as the authorization and empowerment of the supporting enterprise risk-mitigating programs.

For example,

- A corporate behavioral or acceptable-use policy empowers proactive behavioral training as well as reactive behavioral detection mechanisms.
- Corporate administrative policy empowers efficiency initiatives supported by operational metrics and continuous process improvement.
- Corporate legal or regulatory policy establishes nonnegotiable requirements embedded as controls within the ISMS.

Charter Information Security Program

The Information Security Program is the organizational entity authorized and empowered to create and maintain the ISMS to offer the enterprise the services required to meet corporate policy goals.

The Information Security Program not only offers services, but also requires externally provided services to maintain program effectiveness. An example program dependency may be a human resource department that performs background checks for the Information Security Program. A program charter may serve as a vehicle to document the authorization and empowerment, as well as documenting and acknowledging the mutually recognized program dependencies.

Assess Program Risk

Program risk serves as the basis to select controls managed by the ISMS. Some program risk has been analyzed and addressed by others who believe they know the practitioner's environment better than the practitioner, resulting in binding regulations. Some program risk is obvious and intuitive, such as the risk of unpatched information processing systems. Other program risk is more insidious, such as aggregation, when individual inconsequential risks combine to produce risk disproportionate to the sum. For example,

- There is no firewall between Department A and Department B. This is rated a minor risk and has been accepted by both departments.
- Department B then deploys a Web server. The risk of opening Hypertext Transfer Protocol port 80 through the Department B external (Internet facing) firewall is deemed a minor risk and has been accepted by Department B.
- Department A's previously isolated network segment is now no longer isolated.
- A minor risk accepted by Department B caused an unknown risk acceptance by Department A. There is now an unrecognized major enterprise risk.

An ISMS serves as the vehicle to coordinate the management of risk and risk-mitigating controls. Identified risks are quantified and control objectives assigned. Control objectives serve as the glue that justifies and binds each risk to its respective control. The satisfaction of control objectives is prioritized by the risk quantification.

Create Enterprise Information Security Baseline

An enterprise information security baseline serves as a common minimum information security posture for the enterprise. This in turn serves as the basis for trust between operational areas or domains because they all are required to meet this minimum baseline, which may be exceeded as required.

Directives

Directives are controls that define hard and measurable requirements. Directives may be derived from legislation, from industry standards and practices, or in response to risk. Directive controls are typically codified in a suite of standards, with the content based upon informed-choice decision making. Care must be taken in the crafting of the directives because informed-choice decision making implies a degree of risk acceptance. That which is not addressed is by default accepted.

Methodologies

Methodologies are controls that define measurable and repeatable processes. Methodologies may be derived to meet the requirements of directives or may be part of a suite of processes that provide a program service. Methodologies are typically codified as a process flow. Care must be taken in crafting process flows to ensure that the process can be measured and monitored. That which cannot be measured cannot be improved.

Responsibilities

Clear assignment of responsibilities is a control that binds a role to an activity. Activities may be derived to meet the requirements of directives and may be performed by executing a methodology. Responsibilities are typically codified via functional role definitions. Care must be taken when defining functional roles to ensure that role-assigned responsibilities are supported by role-required authorizations and qualifications. Those assigned responsibility must have the requisite authorization, qualifications, and resources.

Create Domain-Specific Implementations

Specifications

Specifications are domain-specific operational controls that define hard and measurable details such as configurations or attributes. Specifications are derived from enterprise information security standards, with each domain potentially deriving unique interpretations for a common standard, dependent on each unique environment. This allows a degree of autonomy in execution. Care must be taken when deriving specifications to ensure domain-specific interpretations; while meeting the spirit and intent of the parent standards, do not cause interdomain incompatibility. To preclude introduction of unidentified risk, specifications must meet the spirit and intent of the parent standard.

Procedures

Standard operating procedures are controls that define measurable and repeatable work instructions. Standard operating procedures are derived from enterprise information security processes, with each domain potentially deriving unique interpretations dependent on each unique environment. This allows a degree of autonomy in execution. Care must be taken in deriving standard operating procedures to ensure parent process attributes are preserved. The execution of domain standard operating procedures is the basis of enterprise information security services.

Tasks

Tasks are activities assigned a functional role executing a standard operating procedure. Tasks are domain-specific and schedule-driven, with frequency of execution based upon risk. Individuals executing tasks while filling a role are performing their employment duties. Performance of duty is an employee metric. Care must be taken when scheduling tasks and assigning duties to ensure the schedule is defensible and the individual competent. Tasking is an employee performance metric.

Assess Operational Risk

Operational risk is based upon the risk that a domain will not be able to meet its enterprise information security baseline-derived obligations, such as specifications, procedures, and scheduled tasks. This risk is many times resource-driven, putting a risk justification to budgeting.

Acceptance of operational risk may change residual program risk, and aggregation may cause this program risk to rise to an unacceptable level.

Measure and Monitor

Measuring and monitoring are the feedback mechanism required for continuous process improvement. What to monitor and how to measure require well-defined metrics. Typical domains will obtain multiple varieties of metrics.

Environmental Metrics

Environmental metrics are based upon the surroundings. The focus is on identifying the enterprise's risk profile. Industry groups are a consideration. Banking and financial services may, for example, attract highly motivated attackers. Level of organizational sophistication may influence the risk level. An ISO27001-certified domain may, for example, have a lower perceived risk level. Location may become a factor influenced by crime rates or fire response times. Risk profiles affect probability. This can be utilized to influence risk ratings in the vulnerability management process. For example, the probability of a specific vulnerability being exploited at a bank is perhaps higher than at a home user site because of attacker motivation and targeting. Consideration should be taken to weighting risk and response based upon these environmental metrics. Another focus for environmental metrics is to establish an information security frame of reference or threshold. Intrusion sensors, for example, utilize environmental metrics to establish detection noise baselines and thresholds.

Program Metrics

Program metrics are based upon effectiveness. The focus is on validating that the ISMS is successfully providing the services that justify its existence. Consider vulnerability management. This ISMS service measures effectiveness, for example, not by how rapidly a vulnerability can be identified and processed (efficiency). Vulnerability management effectiveness is measured by how many vulnerabilities were never identified or fully processed.

Process Metrics

Process metrics are based upon efficiency. The focus is on fine-tuning procedures to maximize performance. Consider a vulnerability tracking process. The acquisition of new software may, for example, decrease the "time to resolve," thus improving metrics efficiency.

When Does an ISMS Protect?

An ISMS protects by degrees.

Responsibility	Owner	Focus
Degree of assurance	Program management	Program risk
Degree of maturity	ISMS management	ISMS process
Degree of implementation	Project management	People, procedure, and technology

Degree of Assurance

In a risk-based ISMS, the risk assessment process is an integral part of the feedback loop that provides continuous process improvement. Because risk can never be completely eliminated, a compromise is sought by which residual risk has been reduced to an acceptable level. This is known as degree of assurance. The Information Security Program is a risk management tool. From the program perspective, the ISMS protects when risk has been reduced to an acceptable level.

The important question is how to define this "acceptable level" threshold. Degree of assurance implies a level of risk acceptance, but risk may be scattered throughout the ISMS. This may preclude a straightforward assignment of risk acceptance authorization. An ISMS, by nature of its structure, recognizes the need to delegate risk acceptance as well as taking into consideration aggregate risk.

Degree of Maturity

A process-based ISMS is conducive to maturity modeling, because processes by definition should produce feedback metrics that enhance the maturation of the process. Maturity modeling scales, such as seen in the Capability Maturity Model schemas and others, serve as a common language with consistent definition of scale. The desired degree of maturity is hence bound to the maturity scale selected, as well as to the specific process under evaluation. A defensible degree of maturity is based upon informed choice. Processes may vary in their acceptable degree of maturity, dependent on external factors such as risk. Nevertheless, the ISMS protects as its processes reach the desired degree of maturity.

Degree of Implementation

Degree of implementation is tied to operations and project management. Information security projects at the operational level are tied to specific operational areas, or security domains. These projects deploy domain-specific controls in response to domain-specific risk, aggregating to raise the enterprise degree of assurance. On project completion, degree of implementation is complete, and the control is now bound to degree of maturity. The ISMS protects as people, procedure, and product integrate into process.

Summary

The management system concept is being applied across many new disciplines. With the ratification of the ISO27001 standard, ISMS have achieved new prominence, in some arenas becoming a de facto requirement.

In conclusion, an ISMS

- Integrates information security risk into enterprise risk management
- Documents informed-choice decision making and due diligence
- Provides a framework for regulatory compliance
- Offers a structure to integrate people, process, and technology efficiently and effectively
- Furnishes a mechanism for monitoring and reporting
- Is business friendly and a market differentiator

Policies, Standards, Procedures, and Guidelines

Chapter 3

Planning for a Privacy Breach

Rebecca Herold

Contents

All Organizations Must Address Privacy Issues

Privacy is considered a basic human right in many parts of the world. Take, for instance, the EU Data Protection Directive (95/46/EC) requirements, "for the protection of the private lives and basic freedoms and rights of individuals." Although privacy principles and laws have been around for well over a decade, it has been only in the past few years, as breaches have become an almost daily event, that organizations have started noticeably to address privacy challenges and dedicate the resources necessary to deal effectively with the myriad of issues and requirements.

The public is savvy with regard to privacy, much more now than it has ever been before in history. Organizations must address privacy, not only because they are legally required to do so, but also because customers demand it and it is just the right thing to do. Organizations must maintain privacy to maintain customer trust, maintain customer loyalty and support, and even improve corporate brand.

Organizations are starting to address some privacy issues, but there are still significant privacy breaches that increasingly more organizations experience. Organizations must prepare for addressing these privacy breaches so they can respond to them in the most effective and efficient way possible, minimizing not only negative business impact but also negative personal impacts to customers.

Incidents Occur Many Different Ways

Incidents can, do, and will continue to occur in a wide variety of ways. These are not just the results of hackers or stolen computers, which are most widely reported, but also the results of malicious intent from outsiders or insiders, mistakes made by those who handle personally identifiable information (PII), and simple lack of awareness of what should be done to protect PII, along with other unique ways.

As examples, each of the following represents a unique type of privacy incident:

■ *Canadian airline refuses customer access.* In January 2007, the Canadian Privacy Commissioner filed charges against a Canadian airline that refused to give a customer access to his personal information.

■ *Cleveland clinic hospital employee theft.* In September 2006, a former employee of Cleveland Clinic Hospital in North Naples and a relative who worked for a Naples-based health insurance claims company were arrested and charged with stealing records of more than 1100 patients.

■ *Connecticut technical high school e-mail error.* In March 2006, the Social Security numbers (SSNs) of the 1250 teachers and school administrators in the Connecticut Technical High School System were mistakenly sent via e-mail to staff. The e-mail was sent to the system's 17 principals to inform them about a coming workshop. The file with the SSNs was attached to the e-mail by mistake. At least one principal then forwarded the e-mail to 77 staff members without opening the attachment containing the SSNs.

■ *DoubleClick cookie use.* In 2000, a series of class action lawsuits were brought against Double-Click for violation of privacy relating to the company's cookie-tracking practices. In January 2000, the stock for DoubleClick, Inc., was at about $135 per share. Following the privacy lawsuits around six months later, DoubleClick's share price dropped to the mid-30s. On top of this was the settlement, which included implementing privacy protections, paying all legal fees, and paying up to $1.8 million.

■ *Eckerd pharmacy use of PII for marketing.* In July 2002, Eckerd had a practice of having customers sign a form that not only acknowledged receipt of a prescription but also authorized the store to release prescription information to Eckerd Corp. for future marketing purposes. The court determined the form did not adequately inform customers that they were authorizing the commercial use of their personal medical information.

■ *Eli Lilly Prozac e-mail incident.* In June 2001, Eli Lilly sent a message to 669 Prozac users who had voluntarily signed up for a prescription reminder service. The message header inadvertently contained visible e-mail addresses for all the recipients.

- *Ernst & Young stolen laptop.* In January 2006, a laptop was stolen from an Ernst & Young employee's car. As a result of the theft, the names, dates of birth, genders, family sizes, SSNs, and tax identifiers for IBM employees were exposed.
- *Microsoft passport security.* In August 2002, Microsoft agreed to settle Federal Trade Commission (FTC) charges regarding the privacy and security of personal information collected from consumers through its "Passport" Web services. As part of the settlement, Microsoft had to implement a comprehensive information security program for Passport and similar services. Each subsequent violation of the order could result in a civil penalty of $11,000.
- *University of San Diego computer network hack.* In November 2005, the University of San Diego notified almost 7800 individuals that hackers had gained illicit access to computers containing their personal income tax data. The compromised data included names, SSNs, and addresses.
- *University of Southern California programming error.* In July 2005, a programming error in the University of Southern California's online system for accepting applications left the personal information of as many as 280,000 users publicly accessible.
- *Ziff Davis Web site error.* Because of how one of their Web pages was designed, a computer file of approximately 12,000 subscription requests could be accessed by anyone on the Internet. As a result, some subscribers incurred fraudulent credit card charges.

To plan effectively to prevent, as well as respond to, privacy incidents, organizations must identify their potential privacy incidents and then address each of them individually.

Increasingly More Breaches Are Occurring

The more mobile PII becomes, being stored upon personal digital assistants (PDAs), laptops, and mobile storage devices and being accessed by people who work from home, work while traveling, or work for other companies, the more risk there is that the PII will fall victim to an incident.

The Privacy Rights Clearinghouse (PRC) logged 705 breaches that they had found reported in the news within the United States between February 15, 2005, and October 25, 2007. These breaches cumulatively involved the information of over 168 million people. Attrition.org also keeps track of breaches, many of which are not on the PRC list. The author has also found many more breaches not on either list, and a very large number of incidents do not get reported in the news.

According to a Ponemon privacy breach study released in October 2006,* losses involving PII cost U.S. companies approximately $182 per compromised individual's record. This was up from $138 per individual's record in 2005. Considering that most breaches impact thousands of individuals, this is significant. Each of the 56 companies surveyed had $2.5 million in lost business as a result of each incident.

Privacy incidents involve much more than just the immediate cost of the incident. Through research with organizations that have experienced privacy incidents the author has found the subsequent and ongoing actual costs of internal investigations, external legal advice, notification and call center costs, investor relations, promotions such as discounted services and products, lost personnel productivity, lost customers, travel and lodging costs to bring business clients on site for assurance meetings, notifications to individuals in other countries, increasing staff, ongoing

---

* http://www.computerworld.com/pdfs/PGP_Annual_Study_PDF.pdf

auditing and documentation requirements, installing new systems and fixing old ones, and so on have a huge impact on an organization.

Prevention Is Much Less Expensive Than Response and Recovery

All organizations, of all sizes, in all industries, in all parts of the world, that handle PII are vulnerable to experiencing a privacy breach. No organization is immune.

Organizations must be prepared to respond to privacy-related incidents. Information security and privacy areas must work together following a comprehensive well-thought-out and tested breach response plan to be effective.

Your organization must understand when you are required to notify the affected individuals. As of October 2007 there were 40 states including the District of Columbia with privacy breach notice laws. There are pending U.S. federal breach notice bills. There are pending proposed laws throughout the world, such as in Canada and the European Union. If you live in some remote part of the world where there is no breach notice law protecting your customers, do not wait until you legally must address privacy and how to respond to breaches. You will have to address this issue sooner or later.

When planning for a privacy breach:

1. Define the possible privacy breaches
2. Create plans for the privacy breach
3. Know when a privacy breach has occurred
4. Know when notification is necessary
5. Continue recovery activities following a breach

Define Possible Privacy Breaches

You must know what a privacy breach is before you can plan how to identify when a privacy breach has occurred and how best to respond to it. There are many different kinds of potential privacy breaches. Most of these overlap with and are part of information security incidents, highlighting the need for privacy and information security practitioners to work together to address privacy breaches.

Some of the types of privacy breaches that organizations have experienced include, but are not limited to, the following:

■ Unauthorized access to e-mails and voicemails
■ Receipt of unsolicited e-mails that can be considered spam
■ Unauthorized access on borrowed or loaned computers
■ Unauthorized access to work areas
■ Illegal use of SSNs
■ Inappropriate access to the network or computer systems
■ Lost or stolen computers, such as laptops, PDAs, and so on
■ Lost or stolen computer storage media
■ Mistakes that leave information vulnerable
■ Dishonest authorized insiders inappropriately using PII
■ E-mail messages with confidential information sent or forwarded inappropriately

- Fraud activities perpetrated by outsiders, insiders, or both
- Hackers gaining unauthorized access to the information
- Information exposed online because of inadequate controls
- Confidential paper documents not being shredded and being given to people outside the organization (e.g., recycled)
- Improper disposal
- Password compromise
- Customer or employee angry with privacy practices

Create Your Privacy Breach Response Plans

Now that you have identified the situations through which privacy can be breached, you need to create your privacy breach response plans. The first, fundamental, action in creating your plan is to identify the PII items that your organization handles. You cannot know if a privacy breach has occurred unless you know what PII exists and where it is located.

Define PII

There is no one universal definition for what constitutes PII. The author has analyzed over 90 worldwide laws and found at least 47 different and uniquely named items that are considered PII as indicated in Table 3.1. Identify the data protection and privacy laws that apply to your organization and document the PII items.

Locate the PII

You cannot know if PII has been breached if you do not know where it is located. A critical component of privacy breach prevention and incident response is locating and documenting where PII exists throughout your organization.

In the course of a business day, organizations collect PII in many different ways. Much of this information is in the form of unstructured data (generally data under the control of end users, such as within Word files, Excel files, e-mail messages, and so on). Be comprehensive in your identification of PII storage locations. Do not forget about those often overlooked and seemingly innocent storage areas where massive amounts of PII could be hiding. Map out how the PII flows throughout the organization.

Following are some high-level steps for locating PII:

1. Identify all applicable laws and regulations
2. Identify and document all types of PII referenced within the laws and regulations
3. Document all types of PII within contracts and Web site privacy policies
4. Create an inventory of all PII used within the organization
5. Identify and document where PII is collected throughout the organization
6. Identify and document where PII is stored and accessed throughout the organization
7. Identify and document all points at which PII leaves the organization

There are many different ways in which you can document your PII data flow. For example, the U.S. Transportation Security Authority (TSA) represented their PII data flow with a somewhat

Table 3.1 Laws Defining PII

Personal Information Item	Law or Regulation									
	HIPAA	*COPPA*	*SB 1386*	*GLBA*	*EU Directive*	*Privacy Act of 1974*	*Drivers*	*FOIA*	*PIPEDA*	*Misc.*
First name or initial	X	X	X	X	X	X	X	X	X[a]	X
Last name	X	X	X	X	X	X	X	X	X[a]	X
Geographic subdivisions smaller than a state (mailing address)	X	X		X	X	X	X[b]	X	X[a]	X
Dates (excluding year for HIPAA)	X				X	X		X		X
Birth	X	X			X	X		X		X
Admission	X							X	X	X
Discharge	X							X	X	X
Death	X					X		X	X	X
Telephone number	X	X		X	X	X	X	X	X[c]	X
Fax number	X	X[b]		X	X	X		X	X[c]	X
E-mail address	X	X		X	X	X		X	X[c]	X
SSN	X	X	X	X	X	X		X		X
Medical records numbers	X				X	X	X	X	X	X
Health plan beneficiary numbers	X				X	X	X	X	X	X
Account numbers	X				X	X		X		X
License and certificate numbers	X				X	X	X	X		X
Vehicle identifiers (such as license plate number)	X		X		X	X	X	X		X
Credit card number			X		X	X		X		X
Debit card number			X		X	X		X		X
California ID number			X		X	X		X		X
Device identifiers (such as serial numbers)	X				X					X

Universal resource locaters	X					X		
Internet Protocol address	X		X	X	X	X		
Biometric identifiers (such as DNA, iris-, finger-, and voiceprints)	X					X		
Full-face photographic images (and any comparable images)	X	X	X	X	X	X		
Other unique identifiers that can be attributed to a specific individual	X	X	X	X	X	X		
Medical care information, such as organ donations, medications, and disability information	X	X	X	X	X			
Any other identifier that the FTC determines permits the physical or online contacting of a specific individual	X				X			X
Information concerning a child or parents of that child that a Web site collects online from the child and combines with one of the above identifiers	X					X		X
Body identifiers (tattoos, scars)	X		X		X[b]	X		
Employment history	X		X		X		X	

(continued)

Table 3.1 (continued)

Personal Information Item	HIPAA	COPPA	SB 1386	GLBA	EU Directive	Privacy Act of 1974	Drivers	FOIA	PIPEDA	Misc.
						Law or Regulation				
Income				X		X		X		X
Payment history				X		X				X
Loan or deposit balances				X		X				X
Credit card purchases				X		X				X
Criminal charges, convictions, and court records				X	X	X				X
Military history					X	X				X
Credit reports and credit scores				X		X				X
Existence of customer relationship				X		X				
Financial transaction information				X		X				X
Merchandise and product order history				X^b		X				X
Service subscription history										X
Fraud alerts				X		X				X
"Black box" data										X
Video programming activity information										X
Voting history					X	X			X^b	X
Conversations (recorded or overheard)					X	X				X

Descriptive listings of consumers			X	X
Education records		X		X
Personnel files		X		X

Often, combinations of more than one piece of information create PII. The following, typically when combined with an element from the above list, are also considered PII. Additionally, these are often considered "sensitive," "protected," or "confidential" information.

Racial or ethnic origin	
Political opinions	
Religious or philosophical beliefs	
Trade-union membership	
Health or sexual activity information	
Marital status	X
Security code	
Access code	
Password	

ᵃ Does not include the name, title, business address, or telephone number of an employee of an organization.

ᵇ Although this law does not explicitly list this item, it is possible that using this item could be considered a violation of the law because the law is written in such a way that it is vague or leaves things open to interpretation. It could depend upon the judge or jury and the other policies, contracts, and documents the organization has published or provided.

ᶜ But not the five-digit ZIP code.

Note: HIPAA, Health Insurance Portability and Accountability Act; COPPA, Children's Online Privacy Protection Act; California SB 1386; GLBA, Gramm– Leach– Bliley Act; EU Data Protection Directive (Personal data is defined very broadly as any "information relating to an identified or identifiable natural person [data subject]. An identifiable person is one who can be identified, directly or indirectly, in particular by reference to an identification number, or to one or more factors specific to his physical, physiological, mental, economic, cultural or social identity."); The Privacy Act of 1974 (amended); Drivers Privacy Protection Act; FOIA, Freedom of Information Act; Canada's Personal Information Protection and Electronic Documents Act (PIPEDA); Miscellaneous other laws.

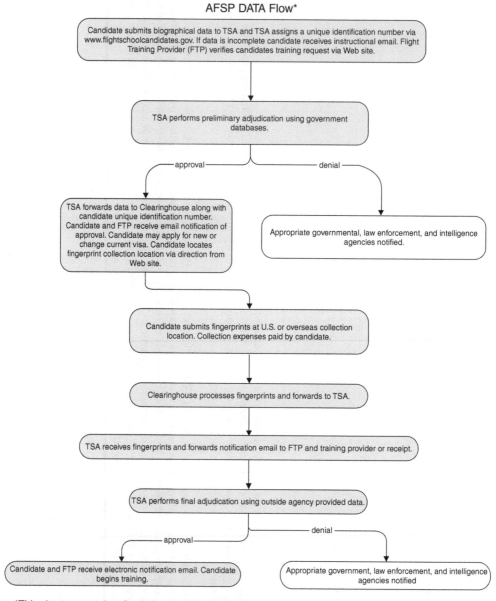

AFSP DATA Flow*

Candidate submits biographical data to TSA and TSA assigns a unique identification number via www.flightschoolcandidates.gov. If data is incomplete candidate receives instructional email. Flight Training Provider (FTP) verifies candidates training request via Web site.

TSA performs preliminary adjudication using government databases.

─approval─ ─denial─

TSA forwards data to Clearinghouse along with candidate unique identification number. Candidate and FTP receive email notification of approval. Candidate may apply for new or change current visa. Candidate locates fingerprint collection location via direction from Web site.

Appropriate governmental, law enforcement, and intelligence agencies notified.

Candidate submits fingerprints at U.S. or overseas collection location. Collection expenses paid by candidate.

Clearinghouse processes fingerprints and forwards to TSA.

TSA receives fingerprints and forwards notification email to FTP and training provider or receipt.

TSA performs final adjudication using outside agency provided data.

─denial─

─approval─

Candidate and FTP receive electronic notification email. Candidate begins training.

Appropriate government, law enforcement, and intelligence agencies notified

*This chart accurately reflects the data flow for all categories of candidates with the following exceptions: There is no preliminary approval for Category III Candidates, and Category IV Candidates receive only notification of application receipt and will not undergo a security threat assessment.

Figure 3.1   TSA PII data flow diagram (http://www.dhs.gov/xoig/assets/mgmtrpts/Privacy_pia_afs.pdf).

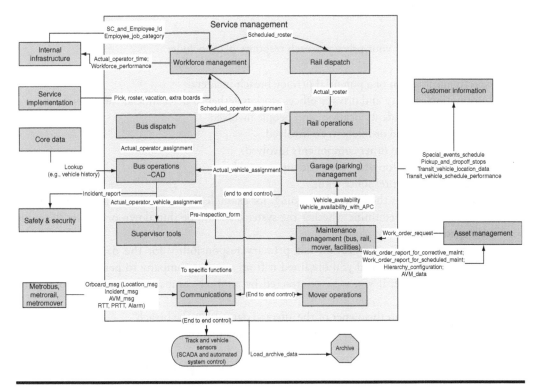

Figure 3.2   TSA PII data flow diagram.

unusual flowchart as shown in Figure 3.1. However, it provides the documentation to show where PII is collected, where it goes, and where it is stored.

Another type of PII data flow that provides more meaningful information is shown in Figure 3.2. This is from Miami–Dade Transit.*

Use the method for documenting your PII data flow that works best for your organization.

Create the Breach Response Plan

Now that you know the types of breaches possible, the PII you handle, and all the locations for the PII, create the incident identification and response plans. Coordinate with and incorporate plan actions with the information security incident response plan. If you do not, you will either have gaps that can defeat your response efforts or have conflicting activities occurring within different parts of your organization that will likely lead to unsatisfactory response results.

Ensure your plan takes into consideration intrusion detection systems (IDSs). Ensure the IDSs are used and configured in the most effective way so that as many of the types of privacy breaches that you have identified as possible will be flagged.

---

* http://www.miamidade.gov/transit/library/pdfs/reports/MDTFinalReportTechnicalAppendixA_1.19.2004_ jfmB2.pdf.

Plan Effectively

The basic components of your privacy breach response plan include:

1. Receive notification of a potential privacy breach incident.
2. Information security and privacy offices work together to determine at the onset.
   a. The type of incident, location, and people involved.
   b. If PII is involved or likely to be involved.
   c. The systems and other components involved.
   d. The timeframe for when the incident occurred.
3. Notify the incident response team.
4. Determine whether the breach is ongoing, for example if a hacker is still accessing the data or systems. If so, determine whether the systems should be shut down or if activity should be logged and watched closely.
5. Determine if your organization has primary responsibility for the data (it is for your clients or customers) or if you obtained it from another company to perform services for them, for example, if you were contracted by another company to process or otherwise handle the data.
6. Immediately inform the owner of the affected data about the breach.
7. Identify the obligations your organization has under its contract with the owner.
8. Fulfill those obligations.
9. Determine if you need to inform any law enforcement agency and, if so, determine which one(s).
10. If your organization is the primary custodian of the data, determine the specific types of data affected and the associated individuals. This may require sophisticated forensics and could take a significant amount of time, but planning ahead for who will perform these actions will keep that time to a minimum.
11. Determine the jurisdictions within which all impacted individuals reside.
12. Identify the notification requirements for each of the jurisdictions.
13. If just one of the notification requirements is met, plan to notify all impacted individuals. Even if you are not legally obligated to notify beyond those in the jurisdictions with the legal requirements, it is a best practice, and it is best for all your customers to do so.
14. Determine the obligations and responsibilities your organization will have to the impacted individuals for such activities as credit monitoring, toll-free information lines, dedicated incident Web sites, expense reimbursement, and so on.
15. Determine the content of the breach notifications.
16. Determine whether the associated state attorneys general or country privacy commissioner must be notified.
17. Determine how to send and communicate any necessary notifications and whether to use in-house personnel or to engage a third party to send notifications.
18. Send the notifications.
19. Remediate and update processes and procedures to help prevent the incident from occurring again.
20. Monitor the ongoing impact of the breach and continue to answer impacted individuals' questions and address concerns.

As you create your breach response plans, keep in mind that the primary goals of incident handling are to

- Quickly control and minimize damage
- Preserve evidence
- Notify individuals if appropriate
- Recover as soon as possible
- Continue monitoring for downstream impact
- Learn from the incident and make changes to help prevent similar incidents from occurring again

Do your documented plans support these goals?

Once you create the breach response plan, effectively communicate it throughout your enterprise. Provide initial and ongoing training for the personnel who will actively be involved with breach response. Test the plans at least annually and whenever major changes are made within the organization.

Know When a Privacy Breach Has Occurred

Incidents may be reported from many different sources, such as

- Personnel
- Customers
- The general public
- Business partners
- News media
- Automated systems

Reports of a privacy breach can be made to many different areas, such as

- Information security
- Privacy
- Human resources
- Call centers
- Technical support

Ensure your plan clearly specifies where privacy breach reports need to be routed and the positions responsible for privacy breach response coordination. Communicate this throughout your enterprise often and in various ways.

When a privacy breach is reported, it is critical to follow your documented breach response plans to ensure that they are addressed in the most efficient and effective manner, that those filling breach response roles fulfill their specific responsibilities, and that the response activities are followed consistently.

Breach Notification

Typically you will need to notify others when a breach occurs that involved PII. Within the United States as of March 1, 2007, there were 35 states with privacy breach notice laws as indicated in Table 3.2.

Table 3.2   U.S. Privacy Breach Notice Laws as of March 1, 2007

State Breach Notification Law	Effective Date
Arizona SB 1338	12/31/06
Arkansas SB 1167	8/12/05
California SB 1386	7/1/03
Colorado HB 1119	9/1/06
Connecticut SB 650	1/1/06
Delaware HB 116	6/28/05
District of Columbia 28-3852	7/1/07
Florida HB 481	7/1/05
Georgia SB 230	5/5/05
Hawaii SB 2290	1/1/07
Idaho SB 1374	7/1/06
Illinois HB 1633	1/1/06
Indiana HB 1101	7/1/06
Kansas SB 196	7/1/06
Louisiana SB 205	1/1/06
Maine LD 1671	1/31/06
Maryland HB208 and SB194	1/1/08
Massachusetts HB4144	2/3/08
Michigan SB 309	6/29/07
Minnesota HF 2121	1/1/06
Montana HB 732	3/1/06
Nebraska LB 876	4/6/06
Nevada SB 347	1/1/06 (10/1/08 for mandatory encryption)
New Hampshire HB 1660	1/1/07
New Jersey A4001	1/1/06
New York S 3492, S 5827, and AB 4254	12/7/05
North Carolina SB 1048	12/1/05
North Dakota SB 2251	6/1/05
Ohio HB 104	2/17/06
Oklahoma HB 2357	6/08/06
Oregon SB583	10/1/07
Pennsylvania SB 712	6/20/06
Rhode Island HB 6191	3/1/06
Tennessee HB 2170	7/1/05
Texas SB 122	9/1/05
Utah SB 69	1/1/07
Vermont SB 284	1/1/07
Washington SB 6043	7/24/05
Wisconsin SB 164	3/31/06
Wyoming SF53	7/1/07

Some of those you may need to notify could include the following:

■ Customers
■ Business partners
■ Telecommunications providers
■ State attorneys general
■ Regulatory oversight agencies, such as the FTC
■ Law enforcement
■ Software vendors
■ Internet Service Providers (ISPs)
■ News media
■ Other incident response teams
■ Owners of the source of the incident (such as if a network attack was launched from another company's network)
■ Lawyers

Incidents can occur that do not involve an actual compromise of, or inappropriate access to, PII. However, if there is reasonable belief, as defined by the multiple breach notice laws, that PII has been inappropriately accessed or compromised, you will need to notify the impacted individuals. Create documented procedures to determine how to make these notifications. Consider the following notification methods.

■ *Written notice.* Send via postal mail or other similar delivery method considered dependable. Send to the individuals' permanent home addresses. Include the cost of postage, envelopes, paper, and staff to assemble the letters within your overall breach response plans to ensure you have sufficiently budgeted for this activity.
■ *Telephone notice.* Individuals will appreciate and respond best to news of a breach using this method. However, this will also be one of the most time- and money-consuming methods of notification. Include the cost of staff, phone charges, and varying times on the phone within your overall breach response plan.
■ *Conspicuous posting of the breach notice on your Internet Web site.* This should not be your primary means of notification, but it is certainly a great supplemental notification method.
■ *E-mail notice.* Even though some state-level laws list this as an acceptable notification method, avoid it if at all possible. Among the many reasons not to use e-mail notification are
  – Recipients may view it as another phishing message.
  – Spam filters may delete it before it gets to the recipient.
  – If it is a shared e-mail address, as many family e-mails are, it is possible the message will never make it to the intended individual if another family member deletes it first.
  – E-mail addresses often are checked or used for a very short period of time; you may have many e-mail addresses that are no longer used.
■ *Notification to major statewide or nationwide media.* This is another method to use as a supplement to a method that contacts each individual directly.

Within your breach response plan, document the type of information to include within the notification message. Also document how quickly notification needs to be made following discovery of the breach.

Generally if notification is necessary it should occur as quickly as possible and account for the time necessary to determine the scope of the breach and restore the security and integrity of the data system, along with provisions for potential law enforcement, investigation, and homeland security-related delays. A suggested best practice is to provide notification no later than 45 days after the date on which the privacy breach was discovered. Not only do many privacy lawyers recommend this timeframe, but at least two state-level breach notice laws (Ohio and Florida) specifically require notifications to occur within this timeframe.

It is important you create your breach response plans with all the state breach notice laws in mind; they are all different. For example, the Illinois law does not allow any extra notification delays for law enforcement purposes.

Recovery

Continue breach recovery activities following your immediate breach response activities. If systems were compromised and led to the breach, eliminate all means of continued intruder access.

Do such things as follows:

■ Restore programs from trusted vendor-supplied media
■ Restore data from trusted backups
■ Install appropriate patches or fixes
■ Modify accounts and passwords as needed
■ Monitor systems for further attacks
■ Modify systems and procedures to prevent subsequent incidents

Identify lessons learned and implement improvements. To do this effectively you must carefully document response actions and track certain metrics. For example,

■ Assess time and resources used and damage incurred. The author has identified at least 40 different types of costs involved with privacy breaches.*
■ Document commands, code, and procedures used in response activities. Update your response plan documentation as necessary.
■ Conduct a postmortem review and investigation to prevent a similar incident from recurring if at all possible.
■ Document all findings and lessons learned and incorporate into a privacy breach report for your executive business leaders.

Do not stop responding to the incident once you have determined the incident has been resolved.

■ Continue postincident monitoring and updating your personnel, business partners, and customers as appropriate about the incident.
■ Continue monitoring inquiries, and ensure the responses are handled consistently.
■ Handle returned breach notification letters appropriately and consistently. Determine what actions to take for those individuals whose letters were returned.
■ Modify incident response plans as needed, including the portions of the information security incident response plans.
■ Implement improvements to information security policies, procedures, and measures.
■ Modify applications and systems as needed. Provide targeted training and ongoing awareness.

---

* See the author's Privacy Management Toolkit: http://www.informationshield.com/privacy_main.html.

Risk Management

Chapter 4

Using Quasi-Intelligence Resources to Protect the Enterprise

Craig A. Schiller

Contents

The times they are a changing

Bob Dylan

Background

Enterprises used to be able to handle the threats themselves. As the threats have grown in scope, they have grown beyond the boundaries of the enterprise.

In the beginning, battling malicious code was a desktop-only concern. The viruses attacked a single computer, our tools defended individual computers. The targets of viruses were files or boot sectors of disks. At first our tools were integrity checkers that confirmed known goodness. Later we began to recognize bad code and created small signatures that we could count on to discriminate bad code from good. The use of antivirus programs was not widespread. During the time that signatures were being developed, several private databases (like Patricia Huffman's VSum) were used by information security professionals to recognize the signs of a virus infection.

Information security professionals compared observed behavior and characteristics with the database entries to determine if they matched a known virus. Using this method, the individual information security professional could find viruses for which no signatures had been developed. Information security professionals would use the database to search for entries that included the behavior or files that they had observed. In this way they might recognize a virus even if no signature had been developed for this particular strain. The behavior was recognizable even if bits had been twiddled to avoid matching an existing signature. It was a heuristic process that was later emulated in antivirus products.

As computers shifted from stand-alone systems to networked workstations, the primary mode of infection shifted as well, from files, to e-mails, and then to network exploits against vulnerabilities. The number of viruses climbed, making it difficult for individuals to keep up without the help of vendors.

Until the 1990s, enterprise security was largely performed in-house, with little apparent reliance on outside resources. That is, most threats of the day could be detected and responded to, in their entirety, within the boundaries of the company using packaged security products. With sensors (e.g., firewalls) along the edge and antivirus (A/V) on the servers and desktops a company stood a pretty good chance of protecting itself from the threats. Even so, the Department of Energy and the Department of Defense realized as early as 1988 that some aggregation and distribution of threat information was needed and thus founded the computer incident advisory capability (CIAC) and Computer Emergency Response/Team Coordination Center (CERT/CC), respectively.

In the late 1990s, enterprise protection was extended through the use of intrusion detection and intrusion prevention tools. The image of self-reliance was an illusion. The threat of these early days was simple enough that intelligence gathering and aggregation of data could be packaged and delivered as commodities. Behind the antivirus software and intrusion detection system/intrusion prevention system (IDS/IPS) packages stood as an intelligence apparatus, harvesting security reports and converting them into neatly wrapped signatures and profiles.

Managed security services (MSS) began to appear. Soon after the introduction of MSS, vendors of these services began to offer the use of their aggregated clients' experiences as an early warning to other enterprise customers. The products offered alerts as well as IDS/IPS and firewall rules created in response to new threats.

With the advent of malware driven by organized crime, the threat has evolved past three points of detection by signature or even single perspective heuristics.

Here is what Gartner's *Magic Quadrant* recently said on the subject:

> Traditional signature-based antivirus products can no longer protect companies from malicious code attacks. Vendors must execute product and business strategies to meet the new market requirements for broader malicious code protection.

> **Arabella Hallawell***

Even A/V vendors have come to the same conclusion, as evidenced by "New approaches to malware detection," an article by Ellen Messmer in the April 30, 2007, issue of *Network World*. The article quotes Brian Foster, Symantec's Senior Director for Product Management, as saying "Everyone agrees signature-based defense is not enough." In the same article, Paul Moriarty, director of Internet Content Security for Trend Micro, said they were looking beyond the signature-based approach, which "has utility but some limitations." Trend Micro hopes to augment traditional signature-based technology with analysis of patterns of traffic to desktops or servers. Further, Trend Micro is looking at promising research regarding blocking traffic to Web sites whose domain names have existed for fewer than five days.

This is not to say that existing antivirus products should no longer be used. On the contrary, it is saying that existing A/V products must be augmented with information and products that address different aspects of the threat to be effective. Increasingly malicious code authors are employing encryption, polymorphism, hide tools, and rootkits to avoid detection. If the attack vector is password guessing or brute force, then the bot-herder takes actions as a legitimate user. The first action one takes is to run a batch file that turns off antivirus products. In addition, more and more code is coordinated and controlled across the network.

All this adds up to a move toward the inclusion of intelligence information and the network perspective in detection. Table 4.1 provides a list of sources of malware information, a description of the data provided, and the security goal to which the information applies.

There are now some attacks that involve no malicious code on the victim's computer (man in the middle, pharming using domain name system [DNS] spoofing). Recently there have been signs of some botnet agents being controlled via terminal services or other remote control technologies rather than by a resident botnet client. These may be using existing remote control software where available (Carbon Copy, virtual network computing [VNC], remote desktop protocol [RDP] terminal services, etc.). This has the advantage of creating botnet clients without the presence of betraying malware. If the bot-herder needs special code for a task, the code need exist only when it is needed (just-in-time malware). This reduces the detectable footprint both in size and in temporal range.

Sometimes the only evidence that a system is owned is data that is collected somewhere else. Sometimes the data is located on other systems owned by your organization. Other times the data is found on systems outside the organization.

---

* From *Magic Quadrant for enterprise antivirus, January 2005: Vendors must address new malicious code threats*, Feb. 22, 2005. www.gartner.com.

Table 4.1   Categories of Intelligence Data Used against Malware

Type	Description	Security Goal
Community virus database	9/1/1998 (last known version); Patricia Hoffman's VSum hypertext listing of viruses. Virus-L, virus.comp, *Computer Virus Catalog*; published by the Virus Test Center in Hamburg. The Wild List (http://www.wildlist.org/WildList/), vendor tables of virus information available from most A/V vendors.	Originally a database to help users figure out which virus they had by comparing symptoms to the list of known virus characteristics. Today's lists are merely a cross-reference of the polyphony of A/V vendor's names for the same instance of a virus. Some vendor lists provide a fair amount of information. The vendor lists usually have limited search capability.
Specific virus removal tools	1987; Two tools (immune and unvirus) created by Hebrew University, one to detect whether a computer had the Jerusalem virus, the other to remove it; more recently A/V companies have produced virus removal tools in response to specific viruses, like Blaster.	Incident response to a virus attack, defensive, no intelligence value.
Integrity checkers	System file checker (SFC), Tripwire	A method or tool for ensuring that static files remain verifiably unchanged since their creation or installation. Similar technology is used today in communications protocols to ensure that messages received are unchanged during transmission.
Virus signature/profile checkers	Most A/V and IDS/IPS tools. A method for detecting and identifying a known virus that uses a small, unique pattern that is present in the virus. Issues occur when a pattern is discovered to be nonunique.	Contributes the identity of many viruses to the total intelligence picture.
Heuristics/anomaly detection	Most A/V and IDS/IPS tools. Heuristic methods flag deviations from a model of acceptable behavior as anomalies. False-positives occur when acceptable anomalous behavior is not understood. False-negatives occur when the model of acceptable behavior is flawed. An alternative to this approach is to catalog known unacceptable behavior.	Heuristic detection has the potential to detect previously unknown viruses.

Organic communication channels for notification of exploits	Abuse e-mail—e-mails sent to the organization's published abuse e-mail address. Help desk trouble tickets informing IT of compromised hosts, reports of abuses, etc.	Identifies compromised hosts, Digital Millenium Copyright Act (DMCA) violations, spam relays, and failures of spam engines; collects miscellaneous abuse complaints from users. Systems identified here can be a potential source of intelligence information.
Enterprise A/V management tools	Central quarantine, central reporting.	Identifies compromised hosts.
External group notifications	Network for Education and Research in Oregon, Recording Industry Association of America (RIAA), Home Box Office (HBO).	Identifies compromised hosts, DMCA violations, spam relays, and phishing Web sites.
Receiving intel from aggregating groups	Information Sharing and Analysis Centers (ISACs), Shadowserver.	Identifies C&C servers; alerts about near-time attacks, new vulnerabilities, technical and operational discussions from peers.
Gathering local intelligence	Workstation and server audit logs, firewall logs, forensic examinations, Ourmon, Snort, CWSandbox, Fiddler, Google searches, darknets.	Identifies compromised hosts that are quiet or use undetectable communications techniques. Identifies intermediate participants in phishing attacks; discovers C&C servers and drop sites; discovers exploited Web sites used for spam, phishing, botnet activity. Discovers attack vectors and local botnet members. Detects and prevents botnets that others have seen. Interrupts communication with known C&C servers.
Sharing intel with aggregating groups	Phishing Incident Response and Termination, Internet Security Operations Task Force, Anti-Phishing Working Group, Research and Education Networking–ISAC	Community aggregation of reports, creating enough of a body of evidence that makes law enforcement participation worthwhile. Letting other companies and organizations leverage what you know. Greater effectiveness in taking down bad sites.

The information in Table 4.1 can lead you to explore new sources of information, which may improve your ability to detect and respond to malware.

Identifying the Kinds of Information an Enterprise or University Should Try to Gather

Organizations need tools that can help detect or reveal botnets and other malicious code even when A/V tools report nothing. They need insights into behaviors and components that can be used to confirm the presence, activity, or effects of malware.

The value of these intelligence sources is that they may reveal botnet, phishing, or spam activity that local network sensors (collection efforts) may not see or do not report. Using these resources you can gain:

- Knowledge of attacks by your own organization's resources on others
- Knowledge of attacks by other systems on your resources
- Knowledge of attacks on other organizations similar to yours
- Knowledge of attempts by your assets to communicate with known C&C servers
- Lists of known C&C servers, ports, and channels
- Results of aggregate data from honeynets, honeypots, and darknets across the Internet
- Access to analysis reports on current threats
- Access to analysis of individual instances of malware
- Access to special tools or special collections of data
- Access to detailed discussions of real uncensored events
- Access to a professional community with similar security concerns
- Access to bleeding edge IDS signatures

External Sources

There are a myriad of sources of information on the various threats, so that it is necessary to choose the most relevant and applicable source.

Places or Organizations Where Public Information Can Be Found

There are many organizations online where quasi-intelligence can be found. Unfortunately, there is no room to cover them all. The author has selected a representative sample of useful organizations. In your sector of the economy there will likely be similar organizations that will provide similar intelligence information.

In response to 9/11, the United States created several Information Sharing and Analysis Centers (ISACs), organized along critical infrastructure boundaries. The umbrella for these centers is called the ISAC Council (http://www.isaccouncil.org/). There are ISACs that serve the communications, electricity, emergency management and response, financial services, highways, information technology, multistate, public transit, surface transportation, supply chain, water, and worldwide sectors. There is also an ISAC dedicated to Research and Education Networking (REN), with which the author is most familiar and which will be described more fully.

Research and Education Networking–Information Sharing and Analysis Center

REN–ISAC (http://www.ren-isac.net) is a cooperative organization for higher education and research institutes that was formally established in February 2003. REN–ISAC is one of many ISACs that were created in response to the needs of the Department of Homeland Security (DHS).

The goal of REN–ISAC (from the REN–ISAC Web page) is to

> Develop a trusted community for sharing information regarding cybersecurity threat, incidents, response, and protection, specifically designed to support the unique environment and needs of higher education and research organizations. The trust community will provide a forum for sharing sensitive information, a source for trusted contact information, a meeting point for peers, a means to facilitate communications, and methods for improving cybersecurity awareness and response.

In addition to sharing information among members, REN–ISAC also has established sharing relationships with DHS, U.S.-CERT, other ISACs, private network security collaborations, and others. It also has relationships with Educause and Internet2. From the REN–ISAC Web site:

> The REN-ISAC receives, analyzes and acts on operational, threat, warning and actual attack information derived from network instrumentation and information sharing relationships. Instrumentation data include netflow, router ACL counters, darknet monitoring, and Global Network Operations Center operational monitoring systems.

REN–ISAC is a membership organization that requires vetting before access to forums and shared data is granted.

Shadowserver

Shadowserver is an organization of volunteers established in 2004. The mission of the Shadowserver Foundation is to "improve the security of the Internet by raising awareness of the presence of compromised servers, malicious attackers, and the spread of malware" (from the Shadowserver Web site). From the Shadowserver Web site, the foundation meets its mission by

- Capturing and receiving malicious software or information related to compromised devices
- Disassembling, sandboxing, and analyzing viruses and Trojans
- Monitoring and reporting on malicious attackers
- Tracking and reporting on botnet activities
- Disseminating cyber threat information
- Coordinating incident response

Shadowserver Foundation is well organized, with teams established to focus on botnets, E-fraud, honeypots, malware, and tools (toyshop), as well as a management team. Criminal activity is reported to the appropriate authority.

Shadowserver provides a mailing list (http://www.shadowserver.org/mailman/listinfo/shadowserver) that will send you a monthly update of the top command and control (C2) servers sorted in various ways. There are valuable white papers, a knowledge base, graphs, and links on the Web page. You can also report botnets directly on the Web page (http://www. shadowserver.org/wiki/pmwiki.php?n=Involve.SubmitABotnet).

Until recently, the Shadowserver Web site provided a list of C&C IP addresses. This list has been taken down to prevent its use for malicious purposes. You can request access to the list by providing your full contact information as well as the purposes for which you require access to the data. Send the request to admin@shadowserver.org. If you do not have access to one of the vetting quasi-intelligence organizations, then this list is essential. You can use this list at the firewall to detect internal botclients trying to communicate to their C&C servers or in your DNS to notify you of queries while preventing communication.

This list, formatted for use in Snort, can be found on http://www.bleedingthreats.net/index. php/about-bleeding-edge-threats/all-bleeding-edge-threats-signatures/.

Bleeding Threat

Bleeding Threat (www.bleedingthreats.net) was founded in 2003 by Matt Jonkman and James Ashton. At that time there was no central repository of open-source IDS profiles. Security professionals had to subscribe to a number of mailing lists and make regular visits to several Web sites to find the latest and best IDS signatures. To address that need, the primary project at Bleeding Threat is the Bleeding Edge Threats Snort Ruleset. This project is staffed by expert information security volunteers.

Castlecops.com or Phishing Incident Response and Termination

CastleCops® is an essential resource in every security professional's tool chest. Here is the mission statement from their Web site:

> **CastleCops**® is a volunteer security community focused on making the Internet a safer place. All services to the public are free, including malware and rootkit cleanup of infected computers, malware and phish investigations and terminations, and searchable database lists of malware and file hashes.
>
> Education and collaborative information sharing are among CastleCops highest priorities. They are achieved by training our volunteer staff in our anti-malware, phishing, and rootkit academies and through additional services including Castle-Cops forums, news, reviews, and continuing education.
>
> CastleCops consistently works with industry experts and law enforcement to reach our ultimate goal in securing a safe and smart computing experience for everyone online.

The Web site has essential information for anyone trying to interpret the log files of Hijack This (http://www.castlecops.com/HijackThis.html). On the main Web page, the index items beginning with "O" and a number refer to a specific section of the Hijack This log. The author has found forum participants on CastleCops to be very knowledgeable. The PIRT database is a primary intelligence resource. Individuals can contribute suspected phishing e-mails to the database. The phishing incident response and termination (PIRT) team is a community of volunteers dedicated to taking down phishing sites (as originally conceived by Robin Laudanski). An overview of the PIRT team can be found at http://wiki.castlecops.com/PIRT. Individuals who wish to report phishing e-mails or Web sites can e-mail the information to pirt@castlecops.com or the information can be entered directly into the Fried Phish tool.

PIRT handlers are selected based on an appropriate background. They are trained in the use of the Fried Phish tools. New handlers work with mentors until the mentor is satisfied with the quality of reports generated by the new handler. Reports from individuals are placed into a suspected phish queue. Handlers confirm the report by gathering data about the reported phish, including retrieving the code from the suspected phishing Web site. Those that are validated are moved into a "confirmed phish" queue. Next, handlers attempt to contact either the server owner or the Internet Service Provider (ISP) in an effort to terminate the phishing site. Successfully terminated phishing sites are added to the "terminated phish" database. There is very little chance of a false-positive surviving this process.

Verified phishing sites are shared with a long list of organizations. As of April 30, 2007, the list included the following:

> 1&1 Internet AG, 8e6 Technologies, Alice's Registry, Anti-Phishing Working Group, APACS Security Unit, Arbor Networks, Australian Computer Emergency Response Team (AusCERT), Authentium, Blue Coat, Brand Dimensions, CERT/Software Engineering Institute/Carnegie Mellon University, ClamAV, Compete, Co-Logic, ContentKeeper Technologies, CyberDefender, Cyveillance, EveryDNS, Federal Bureau of Investigation (FBI), Firetrust, For Critical Software Ltd., Fortinet, Forum of Incident Response and Security Teams (FIRST), FraudWatch International, IronPort, Infotex, Internet Crime Complaint Center (IC3), Internet Identity, Intellectual Property Services, Korea Information Security Agency (KISA), Korea Internet Security Center (KrCERT/CC), Laboratoire d'Expertise en Securite Informatique (LEXSI), Malware Block List, National Cyber-Forensics and Training Alliance (NCFTA), Netcraft, NYSERNet, Okie Island Trading Company, OpenDNS, Pipex, Research and Education Networking Information Sharing and Analysis Center (REN-ISAC), Rede Nacional de Ensino e Pesquisa (RNP), SonicWALL, Sunbelt-Software, Support Intelligence, SURBL, Symantec, Team Cymru, Thomas Jefferson National Accelerator Facility (JLab), TrustDefender, United Online, United States Computer Emergency Readiness Team (DHS US-CERT), Websense, Webwasher, XBlock, Yahoo!

CastleCops provides a free XML feed service into the phish database. The feed is a 30-day rolling window showing both the terminated and the confirmed URLs, their associated Autonomous System Numbers (ASNs), and the PIRT database reference ID number. To request the feed, send an e-mail to Paul Laudanski (paul@castlecops.com) for authorization.

CYMRU

According to the CYMRU Web site (www.cymru.com), Team CYMRU is

> a corporation of technologists interested in making the Internet more secure. We are a group of geeks who are passionate about network security and in helping the community identify and eradicate problems within their networks.

Team CYMRU was founded in 1998 by Rob Thomas as an Internet security think tank. Team CYMRU works with over 700 vendors, researchers, and providers. Team CYMRU provides lists of bogons (Internet Protocol [IP] ranges that should never appear in the Internet, e.g., 127.0.x.x; blocks of IP addresses that have not been allocated to any regional Internet registry; etc.) in a "plethora of formats." Rob Thomas documented the use of bogons against a frequently attacked site in a paper titled "60 Days of Naughtiness." Sixty percent of the attacks used obvious bogons. Their database is updated daily with changes from the Internet Assigned Numbers Authority. The associated Web pages also provide assistance for those wanting to start filtering bogons.

Once you have begun to look for intelligence sources you will run into tables that provide only the ASN or that provide only the IP address for sites. Team CYMRU provides a conversion utility in the form of an IP-to-ASN "whois" page (https://asn.cymru.com/). The ASN is used in Border Gateway Protocol (BGP), which exists at the same network layer as IP. BGP is designed for passing traffic between networks as opposed to within them. A single ASN is used to represent all of the blocks of IP addresses associated with a single organization. When you retrieve whois information about an ASN you can get information about all of the IP blocks belonging to the organization with that ASN. This may help you get to someone who can help shut down a rogue site.

The CYMRU Web site also provides a valuable library of expert papers, presentations, and tools, many of them dealing with BGP security. There is also a section devoted to darknets and how to create your own.

Infiltrated.net

Infiltrated.net is a list of IP addresses that have attempted brute-force password attacks against machines administered by the Web site owner (http://www.infiltrated.net/bforcers/masterlist.txt).

Spamhaus

Spamhaus (www.spamhaus.org) provides a wealth of information useful to spam fighters. They also provide the Spamhaus DROP (do not route or peer) list (http://www.spamhaus.org/drop/index.lasso). This list is a small subset of the larger Spamhaus block list (SBL) list provided for firewall and routing equipment. According to the Spamhaus Web site:

> The DROP list will NEVER include any IP space "owned" by any legitimate network and reassigned—even if reassigned to the "spammers from hell." It will ONLY include IP space totally controlled by spammers or 100% spam hosting operations. These are "direct allocations" from ARIN, RIPE, APNIC, LACNIC, and others to known spammers, and the troubling run of "hijacked zombie" IP blocks that have been snatched away from their original owners (which in most cases are long dead corporations) and are now controlled by spammers or netblock thieves who resell the space to spammers.

Both the DROP list and the SBL list can be used to alert you to any communications between hosts in your organization and known spammer's assets.

Internet Crime Complaint Center

Internet Crime Complaint Center (IC3) is a partnership of the FBI and the National White Collar Crime Center (NWC3). From the IC3 Web site:

> IC3's mission is to serve as a vehicle to receive, develop, and refer criminal complaints regarding the rapidly expanding arena of cyber crime. The IC3 gives the victims of

cyber crime a convenient and easy-to-use reporting mechanism that alerts authorities of suspected criminal or civil violations. For law enforcement and regulatory agencies at the federal, state, local and international level, IC3 provides a central referral mechanism for complaints involving Internet related crimes.

National Cyber-Forensics and Training Alliance

National Cyber-Forensics and Training Alliance (NCFTA) is a partnership of industry, academia, and law enforcement. From the NCFTA Web site, NCFTA

> provides a neutral collaborative venue where critical confidential information about cyber incidents can be shared discreetly, and where resources can be shared among industry, academia and law enforcement.
>
> The Alliance facilitates advanced training, promotes security awareness to reduce cyber-vulnerability, and conducts forensic and predictive analysis and lab simulations.
>
> These activities are intended to educate organizations and enhance their abilities to manage risk and develop security strategies and best practices.

NCFTA participants receive the benefits of cyber-forensic analysis, tactical response development, technological simulation or modeling analysis, and the development of advanced training. NCFTA provides the FBI and Postal Inspection Service with expertise and a place for collaboration with industry and academia.

Internet Security Operations Task Force

Internet Security Operations Task Force (ISOTF) is an anti-cyber-crime group focused on uncovering new trends and tactics to combat phishing, botnets, and other types of online scams. ISOTF is led by Gadi Evron, a security researcher at Israeli-based Beyond Security. In addition to Zero Day Emergency Response Team alerts, ISOTF also publishes member-only mailing lists focused on botnets (http://www.whitestar.linuxbox.org/mailman/listinfo/botnets), phishing attacks (http://www.whitestar.linuxbox.org/mailman/listinfo/phishing), ISP-centric security (Drone Army), malware vendor and security researchers (malicious Web sites and phishing), and registrar operators (Reg-Ops). The last three mailing lists require vetting before you can join. For consideration, contact Gadi Evron at ge@linuxbox.org.

Membership Organizations

The simplest and most direct organization that can provide some intelligence is your ISP. Although ISPs are not traditional membership organizations, you are a member of the ISP community as a customer. The services available vary from ISP to ISP. At a minimum, you should be receiving information from your ISP related to complaints against your organization that they receive. They might also provide you with information they receive about attacks against your organization that they see or are told about.

Quasi-intelligence organizations have varying qualification requirements. Some organizations, like Shadowserver, do not require membership. Most of their information is made freely available to all. Other organizations, like the REN–ISAC, have strict membership and confidentiality requirements. REN–ISAC acquires some of its information from sources that will provide information only on the condition that all who receive it pass a vetting check and agree to abide by tough confidentiality guidelines. This is to prevent the data from getting into the wrong hands. In addition, the confidentiality guidelines create an environment in which members are comfortable discussing sensitive cases because they know the information will not become public.

Each membership organization establishes its own qualifications. For example PIRT shares the information it collects with anyone that wants it. All handlers are volunteers, but to be a handler you must apply and have your resume and experiences evaluated. All newly admitted handlers must go through some mandatory training and a period of time spent working with a mentor. Clearly the focus of handler screening is to ensure the integrity of the analysis process, but the resume review also attempts to identify and block potential bad guys from getting inside, again for integrity reasons.

Another class of quasi-intelligence organization is the paid membership consortium. This includes organizations like the Internet Security Alliance and Red Siren. These organizations tend to be more general in focus, digging into an issue when their constituency expresses a need. This chapter focuses on the free organizations.

Confidentiality Agreements

Some quasi-intelligence organizations are bound to confidentiality agreements by original sources. By agreeing to keep the data or the source confidential, they are able to get quality intelligence that would otherwise be unobtainable.

In some cases, the information cannot be shared with anyone outside your institution. In other cases, you are permitted to share the information only with other individuals that have been vetted by the quasi-intelligence organization. Each cache of intelligence information may carry its own provisions for confidentiality. Here, caches are sets of information from different sources. You need to ensure that each person that might have access to this kind of data understands and agrees to abide by the provisions of each confidentiality agreement.

The Role of Intelligence Sources in Aggregating Enough Information to Make Law Enforcement Involvement Practical

Quasi-intelligence sources provide a valuable service to the Internet community in that they are able to take individual cases that law enforcement would never prosecute and aggregate them with thousands of other related cases. Law enforcement is justified in taking a case with thousands of instances. Organizations like PIRT (Castlecops.com), the Anti-Phishing Working Group (APWG), REN–ISAC, the IC3, and the NCFTA bundle and report cases to the NWC3, which delivers them to the FBI and Secret Service. PIRT and APWG also report the same cases to anti-phishing and antivirus vendors. Sites like Shadowserver make lists of known C&C servers publicly available. Some law enforcement sites like NCFTA are known to use their data.

Without these aggregating organizations, law enforcement would be buried in thousands of individual cases that could not easily be pursued. The aggregating organizations, in addition to collecting and collating the data, bring a great amount of expertise to the task of analyzing and interpreting the information. It is inconceivable that law enforcement would be funded to hire all the expertise provided to them for free by these groups.

Internal Sources

You should not overlook the many internal sources of intelligence information available to you. The most obvious sources are log files of every size, shape, and color. Firewall logs, system logs, and application logs from both servers and workstations. Centralizing your logs can make this data more accessible and can let you develop tools for real- or near-real-time analysis.

For many organizations, Windows workstation logs are not turned on by default. To ensure useful data is being collected the local security policy should include the audit policy settings as follows:

Audit account log-on events	Success, Failure
Audit account management	Success, Failure
Audit log-on events	Success, Failure
Audit policy change	Success, Failure
Audit privilege use	Success, Failure

These settings should be enabled on all Windows workstations. In addition the Windows firewall for all workstations should enable logging and you should ensure that the options "Enable log dropped packets" and "Enable log successful connections" are both checked. This should be done even if you do not intend to use the firewall for filtering traffic.

Table 4.2 lists the potential internal sources of intelligence, a description of the nature of the intelligence, and the security goals addressed by each source.

One fundamental change is necessary in the way help desk teams respond to virus-infected systems that are brought in to be scanned or reimaged. Performing a quick forensic prior to virus scanning or reimaging has proven to be yield valuable information about other infected hosts, C&C servers, payload structures, and more. (See a sample quick forensic procedure at the end of this chapter.) Note that the quick forensic procedure as described here is not intended to support a case for involving law enforcement. The intent of the quick forensic is to expand your knowledge of the breadth of the botnet infection or its links to the outside. If the quick forensic yields information that would indicate law enforcement should be involved (e.g., the presence of child pornography), then the quick forensic should be suspended and a full forensic exam, beginning with taking a forensically sound image, should be performed. As you can see from the sample quick forensic, the procedure will be unique to each organization and to each wave of infected botclients. This sample is version 5. As more information was learned about the nature of botclients infected by this bot-herder, the procedure was modified to gather better information.

What Do You Do with the Information When You Get It?

Organizations need a process for finding candidates (which I call potential intelligence markers) and evaluating them for their suitability. In law enforcement, an intelligence marker may sometimes be placed on an individual's or asset's record to indicate there may be some interest in the individual. An intelligence organization may need to know about activities that are not crimes in and of

Table 4.2 Internal Intelligence Sources

Security audit logs	Check the security logs for failed and successful log-ons. This may provide evidence of password guessing or brute force. Some are obvious, page after page of failed attempts starting with administrator and then changing to different spellings (administrador, etc.). The successful logs that occur during these attempts are likely compromised accounts, particularly if the attempts occur during hours when your company does not usually work. Sometimes it is less obvious, a handful of failed log-in attempts from many machines spread out over time. Have the logs forwarded to a central log server and process them daily using Structure Query Language queries to filter out most normal behavior.	Discover other infected systems by making a list of the machines involved in the failed log-ins. Useful to convince the user who says, "My machine is not infected. I ran a virus scan and it came up clean."
Network firewall, IDS/IPS logs	Traditional security, understand what normal looks like, investigate abnormal entries, look for known attack traffic patterns. Develop rules to block newly discovered attack traffic.	Detect, log, and block traffic at the perimeter. Identify IP addresses transmitting traffic associated with security alerts. Keep logs for analysis after the fact, when intelligence reports identify a problem.
Host firewall logs	Check the host firewall logs for successful inbound connections. Validate that inbound connections are reasonable for that workstation. Check outbound connections on unusual ports, particularly ports for which alerts have recently been issued. Check for communications with known C&C servers.	Evidence of participation in botnet activity. Identify attack vectors, hosts providing botnet updates, spam templates, C&C, etc.
Network traffic anomaly detection	Using Net flow analysis or tools like Ourmon, analyze network traffic for behavioral evidence of botnet or scanning activity. Monitor and report more detailed traffic from suspected botnet clients and servers.	Identify botnet clients and their C&C servers, along with their IRC channel, user ID, and password. Identify malware downloaded by botclients.
IDS/IPS	Snort, Real Secure, etc.—analyze network traffic in near-real-time to spot patterns or anomalies associated with malicious activity.	Signatures come from outside organizations (vendors or open-source organizations like Bleeding Snort).

Darknets	A darknet is a reserved portion of your IP space that is not assigned to any system. Any attempt to communicate with systems in darknet space is evidence of scanning.	Identify systems that are scanning your network. Feed this information to your network traffic anomaly detection systems to further corroborate bot-like activity.
Honeypots, honeynets	An instrumented system set up so that would-be attackers give themselves away. Honeypots and honeynets can be set up to respond to attackers to make them believe they have encountered a new potential host to infect.	Placing a honeypot or honeynet in darknet space permits you to gather information about the scanners and their intentions. Honeypots and honeynets can give you detailed information about attack vectors, C&C servers, location of botnet component storage servers, bot commands, and functionality.
Forensic examinations	A major operations change for most IT shops when remediating virus-infected systems is to perform a quick forensic examination before scanning for viruses or reimaging. Scanning for viruses with an independent virus scanner or reimaging destroys evidence that can help you identify the C&C server and other botclients. Creating a quick forensic checklist can preserve essential intelligence information, even evidence.	Examine the security and firewall logs on suspected virus-infected systems. If you know the time of a suspicious event involving the host, search the computer for files that were modified around the time of the event. If you find malware, look for configuration files associated with the malware. The configuration files may tell you ports used, C&C IP addresses, usernames, passwords, and other infected files.
Sandbox technology	CWSandbox from Sunbelt Software and the Norman Sandbox. Both the CWSandbox and the Norman Sandbox offer a free Web site for organizations to submit individual samples. Submitted samples are analyzed in their respective sandboxes and the results are e-mailed back to the submitter. The sample is placed in the sandbox, in a virtual environment, and executed. The sandbox records all files opened, all connections attempted, all files that the malware attempts to download.	Sandbox analysis can provide C&C server IP addresses or DS names, bot channel names, user IDs and passwords, download sites for malware, scanning software, spam templates, lists of e-mails, and download package names.

(continued)

Table 4.2 (Continued)

Fiddler	Developed by Microsoft as part of the Strider project. Fiddler is a Web browser proxy that records, for analysis, the Web sites through which a browser is redirected when a site is visited and the actions taken during each visit.	Can reveal Web sites that upload malware as well as the structure of sites involved in search engine spam.
Google searches	A method for discovering Web vulnerabilities using search engines. It was popularized by the book *Google Hacking for Penetration Testers*, by Johnny Long. Two useful examples: (1) Use the search phrase "phpbb site:<your URL>" to find phpBB sites. Check these sites for evidence that they have been abandoned by users and taken over by spammers. (2) Use the search phrase "phentermine site:<your URL>" to locate Web sites that may have been co-opted by spammers to sell the popular diet pill.	PhpBB sites that have been misconfigured to permit users to post without being approved by a moderator are often taken over by spammers. Finding Web sites in your domain that are offering phentermine will permit you to take these compromised Web sites offline. If you happen to have Web statistics being gathered about these Web pages, they can yield valuable information about the spammer's infrastructure. Look at referrer sites and the search engine strings used to find the site.
Asset inventory searches	Using tools like LANDesk Manager or Altiris search-managed systems for definition indications of bot control. File names or hashes found on other local botclients, directory structures used by the bot-herder.	Use your knowledge of organic bot information found on local clients to find other members of the botnet. Ourmon snagged Internet traffic containing the name of a file being downloaded by infected botclients. Using Altiris to search for the file, about 40 other infected hosts were located.

themselves but may link an individual to criminal activity or organizations. Sometimes the behavior indicated by the marker is enough to confirm maliciousness without any other confirmation (e.g., a password guessing using the list of default accounts associated with Rbot), but not always.

Other intelligence markers may require a second or third marker to be sure. For example, a workstation scanning your network may be a botclient, but it could also be a bored employee. However, a workstation that scans your network and communicates with a known C&C server has a higher probability of being a member of a botnet. Intel markers can be used to identify infected systems in your enterprise or to let the infected systems ID themselves as in the case of a darknet or honeynet. In this way intelligence markers can contribute to both prevention and recovery strategies.

What makes a good intelligence marker? Intelligence markers that we are interested in consist of data or information that aid in confirming or denying the nature of a workstation or Internet site as malicious. The best markers are unambiguous and defining. That is, by their presence or absence they can confirm or deny maliciousness. For example, network traffic that contains confirmed malicious code retrieved by several sites from the suspect workstation would be an unambiguous and defining intelligence marker.

The usual intelligence marker is less definitive or more ambiguous in isolation. However, aggregating this data can often raise your confidence in a determination. The best markers are well understood, particularly the circumstances under which the marker would mean malicious or nonmalicious use. For example, the Symantec Anti-Virus (SAV) server transmitting to destination Transmission Control Protocol (TCP) port 2967 to several workstations is likely nonmalicious. In contrast, a workstation (not a SAV server) transmitting to several workstations using destination TCP port 2967 is likely malicious and is trying to exploit a Symantec vulnerability.

Evaluation of what makes a good Intel marker will vary with the experience of the evaluator. It takes a skilled evaluator to analyze and vet new intelligence markers. Once vetted, the markers can be described to less-skilled observers so that they may monitor for the presence of the vetted markers. A record should be kept of the vetting process, in case anyone (e.g., a defense attorney) should later question its validity.

Here, for example, is the confidence rating system provided by the Network for Education and Research in Oregon, the author's ISP, for abuse reports related to hosts infected with the Storm Worm.

> The confidence value associated with an entry indicates how likely the host is infected with Storm-Worm and ranges between 1 and 5. A value of 1 means medium confidence: a suspect host connected to a Storm-Worm C&C network but a monitor system could not establish a return connection to verify the suspect host is infected. A value of 5 means very high confidence: a suspect host connected to a Storm-Worm C&C network, searched for strings known to be associated with Storm-Worm, and a monitor system was able to establish a return connection and verify the suspect host's behavior is consistent with Storm-Worm. Values between 1 and 5 suggest that either the suspect host connected to a Storm-Worm C&C network and searched for strings associated with Storm-Worm or a monitor system was able to establish a return connection to the suspect host. When available, the UDP port used to connect to the monitor is provided.

In some cases, markers only add weight to a decision that must ultimately be made by a human. In the bot-detection algorithms found in Ourmon, developed by Jim Binkley of Portland State University (PSU), several markers are monitored and evaluated. Each marker is assigned a letter, which is printed in reports whenever that condition is detected (Table 4.3).

Table 4.3 Intelligence Markers Used in Ourmon

E	Presence of Internet Control Messaging Protocol errors
W	Work weight—essentially the ratio of content to control data
O	One-way or two-way traffic
R	Presence of RESETs
M	Lack of FINS

Table 4.4 Application Flags

B	BitTorrent Protocol
G	Gnutella Protocol
K	Kazaa Protocol
M	Morpheus Protocol (P2P too)
P	Honeypot (darknet) violation
E	E-mail source port (e.g., port 25) seen
H	Web source port (e.g., port 80 or 443) seen
I	IRC messages seen
S	User Datagram Protocol only; indicates spam for Internet messenger

If only one marker's letter shows up, then the system may not be part of a botnet. If several letters are printed, then the likelihood of the system being part of a botnet is increased. In Ourmon, a busy botnet will light up the letters, spelling out EWORM. Ourmon adds other intelligence markers to increase confidence. One indicator shows whether the system is communicating with a known C&C server. Another indicator displays whether a system is acting in isolation or is part of a communicating network of some kind (IRC, P2P, etc.). An intelligence marker displays the ratio of unique IP addresses to destination ports. If you see a host that talks to few IP addresses with many destination ports, you may have a scanner looking for active ports, particularly if the one-way flag is set. If you see a host that talks to many IP addresses with a few unique destination ports, you may be seeing a typical fan-out pattern for a bot that is recruiting. Most bots have tools that scan only a limited number of vulnerabilities.

To reduce the number of false intelligence markers, Ourmon also keeps track of protocols that exhibit botlike characteristics but may actually be legitimate. Similar to our intelligence markers, identifying a host as one that uses a protocol with wormlike characteristics does not discount the fact that it might still be a bot. Instead, it says that worminess alone is not sufficient to conclude that it is part of a botnet (Table 4.4).

You will notice that some of the flags indicate potential good, whereas some indicate potential bad (honeypot or darknet violation, e-mail source port seen, User Datagram Protocol (UDP) only—a spam using Internet messenger indicator).

For a more detailed look at Ourmon, check out Chapters 6–9 of *Botnets—The Killer Web App*, published by Syngress, or go to http://ourmon.sourceforge.net/. To see Ourmon in action go to http://ourmon.cat.pdx.edu/ourmon.

Ourmon also uses data from other intelligence sources to corroborate its suspicions. Several sources, like Shadowserver provide lists of known C2 servers. Ourmon checks the IP addresses associated with a suspected botclient to see if any of them are known C&C servers. The combination of communication with a known C&C server and botlike activity is usually enough to conclude this is a positive determination of a botnet.

PSU obtains this flag by using the list of known C&C servers in our internal DNS server. Any host that queries one of the known DNS servers is returned a special address. The system at this address records the IP address and port number for any system that contacts it. This information is fed into Ourmon and correlated with other intelligence markers for the same IP address. Another approach would be just to return a blackhole address for any queries made to known C&C servers. Similarly, some organizations use BGP to the same effect (turning off routes instead of giving fictitious DNS entries).

Some intelligence you receive from external sources (e.g., from your ISP or from your abuse e-mail address) is about the activity of systems in your IP space. If the intelligence indicates the likelihood of an infected host, you should activate your response process. In the case of PSU, our networking team quarantines the suspected infected host, restricting its access and referring the user to the help desk. Our computer support analysts identify the location of the computer and the user to whom the computer is assigned. The desktop support team retrieves the computer and performs the quick forensic exam. If anything extraordinary or illegal is seen during the forensic exam, an image is taken and information security is notified for a more complete forensic exam. In the course of examining the system, any new intelligence that is uncovered is fed back to Ourmon or other sensors.

Counterintelligence: The Next Step

Security professionals are now beginning to look at these threats in a new light. This chapter urges organizational security officers to begin to look beyond their own boundaries for information to combat the growing darkness. As we have begun to learn more about the threat, a few have made forays into the realm of counterintelligence. The white paper "Revealing Botnet Membership Using DNSBL Counter-Intelligence," by Anirudh Ramachandran, Nick Feamster, and David Dagon from the College of Computing, Georgia Institute of Technology, is one of these. By analyzing the efforts of bot-herders to market their spamming bot activities as free of blacklisting, Mr. Dagon et al. noticed that they made DNS blacklist queries in a manner that could identify them as spamming bots. Their method uses heuristics to distinguish between legitimate and bot-related queries. Their study suggests that bot-herders perform reconnaissance to ensure their bots are not blacklisted prior to conducting attacks. Using techniques described in this paper could yield an early warning capability.

Recent work in the area of passive DNS analysis has yielded great insights into the working of fast flux DNS related to phishing sites. You can see a visual representation of fast flux DNS used in a persistent phishing cluster located at http://www.internetperils.com/perilwatch/20060928.php. This animated .gif was created by taking 20 dumps of the APWG database, gathered from May 17 through September 20, 2006, and combining them with ongoing network performance and topology data collected directly by Internet Perils. The result is a view that no individual target of phishing could have provided. Law enforcement and anti-phishing groups can now see the big picture of systems involved in phishing attacks. In addition they see the effects of fast flux DNS in a striking graphic presentation.

More analysis of the aggregated data collected by these quasi-intelligence organizations is needed. It is here that we will find the weapons to begin to fight the fire currently fueled by organized crime. There are reports that spammers using botnet technology are making incredible amounts of money. One court document says that Jeremy Jaynes was making $750,000 a month from his spamming activities. Rumor has it that Pharmamaster, the Russian spammer that brought down Blue Security, was making $3 million a month from spam. With this kind of money, they can fund significant research to keep their enterprises operational. As evidenced by Blue Security's fate, they can also bring tremendous resources to bear on anyone or any company that begins to impact that income. Governments must begin to recognize this and respond accordingly. At present, there is no concerted effort to ensure that research is being done in all areas that might yield productive results. More important than the technical issues, there is little being done in the realm of law and law enforcement that will effectively meet this global threat.

Summary

A/V products must be augmented to protect your organization against today's threat. Intelligence information from both internal and external sources is needed to address new threats that are not handled by A/V products. Each intelligence source is different. Information security professionals should review the objectives addressed by each intelligence source to determine those that will enhance your organization's ability to detect botnets and other malicious activity.

A rating system should be associated with each intelligence source. The rating should indicate the level of confidence that the organization should place on the information. Information from different sources should be gathered and correlated to raise the confidence level in a determination that a suspicious host may be part of a botnet or other malicious activity.

Organizations should change their process for handling virus-infected systems to require the collection of intelligence data prior to clean scanning or host reimaging. Ensure your workstations are configured to gather useful log information.

Using these intelligence resources to augment your existing security measures you can gain:

- Knowledge of attacks by your own organization's resources on others
- Knowledge of attacks by other systems on your resources
- Knowledge of attempts by your assets to communicate with known C&C servers
- Lists of known C&C servers, ports, and channels
- Results of aggregate data from honeynets, honeypots, and darknets across the Internet
- Access to analysis reports on current threats
- Access to analysis of individual instances of malware
- Access to special tools
- Access to detailed discussions of real uncensored events
- Access to a professional community with similar security concerns
- Access to bleeding edge IDS signatures

Arrange to use this intelligence data with your DNS system, your wide area networks routers, your network monitoring systems, and your IDS/IPS systems.

Finally, find aggregating organizations in your sector and become a contributing member. As a profession, we cannot win the war against bots and other malware unless we work together.

The sample First Responder procedure

Version 5
12/14/06

First Responder Examination of Compromised Machines

Read each section before beginning.

Do not scan the computer for viruses before taking these steps. The scan may delete useful files. Do not edit, view, sort, or otherwise manipulate the event files before saving them.

First, copy the Event Viewer logs to a universal serial bus (USB) drive.

■ Go to Control Panel > Administrative Tools > Event Viewer
■ Right click on each log, and click on "Save As."
  – When saving the first file, create a directory with today's date (YYMMDD) and the name of the computer being examined and the help desk ticket number (e.g., 061102 CAMPUSREC-04 RT2349).
  – Save each log to this folder on the USB drive, using the naming scheme [computer name] [log description] [six-character date, YYMMDD] (e.g., "CAMPUSREC-04 Security 061102").

Keep Event Viewer open, as the logs will be useful later in locating entry events and helping to locate corrupted files. The other logs to export are the antivirus (SAV or McAfee) logs. The McAfee logs are located at:

%DEFLOGDIR%\AccessProtectionLog.txt
%DEFLOGDIR%\BufferOverflowProtectionLog.txt
%DEFLOGDIR%\EmailOnDeliveryLog.txt
%DEFLOGDIR%\OnAccessScanLog.txt
%DEFLOGDIR%\OnDemandScanLog.txt
%DEFLOGDIR%\UpdateLog.txt

On the author's system %DEFLOGDIR% translates to C:\Documents and Settings\All Users\Application Data\McAfee\DesktopProtection

The SAV logs are SAV risk, scan, tamper, and event histories and can be exported by running the SAV graphical user interface.

■ If the log is empty, disregard.
■ If the log has items in it, select the log, then click "Save" on the toolbar.
  – Save them to the USB drive
  – Use the same naming scheme as for the Event Viewer logs
  – These are saved as comma-delimited files

Once the logs have been saved, the next step is to locate any corrupted files or files of copyrighted information (movies, games, etc.) as well as any other unusual files.

At this point you can use the SAV logs to see if they identify any folders that may have infected files. The risk history file will identify folders that contained infected files. These folders should be examined for other potential evidence. The SAV event history may identify folders that contained files that could not be examined, called scan omissions. These folders are good places to look for the bot-herder's payload. Note that saving the SAV logs does not save the individual entry detail. If there is an interesting individual entry, you can copy the text from the entry into a notepad text file.

In the current set of infections, one place commonly used to store stolen intellectual property is in the recycle bin. Looking at hidden files in the recycle bin is tricky. Open Windows Explorer and click on Tools and Options. Change setting on Tools options so that hidden files and folders are visible (enable Show Hidden Files and Folders). Change the settings (disable) for the attributes "Hide Extensions for Known File Types" and "Hide Protected OS files."

Using Windows Explorer, go to C:\ and locate the file C:\Recycler\. If you list the files, you may see a directory that begins with .bin{SID}. This is the directory in which we have found stolen intellectual property. However, the files in this directory do not show up in Windows. To see the files, first double-click on the directory that begins with .bin. This will place a copy of the path in the address bar. Highlight the path in the address bar, then press Ctrl C. This will place a copy of the path on the clipboard.

Next, open a Disk Operating System (DOS) window. Switch to the C: drive if it is not already there. Type cd followed by a quote mark. Right click on the top blue bar of the DOS window. In the drop-down menu locate the Edit selection. Left click on Edit to bring up another menu. In the Edit menu select Paste. Add the closing quotation mark ("), then press Enter.

To check if files are there, you can type the dir command. If there are files, then you will want to type the command again with the forward slash ("/") s option (list subdirectories) and redirect the output to the USB memory stick into a file with a name that includes the name of the computer, the phrase "Hidden Directories," and the date in YYMMDD format, for example:

C:\RECYCLER\bin.{645ff040-5081-101b-9f08-00aa002f954e} > dir /s > e:"{computername} Hidden Directories 061103.txt"

The easiest way to locate files associated with the break-in or the data collected by the hacker is to find the dates of intrusion. Go back to the security log.

■ Sort by date and scroll through the log looking at the "Failure Audits."
■ These indicate failed log-ins, and the most suspicious of these are when there are several failures within a second. However, it is best to open up the properties of the first few and look at them in turn.
■ On the properties page, there are several items of interest that indicate break-in attempts.
  – Make note if the domain field of the Event Properties entry contains anything other than your domain name or the name of the workstation being examined. Also make note if the Workstation Name field contains the name of anything other than the name of the workstation being examined.

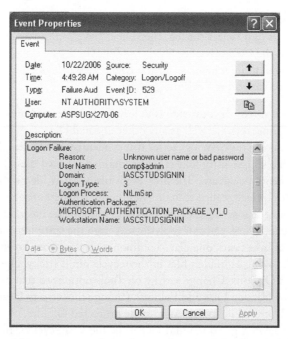

When you find a record like this, record the date and time of the first failed attempt, then move on to another date.

You will use the dates and times of the break-ins to search the file system for other evidence. If the security log is empty or contains only successes, use the dates from the Symantec risk history or event log. If Symantec has also has no logs, check for activity on a recent common break-in date (from other intelligence) or the date the suspicion of infection was raised. For each date you found you can search the files and folders with the options mentioned earlier for showing hidden files and folders and not hiding the system files. Once the search has been completed, sort the files by the date/time field. Look for files that were modified around the time of the break-ins. There may be some normal files at the same time but after a few machines you will be able to recognize most of them. If you want to look at some to check them out, use Notepad. You should not execute any of the files you find. In these files you are looking for things that may tell you how they got in or user IDs and passwords they may have collected or broken. Any hacker tools and the configuration files associated with them can provide valuable insights.

One file that we found on several systems that was worth looking for was a set of five files starting with JAs.

JAsfv.dll
JAsfv.ini
JAstat.dll
JAstat.ini
JAstat.stats

In the request tracker (RT) ticket you should also locate any files that are listed that were detected by an Altiris scan. These files and files either near them or with the same date and time as them may be of interest.

If you find any file with credit card numbers, Social Security numbers (SSNs), or other data that might be personally identifiable information, stop the investigation and contact the security officer. A computer with this kind of data in proximity to hacker data will need to have an image taken and a more thorough forensic examination performed by security.

In the Windows directory (WinNT for Win2K) copy to the memory stick any files that have the word "firewall" in them (Firewall_Zone_A.log, Firewall_Zone_A.log.old, pfirewall.log, etc.)

Open a command window. Change to the drive on which the memory stick is located. Change the directory to the folder for this computer. Change the drive to the C: drive. Change the directory to the root "\" directory. List the directory first with the "/s" parameter, then with both "/s" and "/ah" parameters and redirect the output to the drive with the memory stick. If the memory stick is on drive E: the commands would look like this.

```
C:\Documents and Settings\comp$admin> e:
E:\>dir
Volume in drive E has no label.
Volume Serial Number is 05D1-4545
Directory of E:
11/02/2006 01:46 PM   <DIR>        061117 ESL-TECH
11/17/2006 05:13 PM   <DIR>        061117 ATH-PSC167-XRAY
             0 File(s)          0 bytes
             2 Dir(s)    876,937,216 bytes free
If the computer you were working with was the ESL-TECH computer,
 you would change the directory to 06117 ESL-TECH.
E:\< cd "061117 ESL-TECH"
E:\061117 ESL-TECH> c:
C:\Documents and Settings\comp$admin>cd \
C:\>dir /s >"e:061117 ESL-TECH directories.txt"
C:\>dir /s /ah >"e:061117 ESL-TECH hidden directories.txt"
```

In the root directory (C:\) you will find a directory called "System Volume Information." To look at this directory you will add the account you are using to the security tab of the folders Properties; the default access that it gives you is OK, you will need only to read the files. After applying the change, click OK.

Open the system volume information folder. There may be a folder that looks something like the following (the numbers in the braces will be different):

_restore{FABD0D3E-B186-4217-A903-D6F355385163}

Double-click on this folder. Here do a search for *.old. Copy any file it finds to the memory stick and place in a folder called <machine name> Firewall logs.

Execute system internals Process Explorer and save the results to the memory stick.
Execute system internals TCPView and save the results to the memory stick.
Execute system internals Autoruns and save the results to the memory stick.

When you are done, bring the memory stick and any notes you took to information security and note in the RT ticket that the system is ready to be reimaged.

Chapter 5

Information Risk Management: A Process Approach to Risk Diagnosis and Treatment

Nick Halvorson

Contents

Introduction

Information security, as a subset of an organization's overall risk management strategy, is a focused initiative to manage risk to information in any form. Risk management concepts, when applied to information risk, are readily managed within the context of an information security management system (ISMS). An ISMS is a process-based management approach and furnishes a framework to administer risk management processes.

Robust risk management processes identify and quantify areas of information risk and allow for development of a comprehensive and focused risk treatment plan.

- ■ A clearly defined risk assessment methodology is a mandatory component in legal or regulatory compliance.
- ■ The corresponding risk treatment plan documents informed-choice decision making and organizational due diligence.

The Nature of Risk

Risk may be strategic, tactical, or operational.

Strategic Risk

Strategic risk is risk to the existence or profit of the organization and may or may not have information security significance. Such risk includes regulatory compliance and fiduciary responsibility, as well as risk to the revenue and reputation of the organization.

Tactical Risk

Tactical risk is risk to the information security program's ability to mitigate relevant strategic risk to information. Such program risk includes the ability to identify relevant regulations, identify and justify control objectives, and justify information security initiatives.

Operational Risk

Operational risk is concerned with the ability to implement the tactical risk-based control objectives. Such risk includes budget, timelines, and technologies.

The Process of Risk Management

In its most basic form, the risk management process is closed loop, or iterative, providing a feedback mechanism for continuous process improvement (Figure 5.1).

The current ISO17799-3 standard addresses the application of this process as an information security technique. A process-based ISMS provides the framework within which to implement this technique.

Information Security Program

A comprehensive information security program should address strategic, tactical, and operational risk (Figure 5.2). An information security program is a strategic risk initiative, managed by a tactical risk-based ISMS. This structure allows ready identification and mitigation of operational risk. For example,

- The scope of strategic risk is enterprisewide and focused on the risk-mitigating services required by the enterprise.
- The scope of tactical risk is programwide and focused on the risk-mitigating processes required by the strategic services.
- The scope of operational risk is based upon a discrete domain that stores, transmits, or processes information in any form. This domain-specific risk is focused on the people, procedure, and products that integrate into the risk-mitigating process.

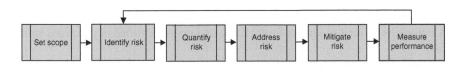

Figure 5.1   Risk management process.

Figure 5.2   Step 1: Set scope.

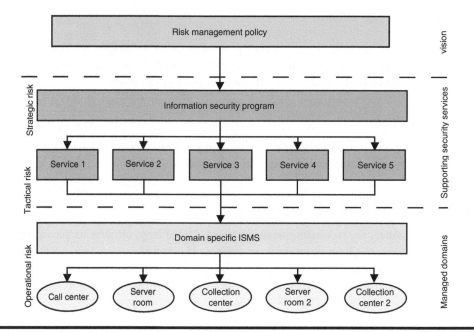

Figure 5.3   ISMS-based information security program.

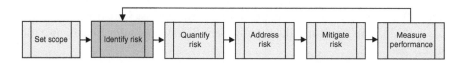

Figure 5.4   Step 2: Identify risk.

An ISMS-based information security program is conducive to scoping and managing multiple risk domains while simultaneously identifying and maintaining both vertical alignment and horizontal dependencies (Figure 5.3).

Threat Forecasting

Threats are negative events that occur when a vulnerability or weakness is exploited. Threat forecasting is a proactive process to predict future risk based upon identified or perceived vulnerability (Figure 5.4).

Threats span the organization at all levels.

- Threats may be strategic, or enterprisewide, such as regulatory noncompliance.
- Threats may be tactical, based upon organizational vulnerabilities, such as ineffective programs.
- Threats may be operational, based upon technical vulnerabilities.

Threat forecasting examines multiple information sources or sensors. Threat sensors may include

- Legal or regulatory analysts
- Program reviews
- Technical bulletins from vendors or analysts

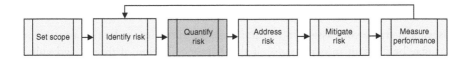

Figure 5.5   Step 3: Quantify risk.

The potential rate of change to the threat environment must be considered and may drive the frequency of triggering the threat forecasting processes. For example, a strategic threat such as noncompliance with emerging regulations typically has a longer tolerable reaction time than an operational threat such as emerging technical vulnerabilities.

Incident Evaluation

Incidents are threats that have taken effect, or in other words, a vulnerability has been exploited to cause an event resulting in an incident. Incident evaluation, although triggered reactively, is proactive because of the "lessons learned" that can be utilized to both identify the underlying vulnerabilities and predict the future probability of reoccurrence. Forensic, or "root cause," analysis will illuminate technical and procedural weaknesses, and performance analysis will illuminate strengths and weaknesses.

Risk Assessment

The processes of threat forecasting and incident evaluation identify relevant threats and vulnerabilities; however, relevant threats and vulnerabilities are not necessarily risks. Identified threats and vulnerabilities must be quantified to determine the existence and magnitude of risk within the applicable environment (Figure 5.5). Quantified risk allows for defensible prioritization of remediation efforts as well as informed-choice (defensible) decision making.

Assessment Scope

Strategic Assessment

Strategic risk assessments look at enterprise business processes that span multiple domains. Not all assessed business processes have information risk.

Tactical Assessment

Tactical risk assessments look at the ability of the information security program to identify and mitigate relevant strategic risk to information.

Operational Assessment

Operational risk assessments look at a domain's ability to meet tactical control objectives in protecting specific information assets. Technical vulnerability assessments are an example of a specifically focused type of operational risk assessment.

Assessment Framework

A risk assessment framework assists in maintaining structure during the risk assessment process, because it may be difficult to make sense of the diverse collection of threats and vulnerabilities that flows from "worst case" scenario brainstorming. A risk assessment framework allows both organization of thought and recognition of relationships among this diverse collection of threats and vulnerabilities. Starting with the premise that information risk is based upon breaches of confidentiality, integrity, and availability, a risk assessment framework can be further subdivided into, for example, intentional and accidental components. Further subdivisions result in creation of a "threat tree" that allows organized "cataloging" of risk and enhances the ability to ask and analyze appropriate risk questions. For example

  Threat: Breach of confidentiality
  ■ Intentional disclosure
    – Vulnerability: Unvetted employees
  ■ Unintentional disclosure
    – Vulnerability: Unencrypted information
    – Vulnerability: Ineffective media disposal

Note the structured thought process resulting in discrete vulnerabilities being mapped to a common threat.

Risk Quantum

Risk quantification is based upon identification of relevant variables that are then incorporated into a risk-rating algorithm. A quantitative assessment requires much more effort than a qualitative assessment, but may be necessary when, for example, using the resultant risk rating to make financial (quantitative) decisions. Typical qualitative risk quantification utilizes two independent variables, probability (likelihood) and harm (impact). Risk-rating algorithms vary in sophistication depending on the level of detail and accuracy required to be furnished by the assessment.

Probability

Probability may be seen as having three attributes. Total probability must take into consideration all aspects:

  ■ Frequency: How often the scenario can be expected to occur
  ■ Simplicity: The level of effort required to create the scenario
  ■ Motive: The determination of the attacker

Frequency and simplicity are relevant for each vulnerability, whereas motive is relevant to the organization. For example, an externally facing firewall has a high probability of penetration attempts (frequency) but a low probability of success (simplicity). A defense contractor or financial institution may generate more focused attention than a home personal computer user (motive).

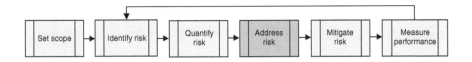

Figure 5.6   Step 4: Address risk.

Harm

Harm is the impact successful execution of the event would cause the organization. Because harm is many times aligned to a particular tangible asset, another view sometimes used in risk assessment is value, where value is perceived in terms of availability and harm perceived as absence. This view is more common in enterprise business process risk assessment.

Raw Risk

The identified vulnerabilities quantified through an algorithm (of your choice) utilizing the independent variables of probability and harm constitute raw risk, or risk before the application of controls. Raw risk serves as a baseline for threat exposure, or risk environment. Raw risk also acts as the basis of "before and after" views, modified as controls are factored in to calculate residual (postcontrol) risk. An unacceptable level of raw risk serves as the justification for implementing mitigating controls.

Risk Tolerance

Having identified and evaluated the risks attached to specific vulnerabilities, the risks must be addressed (Figure 5.6). Decisions on risk are based upon the organization's risk tolerance thresholds and include the following options.

Avoid Risk

Risk may possibly be avoided, for example, by relocating a data center.

Transfer Risk

Risk may be transferred to someone with a higher risk tolerance, for example, an insurance company.

Accept Risk

Risk may be accepted, although diligence requires care regarding

- ■ Who is authorized to accept what level of risk
- ■ How is risk acceptance based upon informed-choice decision making
- ■ Whether the aggregation of accepted risk remains tolerable

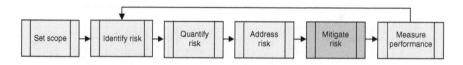

Figure 5.7 Step 5: Mitigate risk.

Mitigate Risk

Risk may be mitigated to an acceptable level through the application of compensating controls. It is not practical to eliminate risk completely, only to reduce risk to an acceptable level.

Control Objectives

Control objectives serve as the glue to bind specific vulnerabilities to specific controls. Defining control objectives is the first step in deriving the corresponding control requirements to mitigate the risk associated with the vulnerability (Figure 5.7). Control objectives give a risk-based justification to allocation of resources.

Selection of Controls

Once control requirements have been derived from control objectives, tangible controls may be selected.

Discretionary Controls

Discretionary controls are controls that can weigh cost versus benefits. In general, the cost of mitigating a risk needs to be balanced by the benefits obtained. This is essentially a cost–benefit analysis on "at what cost" the risk is acceptable. It is important to consider all direct and indirect costs and benefits, whether tangible or intangible and measured in financial or other terms. More than one option can be considered and adopted either separately or in combination. For example, mitigating controls such as support contracts may reduce risk to a certain degree, with residual risk transferred via appropriate insurance or risk financing.

Mandatory Controls

Mandatory controls differ from discretionary controls in that cost has no bearing on the selection of mandatory controls. These are controls that must be implemented to mitigate specific risks. There may be no risk acceptance option due to legal and regulatory requirements, for example.

Risk Treatment

Development of Action Plan

The organization requires a treatment plan to describe how the chosen controls will be implemented. The treatment plan should be comprehensive and should document all necessary information about

- Proposed actions, priorities, or time plans
- Resource requirements

- Roles and responsibilities of all parties involved in the proposed actions
- Performance measures
- Reporting and monitoring requirements

Action plans may have strategic, tactical, and operational components and should be in line with the culture, values, and perceptions of all stakeholders.

Approval of Action Plan

As with all management plans, initial approval is not sufficient to ensure the effective implementation of the action plan. Senior management support is critical throughout the entire life cycle of the plan. By its nature, an ISMS is an empowerment vehicle for risk treatment, with clear trickle-down authority documenting management support and authorization to the highest levels.

Implementation of Action Plan

An important responsibility of the action plan owner is to identify requirements and procure necessary resources to implement the plan. This may include such tangibles as people, process, and products; the component parts selected to meet the required control objectives. In the event that available resources such as budgets are not sufficient, the risk of not implementing the action plan must ultimately be accepted by someone. The risk management model allows transference of risk to a willing risk acceptor, and the ISMS framework provides the means of transference.

A critical success factor (CSF) for the risk management process is to strategically reduce risk to an acceptable level. A key performance indicator is the tactical ability to reach this steady state, or equilibrium, through the judicious selection and deployment of efficient and effective controls. Operational metrics can be used to evaluate control efficiency and effectiveness.

Risk Metrics

There are various types of risk metrics that may benefit the information security program (Figure 5.8).

Process Metrics

A process by definition has a CSF defining the successful execution of the process. The CSF is evaluated via process key performance indicators. Key performance indicators are evaluated via process metrics. Whereas process design deals with process effectiveness, process execution deals with process efficiency. For example, a risk-mitigating operational "incident response" process (a reactive control) has been designed to be tactically effective, but the performance indicators look at operational efficiency factors such as "time to respond."

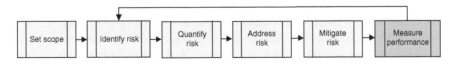

Figure 5.8   Step 6: Measure performance.

Program Metrics

Program metrics typically measure process effectiveness. These tactical process effectiveness metrics require a "history" against which to measure, with value being enhanced by history length. This type of evaluation is synergistic with maturity modeling, because maturity modeling is by nature history-based.

Environmental Metrics

Environmental metrics are of value when trying to evaluate an organization's risk profile and resultant risk strategy. For example, a response process (reactive control) may be triggered frequently, giving insight into the external environment. This metric says nothing about the efficiency or effectiveness of the information security program, but may add justification to its existence or tactics.

Control Attributes

Controls in this context may be seen to have two independent attributes, maturity and weight.

Maturity

As risk treatment progresses, controls remain in varying degrees of maturity. Factoring in the maturity level of the various types of controls on a standardized scale allows one to quantify effectiveness in progress toward meeting control objectives and the resultant reduction of risk.

Weight

The following controls may be considered:

- Directive
- Preventive
- Detective
- Reactive

In some environments there is merit in weighting the value of a specific category of control. For example, in a risk-intolerant environment such as the nuclear industry, a preventive control may be far more valued than detective and reactive controls and should be weighted accordingly.

Residual Risk

Residual risk is the risk that remains after risk treatment. Residual risk is derived from raw risk, with an algorithm typically utilizing risk-mitigating control attributes to modify the raw risk environment. Untreated residual risk is essentially de facto accepted risk. Because the objective of the iterative risk management process is to reduce residual risk to an acceptable level, the risk management process may require multiple passes to reach this goal. For example, a vulnerability management process that tracks the system patching life cycle may require multiple iterations before an acceptable residual risk of 5 percent unpatched (95 percent patched) is achieved.

Summary

Information security is a focused application of risk management, managing risk to information in any form based upon the risk criteria of confidentiality, integrity, and availability. An information security program is hence a subset of an organization's risk management program and is readily managed within the context of a process-based ISMS. ISMS and risk assessment frameworks add structure to the information security program, clearly delineating risk roles and responsibilities. A process-based approach is repeatable, defensible, and extensible, offering metrics to optimize efficiency and effectiveness while reducing risk to an acceptable level.

Chapter 6

Department-Level Transformation

R. Scott McCoy

Contents

Introduction

The main complaint among security professionals is that they lack the resources they need to do their job. There are classes on metrics, strategy, how to sell a program to upper management, and even how to write a business case. What seems to be missing is a concise explanation on how all there fit together with a step-by-step "how to." This is an attempt to do just that, by fully explaining how the process works in detail and the pieces necessary to transform a department so that it can meet the particular requirements of an industry and company. Every day security managers, be they information technology (IT) or corporate, are torn between conducting their daily work and trying to improve their programs. Time must be taken for the latter, or the former will never get better and may get a lot worse.

To change the current state of a department, there must be an honest and complete view of the department's scope and its performance in accomplishing that scope. There must be an understanding of what the current challenges are, whether they are threat-based or competition or regulatory, and an educated guess as to what the challenges will be in the next three to five years. The security professional must understand his or her own organization, from an operational detail level down to the internal politics and key players. Finally, security managers must know themselves and their staffs' strengths and weaknesses.

In 500 BC, Sun Tzu wrote, "If you know the enemy and know yourself, you need not fear the result of a hundred battles." Some people find it odd to think of people in their own company as the enemy. Perhaps opponents would be better, but because there will always be fewer budget dollars than requested and because that budget is distributed between all departments, if one department's budget is raised by even 5 percent, some other department is going to get less. Before going down the path to growing their department, security professionals need first to understand themselves, their department, and, at a minimum, the other departments that report to their boss. If there is time or if the security professional has been in place long enough, a thorough analysis of all noncore departments should be made. In this way, the outcome of a thousand budget battles, and make no mistake, they are battles, should not be in question.

The goal of this evaluation should not be to increase budget, because it is possible that, once complete, the analysis may point to either doing less or doing the current workload differently, which may actually reduce spending. The odds are that few security departments overspend, but the point is not just to seek more money, because money without a plan is not a recipe for success.

The goal is to build a department that has a well-defined scope of responsibility that will mitigate risk at the level the company is comfortable with and use the smallest amount of resources to accomplish that objective. It is hoped that these objectives will include things like recruiting, developing, and retaining qualified personnel. There are several ways to approach this, including just throwing money at the situation, but good managers find ways to supplement the money (and it does take some money) and to motivate and engage workers without relying solely on a bunch of conferences, but this will be covered in more detail under Worker engagement.

There are six steps in department transformation:

- Strategic vision
- Gap analysis
- The business case
- Implementation
- Department performance
- Worker engagement

The Strategic Vision

The strategic vision document should have three components: current state, future state, and a detailed description. Most departments have been around for a while and have some historical reasons for why they are configured the way they are and how they do certain pieces of the job. Those reasons and origins may or may not be known by those currently in the department, but it is actually better if they are not. With knowledge comes emotion, especially if a well-liked current or former employee created a process that is still in use. In tackling the first step, creating a strategic vision for a department, it is essential to have a complete and realistic understanding of its current state. To accomplish this, break down the pieces of the department into functional areas and write down a few statements that describe them. The goal is not to be all negative or all positive, but describe each segment honestly. This may be difficult, and if so, an outside consultant may be able to help. Outside perspective does not have to cost a lot of money; it could be an auditor from your own company or even a peer from another company, especially if they are willing to go through this same process.

It is important to stay current and to help explain things in a way upper management can quickly grasp. In a paper by Booz, Allen, and Hamilton titled *Convergence of Enterprise Security Organizations*, http://www.boozallen.com/publications/article/1439866, dated September 8, 2005, the areas in a converged department were broken into the functional areas of physical security (access control), corporate security (investigations), and IT security (network). Upper management has an easier time understanding the security areas when they are broken down into these major headings and all of the applicable components are listed under them with a bullet for each. It is also important to get input from department staff, but it may help to complete a first draft. This will focus the input on the content and not waste time on format.

The next piece of the paper should be identical to the first (the current state) in format, but be called future state and have bullets that describe how you want the functional areas to either perform or be viewed. The last piece is a detailed description of your department scope. This section goes into a lot of detail that no one may read completely, especially your boss, but it is more for you or whoever has your job in the future. It is important to remember the drivers and the conditions under which you made your decisions. This section goes into a more detailed description of each program and has three or, depending on the industry, possibly four parts. Those parts are

■ Scope
■ Trends
■ Future plans
■ Regulatory considerations

Here is a generic example for reference only; any real description would be more detailed.

Current State

■ Guard force
    – High turnover (90 percent)
    – Minimal training
    – Poorly educated officers
    – Customer complaints
    – Existing coverage has no risk-based justification

Future Desired State

■ Guard force
    – Low turnover
    – First-responder training with continuing education

- Minimum requirements
- Sites with coverage are determined by a risk-based assessment

Detailed Program Description

Guard Force

Scope

There is security officer coverage at five locations. All officers are contracted with the Really Good Officer Co. and as of December 2007 the contract is in its third year of a four-year contract with a one-year extension clause. Security officers are unarmed and trained as first responders. Turnover is at 80 percent and a recent survey showed the officers are paid an average of $2 per hour less than at other companies in the area.

Trends

Current trends still show a preference for contract security officer coverage, though the quality of officers and corresponding increase in pay suggest that many companies are expecting more from their officers in education, training, and professionalism.

Future Plans

Assess the current level of coverage, both for where officers are posted and for what else we may require of them. Send out a request for proposal (RFP) when the contract expires and put forth a scope that will meet the evolving needs of the company.

Regulatory Considerations

Although there are currently no regulations requiring security officer coverage at critical sites, adding such coverage may either help avoid or minimize the intensity of new regulation.

A five-year plan is common because it is far enough into the future that there is time to make changes but not so far out that your plans could fall apart due to too much change. This is a good time to get some perspective from both upper management and direct reports. Think about all of the issues that are currently impacting the department and try to put the issues in perspective.

This is a golden opportunity for security professionals to prove they are business managers first and security professionals second. It is the security practitioner's responsibility to protect the company, but it is not possible or cost-effective to attempt to mitigate all risk. Some risk, especially with lower impact, must be accepted.

When going through this exercise, try not to limit the analysis within the confines of the department's current scope. Ask the tough questions, like whether the security department would be the best place to perform other tasks currently provided by another department, and the converse, whether another department would be the best place for some work currently being done by the security department. Not everyone believes in the convergence of IT security and more traditional security roles. Look beyond preference and bias and determine if the company would benefit before ignoring it outright. As an example, what about background checks? A survey in the Institute of Management and Administration's July 2006 edition of *Security Director's Report* showed that 89 percent of companies responding had background screening conducted by

Human Resources (HR) and not Security. One of HR's main functions is to bring people in, not to keep people out. Keeping people out is something Security excels at, so which department is better equipped to perform background screening?

Every company's experience will be different and it may take several drafts and about three months, with about two to four hours of work a week, to complete. The time spent will be worth it, because it will be the basis for the transformation.

Once completed, remember that this is only the first step. The next step is to complete a gap analysis between current and future desired state. This analysis will determine what will be done differently, how it will be done, what staff will be needed, and what skills the staff will need to be successful. This may include new policies, new products, new people, and new partners. Try not to rush toward a solution at this point, stay focused on identifying the gaps for now.

Using the previous guard force example, the gap analysis between current and future state might be

- Last RFP lacked minimum requirements for officers or performance measures for the contract
- Low pay for officers compared the rest of the region
- Lack of companywide business impact analysis or enterprisewide risk assessment to identify critical sites

Be careful not to try to solve the problems in the gap analysis as it is created. The way to get better qualified and better skilled officers is a more obvious problem to solve than most people will find, but none of the problems should be difficult to solve. Without this exercise, you may be able to come up with solutions to individual problems, but without the discipline the exercise requires you may not capture everything that needs to be improved. You may also not get wholesale support from your management if you bring items to them piecemeal. Department heads should be able to think strategically, and even if it is easy for you to see the total picture, as with algebra, it is important to show your work to get credit or, in this case, buy-in from upper management.

The solution to guard officer coverage is definitely not complex, but in the course of gathering data there will be a need to put together something more than opinion. Gather the facts that will help put together the business case, and bring upper management along the way during the process so the business case will not be new to them when it is presented.

Gap Analysis

Now that there is a strategic vision with buy-in from upper management, it is time to determine how to get from point A to point B.

The first step is to complete a gap analysis between the current and the future. Once the gaps are described, ask some questions:

- Do I have all the programs that I need?
- Do the programs I currently have in place meet the objectives?
- What are the outcomes or work products that need to be routinely produced by my department in the future scope and how many hours does it take to accomplish them?
  - Risk assessments
  - Giving security awareness training
  - Background investigations

- Creating or revising site-specific security plans
- Conducting penetration tests
- Auditing security settings
■ What is the average number of unscheduled items per year and how many hours does it take complete them?
  - Investigations
  - New application assessments
  - Computer incident response team events
  - Supporting audits
■ Do I have the right position descriptions to get the work done?
■ Do the current staff have the right skill sets?
■ Do I have the right number of people?
■ Is there a way other than traditional staffing to accomplish my objectives?

This takes a lot of analysis, but it is worth the work, because only by doing this level of analysis can someone fully understand what a specific company needs from its security department. There is nothing wrong with finding a consultant to help with this process.

The outcome of the gap analysis will be a work plan, which can be as simple as a table that shows the milestone dates and success measures. The final step will be to prioritize the work plan into a multiyear format that organizes the steps in the order necessary to execute.

When this process is started, it is impossible not to have certain preconceptions, but realize that the final result may be different. Also remember that this is a living document; when things change it is important to reevaluate the portion affected by that change and perform a new gap analysis. The gap analysis may identify the need for several things or potentially nothing if there is no need for change. If any of the things needed require more money, it will most likely require a business case to get.

The Business Case

All of the documentation that was created during the process of figuring everything out needs to be kept, but this documentation is not the business case. These are documents that the data is drawn from. Every company does things differently and business cases are no exception. Some companies have elaborate formats that resemble novellas, some have only one page, and most have no format at all. The one-page business case has a lot of appeal, but it can be a challenge to articulate all of the justification with so few words. Breaking down all of the pieces needed for a department transformation into separate cases, like guard force management as one and department reorganization as another, is recommended over trying to change it all at one time. Also try not to present more than two business cases a year that have a significant financial impact.

The relationship between a department head and the next level of management will determine how much prep work and socializing for the business case are necessary. This is the most difficult area to give advice on, because every situation is so different. If the relationship between department head and upper management is new or in question, seek advice from a trusted mentor in the organization. Whether advice is available or not, it is important to determine what motivates the next two people in the chain of command. This is critical when communication of the change is created. In some cases power points and a high-level executive summary will do the trick; in others, more detail is required. The higher up the case goes the less detail should be needed if there is trust in the chain of command. Usually the next level is the hardest audience, but this is not always so.

Implementation

The implementation plan will most likely be a multiyear prioritized work plan that is broken down into logical and measurable milestones. Because there could be many steps between the current state and the final desired state, it is important to lay out all of the steps for all of the initiatives and spread them out over a few years, especially where budget dollars will be required. Some of the initiatives must be done first, so the order in which the work is laid out is important, both within each initiative and between the initiatives. Some actions can and should be done in parallel, whereas others are by their nature linear and dependent on others to be completed first. Make sure not to take on too much in any given year, because the departmental workload must also be completed during the transformation; this is the most common mistake made by any team.

Measuring Department Performance

Most companies run their businesses by facts: What services do they provide or what products do they make? How much can they charge for their product or service? Can they make new products or perform new services? Should they do it better or cheaper than the competition? Every bit of spending in a company is broken down into two categories: cost of goods (COGs) and overhead. If it is a manufacturing company, then all the raw materials, the electricity to run the machines, and the salaries for the labor to produce the product are COGs. Everything that does not contribute directly to the creation, storage, distribution, and sale of the product is overhead. Security is not a core part of any business except a security business. Security is overhead. This does not mean that it is not important, but being important also does not make security core. The loss of an IT or corporate security department to a business would exceed the cost of that department, but because most companies already have these departments and have had them for some time, it is very difficult to prove. So, security is seen as a necessary evil at worst and a valuable asset at best. The best way to move toward the perception as a valuable asset is to show the value in business terms. Retail companies have loss prevention departments that measure the percentage of shrinkage and can show the effectiveness of their programs by how they can reduce the amount of shrinkage. A combination of preventative and reactive programs must be in place and deployed with skill. Other companies that have more traditional security departments have programs that are more difficult to quantify. All of these programs, as well as all other work products and services, should be measured.

There are two types of measures: those that you can set performance targets to and those that you cannot. The measures you should not set targets on are things like number of thefts per year. This is work volume and should be tracked, but specific targets on metrics you cannot predict or directly affect are demotivating and counterproductive. Even if a company does not require measuring the performance of its security department, that department should at a minimum keep track of workload like how many investigations were conducted, alarms monitored, people escorted, guard tours conducted, etc. This data will be invaluable in building a case to increase staff or to defend existing levels.

Budget

The measure of successful budget performance is not simply to avoid spending more than the budgeted amount by the end of the year. You must also be able to forecast your spending accurately from month to month. A valid measure for operating expense is to be able to forecast one month in advance, within ±5 percent, what the actual spend of operating dollars will be. Capital projects are more dynamic and may have a forecast target of ±10 percent. The second measure might be not to exceed the budgeted amount by the end of the year, because this also has a direct impact on earnings for the company.

Customer Satisfaction

Measuring the satisfaction of customers, or even the idea that security departments have customers, may be a foreign concept to some security professionals. Security departments are internal service providers who directly and indirectly support the core operation of their company in dozens of ways. The key is to identify these services and then to gauge the satisfaction of, at least, supervisors and above with the delivery of those services. Doing a survey around investigations is not recommended, but granting access control or completing a background check or issuing a badge all take time and cost money, so most likely the customers want these things to be done more quickly or cheaper or possibly more accurately.

The first step is to issue an annual survey asking for overall satisfaction and specific satisfaction around key services. Make sure it is anonymous and that there is a space for comments. Be warned, if this is the first time customers are asked for feedback, the first survey results and comments may be a little hard to read. The results of this survey can be used as supporting documentation for your business case and even to spark ideas for the five-year strategy.

Cycle Times

How fast services are provided can be a large source of dissatisfaction if the perception is that they should be faster. Time to issue a company ID, time to complete a background check, time to issue a new laptop, time to grant logical access, or time to roll out a new application—all of these things frustrate customers and damage credibility when the perception is that the services provided take too long. Sometimes this is because the services are too slow, but other times it is a matter of adjusting the expectation of the customer through honest and open communication. To be successful and get voluntary cooperation with security policies, a security department must have credibility at a minimum, and treating customers with respect and meeting performance commitments is a large step toward gaining that credibility.

Worker Engagement

The fact is, the employees are the ones that get the work done and can either make or break the strategic initiatives that have been agreed upon. Every manager should devote the appropriate amount of time to employee engagement for the culture of his or her company and department, which varies greatly by industry and country. The first thing to do is to determine the current level of engagement. There is a standardized survey provided by Gallup that many companies use to measure the level of engagement of a company's workforce. It is backed up by years of research that shows a direct correlation between an increase in engagement scores over time with a decrease in workplace injuries and an increase in productivity and earnings. It is possible to come up with a company-specific survey, but regardless of how it is done, there should be some way to measure engagement to track if actions taken to affect it positively are working.

Areas that should be given focus are

- Having a formal development plan for all workers
  - Continuing education
  - Cross training for advancement or to build depth
  - Development of management skills where appropriate
- Giving recognition when it is earned (it is not recommended to mandate a program as that seems to take the value out of it)
- Inclusion of workers in strategic and annual planning
- Team building events, if appropriate
- Having at least two levels for individual contributor positions so workers have a path for advancement

What employee engagement boils down to is caring about the well-being of the workers and expressing it professionally through word and deed. It is also about having an atmosphere of trust, in which people know they can survive a mistake and they are not afraid to express their opinion. As with all things, the first time an opinion is measured, be it on this or customer satisfaction, the scores are artificially low. If this is the first time a group is asked, they have years of issues that come boiling out. The key is to know this going in and be prepared for it. The most important thing that to do once something is measured is to take action on the outcome of the survey. If no actions are taken, it is worse than if there had never been a survey, because there is an expectation of potential change associated with being asked an opinion in such a formal way. It is not practical to fix everything, but it is important to put forth effort and take reasonable steps to improve one or two of the highest priority issues as ranked by the workers. The action planning from the survey data is best accomplished with an outside facilitator and the workers for the surveyed group (no more than 20; if larger break the group up). The "boss" should not be in the room, because even bosses are human and have a hard time not being defensive, whereas workers have a hard time opening up in the presence of their boss.

Conclusion

It is extremely helpful to have someone in the department with project management experience. If no such person exists, it may be necessary to get someone on board or use the services of a consultant. Because every department will have completely different gaps and challenges, it is impossible to give a more detailed description, other than to say that it may take less or more time than five years to get from point A to point B, especially with course corrections along the way as things within the environment change. Once started, the journey is not meant to be locked on cruise control; remember that the destination itself may look completely different from that originally envisioned and that the destination is not final. Once the original transformation has been completed, it is likely time to begin the process all over again.

The things that define a security department as successful or unsuccessful are department's capacity to prevent where possible, respond effectively when required, and aid recovery to normal operations as quickly as is practical. This is the same whether there is a denial service attack, the intrusion of malware, or an actual disaster. To accomplish these goals, the people in the department must know the security requirements that are unique to their industry and design a department that is appropriately organized, staffed, and funded to meet the evolving challenges that are specific to that organization. Even within the same industry, with similar threats, there are differences that must be accounted for. This can be done effectively only if the people in that organization take the time and effort to perform the detailed analysis that is required for strategic planning. Once this is accomplished, the department members must also have the skills and abilities needed to execute those plans. A department should not ask for more dollars than is required to accomplish the mission, and if it is accomplished for less, then the sum must be returned. These are security departments, whether they are IT or corporate, and as such will always be seen as cost centers first. Only by building a reputation of integrity and competency in business can a department rise to its full potential.

Chapter 7

Setting Priorities in Your Security Program

Derek Schatz

Contents

Introduction

A well-run information security program provides a structured approach to the management of risk to an organization's information technology (IT) infrastructure and the information that it handles. In a typical business that continually faces new threats, the information security managers must ensure that they focus their efforts and budget money on the right initiatives and tools to gain the greatest risk reduction for the business at the least cost. This is not an easy task, as these decisions must be made in the face of a number of significant challenges.

- Security spending is continually scrutinized by an organization's management for business value, requiring the security manager to become adept at justifying spending in business-relevant terms.
- Certain risks may increase rapidly in importance in the middle of a budget cycle, requiring reallocation of funds. An example of this may be an important new R&D project that requires extra protections against industrial espionage and the resultant loss of highly sensitive intellectual property.
- Security must overcome the reputation of being the group that says "No" and acting as a roadblock to new IT initiatives and instead be the group that says, "Yes, but let's do it this way so risk is reduced."
- Increasing regulatory compliance requirements threaten to absorb the entire security budget.
- Difficulty in attracting and retaining skilled information security personnel can introduce risk that security projects will not be completed as planned or with adequate quality.
- Internal political issues and turf battles may hinder the implementation of new processes and tools.
- A major security breach may call the effectiveness of the entire security program, and even the competence of the security manager, into doubt.

For many information security professionals, one of the greatest attractions to the field is that there is always something new going on: new threats, new technologies, new business initiatives, new regulations. This is often one of its greatest frustrations also, as it is impossible to ever achieve a state of perfect security in which all risks are mitigated to a level that is acceptable to the business. After all, "security is a process, not a product." The security manager must constantly reevaluate the risk environment, gain agreement from the business side on risk prioritization, and adjust the focus of his or her program as needed to address new threats and requirements as they arise. But the end objective should not simply be to reduce information risk in the organization—this is the objective of a merely good security program. Rather, it should go beyond that, enabling the business to take on new ventures to increase revenue and shareholder value that would be too risky without an effective security program in place. It is this that makes a security program great, makes it invaluable to the business, and earns it a place at the big table.

This chapter looks at some guiding principles for security managers to follow when deciding on priorities for their organization's security program. As will be seen in the following section, however, priorities depend on the program's maturity.

Levels of Maturity of a Security Program

As with Carnegie Mellon's Capability Maturity Model Integration (CMMI®) for process improvement in software engineering, security programs go through phases of maturity that are based on how well policies and processes are documented, how broadly they are adhered to across the business, how well their effectiveness is measured, the level of support from senior management, and how developed the security infrastructure is. The IT Governance Institute® and the Information Systems Audit and Control Association also publish a security governance maturity model as part of the Control Objectives for Information and Related Technology (COBIT®). Understanding where an organization stands on such a scale is important for a security manager new to the job, because initiatives that would be successful in a more mature program would likely fail in one that is less mature. For example, developing a strategic plan for security is more likely a fruitless effort in an organization that suffers regular security breaches because of inadequate infrastructure protections. The focus in such a situation must be to stabilize the environment so that the security manager can begin to look beyond the purely tactical responses, becoming proactive and not purely reactive. It should be clear that an organization at the lower levels of security program maturity will be challenged to manage risks to its information assets effectively and will therefore have a hard time demonstrating business value. But achieving and maintaining the highest levels of maturity are very difficult and require substantial dedication on the part of the security team and very strong support by the organization's leadership.

CMMI uses five levels, and COBIT uses six, but for purposes of this chapter, a simplified model with four levels is presented. For each level, 12 major areas of concern that are good indicators of an organization's security program maturity are used as the basis for assessment. Note that there is some correlation between an organization's size and its maturity level—as an organization grows, ignoring or simply underfunding security becomes increasingly perilous as information risks become unmanageable. In addition, there are few large companies that are not publicly traded and therefore subject to Sarbanes–Oxley (and likely a raft of other regulations), which requires implementation of a solid security program and system of internal controls. Yet on the flip side, there are many smaller privately held companies that face significant risks due to the nature of their business but lack a more mature program to manage them effectively.

Before looking at the characteristics of the maturity levels, a sampling of key questions that can help in an assessment of maturity is provided in the following section. In general, the hallmarks of a mature program are strong management support earned through credible activity, adherence to repeatable processes with measurable feedback loops, and the ability to respond and adapt rapidly to a changing risk environment.

Key Questions to Help Assess Security Maturity

1. Security policies
    1.1. Has the organization created and published security policies, standards, guidelines, processes, and rules?
    1.2. Has a control framework been defined and implemented for regulatory compliance (or other) purposes?
    1.3. Is the organization's information labeled as to its sensitivity and criticality to the business, and do policies clearly state the roles and responsibilities for its protection?
2. Management support
    2.1. Does senior management recognize the importance of information security and communicate this to the rest of the company, perhaps based on a communications plan created with the security department?
    2.2. Are budget requests for security given due consideration when funds are being allocated?
    2.3. Does the security function report into an appropriate place in the organizational hierarchy?
3. Security integration into the system development life cycle (SDLC)
    3.1. Are security experts involved in new system development or implementation projects from the beginning?

    3.2. Are design reviews conducted on security features of new systems?

    3.3. Are new systems and applications tested for security standards compliance before being released into production?

    3.4. Are programmers trained in secure coding practices?

4. Security personnel

    4.1. Do dedicated information security staff positions exist, and are the people in those roles adequately skilled?

    4.2. Are training funds allocated to training to keep those skills current?

    4.3. In a distributed/federated environment, does security management exert sufficient influence over personnel in other areas who perform security functions?

    4.4. Are security experts sought out by others in the organization for advice and counsel?

5. Security infrastructure and tools

    5.1. Are the right tools in place to perform functions such as malware detection and removal, firewalling, intrusion detection, encryption of data at rest and in transit, identity management, strong authentication, spam filtering, and patch management?

    5.2. Do security personnel have the time and skills to configure and operate these tools properly?

    5.3. Is the organization's network designed for security?

    5.4. Has a reference architecture for security been defined and documented?

6. Threat and vulnerability management

    6.1. Is a comprehensive view maintained of the organization's vulnerabilities?

    6.2. Are discovered vulnerabilities prioritized, tracked, and fixed?

    6.3. Are patches quickly tested and applied to the organization's systems after they are released by the vendor?

7. Configuration management

    7.1. Are system configurations change-controlled?

    7.2. Is a limited group of specific individuals authorized to make changes to production systems?

8. Access control

    8.1. Is network and system access strictly limited to only those with a business need for it?

    8.2. Are user accounts disabled or deleted immediately after employees leave the organization?

    8.3. Are standards for password strength enforced?

    8.4. Are strong authentication mechanisms used on the most sensitive and critical systems?

    8.5. Are system access logs regularly monitored for unusual activity?

9. Audits and assessments

    9.1. Are outside firms hired to conduct security assessments on at least an annual basis, and are the findings from those assessments acted upon?

    9.2. Is there a close working relationship between the internal audit and the information security departments?

    9.3. Do audits incorporate requirements for regulatory compliance?

10. Business continuity

    10.1. Have business impact assessments (BIAs) been conducted?

    10.2. Does a comprehensive documented business continuity and disaster recovery plan (DRP) exist?

    10.3. Is the plan exercised annually for training and test purposes?

11. Incident handling
    11.1. Has an incident response (IR) process been documented?
    11.2. Have key personnel been trained on this process?
    11.3. Are there regular drills to reinforce the training?
    11.4. Are outcomes and lessons learned from previous incidents used to improve the process?
    11.5. Has management provided clear direction as to involvement of law enforcement on incidents?
    11.6. Is there adequate technical expertise available either in-house or on contract for forensic analysis?
12. Training and awareness
    12.1. Is there an employee security awareness program in place?
    12.2. Do employees understand their roles and responsibilities in helping to maintain the security of the organization and protect its information assets?

Characteristics of Security Program Maturity

The following sections describe characteristics of security programs at each of the four levels of maturity defined in this chapter. Note that organizations will not typically exhibit all of the characteristics within a given level. Instead, they may be more advanced in some, less in others. It of course depends on what areas have been emphasized to that point in time.

Maturity Level 1

At this level, there is really no security "program" to speak of. Organization management has paid little to no attention to information security matters, and information protection activities are conducted in an entirely ad hoc manner. Note that in today's environment of pervasive threats and ever-expanding regulatory requirements, there are fewer and fewer organizations still operating primarily at this level. Characteristics of the following categories include

Security policies. No documented policies exist, and procedures for security tasks are entirely ad hoc and nonrepeatable. Security failures reoccur due to lack of understanding of the security impact of staff activities. No distinctions are made in the value of the organization's information assets.

Management support. Management pays little or no attention to the subject of information security, and there is no separate budget for security activities apart from general IT (because there is no separate manager for such a budget). Staff performing security functions are buried at the lowest levels of the IT hierarchy, exhibit little to no understanding of what is important to the business, and are focused solely on technical matters such as firewall configuration and user account management. Business management views information security as a cost of doing business that does not produce measurable benefit. Note, however, that this situation is increasingly rare and approaching nonexistence in large or publicly traded companies due to regulatory requirements for security that have visibility at the level of the board of directors.

Security integration into the SDLC. Information security is not involved in the development of new systems and at most is asked to rubber stamp the move of new systems into production. Systems developers and programmers are unfamiliar with the concepts of secure programming and therefore produce applications rife with security vulnerabilities.

Security personnel. There are no personnel dedicated to information security in the organization. Security functions are performed as just another "hat" worn by someone in the lower levels of the IT systems administration staff. Lack of training means these individuals are unfamiliar with the key requirements of these functions.

Security infrastructure and tools. Only the bare minimum of tools is deployed on the organization's network, typically a firewall and some antivirus, that is not updated regularly. Perhaps the firewall has been configured by someone untrained in its operation, leaving holes open for exploitation from the Internet. Lack of thought about security in the network design creates yet more holes from branch offices or connected business partners. Wireless local area network (LAN), if used, is uncontrolled and unsecured.

Threat and vulnerability management. Because there is little common understanding of where the organization's critical assets are housed, vulnerability information cannot be prioritized and therefore patches cannot be, either. Application of patches to systems is irregular and in many instances is far behind. This allows further exploitation and damage to systems by hackers and malware, thus causing additional downtime as systems must be cleaned up and restored to operational status.

Configuration management. Developers have unfettered and unmonitored access to production systems, and the flow and control of systems from development to test to production are uncontrolled and unstructured. Changes to systems are ad hoc and untracked, and downtime results from unauthorized and untested changes.

Access control. More active user accounts exist on systems for past employees than for current ones. Authentication mechanisms are weak, and employees are uneducated about using good passwords. No password policy exists to force regular changes to passwords, and employees often write their passwords on a sticky note left on their monitor. No monitoring of access logs is performed.

Audits and assessments. No outside assessments of the organization's security posture are performed, and financial audits pay little attention to information security issues.

Business continuity. No business continuity plan or DRP exists. Little attention has been paid by management to the possibility of a business-ending catastrophe. No BIA has been conducted to identify the critical information assets of the organization.

Incident handling. Response to security incidents is entirely ad hoc and inadequate and is conducted by untrained staff. Unfortunately for a level 1 organization, incidents are frequent, so staff spend a great deal of time cleaning up malware outbreaks and system intrusions.

Training and awareness. No security awareness program has been created, and therefore employees are unfamiliar with what is expected of them in protecting the organization's information assets.

Maturity Level 2

At this level, a basic security program has been established. Management has some awareness of security issues, but mostly in a reactive sense, for example, a virus outbreak has underscored the need to keep the desktop antivirus software current. Characteristics include the following:

Security policies. Some basic policies have been created, such as for employee e-mail use. Key systems containing business-critical data have been identified but not fully documented; they receive more protection attention than other systems.

Management support. Management is aware of security issues and views some level of security control as desirable to reduce downtime and protect company information assets, although security spending as a percentage of the IT budget still trails industry norms. Management does not lead by example, nor does it communicate its support broadly across the organization. This is primarily due to security personnel having difficulty framing security issues in business terms.

Security integration into the SDLC. Security is involved in the test phase of system development and has some opportunity to require fixes before systems go into production. Some developers have had training on secure programming methods, but are not consistently held to documented security standards.

Security personnel. Management has funded at most a few full-time security staff positions in the IT organization to focus on security issues. Key IT personnel have had some security training and understand the implications of some key risk areas.

Security infrastructure and tools. A set of tools has been implemented in the organization's network and computer systems, although some gaps still exist that could allow significant damage from an attack. Antivirus is updated automatically, and network intrusion detection sensors have been deployed on some key segments, although they are not tuned well and the alerts generated are often ignored due to administrators' experiences with high levels of false-positives. Filtering of traffic has been implemented on business partner connections.

Threat and vulnerability management. The identification of the organization's key systems has enabled some rudimentary prioritization of patching activity, although it often happens that Web servers on the perimeter get less attention than an internal database server despite the fact that they are exposed to greater threats. Critical patches get applied, albeit too slowly because of continued use of manual processes.

Configuration management. Developers still have access to production systems because they are the only ones who understand how to fix the applications those systems are running, but at least they have to first get approval to do so from the IT operations manager. Downtime is reduced but still happens due to incomplete testing, perhaps because of a lack of good integration testing.

Access control. User log-in accounts are somewhat better controlled, but many accounts are still not deactivated in a timely manner, perhaps only monthly or quarterly. Some guidance on selection of good passwords and protection of them has been given to employees, but enforcement of password quality is spotty across systems. Some key systems use strong authentication for administrative access. Access logs on critical systems are monitored manually.

Audits and assessments. An outside firm is brought in to conduct annual security audits and assessments, but the report never makes it above the IT manager or director level, as the security holes it enumerates would be too embarrassing. Some significant issues remain still unfixed on subsequent reports.

Business continuity. A basic DRP for IT systems has been created, but never tested. Perhaps a recovery center contract has been signed with a vendor. But senior management has not paid much attention to the issues involved with business recovery. Data backup tapes are rarely tested for restorability, if ever.

Incident handling. A basic process for incident handling has been documented and a few key team members have received some training. But no formalized team has been created, and frequent security incidents often result in ad hoc panic-driven responses.

Training and awareness. Security awareness efforts are rudimentary and infrequent. Many employees are still unaware of key safe computing behaviors, which means that malware outbreaks still happen with some regularity.

Maturity Level 3

At this level, the security program is running fairly well and has the support of the organization's management. Tactical response is mostly under control, allowing the security manager to focus more on strategic efforts. Areas where initial capital expenditures will result in ongoing reduction in operating costs are identified. However, gaps still exist and some processes are still too labor intensive because of the lack of good tools to automate them further. Characteristics include the following:

Security policies. A comprehensive set of policies, standards, and guidelines has been developed and promulgated across the organization. Compliance is monitored in some areas but not in others, resulting in increased risk (as well as increased scrutiny by auditors). Some areas could use more effective enforcement tools, perhaps a Web-traffic monitoring tool to detect users violating a policy against sharing of copyrighted media.

Management support. The security budget is within industry norms. Management has a good understanding of the information risks that face the business and therefore fully supports a solid security program. Management also takes many opportunities to voice support for security to the rank and file. Security management provides regular reports of metrics and status to the chief information officer (CIO) or other senior management.

Security integration into the SDLC. Security is regularly involved in the development of new systems from the beginning, and has the ability to escalate security issues prior to production deployment. A process for risk acceptance of noncompliant systems has been implemented. Most developers have received some training in secure development methods.

Security personnel. A dedicated security team of multiple experienced and certified individuals exists, led by a senior manager or even a chief information security officer. To attract and retain talent, compensation is on the upside of industry averages. Achievement of security objectives is assisted by key people in other departments.

Security infrastructure and tools. Tools have been deployed throughout the network that provide a comprehensive set of preventive and detective controls to prevent, monitor, and report on things like malware activity, network intrusion attempts, attacks against the wireless LAN, and Web application attacks. However, this has resulted in a plenitude of point solutions that require significant operational attention and a complexity that increases risk of errors or failures. A security event management (SEM) tool set and process are used to normalize and correlate alerts from log feeds from the intrusion detection system (IDS), firewalls, and critical systems. But some areas could still benefit from greater automation, such as centralized identity management. A basic reference architecture for security functionality may have been developed.

Threat and vulnerability management. Most critical systems are patched within a week, using a specialized patch deployment tool. Challenges may still exist—for example, an enterprise resource planning or customer relationship management system may get delayed patches due to heavy customization, increasing the risk of patches breaking the application. Also, there may not yet be good correlation between specific threats and the systems on the network of varying criticality.

Configuration management. Access to production systems is restricted to operations personnel only, and all fixes are first tested in the development environment. System configuration data is stored manually in federated repositories.

Access control. User log-in accounts are fairly well-controlled, albeit still mostly manually. An enterprisewide identity management system has not been deployed. Some key application systems, as well as superuser-level administrative access to network infrastructure and host systems, require strong two-factor authentication. The data center is in a secured facility with tightly controlled access. The concept of data ownership with owners being responsible for access decisions has taken root.

Audits and assessments. Audits and assessments occur on a regular basis, with results communicated to key stakeholders who collectively respond with corrective action plans. High-risk findings are addressed fairly promptly, and the loop is closed on the reporting to senior management. Security is also somewhat involved in the due-diligence process when significant new business partnerships are initiated, establishing requirements for third-party security evaluation of the business partner's security practices. There is a good partnership with the organization's internal audit department. However, audit and assessment efforts are not always well coordinated, causing duplication of work, particularly in the area of audits for regulatory compliance.

Business continuity. A reasonably complete plan exists and has been tested at least once in the past year. But it may not have been updated to reflect new business initiatives or new sites performing critical IT functions. Upper management supports the plan, however, and has allocated adequate funding for it. Backup media for some of the key systems are tested for restorability as part of the regular rotation.

Incident handling. A virtual incident response (IR) team that consists of trained people from key departments has been identified. The IR plan is tested at least once a year, and the team is able to respond reasonably well to the security incidents that occur. However, there is a lack of coordination with other key departments in the organization such as legal, communications, and, most importantly, senior business management.

Training and awareness. New employees are briefed on security policies, and there is an annual effort to remind the employees of the importance of certain security practices. Malware incidents have been reduced in frequency due to employees' improved practices. Protection of intellectual property has likewise improved.

Maturity Level 4

At this, the highest, level the security program is operating in an optimized and very effective manner and has support up to the board level, creating a risk-aware organization that does not rely only on the security team to keep things secure. Security is regarded as integral to the business and enables the business to proceed into areas that would otherwise be too risky. A comprehensive set of security controls, both technical and procedural, is in place and employees participate in protecting the company's information assets. Automation of key processes and reporting mechanisms ensures that the security team is able to respond quickly to new threats.

Security policies. Comprehensive policies and standards are reviewed and updated annually, and compliance is monitored in a number of ways. Deficient areas of compliance are responded to with additional technical controls or increased training as needed.

Management support. Senior business management evinces full support for security objectives and has included information risk in the business's overall risk management planning.

The chief security officer has established significant credibility and regularly solicits time to brief senior business management on the status of and plans for information protection in the company.

Security integration into the SDLC. Security has been baked into all phases of the SDLC. Security requirements are defined before any development on a new system commences. Most or all developers are trained on and follow the company's secure system development practices, and functional security testing is performed on all applications prior to going live.

Security personnel. Excellent compensation and a stimulating environment attract top-notch talent to the security team. They are not focused solely on technical matters, but instead work to understand the business and speak its language to frame risks in a way that is relevant to business decision makers. Team members have access to all the training needed to be successful and are rotated through different positions to round out their skill set.

Security infrastructure and tools. Automation of security tasks has been implemented where possible for labor savings and reduction of errors, and the security infrastructure is managed centrally in a dedicated security operations center. Suites of tools provide an integrated operational capability. Tools generate comprehensive metrics that enable pinpoint identification of areas that need additional attention and enable better quantification of risk reduction.

Threat and vulnerability management (TVM). A comprehensive and regularly updated configuration database of all critical systems enables rapid patch deployment across the enterprise. Patches are prioritized according to risk exposure.

Configuration management (CM). Evidencing the close relationship between CM and TVM, automated feeds of configuration data is stored in a centralized database that serves as a powerful tool to manage the organization's overall security posture.

Access control. An enterprisewide identity management system is used to manage user and system credentials and ensure that they are added and deleted in a timely manner. Self-service password reset has reduced the burden on the help desk (enabling it to spend time on higher-value activities), and two-factor authentication for sensitive systems has likewise reduced the need for frequent password changes. Superuser access is tightly controlled to protect against insider sabotage and other malicious acts. All application systems have documented owners that make access decisions.

Audits and assessments. Activities are well coordinated across the business, with security, compliance, and audit working in sync to continually improve the system of controls. Reporting enables a clear path to industry certification such as ISO27001.

Business continuity (BC). A comprehensive cross-team plan that enables rapid resumption of key business activities at an alternate site is in place and is rehearsed at least annually. It is baked into the development process and developers help identify critical business processes that need recovery plans. The BC/DR function is led by a dedicated, experienced manager and staff who ensure that the plan is regularly updated to reflect new sites and initiatives.

Incident handling. An enterprise-level IR plan is in place that has been coordinated across all key departments. Scenario planning ensures that the highly trained IR team is able to respond to almost any situation in a rapid and effective manner.

Training and awareness. A broad-spectrum awareness program ensures that employees are continually educated about and reminded of their responsibilities to maintain the organization's security. Metrics for awareness program effectiveness are used to tune the messages and identify areas that need more attention. Data custodians and IT personnel receive specialized training.

Setting the Right Priorities

For the security manager new to an organization, or an existing one working to achieve maximum leverage with his or her limited budget, focusing on the right issues is critical to success. For example, in a less mature program it may be folly to spend time and money on advanced projects like identity management when much more fundamental things are broken. Some activities, however, are *de rigueur* for the security professional entering an organization at any maturity level: understand the business, understand the culture, understand the IT infrastructure, and win allies in key areas of the organization.

Now let us take a look at each maturity level and the prioritized areas that the security manager should focus efforts on. Consider these priorities to be cumulative—as the security program gains resources, skills, and maturity it will be able to take on more advanced initiatives while continuing to maintain existing tools and processes. These existing activities must continue to evolve toward greater automation and definition of repeatable processes. For brevity, the activity descriptions are kept to a high level—consult other chapters in this book for more details. Of course, differences in organizations may require adaptation of these recommendations to fit the specific environment and culture.

Maturity Level 1

At this level, it is entirely likely that the first full-time security professional hired is for a staff-level position, reporting to a manager in IT or perhaps audit or finance. Such a hiring represents the first significant indication of management support for information security.

The security practitioners in an organization with an immature program at this level will be primarily in tactical mode, performing triage and firefighting on an almost daily basis. Because of this, they will be unable to focus on any more strategically focused work because of time constraints and the simple fact that management and the organization are not yet ready for such thinking from the security function. Nor should the security practitioner yet attempt to create a complete security policy—policy is not very effective at stopping bleeding. Instead, they should focus on the following areas.

Build relationships with key managers and staff. In an immature security program, it is essential to gain allies in other parts of the organization for maximum leverage of very limited security resources. Ideally, these allies will buy into the security effort and help create a federated type of security team.

Implement comprehensive malware detection. Antivirus and spyware-detection tools must be installed and regularly updated on desktops, laptops, servers, and mail gateways. A 2007 report by Webroot Software found that 43 percent of firms they surveyed had been hit by malware that caused disruption to their business. Although a growing percentage of malware is rapidly evolving and not detected by many of the tools out there, detection tools remain a critical line of defense that must be deployed as effectively as possible.

Shore up the network perimeter. Assess the network's firewall defenses at all entry points into the network. Review the filter configurations and ensure that each permission is fully justified by business need. For environments with complex yet porous firewall configurations, it may be most effective to examine logs of traffic flows over a couple of weeks and then start with a clean "deny-all" slate and build it back up by soliciting input on needs. Conduct a survey to track down wireless LAN access points and begin securing them.

Develop a patch management process. Keeping desktop and server systems up to date on patches is a critical ongoing task. At this maturity level, however, patch deployment is likely a manual process, so concentrate on Internet-facing systems first, then user desktops, and then key internal servers. For Microsoft Windows desktops, just set them up to use Windows Update—at this stage the risk of a bad patch is far outweighed by the risk of remaining unpatched. This goes for Windows servers as well.

Delete or lock dormant user log-in accounts. Inactive log-in accounts are a common avenue of compromise by disgruntled ex-employees. Review key systems to get a list of accounts that are no longer authorized and accounts that have not been accessed in 90 days by existing employees, then get them deleted or locked.

Begin identifying critical application systems. Although simply identifying critical systems does not improve a security posture by itself, it will help focus future protection activities on what is important to the business.

Conduct a security vulnerability assessment. If funding can be secured to hire a third party to conduct an assessment, then the objectivity of an outside entity will be worth it. It will be a challenge to fix all of the vulnerabilities that will be found, so first obtaining support for the effort from system owners and management is important. Gain consensus on a timetable to fix the worst problems by a target date. Refer to best practices documents for guidance to point to when justifying how the vulnerabilities should be fixed—the National Institute of Standards and Technology (NIST) is a good source for this (see Special Publications 800-30 and 800-53 in particular).

Because the security practitioner's time is limited and the organization is not ready yet, some areas that should be avoided at this stage include anything more than basic policies, security awareness training, insertion of security into the SDLC, and disaster recovery planning. Looking for quick wins to show management will build credibility for the program and lay the groundwork for further efforts. Security metrics will be hard to come by at this point, so focus should be on the rapid reduction in risk to the network that has been achieved.

Maturity Level 2

At this level, a basic security infrastructure is in place and functioning, and primary focus can be shifted to somewhat more evolved security activities. Remember that activities are cumulative—priorities at level 1 must continue to be worked, as they will need ongoing support and improvement to reduce risk further.

Policies, standards, procedures, and guidelines. Begin developing a set of security policies that take into account the business's culture, relevant laws and regulations, and the company's appetite for risk. Having the chief executive officer sign off on the policies will demonstrate to the organization that senior management takes security seriously. Policies also carry legal weight and help reduce liability—something the general counsel will appreciate. Once high-level policies are published, develop standards that spell out specific, measurable technical controls that can be verified for compliance. Documented procedures that detail for users and systems administrators the steps needed to implement the policies and standards may then be created. Last, guidelines that provide recommendations for action may be generated.

Understand the business. Seek out the key players in areas such as sales, marketing, operations, legal, human resources, and audit to build knowledge of how the business operates, what the key objectives and strategies are, where management sees areas of risk, what the perception of security's role is, and who the key players are (they are not always in management roles—the senior UNIX guru who has been at the company for 20 years may be one of the most important people to make friends with).

Vulnerability assessments. Assessments and audits should be planned to take into account multiple reporting requirements for compliance, internal tactical planning, and metrics. Otherwise, significant time and effort may be wasted redoing the same assessments for different recipients.

Security monitoring. Ensure that firewalls, virtual private network (VPN) concentrators, and critical server systems are generating useful logs. Begin centralizing the log output to a main log server. Deploy IDS on key network segments, using a limited set of alerts focused on major threats. Otherwise, IDS alert output will easily overrun the time and capabilities of the security team at level 2.

Incident response. The annual Computer Security Institute/Federal Bureau of Investigation security survey has found that more than 70 percent of organizations have had at least one security incident. The rest probably just did not know it. It is therefore very important to define and document an IR process and identify the key personnel that would be needed to respond to a breach of security. Ensure that everyone involved is trained on the process and knows how to respond in an organized and efficient manner. Rehearse the process every six months if there are not enough actual incidents to practice on.

Disaster recovery planning. Having identified the critical IT systems and developed an understanding of the business and its recovery time objectives, and the major business-interrupting threats it faces, develop a recovery plan that will help get critical IT systems back up and running in the event of a disaster.

Continued effort and focus at this level will help move the organization up the maturity scale. At this stage, avoid complex tool deployments like SEM and identity management and directory services, any large security awareness programs, and data classification efforts. Getting the infrastructure secured to a basic level will free more time to work on building support and relationships and developing better processes around the tools that have been deployed. Management should be aware of the work that the security team is doing and understand the value it brings to the organization.

Maturity Level 3

Organizations at this level of security maturity are doing the basic blocking and tackling well and can devote resources to more advanced efforts. However, the security manager should be careful not to shortchange the fundamentals while working on these more advanced projects. Continuing to do that well helps ensure that management will appreciate the security team's value and fund additional projects. The manager must not underestimate the skills and resources that advanced projects like these require. Nothing will destroy security's credibility faster than spending a large amount of money and having only a broken, half-functional tool to show for it. Bring in consulting expertise as needed to ensure success, and break down the project into manageable chunks that each has a strong chance of success. Project failure is one of the major reasons that many organizations cannot get their security program up to a higher level of maturity. At this level of maturity, the following areas deserve attention:

Security tool integration. Once an organization has deployed a plethora of security point solutions, the new challenge is to integrate them into a cohesive whole that enhances security visibility across the enterprise while reducing the effort needed to manage the tools and the huge amount of data they generate. Security information management tools, sometimes also called SEM, enable this by pulling in the myriad sources of security monitoring data like firewalls, IDSs/intrusion prevention systems, VPN servers, routers and switches, servers and desktops, vulnerability scanners, and antivirus gateways.

Secure application development training. To achieve stronger integration of security into the SDLC, the software developers should be trained in secure coding practices, especially for Web applications—a major source of risk. Seek out one of the training consultancies that specialize in this. Also refer to NIST Special Publication 800-64 for more information on integrating security into the SDLC.

Awareness training. Once the infrastructure is reasonably well secured, focus on getting employees familiar with the current security threats, their responsibilities for keeping information secure, who to call to report incidents, and proper behavior when using e-mail and the Internet. Use multiple media that continuously reinforce the security message.

Strong authentication for critical data. Passwords are not enough for strong access control. Having identified the systems that hold and process critically sensitive data, implement two-factor authentication for those systems and ensure that there are no privileged accounts left out from under that umbrella. Pilot the project with a small group of systems and users first to avoid any problems later.

Data classification. This is perhaps one of the most challenging security projects, taking years to implement as the culture and awareness of the organization changes. But it is very important, as it helps legally protect the company's trade secrets and ensures that access to sensitive documents and data can be properly restricted. Work with the legal department and begin with a classification policy, educate users, and begin labeling documents as they are newly created. As existing documents and applications are updated, they should be labeled as well.

Compliance tools. The ever-growing raft of regulations that companies, especially public companies, must comply with has resulted in a very difficult environment. Many companies deal with new compliance reporting or audit requests on at least a monthly basis and find themselves repeating the same work over and over. This is a big drain on resources and often does not make the company measurably more secure. Evaluate and implement tools to help streamline compliance reporting and avoid duplicated effort. Also, pursuing certification against ISO27001 can help in this area.

Security strategy. A 2004 study by PricewaterhouseCooper and *CIO Magazine* found that 50 percent of security managers do not have a security strategy. But once the security program has matured to this level, the security manager must start building a strategic plan to fit the business and provide a framework for all of the security efforts. To do this effectively, however, requires that they are closely aligned with the business and involved in the overall strategic business planning process. The security strategic plan should be revisited every year and adjusted as needed.

Business continuity. Although DRP focuses on restoration of the company's IT infrastructure, business continuity planning focuses on restoration of business operations when the availability of supporting resources like the network and facilities is lost. Although this planning function is not purely security, it is a key part of enterprise risk management and the security manager will play a key role in this effort.

Maturity level 3 is the highest that many organizations get before plateauing. This is due to many factors, but discontinuity of security program management is one, overall lack of rigor in the organization's processes and risk management approach is another. To reach the highest level of maturity requires substantial discipline and expertise, and a great deal of effort to stay there. But there are more and more companies that achieve this as best practice are shared and institutionalized.

Maturity Level 4

The most mature security programs are fully optimized and have well-documented (and used) processes that provide a feedback loop to continually improve security. Although tools are still important, the greater focus at this level is on business alignment and standardization of processes.

> *Identity management and public key infrastructure.* As the numbers of systems and users in an organization grow, the effort required to manage user accounts effectively and access privileges quickly becomes overwhelming. Build and deploy an enterprisewide identity management system to centralize user accounts and privileges and reduce the risk of overassignment of access and of incomplete termination of access when an employee leaves the company.
>
> *Comprehensive metrics reporting.* To continue building management support for new security initiatives and ensure that security is baked into the business, develop a suite of metrics that enable tracking of security spending effectiveness and that can help to identify problem areas that need more attention. Ensure the metrics are properly tuned to the audience.
>
> *Enterprise risk management.* The manager of a mature security program should be fully involved in the organization's overall enterprise risk management program. The top-performing security officers have created a risk-aware culture in their companies in which employees fully understand their role in protecting information and management evaluates all decisions in terms of risk (and therefore cost to the business).
>
> *Formalized security governance.* IT governance is a topic on more and more CIO's minds, and prominent resources like the IT Infrastructure Library are available to help establish and maintain a governance structure. Establish a security governance structure that includes key stakeholder representatives to ensure that security is continually aligned with the business and responsibilities are clearly defined. Governance efforts will also help the security department position itself as an internal service resource for the rest of the business.

Another tool that top-performing organizations use to ensure they are moving in the right direction is industry benchmarking. By leveraging contacts in the industry, a group of security managers can build off of one another's successes to achieve higher levels in their security program—"steel sharpening steel."

A security manager that has built or manages a program at a high level of maturity is a very valuable asset to his or her organization and will be frequently sought out by others looking to leverage their expertise.

Conclusion

The reader should now be familiar with the characteristics of security programs of differing levels of maturity and what the security managers need to focus on when starting in an organization at each level. It is important that they are able to evaluate program maturity objectively so that effort and resources can be assigned to the most appropriate activities that result in the most risk reduction for the business.

Chapter 8

Why and How Assessment of Organization Culture Shapes Security Strategies

Don Saracco

Contents

Why Be Concerned with Organization Culture?

To answer this question we must first answer the question, "How are security and culture linked?" The answer to that question lies not in what we know but in what we do not know. Although we take it for granted that security is an indelible part of individual and organizational life, the definition and extent of its need vary greatly across any population of people and organizations. After all, if it is simply "common sense" to ensure security, of what use is the answer to the question? We should simply implement as much security as we possibly can and consider the job done. Of course, such a simplistic application of common sense could lead an organization into excessive spending and crippling constraints on employee productivity.

As it turns out, every management practice in an organization will support or inhibit that organization in proportion to the extent that the practice is aligned with the culture. Failure to align with culture is the hallmark of "programs of the month" that come and go and end up on the trash heap of good intentions badly executed.

> Effective alignment of practice with culture enables security managers to design and implement necessary and sufficient security, and the provision of no more and no less than that is the security manager's job.

The purpose of this chapter is twofold. First it will explain why you must understand the link between culture and security practices. Second it will describe how you can go about assessing your organization's culture and linking that assessment to security strategies.

Learning to Be Secure

Security needs in people begin with what are apparently instinctive reactions to perceived threats. Humans seem to have a survival instinct hardwired into the organism. It is initially visible in the form of reflexes and later becomes more sophisticated. An infant reacts to loud noises or jerky motions with alarm. As the child grows and develops more sophisticated perceptions, reflexes are augmented by thinking processes. Reactions to threats include not only simple perception but also analysis of the threat and the choice of an appropriate response.

As sophistication grows even further people become able to develop actions based on an assessment of the probability that a threat might exist. Our personal security becomes more proactive and less reactive. A person walking down a dark street in an unfamiliar neighborhood hearing footsteps approaching from the rear is likely to experience an elevated heart rate and other physical signs of psychological arousal. There is no clear and present danger but the person makes an analysis of the facts listed earlier, blends it with past experiences as well as stories heard, and reaches instant conclusions regarding the presence of threat. These conclusions produce the physical feelings with which we are all familiar when danger is sensed. The default response for people is to prepare to flee or fight. It seems that the very design of the organism is toward protection and survival. It is important to note that reflexive reactions never completely disappear. They have always been necessary for the survival of the organism and are not likely to evolve out of existence any time soon.

A truly interesting thing about this process is that as learning continues, the proactive process can come to appear reflexive as the processing of information regarding familiar stimuli becomes "automated" in the brain. Familiar threats begin to produce what appear to be reflexive reactions, which are actually learned responses that bypass conscious analysis as an unnecessary step in dealing with that stimulus. Essentially, a person forms an "association macro" that runs an automatic analysis of the stimulus and then runs a programmed response. The person walking down the dark street did not think about the danger. In fact the physical feelings were probably felt before any conscious thought occurred. Thus the foundation for the person's tendencies throughout life to approach or avoid various stimuli is laid.

In a sense the processes come full circle from reflex to conscious thought and back to what appears as reflex again (see Figure 8.1).

Such learned automatic behavior is even called "knee jerk" in popular literature. The allusion to what happens when the doctor taps a person's knee to test reflexes is not without foundation. For all intents and purposes it is the same thing. The only meaningful difference between the two responses is that the latter, learned response can be altered by conscious cognitive intervention.

As cognitive mechanisms continue to develop automated responses can become incorporated into larger schemes of thought such that the person anticipates discomfort and avoids walking unaccompanied in unfamiliar neighborhoods at night. After all, would not a reasonable person avoid perceived danger? You can probably see how this process proceeding out of control can also produce "unreasonable" patterns of behavior that we might call paranoid or otherwise excessive.

So What?

By now you are probably asking yourself why this discussion of assessing culture began with a walk through Developmental Psych 101. It is important because this "biological inertia" to survive and to use programmed responses is also true for other organic forms in our world, including human organizations, and it finds its expression in the patterns that we call organization culture. That which is born does not normally want to die and there is a will to live apparent in all viable organizations as well as in viable people. In fact managers in organizations accept their accountability for the protection of the organization's continued growth and survival unquestioningly. I have not seen a position description (except at the chief executive officer level) that spells out this

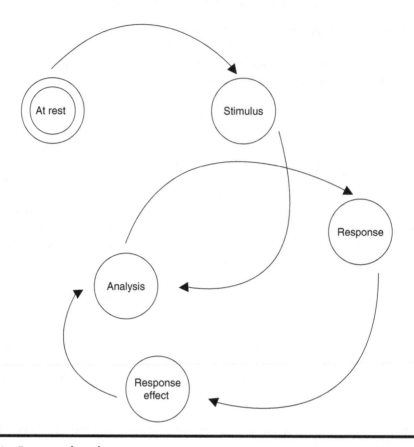

Figure 8.1 Response learning process.

accountability for managers but I doubt that any would deny that it exists. It could be argued that this reflexive will to survive is hardwired into the organization or is at least automated in management practices (Rousseau, 1995).

The problem is that reflexes are not enough and reactions to risk must become thoughtful anticipation of risk. Rapid discovery of a security breach must be secondary to effective reduction of a security risk. The design of the process of reducing risk is the point at which all organisms and organizations differ and that difference follows from either personality in the individual or culture in an organization.

> So, just as we would need to understand the personality of an individual to understand his or her needs for security, so must we understand the culture of an organization to design an appropriate security program.

Different personalities are likely to perceive personal risk differently and different organizational cultures will also differ in their perceptions of what is most important to their survival. As will be discussed later, culture can trump good common sense when it comes to management and security practices and this is the compelling driver for including a useful assessment of culture in the development of a security program. After all, effective management is doing the right things right, not just doing everything that can be done.

The Requirements of Assessment

The first requirement of cultural assessment is support from the most senior levels of management for the conduct of such an assessment. It cannot be assumed that owners and other top managers of organizations want any such assessment to be performed, so portion of this treatise will be devoted to selling the idea of assessment.

There are a number of definitions of assessment. For our purposes we will use the one that refers to assessment as a categorization, sorting, or classification. If we can provide a useful classification system for organization cultures, we can identify security strategies most appropriate for each class. So, the next requirement for assessment of organization culture is a classification system. We will use a fairly simple system that provides adequate direction without unnecessarily complicating the work.

The next requirement is a method of assessment. The method must provide sufficient information to differentiate among organizations and be compatible with practices in the organization. Both survey and interview methods may be used. Both can be valid and can be used independently or together.

The next requirement is a logical connection between the classification and the specific security strategies. This requirement is partially met by the use of a robust classification system that is founded in valid and reliable principles of human and organizational behavior. It also calls for openness to changes in management practices where such changes will enable or enhance the effectiveness of strategies.

The final requirement is effective presentation of the assessment results and recommendations to organization decision makers, without whose support no effective program can be implemented. Both new and enhanced security strategies and changes to management practices are likely to include costs of some kind, so this step is crucial to getting the right program in place. Without appropriate management support, many security personnel are relegated to the role of "virus and porn police" with no strategic impact on the business.

Selling Assessment

Selling the assessment may be the most important part of the entire process, for without it the assessment is not likely to move forward. The process is fairly simple, as shown in Figure 8.2.

Selling Yourself

It all begins with the ability of security professionals to be perceived as competent and trustworthy partners in the pursuit of business goals. If you do not really know how you are perceived you will have to find a way to ask people. This is the first necessary step toward ensuring the value of your security program as well as your own influence in the organization.

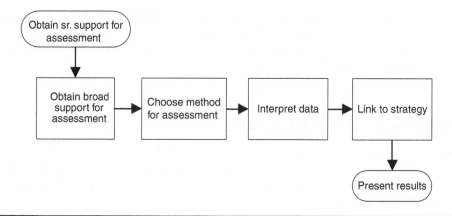

Figure 8.2 Assessment process.

Of course the first source to use should be your direct supervisors. They may be willing to give you some unvarnished feedback about your perceived effectiveness and can also help you to plan the reinvention of yourself in your role. If your supervisor lacks the skills or willingness to give you useful feedback and developmental support you will have to go to your peers and customers. Frankly, you should never spend any significant length of time in a staff position without getting feedback from your customers anyway.

Soliciting feedback can be a risky process. People who are asked face to face to assess your effectiveness are just as likely to tell you what they think you want to hear as to give you an honest appraisal of your relationship with them. An anonymous method is probably better. There are two ways to get anonymous feedback. You can develop a valid questionnaire and distribute it to a sample of your peers and your customers at every level of the organization that is as large as possible or you can have a surrogate interview people on your behalf using a structured interview protocol that you have helped to design. The former is faster and probably less expensive. It will also be statistically defensible. The latter method will get you nuances of perception and a richer pool of information but will take longer, cost more, and lack statistical power. In either case you should enlist the aid of a skilled assessment professional to help interpret the results of your data collection and help you to make specific plans for improvement.

If the current security staff already enjoys the confidence of peer and superior customers, selling the idea of culture assessment should be relatively easy, but it will not necessarily be a "slam dunk." In the past years when my colleagues and I at MLC & Associates, Inc., were first developing our assessment methods, we had the experience of getting agreement from a senior management sponsor to do the assessment only to find that when we tried to roll out the method, there were others who objected to it. We quickly learned that an assessment of culture will succeed only if there is broad management support for doing it. At a minimum, this support should include the senior business operations managers, human resources, risk management, audit, the chief information officer, the chief administrative officer, and a significant sample of middle managers throughout the organization.

Selling the Assessment

We and our clients have found that a well-designed and planned "road show" can be a very effective method of gaining the broad base of support that you will need. A road show has two central elements. It contains factual information and it succeeds in generating dialogue. The factual information is necessary because people want to know exactly what they are being asked to support (or at least not object to) and how it will help them to reach their goals. The dialogue is necessary because you will need to know what those goals are before you can position the assessment as helpful.

In most cases, this selling process involves multiple iterations of face-to-face meetings with key people. Initial meetings can be exploratory for the purpose of exchanging general security program and business unit goals. One of the most common mistakes that we have seen people make is to assume that they have the support or agreement of someone as a result of a single conversation. Support and agreement must be treated like living things that require constant nurturing and renewal. Organization life today is much too dynamic to assume that any relationship is permanent.

Skilled security managers will do much more listening in these meetings than talking. They should be certain about the strategic goals that provide the direction for the program in case peers and superiors want to know, but there is little or no value in long-winded speeches filled with technical jargon intended to impress people with your brilliance. There is tremendous value in sincere inquiry about the things that are important to business operations. So, if you are asked to describe your program respond with a brief but complete statement of your strategic goals followed by a question such as, "What can we do that will best support your business goals?"

Of course the people with whom you are meeting will be curious and perhaps even suspicious about what you want from them. We have found that it is always best to be brief and honest about that. You will be asking for support in the conduct of an assessment of the organization's culture. It is important to formulate a succinct statement that says what you want and what it is likely to cost the other person, if anything.

Your purpose in assessing the culture is not to try to change it or be critical of it, but to understand it, so that your program will be appropriately aligned with it.

You should operate under the assumption that the culture is what it is and represents part of what makes the company successful. Unless the company is in serious trouble, this is usually a safe assumption.

If you are asked for details, focus on providing "minimal truth." Avoid technical jargon and be prepared to give a simple example of how you will use the information. Such an example might be that you need to develop security policies that are consistent with the culture, because to do otherwise puts you in danger of being either overly restrictive or not sufficiently diligent. Security policies and practices must blend with the culture rather than attempt to change it—unless such a change is necessary to reduce or eliminate a legitimate risk.

Some security chiefs find it useful to assemble a steering committee or program management office involving key personnel from around the organization willing to serve. If you choose this management strategy, it should be the first thing that you do before framing any initiatives. Such an advisory group can be a powerful ally but it will take some time to get it up and running. A key to success for a steering committee or advisory board is to ensure that they have real work to do and real decisions to make. For example, you can use such a body to bless your drafts of organization security policies, thus ensuring that your policy framework is both widely accepted and aligned with the interests of key players in the organization. A steering or advisory committee is a double-edged sword that can hurt your efforts as well as help them. If you choose to use one, assemble and nurture it with great care. Communicate often and effectively with its members and never assume that everyone is automatically on the same page with you or that you can use the committee to "rubber stamp" anything.

Choosing Assessment Methods

The choice of assessment methods is critical to the success of the process. Organizational activities associated with programs and initiatives must gain fairly wide acceptance not to be disruptive or face resistance.

Disruption can come from poor understanding of the motives for the assessment. In these times when people are increasingly likely to distrust an employer's actions, any assessment may be viewed as a step toward restructuring or right-sizing, with the consequences of reduced productivity and malicious compliance.

Resistance, both open and passive, can also derail an assessment. As people become successfully socialized into their organizations, they learn how not to do things as well as how to get things done. Research tells us that when they are threatened, people will often plead lack of time or insufficient priority to avoid engaging in a mandated activity without clear purpose. Passive resistance is very difficult to identify as people will invoke reasons for not doing their part apparently rooted in a focus on central organizational goals. Senior managers are unlikely to be critical of people who appear to be supporting management's primary reasons for being.

You might be persuaded to think that obtaining senior management support for an assessment would be sufficient to overcome resistance, and for some percentage of the population in some organizations that would be true. There is, however, no substitute for gaining broad support from all levels of management as well as from the rank and file of employees.

If by now you are becoming discouraged by all that must be done to get this right, do not worry. There is also good news, and that is a little truth telling works wonders. The most important truths to tell are about how the assessment information will be used without hiding any secondary purpose and that individual inputs from people will remain anonymous.

For example, you may see that an assessment of the culture can be incorporated into any analysis of readiness for organizational change as well as into actual change initiatives. If the organization plans to leverage the cost of the assessment by using the information for more than security program development, that fact must be shared with people in the beginning.

It is also necessary to guarantee anonymity for individuals. There will always be those who suspect the information will be somehow used against them in administrative proceedings. Of course to do so would be both unethical and in some states illegal. Verbal assurances may not be enough to support a guarantee of anonymity. You may need to share an explicit description of how that anonymity is going to be protected and make the process open to inspection.

Well, that's enough discussion of things about which you should be concerned. Let us get to the "how to do it" parts.

Interviews

Effective interviewing is an art. It requires both discipline and sensitivity to what is not being said. The discipline can be rooted in the interview protocol but even skilled interviewers can succumb to the temptation to stray from the protocol just for the sake of variety. Reliance on the protocol should be absolute as a consistent framework for interviews. Properly done interviews can provide a very rich body of data from a relatively small sample of subjects but interpretation must be done with the highest standards of professional discipline to avoid overly subjective interpretation of results. Having the data collection and the interpretation done by different people can overcome this pitfall and help to ensure that conclusions about the culture can be supported.

Sensitivity to what is not being said enables interviewers to demonstrate that they are sincerely listening, makes the interview more conversational, and allows the interviewer to probe beneath the surface for foundation beliefs about the culture and experiences within it. This is the part of interviewing that is the most artful and that takes significant experience to learn. We do not recommend that inexperienced people use interview methods. An unskilled interviewer can come across as an interrogator and that will do nothing less than confirming any negative suspicions about the purpose of the interview that the subjects may have had at the outset. We do recommend that anyone hoping to be successful in staff roles learn effective interviewing skills. They will serve you well throughout your career.

Interview Protocol

The interview protocol is the essential structure of the interview process as well as the list of questions you intend to ask. The core questions of all subjects must be asked to ensure accurate interpretation of results. The core should consist of enough questions to develop sufficient information for analysis but not so many as to cause you be rushed near the end of the scheduled time. We have found that somewhere in the neighborhood of 10 to 15 open-ended questions fits fairly well into a one-hour time slot. This allows you to get enough information to contribute to a classification of the culture archetype and enough time to maintain a friendly, conversational tone to the interview.

Selecting Interview Subjects

The selection of interview subjects should be done with input from stakeholders or neutral parties. We have found input from senior managers as well as from senior administrative assistants to be very useful in selecting a good cross section of the population. The subjects should include managers at several levels as well as rank and file staff of all types (e.g., exempt and nonexempt). Include both people with significant tenure and those who have fewer than 18 months with the organization. Most people should be able to provide enough information to help with classification of the culture after they have been on board for about 90 days, but a little longer is probably better. Frankly, it depends on things like the actual age of the organization. It is important to get a good cross-sectional representation of organizational functions to ensure that you account for internal differences in departments. A large organization with rigid "silos" can have important differences across departments and these differences can influence how you implement security measures.

We have done an analysis in an organization in which more than half the personnel had been with the organization for less than a year and were still able to make an accurate assessment. The rapid growth of the company called for people to truly "hit the ground running" and the recruitment process aimed at fully informing new hires about how things were done in the company. We were able to get a very good representative sample of the various functions and thus to understand the differences with which the program would have to cope.

Interview Structure

The overall structure of the interview should help to ensure an appropriate tone and that you get the information you need. The general process structure should look something like the following:

- Introduction
    - Purpose and affirmation of anonymity
    - Process description
    - Check for understanding
- Opening questions (ask about the subject's role in the organization, tenure with the organization, experience with security, etc., to establish a conversational tone)
- Core questions (start with the most general and unrelated to the person's own experience and work toward more specific examples of the subject's personal experiences)
- Finish by giving the subject an opportunity to ask questions of you, offering thanks, and by sharing what the next steps in the process will be

Interpreting Results

Interpretation of interview results calls for intimate familiarity with the culture classification system that you use and the implications of each class for security strategies. The process for drawing information from interview data is called "thematic analysis" because what you are doing is identifying relevant themes that appear across interviews. These themes lend support to your conclusions about the classification of the culture and subsequent application to your program. A theme is a response to your core interview questions that appears more than two or three times in as many separate interviews. We have found that in an organization of medium to large size between 20 and 40 interviews should be sufficient.

In a land development organization in which we conducted an assessment, we repeatedly heard that decisions were seldom made below the executive level. In our classification system this theme clearly points to a vertical archetype. Other information that supported this conclusion appeared in stories of a sort of "bipolar" way of doing things. It either took "forever" to get anything done or things had to be done immediately so as to not suffer the disfavor of a senior manager. This is another clear indication of the vertical archetype that will be described under "A Classification System for Organizational Cultures."

Surveys

Assessment by survey is more about science than about art, although the artful preparation of the survey is still necessary. You may even find that some people are more suspicious of a survey than of interviews. Any survey that smacks of psychology or social research can provoke hostile reactions in some people. People sometimes have bad experiences with surveys badly done, so that they will never greet one without deep suspicion or resentment. You can protect against hostile reactions by sufficiently and honestly communicating the purpose of the survey, affirming the anonymity of respondents, and fully describing how the data will be handled and processed.

A survey is more science than art because it can avoid any tendencies for the data-collection process to be biased by subjective interpretation of data. It provides an objective measure of opinions and usually allows for a much larger sample of organization members to be included in the data-collection process. However, science calls for a certain level of rigor in the creation of the survey instrument and the treatment of results.

The Instrument

There are two major concerns when it comes to using survey instruments: validity and reliability. In the simplest terms, the instrument must measure what it intends to measure (validity) and produce similar results with repeated use (reliability). At the time of publication, we have not been able to find a standard instrument that can be used in the design of a security program. There are several instruments that have been developed to assess cultures with regard to safety issues as well as tools intended for use in general assessment of organizational climate. There are apparently none based on a classification system that can be related to security strategies.

This is not particularly surprising when one considers the fact that most security experts avoid the subject of culture as a factor in program implementation, preferring to focus on the power of technology and policy to achieve security program goals.

Developing Your Own Instrument

We have been using a survey instrument of our own design for culture assessment for the past decade. It is based on a classification system that readily provides guidance for a wide variety of organizational development activities and initiatives. Although the instrument has not yet been statistically validated, it consistently returns internal reliability coefficients above 0.90 (above 0.80 is considered fairly reliable and above 0.60 is often considered acceptable in social research). This suggests that the instrument is essentially coherent and is measuring something consistently. We believe that it is measuring the factors that we assume characterize the major archetypes of culture that we believe exist, but we have not yet secured a research partner to help us to validate our assumption.

The foregoing information is not included as an advertisement but to demonstrate that developing your own instrument can be difficult and requires adherence to rigorous research rules. We are neither willing to offer our tool on the market nor do we suggest to clients that it is more than it is, because it does not yet meet the standard for a research tool. Neither should you pretend that your homegrown survey is valid and reliable without appropriate statistical evidence. Questionnaires are fairly easy to write, but scientific instruments take years to develop and require a solid theoretical basis. Perhaps some of the purveyors of security technology and program support will become willing to invest in the development of useful culture assessment tools as they learn about the need to align programs and technology with culture.

This does not mean that you cannot design your own survey instrument and use it. It means only that you will need a robust classification model upon which to base your questionnaire and that you must include the limitations of your tool in any report of results that you produce.

The following is offered as basic information relative to developing survey items.

The instrument items are usually written in the form of statements with which people are asked to agree or disagree on a scale from "strongly disagree" to "strongly agree," because what we are looking for is where the person's perception falls on a continuous scale. For example, if, as the first item in the following list states, leadership is emphasized more than control, we get an indication that the organization culture archetype is more horizontal than vertical. There must be multiple items in the instrument that seek the same determination until a single item is validated statistically to provide the information alone. In our instrument we use 36 items to identify placement in three categories. That gives us 12 items for each archetype looking at six different factors, so each factor is measured two times.

1. Leadership (inspiration) is emphasized and rewarded much more than is management (control).
2. My primary customer (the person I must please) is my supervisor.
3. People are rewarded and recognized primarily because of their individual accomplishments.
4. There are things that are not "discussable," that is, things that everyone knows, but it is not OK to talk about.
5. Innovation is highly valued despite the risk of failure.
6. People must get permission to do anything new or different.

The Survey Protocol

There is a standard general protocol for the use of social research tools. It is designed to avoid contamination of survey results that can come from conscious or unconscious bias. The following steps are an adaptation of the protocol for the use of individual assessment instruments:

1. Administer the instrument
2. Score the instrument and collect relevant statistical results
3. Interpret the results in terms of the classification system and implications for strategy
4. Report the results to stakeholders, including implications for security strategies

The critical part of this protocol is administration before the classification system model is discussed with any of the participants in the survey. Results can be skewed by knowledge of the model unless the survey includes enough items of the right kind to identify deliberate bias in the responses. For custom-designed tools and most others that are commercially available this kind of robust instrument design is seldom available.

A Classification System for Organizational Cultures

Cultural analysis is defined in the organizational psychology literature as a stream of investigation that seeks to understand and map trends, influences, effects, and affects within cultures (Aronson, 1995). Standard analysis of culture is based upon an idiosyncratic array of symbols, norms, myths, legends, and character archetypes. The analysis and classification framework that we use is derived from research and practice concerned with psychological contracts and core relationship dynamics within organizations (Rousseau, 1989; Rousseau, 1990; Rousseau and McLean, 1993). Psychological contracts are the operant agreements regarding the understood exchange of value between employees and their organizations. The exchange of value generally calls for employees to give things like their attendance, best efforts, loyalty, and adherence to organization values in exchange for adequate compensation, benefits, opportunity, and quality of relationships. These contracts tend to be unique on an individual level owing to the unique

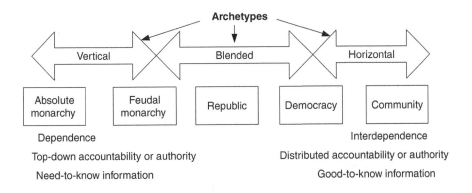

Figure 8.3 Archetypes governance model.

psychology of individual people. At the level of organization archetype, the contract is a normative one that is shared by all employees with the organization. The research of MLC & Associates has identified organizational archetypes that are characterized by certain underlying beliefs, practices, and elements of the psychosocial contract that are common across the vast majority of relationships between the organization and its members. These archetypes can be described as analogous to fundamental models of governance ranging from absolute control by an individual to widely distributed control as may be seen in a community (Figure 8.3).

The Organization Imperative

Humans will organize. Whenever people commit to work toward shared goals, they will organize to reach those goals (Biddle, 1979). Granted the organization may not always be elegant or functionally effective but it will exist. It appears that people will organize because there is a need to know how we relate to others with whom we work and an organization can define relationships according to commonly accepted definitions of roles.

Organization relationships are most significantly influenced by the distribution of authority and accountability (A&A). This distribution informs people about how they can learn what is important and how things get done in the organization. It also defines formal freedom to act, which is a de facto control on the extent to which people can be creative.

The Psychological Contract: The Heart of the Culture

Psychological contracts are both individual and collective (normative). Each organization has a normative contract in place that can serve as a basis for the classification of the culture. Many elements or clauses are included in the contract (see Figure 8.4) but there are some that represent a core of critical factors. These revolve around the distribution of A&A and include how information is managed and how much dependence is expected from people. Such a classification system allows us to make the connection between the culture and how we must design the organization's policies and practices, because each archetype calls for specific patterns of behavior and belief.

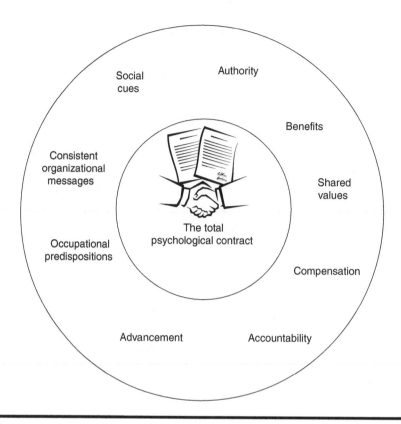

Figure 8.4 Inputs to the psychological contract.

The Formal Organization

In most organizations the formal distribution of A&A is shown in organizational charts that are drawn in the form of pyramids with the least of both authority and accountability at the bottom. The more layers in the pyramid the less A&A is vested in the lowest rungs of the ladder. Pure forms of this distribution are somewhat confounded by the existence of unions in the workforce. In those cases certain forms of power exist in the collective bargaining unit that no individual would have. There is also a lack of some forms of individual power that are co-opted by the union. In no case does the existence of a collective bargaining unit change the fundamental characteristics of a cultural archetype. The impact of collective bargaining is primarily to remove management power to abuse and exploit and to remove individual power to excel by exceeding performance standards. The fundamental distribution of A&A remains aligned with the extent and depth of the verticality in the formal organization.

Informal Organization

Where formal organizations reflect the intentions of their designers, informal organizations reflect how things actually get done and relate to one another. Where formal organizations tend to be stable and unchanging in their basic design, the informal organization is more fluid (Aronson, 1995).

The dynamics of the informal organization are driven by the influence of politics and personalities as well as by people with leadership ability that exceeds what is formally expected from their roles.

In every one of the hundreds of organizations with which we have worked over the past two decades, there have been people whose influence far outstripped their formal authority. Sometimes that influence has positive effects on policies and practices and sometimes not. One example can be seen in a client of ours. This manufacturing organization implemented a wireless radio frequency system in support of its logistics control and communication functions. A single individual from outside the information technology (IT) department held sway over what was done with the system including the extent to which it was made secure—or not secure. Despite our urging that the system "ownership" be shifted to IT to ensure adequate support and security, management was unwilling to confront the current owner to effect the change because it might call into question the need for his role and pay grade. We had to resort to having one of our consultants gain access to the organization's network from a laptop in a car in the headquarters parking lot to demonstrate the extent to which the organization was in jeopardy. Remember this story as we look at the vertical archetype in the following section; we will return to it as an example of the predictable patterns of behavior in the archetypes.

Vertical, Horizontal, and Blended Cultural Archetypes

Generally an archetype is defined as "the original model of which all other similar persons, objects, or concepts are merely derivative, copied, patterned, or emulated." In psychology, it is often described as an unconscious predisposition to perceive in categories, though not to be confused with stereotypes. Archetypes are more fundamental and tend to endure over time and social system changes. The archetypes in our model reflect commonly understood models of relationship that can be traced to the beginnings of human organization such as families and military or religious organizations (Aronson, 1995).

The Vertical Archetype

The vertical archetype is based on a fundamental model for organization relationships—the hierarchy. Although it may be arguable that there is some degree of hierarchy in all organizations, there are significant differences in culture tied to the depth and rigidity of that hierarchy.

Deep and rigid hierarchy is visible in the earliest models of organization. Whether it is in a family, an army, or a church, position in the hierarchy defines formal A&A. Of course there are those in the lower levels of the hierarchy that wield power beyond that vested in their formal roles; but that is a subject for another treatise. Here we are concerned with the expected characteristics of the formal organization.

Let us look at the characteristics of a well-run vertical organization:

- Membership comes from actual or virtual belonging to a familial system. For example, the owner's relatives may be employed by the company and others are told that they are joining a virtual family when they are recruited or interviewed for employment. In most cases this promise of work life analogous to family life is presented as a positive aspect of the culture. This promise will become a key feature of the individual psychological contracts of employees and unless what it means is made very specific, it is subject to wide variance in individual interpretation. Some people grew up in loving extended families with strong rituals and close relationships. Others grew up in families that provided identity and economic support but little in the way of togetherness and affection.

- Continuation of membership is dependent upon compliance and loyalty to leaders. More than a few people have been let go from organizations for violating the expectation of loyalty.
- Ideal leader is a strong, caring parent. Deeply vertical organizations led by cold and distant parents tend to be dysfunctional in the same way that families would be. That is to say that behavior of subordinates is driven more by fear than by desire to please a loved and respected leader. Remember our gentleman with control of the radio frequency identification system in our manufacturing client. He had managed to create an aura of fear around himself such that people were unwilling to confront his clearly dysfunctional behavior. The fear probably had its origins in his own fear of being perceived as redundant. If he owned something both mysterious and important his personal job security could be enhanced. His "crime" was compounded by a largely disinterested senior management that the IT staff were sure would not intervene in the name of a more secure network. Of course there was no truth to the belief that management did not care; they were merely ignorant and no one was willing to risk being the whistle-blower. It took an outside agent to raise awareness and change the dysfunctional dynamic. This was clearly an example of poorly executed senior management because in any vertical system the parent figures have to express caring or concern before people will believe that they have it.
- Leadership role is assigned along with legitimate status and authority. The extent to which a person is expected to be a leader is determined by whether there are subordinates to his or her position.
- Ideal member is a dependent, well-adjusted child. This contract for dependency is a critical part of the psychological contract in vertical organizations.
- Authority and accountability are distributed in direct proportion to vertical position.
- Superiors are the primary source of direction, feedback, and recognition or reward. It is common for leaders to tell subordinates that their job is to "make me look good" in exchange for benevolent treatment.
- Information is handled on a strict need-to-know basis. This is obviously crucial in the shaping of security policy and practices.
- Permission is generally required before acting. This is also especially important to security programs.
- Members relate to one another as parent to child (leader to follower) or as siblings (peers). This is a more subtle but nonetheless important feature when we look to align security policy and practices with the culture.
- Work and people are organized along department or functional lines. The good (or bad depending upon how you view it) news here is that a significant amount of organizational behavior is fairly predictable.
- Change initiatives such as program or system implementations can be propelled to success by directives from respected (or feared) senior people who can compel compliance.

The Horizontal Archetype

Still fairly rare but visible on the horizon of organizational evolution is the horizontal organization, which claims maximum versatility, resilience, and speed of both operations and adaptation. A well-run horizontal culture looks like the following:

- Based upon a "community of well-adjusted adults" with minimal hierarchy as the model for organization (flat structure).

- Emerging as an organizational model along with the spread of technology. The nature of technology urges the work surrounding it to be more team-based and customer-driven. Thus the influence of technology on the design and conduct of organized work is to flatten organizations to enable faster processes and increased throughput.
- Membership hinges on effectiveness in adult-to-adult relationships. Single superior–subordinate relationships are not the key to personal effectiveness. People must be able to function effectively in teams and often in multiple teams.
- People are organized in teams responsible for projects (long and short term).
- With the exception of a team or person at the top with responsibility for strategic plans and noncustomer external relations, leadership is a more distributed function.
- Information is handled on a good-to-know basis. The default position is for information to be pushed at people rather than held from them. Selecting the important from the unimportant becomes a core human competency.
- Permission from superiors before acting is seldom required though assent from affected members may be commonly required. Getting the team or the customer on board before acting is the ongoing challenge. Highly confident people will take risks when time does not allow for consensus building.
- Direction is primarily informed by customer's needs and team culture. The assumption is that meeting customer needs in a fashion consistent with healthy team norms is the path to effectiveness.
- Feedback comes from customers and teammates as well as directly from the work. The now familiar 360-degree feedback does not have to be solicited because it is frequently available.
- Authority and accountability are widely distributed and sought by those in a position to impact customer satisfaction, revenue, and organizational continuity. Acquiring more authority, which is often a goal of politically active people in more vertical organizations, is of little value in a flat organization where the structure of work is more dynamic.
- Change initiatives such as program or system implementations will normally require significant investments of time, effort, and materials to educate and enlist the cooperation of organization members. Such investments are returned in the speed with which actual implementation can be achieved.

Archetypes in the Middle

The vast majority of organizations today have a culture that is a blend of vertical and horizontal elements in the contract. It could be said that such an organization is "neither fish nor fowl" and unsure of its own identity, but that is not really the case. As it turns out, an organization culture can have elements of both vertical and horizontal archetypes. Such an organization may be more complex to manage but it can run well so long as everyone is aware of the contract requirements such as:

- Fundamental hierarchy that includes elements of a horizontal archetype. People are primarily accountable to a superior but get significant direction from customer needs.
- Probably the most common type found today. As organizations evolve along with the spread and development of technology pure verticality is disappearing. This is even true for military organizations that are now considering the combat team as their primary unit rather than a large organization of soldiers.

- People are organized by function, and work may be organized by function or by project. The value of projects is understood but effectiveness in project and portfolio management is often confounded by behavior driven by hierarchy.
- Direction may come from superiors or customers but evaluation of performance is primarily by superiors.
- Authority and accountability tend to flow upward but may be temporarily distributed to teams working on key projects. High-profile projects are often a path to recognition and advancement.
- Management is significantly more complex owing to the blending of vertical and horizontal archetype characteristics. As an organization becomes more horizontal, managers must be effective in all directions. Professional staff members are often more comfortable working directly with customers than they are taking direction from functional superiors.
- Permission to act is generally necessary but successful risk-taking will be rewarded.
- Leadership in functions is vertical and in project teams may be distributed.
- Accommodates the widest variety of psychosocial contracts because messages about organizational expectations will contain emphasis from both ends of the continuum, from vertical to horizontal.
- Reference to both vertical and horizontal systems produces a highly political climate in which power, the trappings of power, and pursuit of power are constantly visible as features in day-to-day dynamics.
- Both formal/public and behind-closed-doors are important methods of communication.
- Change initiatives such as program or system implementations are dependent upon top-management commitment and support as well as successful engagement of affected organization members.

The key feature that changes among archetypes across the continuum is the distribution of ownership, both felt and actual. It is this feature that most strongly influences the array of characteristics in any organization culture. In recent history, monarchy has all but disappeared as a governance model for nations, and community has been successful only in small experiments for relatively short periods of time. Thus, the most frequently appearing archetype will be a blended one possessing characteristics of both vertical and horizontal archetypes. IT organizations are urged by the nature of their work (often complex and requiring team effort) to be more horizontal than vertical and to organize in teams rather than functions. This is a key factor in complicating change initiatives in mature organizations.

Not Only What but How Well

The key reason it takes some skill to interpret the results of an assessment of culture is that it is not quite enough to know what archetype is operant in an organization. It is also necessary to have some insights into how well that archetype is being expressed. For example, a purely vertical organization can be very effective but only if there is strong, competent, and caring leadership at the top as the model for other leaders in the organization. We have worked with a privately held company that is managed at the top by an owner/manager whose lack of leadership is reflected in a poverty of leadership throughout the organization. Political infighting, poorly founded decisions, wasted resources, and fearful people are the inevitable results. For reasons not discussable here, the company is successful but not because it is a well-run vertical archetype. In fact there is tremendous

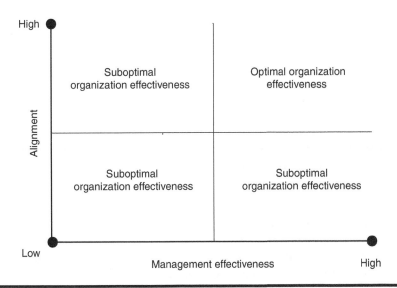

Figure 8.5   Optimal culture—Management alignment.

potential in the company that is unlikely to be realized so long as the present leadership is in place. Its security policies and practices reflect this lack of leadership. Security policy is unclear and there is no coherent strategy driving security practices. Talented security professionals are relegated to policing functions and are not invited into the design stages of new systems and processes. Security is treated largely as a necessary but not particularly welcome afterthought. Morale in the security office is low and turnover exceeds normal expectations. All in all and despite excellent cutting-edge technology this is a security function without a positive impact on the business (Figure 8.5).

To understand the impact of management effectiveness, it is necessary to look at the stable characteristics of the organization and make an educated assessment as to how well they are being expressed. For example, in a blended archetype organization, information will be managed essentially on a need-to-know basis, but there must also be a strong internal communications function that can push necessary and sufficient information out to the population so that the employees can adequately serve customers and represent the organization to them and other outsiders. Drawing the links between culture and strategy demands a profile that identifies the archetype and assesses its effectiveness, but of the two factors the archetype will always be the more powerful.

Linking Strategy to Culture

By now you may have begun to see how the classification system based on vertical, horizontal, and blended archetypes can inform the design and implementation of security policies and practices. The linking process is shown in Figure 8.6.

The more vertical the organization, the more top–down its dynamics and the more employee behavior can be influenced by demands for compliance.

As organizations become more flat and horizontal, the drivers of behavior are more varied and include customer and peer influences. The business case for behavior becomes more important than compliance when change is implemented in flatter organizations. How people define value is driven more by customer needs and actual impact on operations than by how much superiors approve.

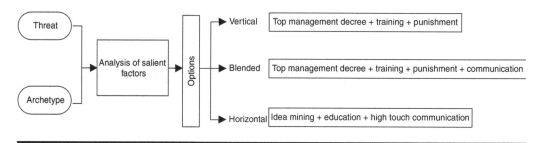

Figure 8.6   Linking culture to strategy.

A characteristic of flat organizations that flies in the face of many people's fundamental assumptions about the workplace is that the most knowledge about what must be done to meet customer needs and advance business objectives resides in the lower levels of the company rather than only at the top. Many in the workplace are comfortable with the assumption that the more senior the persons are the more they know. Of course, when information is managed on a very strict need-to-know basis this is often true, because low-level people are not asked to clutter their thinking with real business knowledge, so it is kept from them.

If the contract that an individual accepted along with employment calls for appropriate dependence (vertical archetype), people are less likely to resist security controls. If the vertical organization is led by a truly caring leader, resistance is even less likely because such a person will be assumed to have the best interests of the business and of the people in mind when creating and applying policy.

In vertical organizations people feel powerful because they hold titles, have inside information, and have strong relationships with others who also hold titled positions. In flatter organizations people feel powerful because the feedback they get tells them that they are having the desired impact on customer satisfaction and are working well with teammates. These are nothing more or less than different definitions of competence. The strategies that a security program chooses must recognize this sort of fact. Consider this example of how different types of organizations can respond to a common threat to security—social engineering.

Recognition of the social engineering threat includes acceptance of the fact that this is one of the most difficult threats to reduce, because both the threat and the solution involve influencing human behavior. Let us assume that the cultural archetype in this organization is blended, so we may infer that behavior is influenced both by strong leadership and by customer needs. The archetype also suggests that our efforts will be positively influenced by effective performance management and employee relations practices. Let us say that our organization is fairly typical in that performance evaluations are done on an annual basis by direct supervisors who may or may not have input from customers and peers of subordinates. Further let us assume that our employee-relations practices are focused on reducing risk to the organization, as is the case in most organizations today. Of course there are likely to be other factors, but let us focus on these for purposes of explanation.

Formal written policy is organization law. For our security policy with regard to social engineering to have weight it will have to be visibly blessed by top management. The policy should also define infractions as well as including a general description of administrative consequences for violations of the policy, so its language must be coordinated with the human resources office as well as legal counsel.

If there are administrative consequences for infractions, there must be some method of enforcement implemented and publicized to deter policy violations. If we believe that our perimeter security is weak because people are frequently allowing "tailgating" by strangers, we might install video surveillance at the entrances both as a deterrent and to capture a record of infractions.

We might also implement training to ensure that everyone in the organization understands both the nature and the threat of social engineering, because the phrase is not self-explanatory. Initially this training will have to be done across the population and the best method might be a video- or computer-based approach that ensures access to the information but does not place great demand on people's time. Media materials in support of this policy should include the image and voice of top management to lend credibility to the messages. In our organization, policy and training language should also include information about impact on the customer experience and company profitability (especially important if employees have an ownership stake in the company). For ongoing training the introduction to security policy and practices should be a part of formal and informal new-hire orientation.

If we were addressing this threat in a horizontal organization, our approach would be different. Our focus at the outset would be on developing ideas from among the employee population about how the threat can be addressed by policy and practices. The responsibility for enforcement would be distributed among the population and education about this part of role expectations would be "high touch" rather than "high tech" and directly involve the most senior managers in the organization. Discussion of security threats of all kinds would include metrics that describe the impact of breaches in business terms. The extent to which people at various levels in the organization are directly involved in strategy and program development varies with cultural archetype as is shown in Figure 8.7.

You may be able to see from our example that understanding the culture in terms of the most positive aspects of the archetype logically leads to workable strategy. The archetype also discourages the endless analysis of culture that can come from inclusion of every idiosyncrasy of a physical or social behavioral nature in a description of culture. The principles underlying the archetypes give you a solid foundation upon which to base policy and practice recommendations.

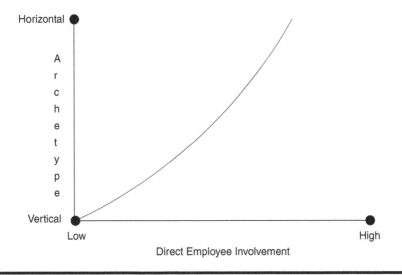

Figure 8.7   Employee involvement by archetype.

Presenting Assessment Results

Focus on Strategy

It is not necessarily required that the results of an assessment of culture per se be presented to anyone. This is truer if the organization is more vertical. It is the strategies that matter to people because the strategies will impact operations and behavior. So, it can be enough to say that an assessment of organization needs with regard to security policies and practices has led to a set of strategies that are aligned with the current culture and business needs. Thus it is the strategies that are presented and not the direct results of the assessment.

If They Really Need to Know

If there is an organizational interest in what drove the creation of strategies, choose the briefest description of the assessment process that you can. You may want to dazzle people with your brilliance but we have learned that there is little value in overinforming senior people. They have neither the time nor the patience to wade through a lengthy dissertation on the theory behind your conclusions. Lead with results (strategies suggested or implemented), even if you have been asked to talk about methods, and then describe methods briefly. Finish with how the strategies are expected to support organizational goals. Remember to give credit to your steering committee or your program management team or whoever supported your efforts in developing the strategic direction of the security program.

It is generally a good idea to make presentations to management as if what you have done has been a roaring success. If you have botched the job badly nothing you say is going to help. If there is any kind of case to be made for a positive view it may have the effect of mitigating a negative minority opinion.

Some Final Thoughts on Culture

Is there an ideal culture for optimal security? Given the conventional wisdom about what culture is and how to understand it, this could be a reasonable question. Actually the answer is "no," if we are talking about an ideal archetype. There certainly can be a well-executed cultural archetype combined with strategies that are appropriately aligned with that archetype.

A basic assumption behind the existence of security programs and practices is that there are limits to the extent to which people can be trusted. These limits are drawn by our inability to predict perfectly what any individual person will do in a given situation. Although we can and do know a fair amount about the general processes of individual motivation and social interaction, there is at least an equal amount that we cannot and do not know about what an individual is likely to do in a given situation. Thus we are driven to make ourselves and our property secure from human mischief and malevolence in that realm of uncertainty.

Human behavior is driven by both individual and social influences. Organization leaders shape the attitudes and behavior of the people within their sphere of influence by the policies and practices they promulgate and the behavioral models they present (social influence). Managing well, which to us means managing in positive alignment with the cultural archetype in place, is the path to reducing the likelihood that your security program will have to focus most on protecting the organization from its own people.

The social influence of leadership is one of the most powerful forces available to ensure the security of people and property.

As a security professional you have an obligation to provide leadership by aligning your program with the cultural reality in your organization.

If it looks like a duck and it quacks like a duck and it waddles like a duck, there is a fairly good chance that it is a duck. Your job is to help it be the absolute best duck that it can be.

Excellent alignment of programs with culture fosters faith in leaders.

Faith in leaders encourages trust in policies and practices. Faith and trust within the organization makes your job much simpler in that you can focus on the threats from outside and on helping business operations to have necessary and sufficient security without it having to be an inhibiting influence. Rest assured that if your security measures are not aligned with the culture and with the needs of business units they will be ignored eventually by your own people. As a staff professional, you do not want enemies within the management ranks of your organization.

You want to be perceived as an ally in reaching the business goals of the organization and it is your job to align your program with those goals, not the other way around.

Can culture be changed? Most certainly culture can be changed. There are numerous examples of cultural change in management history. Most rapid and dramatic changes, though, have come about because organizations are in serious trouble. Under these conditions, change is both possible and relatively easy, though not painless. A much more productive path to change is found in accepting the archetype for what it is and optimizing the way that it works. For example, if the culture is vertical, then strong, caring leadership is necessary. If the culture is horizontal, then team performance metrics and frequent customer feedback must be in place. For a blended culture to work well, there must be strong, caring leadership and very effective project management. Of course there are numerous other management practices in all cases that can be optimized. The key is to accurately assess those that are out of alignment in any way and change them.

In one organization with which we have worked there was a deep crisis period that caused extensive force reduction and broad financial restructuring. One of the most powerful changes that helped the company to bounce back was to change the work schedule. They lengthened the workday slightly Monday through Thursday and ended the formal workweek at noon on Friday. The culture in this consumer products company was a blended one that had grown up from an owner-managed family business to a billion-dollar giant in its industry. Both product development and technology projects were in need of vastly improved management. The changes that the remaining people were being asked to accept would certainly have been resisted more if not for the enormous morale boost that came from giving employees Friday afternoons off. In fact, informal measures of attendance some months after the change showed that a significant number of employees were working into Friday afternoon anyway.

In this company, the transition from pure verticality to the blended archetype took place over a period of 40 years and change was still under way at a glacial pace. Some might say that the culture changed when emphasis was placed on improved project management and support for employee morale. In fact the changes did nothing more or less than bring policy and practices more into alignment with the blended archetype.

Real culture change can be seen in other companies. Jack Welch took a very large monolithic company with a very vertical culture and broke it into smaller business units with increased accountability for performance. This forced the company to move toward a more horizontal archetype that was more nimble and competitive in the changing markets in which General Electric (GE) operated. This example of deliberate change for the purpose of improving a company that was generally profitable and healthy is significant in part because it shows how long it takes for change in a cultural archetype to take place. Mr. Welch spent the better part of 20 years achieving the changes he set out to implement and there were many instances in which there was a temporary misalignment of practices with the emerging culture. Both people and processes had to change and change generally brings some measure of discomfort along with its benefits.

Should culture be changed? Just because a thing can be done does not mean that it should be done. In the case of GE the change was led by a visionary manager who could see decades into the future and was willing to do the hard work of sticking to the path that he set. He was a strong leader and opened up opportunities for people to become more accountable and able to have more direct impact on how things got done within GE divisions. The growth that the company experienced during his tenure is testimony to the wisdom of his leadership.

By contrast during the late 20th century a number of companies quickly embraced the bright promise of Total Quality Management (TQM) without understanding that full implementation would require changes in culture to accompany the implementation of quality tools. Essentially the full value of TQM required that work become designed around teams, that structures become flatter, and that more information be made available to more people. Organizations that were unwilling or unable to make that sort of radical change got little benefit from quality tools and practices.

This treatise was intended to provide some practical instruction as well as to demystify the question of aligning culture with security program design. Our experience tells us that if you apply the information thoughtfully, you will increase the likelihood of your program being successful. And if you apply this knowledge, let us know how it worked for you.

References

Aronson, E. (1995). *The Social Animal*, New York: W. H. Freeman.

Biddle, B. J. (1979). *Role Theory: Expectations, Identities and Behaviors*. New York: Academic Press.

Chilton, K., and Orlando, M. (1996). A new social contract for the American worker. *Business and Society Review*, 96(Winter), 23–26.

Laker, D. R., and Steffy, B. D. (1995). The impact of alternative socialization tactics on self managing behavior and organizational commitment. *Journal of Social Behavior and Personality*, 10(September), 645–660.

Morrison, E. W., and Robinson, S. L. (1997). When employees feel betrayed: a model of how psychological contract violation develops. *Academy of Management Review*, 22(1), 226–256.

Nelson, D. L., Quick, J. C., and Joplin, J. R. (1991). Psychological contracting and newcomer socialization: an attachment theory foundation. Special issue: Handbook on job stress. *Journal of Social Behavior and Personality*, 6, 55–72.

Rousseau, D. M. (1989). Psychological and implied contracts in organizations. *Employee Responsibilities and Rights Journal*, 2, 121–139.

Rousseau, D. M. (1990). New hire perceptions of their own and their employer's obligations: a study of psychological contracts. *Journal of Organizational Behavior*, 11, 389–400.

Rousseau, D. M. (1995). *Psychological Contracts in Organizations: Understanding Written and Unwritten Agreements*. Thousand Oaks, CA: Sage Publications.

Rousseau, D. M., and McLean, P. J. (1993). The contracts of individuals and organizations. In L. L. Cummings and B. M. Stow (Eds.), *Research in Organizational Behavior*, Vol. 15, Greenwich, CT: JAI Press, pp. 1–47.

Chapter 9

A Look Ahead

Samantha Thomas

Contents

This chapter is meant to provide the information security professional an awareness of the coming years' information security challenges. There are a variety of observations offered with suggested solutions. This chapter should leave the reader armed with the readiness to solicit thoughtful questions from and offer solutions to his or her organization, business partners, and customers for planning of and success with their information security efforts.

Opening Remarks

It is a necessary and difficult challenge to plan deliberately for information security. Short-term, one-year-ahead planning tends to be tactical in nature and firefighting in reality. Strategically, organizations are charged with attempting to plan two to four years ahead, as most chief information security officers (CISOs) are required to provide strategic plans to chief financial officers for budget purposes, for direct reporting to executives and directors for cultural support, and to internal business partners for stratifying relationships. Both areas of tactical and strategic planning require CISOs continually meet multiple challenges. Consistently certain challenges have reoccurred over the past 20 years: a significant shift in the manner in which society views privacy, a multigenerational workforce, and the rapid evolution of technology. These challenges embrace all areas of business, be they academia, medicine, government, environmental science, manufacturing, etc. Although these challenges will likely not change in the coming few years, the nuances within each will continue to evolve.

Future Challenges

Policy

As the security of critical infrastructure for most countries continues to be a priority for top leadership, there will be consistent and continual growth of national policy (e.g., law, regulations, and civil codes) related to privacy and confidentiality of information. Certain specific information security policy and standards, including ISO17799 and BS7799, have experienced multiple updates, and there will be continued iterations and amendments. The European Union, Canada, and Australia already feel the tug of their constituents' sensitivity to privacy and data protection in privatized corporations. These three collectives will continue to have parliamentary struggles in maintaining the balance of previously published privacy regulations and the future needs of their constituency for privacy. The Organization for Economic Cooperation and Development and affiliated countries will be creating more defined specifications, particularly in the areas of Computer Emergency Response Teams. Picking up the pace in this area we may also see an active increase in information security efforts in Turkey and several South American countries and related regulations in Poland. The creation of a Basel III Capitol Accord may also include more input from U.S. financial firms. In the United States the Real ID Act requirements may not be reinstated in 2009, whereas Patriot Act controls continue to cause controversy. With these far-reaching changes in policy, CISOs should develop a plan to work among and regularly meet with their risk managers and privacy officers. Awareness of the level of information security risk the company is willing to assume, and privacy and compliance concerns of these two key business partners, will be essential for CISOs to assist in maintaining the appropriate balance of risk tolerance of the organization and proper information protection controls. This is the perfect opportunity for information security professionals to stand out as valued partners by demonstrating the ability to be an advocate in these areas, and by acting as a bridge for these partners to connect with the key program areas of a company by way of building risk reduction and compliance measures within business processes. It is also important to point out in the midst of continued confidential and sensitive information disclosures, that working with risk managers and privacy officers provides an opportunity to make clear that security breaches of all types will most certainly continue, to accept this reality as a risk of doing business, and to ensure the organization has a plan to handle them. This point cannot be stressed enough, as in this regard the information security professional position evolves into that of trusted guide and first responder. Popular media will continue to dote on finding organizations to blame for breaches and repeat that blame time and again for months or even years. For the CISO to ensure that his or her leadership has a plan to respond that complements compliance with current and impeding policy, without taking blame but by accepting responsibility, the partnerships with chief legal counsel and public affairs will continue to be as critical as ever. To support decisions in this area, CISOs should also maintain consistent relationships with their legislative offices, policy committees, and research and development bureaus to stay abreast of policy and strategic business developments that will affect the tactical and strategic planning of the information security program. The CISO should keep those areas of business appraised of information security concerns, make recommendations of issues to be "on watch for," and suggest changes or modifications in current business practices to support the standard of due care set forth by the organization.

Workforce

The end of the first decade of the 21st century brings companies worldwide to a very significant turning point regarding the generations of their workplace. The majority of the "Greatest Generation" World Wars I/II-era workers in most countries will be leaving the workforce from what were the "second" jobs acquired after officially retiring from their pre-65-years-of-age company jobs (Table 9.1). Their first children, the leading cusp of the "baby boomers," will be eligible for what many developed countries offer those citizens: pensions after 60 years of age. To this end there will be an enormous impact within the internal culture of all organizations. Not only will companies ill prepared for this exodus of knowledge come face-to-face with high personnel turnover rates, but also the information protection implications will be grave as company histories, intelligence, wisdom, and in-mind undocumented business processes leave factory floors, hospitals, laboratories, data centers, government entities, technology companies, utilities, and universities.

Many information security challenges lie immediately ahead for those left to pick up the pieces—the tail end of the Baby Boomer Generation and early Generation X. Not only will these people be charged with leading organizations without the knowledge of the early edge baby boomers and the (work) ethics of the World War II generation, they will also be the upcoming driving leadership in most worldwide organizations. These workers will also be managing very different generations: the ending cusp of the baby boomers, their fellow Generation X-ers, and all of Generation Y. While the tail-end Baby Boomer Generation prepares for retirement and "second-career" pursuits, the early cusp Generation X leaders have many slippery slopes to overcome with information security, most notably the internal management of how the three generations working together perceive and manage information security. The issue is not so much the end result of compliance with policy and company regulations to protect people, information, and assets; more so it is the different pathway each generation feels is appropriate to use to get there. To this end, CISOs should work closely with their privacy representatives and human resources/personnel departments and stay acutely abreast of organizational change management efforts.

Another key issue in the area of workforce will be secure communication. Although the exiting generations previously mentioned prefer communication by personal contact, live telephone conversation, and, to some extent, e-mail, the incoming leadership has used and will continue to use e-mail heavily and prefers employment as independent contributors by telecommuting,

Table 9.1 Description of Generations

Greatest generation	Late 1900s–mid-1930s
Baby boomer generation	Late 1940s–early 1960s
Generation X	Mid-1960s–early 1980s
Generation Y	Late 1970s–early 1990s

push-button technologies (e.g., interactive voice-response systems), and to some extent text messaging on handheld devices. Following this will be the work(ing)force majority Generation Y. This generation is most at ease and even demanding of a work environment that uses Web-based software applications, instant messaging, text messaging, and Webcam interfaces and desires a variety of these communication avenues available for them to pick and choose as they deem appropriate. Conversely this generation does not aspire to scheduling face-to-face meetings or using "regular office" e-mail to conduct business, as they feel this takes away from their ability to multitask and provides for an unproductive work environment. Along with the observation that the communication preferences of Generation Y and those of the incoming leadership generation directly conflict with each other, the information security implications open up extensively in obtaining and maintaining a high variety of communication avenues. Although secure communication challenges have always existed, the extent to which information is used, maintained, transmitted, shared, and disposed of increases many fold to accommodate this varied workforce. Also of note: the internal pressures of the workforce will increase due to the lack of Generations X and Y entering the typical corporate and government environment, as trends continually indicate these generations opting to pursue small businesses and entrepreneurial opportunities of their own. CISOs should continue building relationships with their Web-application developers, telecommunication specialists, and human resources/personnel staff and maintain heightened awareness of communication trends in their global and satellite offices. These relationships will continue to be critical for assurance of properly implemented information security architecture methods and controls, meeting evolving compliance concerns, and having staff "separation and transfer" plans in place.

External Customers

In many instances the same information security concerns in the workforce will be mirrored in serving a similar demographic of the outside customer. To expand on the observations made earlier, in many instances the customer base will be more youthful or aged than a standard workforce age base. The same theory mentioned above of offering a variety of communication vehicles in the workplace to attract top personnel in many cases also applies to obtaining, maintaining, and enhancing the external customer experience, as well as making those offerings palatable to a customer base that is a larger span in age. With a majority of business and government services offered with continued global focus, the demand for secure computerized data and paper information has never before been such a significant factor in the company-to-customer interface. Beyond the effects of security for conducting international business, customer expectations of organizations to have knowledge of, abide by, and have business and system processes that allow for compliance with regulations and policy will be met with little or zero fault tolerance. As the public continues to hear and understand that information security breaches (continue to) occur, their lenience toward an organization's lack of proper processes will wane. This means an increase in constituency calls to government leaders to create and modify policy, letters to board members, pressure from stock holders, and waves of turnover rates in customer loyalty. It also means that the role of information security will grow from merely an integral program inside a company's overall strategic direction to a more significant public relations issue and transparent role within and outside of an organization. The challenge will be for CISOs to determine when and how to include their media relations staff and legal counsel when making decisions for what may not be obvious information security risks and what the company deems appropriate mitigation measures and controls related to public interpretation and trust. Further, these decisions are complicated by the globalization of business, the extreme variety of cultural expectations, and the continual changes in an individual nation's information security and privacy policy.

Information Technology

Today the majority of an organization's critical information has been converted into or originally developed within an electronic medium using computer systems. This fact brings significant challenges to both an organization's CISO and its information technology business areas. The work plan developments for technology staff charged with managing enterprise architecture and business continuity programs rose high in 2002–2004, then dipped down after 2006. Attention to these plans, and their security, will rise again in the next few years. With technology and related disaster recovery processes too quickly executed in response to the events on and after September 11, 2001, the time is ripe, nearly ten years later, to revisit and revise business methods for the upcoming decade. For this revision, the enterprise architect and chief information officer (CIO) (or chief technology officer, CTO) play pivotal roles in laying the foundation of success for the CISO to ensure that modifications to an organization's business continuity planning have at the forefront the secure availability of assets and information. Other affected areas of information security related to information technology will be an increase in the use of smart-card and biometric technologies. Although the United States differs from most other countries, with heavy use of the magnetic strip for various financial and identification card uses, the overall use of smart cards and radiofrequency identification will increase and continue to evolve. To this end the hiring of telecommunications specialists and outsourced telecommunications consulting services will rise as the demand for mobility, connectedness, and secure responsiveness increases. This also comes at a time when, along with using smart cards, the individual consumer (staff and customers) can afford to purchase his or her own personal satellite telephone. The increased purchases of these phones bring about the evolution of handheld services to a highly integrated technology space—palmtops with rich data-center-type capabilities. This convergence of connectedness gives leeway for mind-bending types of new communication vehicles, including not only the sharing of text and attachments from one handheld satellite device to another, but also packets of reduced video files that may be transported via satellite and, when uplinked by the receiver, viewed as a holographic display (à la Star Wars) with several people simultaneously interconnected. As these evolutionary communication vehicles continue to push the envelope of technology and consumers' demand for connectedness increases, the upcoming 2010 decade will see dramatic discoveries in these areas. For the organization's internal technology administrators these quickly evolving changes mean a continual update of security parameters, notably the security aspects of a company's system development life cycle. Another interesting side effect of a company continuing to meet the secure communications demands of its staff and customers is a stronger push for vendors and product developers to resolve the ever-present security issues of bugs that continue to plague operating systems and commercial software applications. Depending on the severity of the issues this push may ascend to the regulatory level. Until then, certain information technology security-specific software, such as vulnerability prevention, detection, and correction applications, will likely maintain its slow but steady climb. Also related to communication, there will be continued growth in both breadth and depth of search engines for use inside the organization. CISOs may thus see an increase in enterprise document management, digital rights management, and challenges in electronic discovery and forensic issues as they relate to access, appropriate use, and log monitoring. Related to all of these future areas of information security and information technology lies a responsibility of the CISO to partner with his or her

CIO, CTO, enterprise architect, and Web-application developers and ensure collective agreement on and diligently search for the most secure and least intrusive communication vehicles for staff and customers.

Footing for the Future: Buy-In and Communication

For many CISOs gone are the days of "selling" the idea of information security to their executive leadership. Now are the days in which information security professionals must consistently and concisely show their value in the organization. Rubbing directly against this effort is the acceptable tolerance of time required for securing the physical, administrative, and technical areas of information and assets. In the past decade tolerance for a business's downtime has been reduced from days to hours to minutes to effectively nothing. As CISOs have moved from concentrating on detecting an event to event-driven planning, there has been an immense push on prevention since 2000. This push has led to an increase in work for the information security professional to be involved with much of the execution in front-end engineering and testing of business processes in attempts not only to prevent incidents but also to decrease business disruptions from downtime.

Acquiring Buy-In

CISOs must directly express to leadership the idea that information security not only is the responsibility of the organization for ensuring controls but also could and should be a realized financial opportunity from which every area of a business can reap benefits. To do this, information security professionals must not only advise, but also roll up their sleeves to assist colleagues when they need to integrate information security and privacy strategies into their own areas of business. This work moves beyond setting oversight policy and monitoring. It means making available the opportunity for other leadership in your organization to achieve measurements and milestones and to show innovation and creativity in information security within their own areas of business—notably strategic outcomes to report to executive staff and the board of directors as well as tactical outputs for internal business partners and other advocate areas. Key areas for acquiring buy-in include business resilience, competition, regulations, and legal constraints.

> *Business resilience.* This topic is often the most difficult area in which to acquire buy-in. Often there is a complacency among other areas of business that information security issues are by and large the sole responsibility of the CISO and there tends to be a quick forgetfulness of incidents as we become more agile with quick recovery that allows business to swiftly move forward. This is particularly obvious in regions where organizations are keenly aware of disruptions caused by natural disasters and power outages. Within the past decade there has grown a stronger interest in issues surrounding terrorism and personal safety for which tactics have greatly changed. For physical security there are fringe concerns, like climate influences such as gas emissions and mismanagement of toxic waste and how these two areas affect environmental factors, which in turn affect the physical security of our information, assets, and employees.
>
> *Competition.* An area often overlooked by CISOs is the information security implications of research and development, sales, and marketing on meeting their goals for being a leading contender in their market space. CISOs need to be continually diligent in examining

how information security will affect an organization's ability to communicate worldwide and increase or reduce market shares, particularly after stocks dipped in the earlier part of the 1990s. This, along with the qualitative nuances surrounding international public image (which due to the Internet and media can be argued as all inclusive), demonstrate how the consequences of a poor image affect an organization's ability to be more agile and innovative than its competitors. If not carefully examined and executed, information security efforts in this space will continually place constraints in these competition-type arenas.

Regulations. Policy has received much attention in since 2005. Many countries—Taiwan, Tunisia, Uruguay, Argentina, Hungary, Ireland, Canada, Australia, Turkey, Brazil, Pakistan, Cambodia, Philippines, the list goes on—continue a hard line striving to improve their security infrastructure and increase privacy directives. Third- and even fourth-party caveats written into comprehensive information security programs and business contracts will be looked upon to decrease risks by allowing examination of authorized access, use, etc., by a network of business partners who in turn have their own service provider and business partner agreements and controls that require agreement on how information security and privacy directives will be met.

Legal constraints. Simply put, financial obligations to protect company information and assets, and to keep liability to a minimum through risk management, must be finite. Allowing leadership to have the legal discussion of risk, budget, and strategic goals allows the organization as a whole to mitigate and accept certain risks while setting a standard by which the CISO can follow and adhere. Interestingly this also allows for an often-overlooked opportunity in the return on investment in information security, or better put, an area of cost savings overall in an organization. These savings may be found in the examination of risk reduction as it applies to a company's ability to negotiate a reduction in the amount of premiums and insurance coverage requirements.

This overview of key areas leaves CISOs with two inescapable truths for acquiring buy-in: (1) Although information security issues continue to be a heightened consideration for the manner in which an organization conducts its business, the security professional will still be required to continue focusing on the narrow areas of protection, detection, and correction of breaches, while at the same time be challenged with the broader aspects of "the business" of its organization. However, today and in the near future, security-related incidents that affect public image and unauthorized releases of information come in hundreds of different forms and severity, and their effects can be more crippling than ever. As an added concern, with help from the Internet and mass media, security-related indiscretions are reported worldwide when organizations do not respond well to these incidents. (2) Succinctly put, an organization employs a CISO to engage in securing information, as unplanned incidents—be they unauthorized access, modification, or destruction—are guaranteed.

Communication

To assist in addressing these two truths, the foremost advantage will be with those organizations that fervently integrate and weave more than just information security controls into an organization. A successful CISO must communicate intent and build partnerships to create the vision one desires for their organization's information security program. This obligates the CISO to create and lead a strategic and continuously evolving communication plan for the organization's information security program and must include educating customers, dispelling myths with internal business partners, and relating truths to leadership. For a communication plan to be strategic and for each information security effort to be in alignment with that strategy, CISOs must ensure that leadership is aware that although the information security program is facilitated by the CISO, it is owned by the business—it is their program to support, nurture, finesse, and continually improve upon as their own business areas grow and evolve. Another, sometimes difficult, part of a communication strategy is the security professionals must acknowledge to internal staff and management that they realize the business staff understand their specific program areas better than the information security staff. This simple yet possibly ego-swallowing statement assists in establishing a partnership between a security team and a business area because it moves a usually preconceived group dynamic from that of a fault-finding mission to a mutual respect for each program's range of expertise. Another important success factor for the CISO to communicate to business areas that as their own business processes become more secure, logically they (the business areas) reap the benefits of the information security successes. Further, the CISO should explain that the purpose of the information security program is not only to ensure programs and processes are in compliance with information security policy and standards, it is also to create a consultative relationship that allows business areas the opportunity to confer with their information security staff so as to execute risk-mitigating decisions for their own business area. This provides an avenue for shifting business areas from simply trying to be in compliance with policy to actively engaging to make security-minded decisions about their programs. That said, certain business areas may still be resistant to this type of involvement and it will continue to be the CISO's responsibility to consistently and diplomatically remind business areas that by not being an active part of the information security program, they accept the risks of not being fully engaged. This message should also be reiterated to an organization's councils, committees, etc., whose members often make sweeping project and program decisions. The dynamics in those cross-functional groups are different from those of groups in similar working types collectively employed in the same area of business.

Conclusion

The pace at which business in today's world moves will continue to be faster than we have ever experienced, and there will be continual gaps in the ebb and flow of effective communication of information security. In the workplace, technology upgrades and the diversity of how staff interact within a business are more prevalent than ever before. The way an organization conducts business today is different from what it was as little as two years ago and will be different two years from now. In the years ahead the information security professional will continue dealing with the challenges of creating customer-centric information, security-sensitive leadership, and a security-minded culture among its internal staff, business partners, and customers. Taking time to examine the future and being mindful of what lies ahead will assist organizations in effectively recognizing areas for success with their information security efforts.

ACCESS CONTROL

DOMAIN 2

Access Control Techniques

Chapter 10

Authentication Tokens

Paul A. Henry

Contents

Evolution of the Need for Authentication Tokens

Remote access has opened up a new world of possibilities for the Internet-connected enterprise. Today, users can access their corporate network from a hotel room or coffee shop in nearly any city in the world. Network administrators can now manage the entire enterprise network from the comfort of their home, no longer needing to drive back to the office at 3:00 AM to address a critical issue. Thin client technology and virtual private network access have made it possible to gain access to the enterprise network anytime from anywhere.

With the convenience and additional productivity afforded by remote access comes an enormous amount of risk: Keylogger malware surreptitiously installed at 14 public Internet terminals in Manhattan allowed an attacker to compromise the personal information and network access of dozens of people and organizations. One Silicon Valley company endured months of unauthorized access by a competitor before they discovered the breach. In 2006, a well-organized identity theft ring victimized over 300 customers of a well-known financial institution, costing the financial institution over $3 million in direct losses. Phishers plague the Internet on a daily basis, using their social engineering ploys to harvest user credentials for banking and E-commerce customers, allowing them to quickly and quietly drain the customers' accounts.

At the root of all of these exploits and, indeed, the cause of hundreds of corporate breeches, countless identity thefts, and millions of dollars lost every year is the traditional password.

The average computer user has dozens of accounts online and at their job. Access to nearly all of these systems requires a password. Most people cannot memorize a different password for each of their accounts, particularly if they access certain applications only once a month. Here are some ways average users combat their memory problems:

1. They choose one password for everything. Of course, if their password for their personal Web mail is compromised, chances are good that their company network password is compromised as well.
2. They write their passwords down. One online study revealed that over 30 percent of people surveyed wrote their passwords down and "hid" them under their keyboards, on their staplers, or in their desk drawers.
3. They choose information they can easily remember. Many people—up to 35 percent, according to some experts—choose some piece of personal information: a name of a family member or pet or a birth date. The problem is such information is often common knowledge. A potential hacker can make small talk in the lobby with an employee—and come away with dozens of passwords to try.
4. They get clever. In one company's password audit, 10 percent of passwords were "stud," "goddess," "cutiepie," or some other vanity password. Even more disturbing, 12 percent of passwords were "password"—and most of the users who chose it thought that it was a clever choice. The problem is that hackers know all of this. Before they attempt personal information to crack a password, the first thing they try is "password." Hackers will also pretend to work at a company, striding confidently into the front doors with a nod of the head to the security desk or the receptionist. Any passwords on monitors or under keyboards are fair game. Once a hacker has cracked a password, they can view confidential documents or e-mails without the organization ever knowing about it.

Password-Cracking Tools Have Also Evolved

Traditional brute-force password-cracking tools grinding through lists of known passwords or automatically trying each and every letter, number, and symbol in machine-generated password guesses are no longer the primary tool for cracking user passwords to gain privileged access. The traditional brute-force password cracker has evolved to include the use of precomputed password hashes. Rainbow tables—a set of downloadable algorithms—allows a malicious hacker to precalculate each and every combination of letters, numbers, and symbols in various password lengths. Once a set of tables is calculated, guessing the password is no longer necessary; it is simply looked up in the precomputed hash database.

Instead of the time-consuming task of guessing passwords, precomputed hashes allow the password-cracking tool simply to look up the password hash in the precomputed hash database and return the password.

Strong Authentication Mitigates the Risks of Weak Passwords

The answer to this huge problem is strong authentication. This refers to factors that work in combination to protect a resource. Automatic teller machines (ATMs) are the most common example of this: to access their checking account, customers must use two factors to be authorized. First, they must have their physical bank card (one factor: what you have), and second, they must know their personal identification number (PIN) (second factor: what you know). Most people would not want their checking account guarded with just a PIN or just the card—yet companies use password-only protection to guard resources that are many times more valuable than the average person's checking account. Government standards are now making it imperative to protect consumer information. Health care agencies and financial institutions in particular are finding that implementing strong authentication is a step toward complying with recent legislation to protect patients and customers.

Without realizing it, many organizations had been using strong authentication for years: employees had to know passwords to access the company network (one factor: what you know), but also needed to be inside the building (second factor: where you are). But remote access has taken away the location requirement, as demanded by today's business environment, and authentication has become vulnerable as a result.

Tokens as a Candidate for Strong Authentication

Tokens are small pieces of hardware, about half the size of a credit card (but a bit thicker), that often fit on a key chain (Figure 10.1). Like an ATM card, this factor is a "what you have." They often have liquid-crystal displays and give the user a onetime passcode for each log-in. Instead

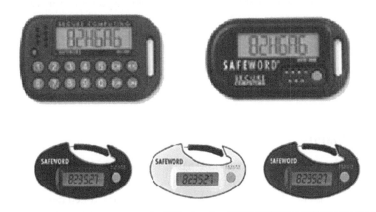

Figure 10.1   Token form factors.

of logging in with a password, the user activates the token and types in the characters from the token display into the password field. Tokens usually require a piece of server software that allows or denies access to the user. The big advantage for most information technology departments is that token solutions do not require a piece of client software on the user's machine. Tokens, therefore, can be used anywhere: on public Internet terminals, on the Web, from any laptop, desktop, or palmtop. Some users resist tokens initially, and some companies are concerned about price: in excess of $70 per user as an initial cost for many solutions. But the solution is cost-competitive, highly reliable, and portable and is one of the simplest options available to deploy.

Common Types of Tokens

Current-generation tokens are available in form factors that are much less intrusive to users than previous-generation tokens. Nearly all token implementations today use onetime-password methodologies. In effect, the password is changed after each authentication session. This efficiently mitigates the risk of shoulder surfing or password sniffing, as the password is valid only for one session and cannot be reused.

Asynchronous Tokens

The asynchronous token, also called an event-based token or challenge–response, provides a new onetime password with each use of the token. Although it can be configured to expire on a specific date, its lifetime depends on the frequency of its use. The token can last from five to ten years and effectively extend the time typically used in calculating the total cost of ownership in a multifactor authentication deployment. When using an asynchronous onetime-password token the access control subject typically executes a five-step process to authenticate identity and have access granted:

1. The authentication server presents a challenge request to the access control subject.
2. The access control subject enters the challenge into his or her token device.
3. The token device mathematically calculates a correct response to the authentication server challenge.
4. The access control subject enters the response to the challenge along with a password or PIN.
5. The response and password or PIN are verified by the authentication server and, if correct, access is granted.

Synchronous Tokens

The synchronous token, also known as a time-based token, uses time in the computation of the onetime password. Time is synchronized between the token device and the authentication server. The current time value is enciphered along with a secret key on the token device and is presented to the access control subject for authentication. A typical synchronous token provides for a new six- to eight-digit code every 60 seconds; it can operate for up to four years and can be programmed to cease operation on a predetermined date. The synchronous token requires fewer steps by the access control subject to authenticate the following successfully:

1. The access control subject reads the value from his or her token device.
2. The access control subject enters the value from the token device into the log-in window along with his or her PIN.
3. The authentication server calculates its own comparative value based on the synchronized time value and the access control subject's PIN. If the compared values match, access is granted.

The use of a PIN together with the value provided from the token helps to mitigate the risk of a stolen or lost token being used by an unauthorized person to gain access through the access control system.

Tokens under Attack

Since tokens became the most popular alternative to traditional passwords only one attack methodology has been successful in actually cracking them, and it was used successfully against only a single token vendor. Hackers reverse-engineered the methodology used in the calculation of the onetime password and using that, in combination with the token serial number and the token activation key, they were able to calculate the next eight onetime passwords that would be calculated by the token. This methodology was implemented in the popular Cain & Abel password-cracking tool v2.5 beta 21 (Figure 10.2) found at http://www.oxid.it/ and was mitigated by storing the activation key separately and securely until the vendor introduced a new version of the token using a different onetime-password computing methodology.

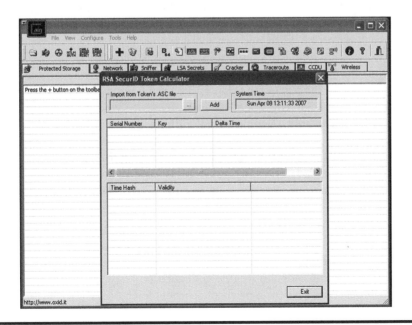

Figure 10.2 Cain & Abel password cracking.

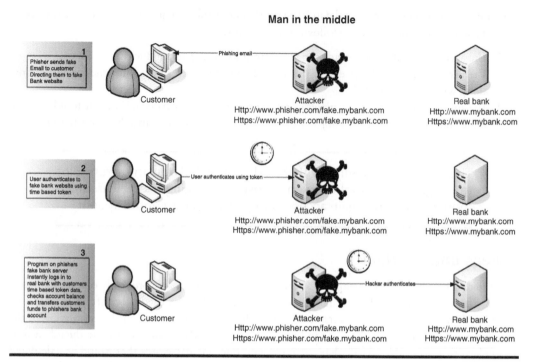

Figure 10.3 Man in the middle attack.

Tokens are inherently resilient to attack, but poor token implementations can provide weaknesses that can be taken advantage of by hackers. As recently as 2006 a man-in-the-middle (MITM) attack (Figure 10.3) was successful in compromising a token implementation for a popular bank. Although the attack relied solely on social engineering and did not exploit a weakness in the token itself it is important to consider this attack methodology in the deployment of any token implementation. One methodology of risk mitigation for this attack that is gaining popularity is the consideration of the reputation (Figure 10.4) of the Internet Protocol address, network, or domain from which the authentication is being requested. By denying authentication from a source that has a "bad reputation" significant risk mitigation can be afforded in consideration of a MITM attack.

Current developments in identity and access management (IAM) solutions are also providing stronger token implementations by taking into consideration the security of the endpoint from which the user is authenticating. It is common in current-generation IAM product offerings to validate that

- The endpoint is running the required antivirus software and the signatures are up to date.
- The endpoint is running the required firewall and the configuration matches the requirements of the enterprise endpoint security configuration.
- The endpoint operating system is patched to current levels.
- The endpoint applications are patched to current levels.

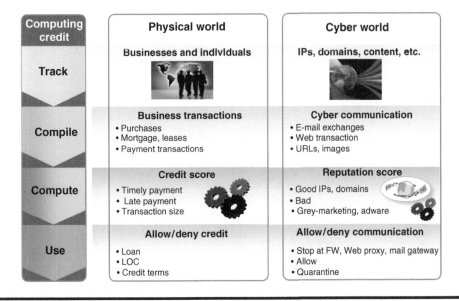

Figure 10.4   Reputation defenses.

If the endpoint is found not to be compliant, access is denied and the user is constrained to an area of the network where the failures can be corrected prior to allowing the user to authenticate again to the enterprise network for permitted privileged access.

In closing, current-generation onetime-password authentication tokens by and of themselves can go a long way toward mitigating the risks associated with traditional passwords. However, to afford maximum risk mitigation to the enterprise, authentication tokens combined with access control systems that use endpoint reputation scoring or security validation of the endpoint from which the user is authenticating should be considered.

Chapter 11

Authentication and the Role of Tokens

Jeff Davis

Contents

Authentication is an important part of any system or application security. It is the basis for any access control that is needed over information that is in the system or authorization for any transactions that could be carried out. To provide stronger authentication, tokens are increasingly being used to add an additional dimension or factor of authentication and to reduce the risk of an attacker impersonating a user.

There are in general three different factors that are used in authenticating a user. These factors are something you know, such as a password; something you have, which could be a token device; and something you are, which may be implemented through biometrics such as fingerprints or other physical characteristics. This chapter will give an overview of authentication, the use of different factors of authentication to establish an identity, and some of the risks associated with the use of the different factors of authentication and how tokens can be used to mitigate some of them.

Overview of Authentication Factors

Authentication is the act of someone establishing an identity that they have declared them to be. In the world of computers the most prevalent example is when the users authenticate to prove that they are the persons assigned to a specific ID that is used to control access to a system. There are three different types or factors of authentication. These three factors are something you know, something you have, and something you are. These can be used individually or together to authenticate an identity.

The first factor, "something you know," also called a shared secret, is generally implemented as a static password that is shared between the person needing to be authenticated and the server that authenticates the access (Figure 11.1). The process of authentication usually starts with the user typing in the password at the client. The password is then sent to the authenticating server and is put through a one-way hash algorithm to generate a hash for the password. The hash algorithm has the property that it will generate a unique hash for different passwords, but it is not possible to reconstruct the password from the hash value. This hash is then compared to the hash that is stored on the authenticating server to see if they match. In some implementations the hash is generated on the client before it is sent to the server. There are a number of ways to attack this method of authentication, one of which is to intercept the password by monitoring or "sniffing" the network. Encryption can be used to help prevent the interception of the password when it is passed over the network. Most Web portals utilize a secure channel implemented by the Hypertext Transfer Protocol when accepting authentication information to mitigate this risk. Another method of attack is through the use of a keystroke logger program that may be present on the end user's device. These programs can record everything that is typed at a keyboard, including passwords, and send it to a third party. Keystroke loggers are used in many computer viruses to collect passwords that can be used for further compromises or actual theft from online banking. Installing and keeping

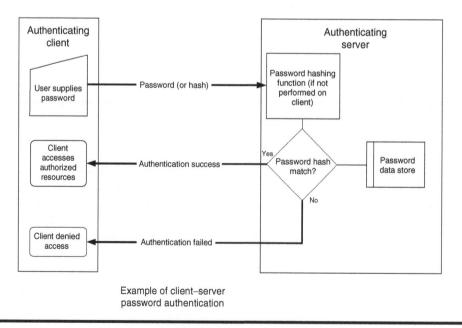

Example of client–server
password authentication

Figure 11.1   Example of client–server password authentication.

up-to-date antivirus software will help prevent these viruses from installing the software. This risk can also be reduced by not using an account with administrative privileges for Internet browsing or reading e-mail. These two activities are the most prevalent vectors used by viruses to infect machines. Typically if a virus is attempting to infect a machine via one of these vectors, it will run in the context of the user who is performing the action. If the user does not have administrative access to the machine then most viruses will not be able to install a keystroke logger. A third type of attack is one that uses social engineering to trick an end user into providing the credentials to a system that is owned or monitored by the attacker. This is commonly done through the use of phishing e-mails. A phishing e-mail is a fake e-mail that appears to come from an official source. The fake e-mail prompts the user to supply their credentials via a Web link that is contained in the e-mail. The Web link appears to connect to the authentic system but actually points to a system that has been made to look like the real system but is owned or monitored by the attacker. These attacks have become more and more sophisticated and can be successful even if a small percentage of users respond to the e-mail because of the volume of e-mails that are sent. Mitigating these attacks is very difficult as it depends on modifying the users' behavior so that they do not trust the links sent via e-mail. Because these attacks depend on user awareness of them they will continue to be successful in gathering passwords from users who are unaware of these types of attacks.

Another attack method against static passwords is to try every possible combination of passwords to determine the correct password. This is commonly referred to as a password-guessing attack or brute-force attack. This is generally done by capturing the computed hash of the password, either through network sniffing or from the server it is stored on, and then running a program to generate every possible combination of passwords, calculate their hashes, and then compare the hashes to the captured hash until one matches it. These attacks can be time-consuming depending on the length and complexity of the password. For example, a password that is made up of six numeric digits ranging from 0 to 9 will have 1 million combinations that will have to be tried, whereas a password that is made up of six upper- and lowercase alphanumeric characters will have over 56 billion combinations. However, with the advances in processing speed, using a computer to generate all 56 billion combinations would still take only a couple of hours. To shorten the time even further, especially for longer password implementations, a brute-force attack can be sped up through the use of precomputed tables of passwords and their associated hashes, which are commonly called rainbow tables. If the hash of a password can be obtained from the authenticating server or intercepted on a network, then its corresponding password can be looked up in the rainbow table in a much shorter time frame. One protection against the use of rainbow tables is through the use of a "salt" as part of the hash algorithm. A salt is a number of bits that are added to the password before it is run through the algorithm. This effectively lengthens the password and makes any brute-force attack more difficult. Also the bits used in the salt may not correspond to any characters used to generate the rainbow table as they may be unprintable and usually not used in a password. This would make a rainbow table generated with printable characters ineffective.

Another implementation of the "something you know" factor is through the use of security questions and user-supplied answers. These are questions and answers that have been registered between the user and the authenticating authority. They are usually established as part of the registration process for establishing the ID for that system. Their most prevalent use is as a way to identify a user who has lost or forgotten his or her password and needs to reset it. This process is threatened if the questions use information that may be obtainable through public records, like mother's maiden name or place of birth. The best implementations of this process utilize questions and answers that are selected by the user from a pool of questions and do not contain information that can be easily obtained by third parties. Questions like "What is your favorite color?" or

"What is your favorite sports team?" are examples of questions that could be used. In practice, more than one question is usually used to verify the individual's identity before any actions are performed.

The next type of factor is "something you have" or something you possess. This is usually implemented through the use of a device or token that the end user carries with him or her. This device or token will provide an authentication code that will be used to validate a user. In some implementations, this authentication code is combined with a personal identification number (PIN) or other password that the user knows to ensure that the device cannot be used by another person. In other implementations, the PIN or password is used to lock the device and prevent it from producing valid authentication codes until it is supplied. When the PIN or password and the device are used together, this is known as two-factor authentication. The devices mitigate the threat to the single-factor implementation of passwords by generating authentication codes that are onetime-use passwords. These password are able to be used only once to authenticate and will be rejected if attempted to be reused. This negates attacks involving network interception or keylogging because of the dynamic nature of the password. Attacks against these devices usually involve the compromising of the communications channel from the end user to the server or are actual physical attacks against the devices themselves in an attempt to copy the device or determine some of its characteristics. These systems involve increased costs for both the device and the people to manage them.

The third factor, "something you are," is usually implemented via a biometric measurement. The most popular implemented biometric today is fingerprint matching. Other biometrics that have been explored and have some limited implementations include iris recognition, hand geometry, and voice recognition. This factor has the advantage of being extremely hard to steal and, as with a token, is usually combined with one of the other factors to increase its effectiveness. There are drawbacks to implementation of this factor as these systems do produce higher rates of false-positives and false-negatives. There is also some reluctance to use some of these implementations because of concerns that the measurement method may cause some harm. Many of these implementations are expensive but fingerprint readers and facial recognition systems have been coming down in price as they become more widely available and are starting to be included as part of standard system configurations. In general, the attacks against this factor usually are attempts to spoof the reader of the biometrics and take advantage of any weakness it has in properly measuring the biometric. This has been especially true of some fingerprint scanners being susceptible to fake fingers molded out of plastic or gelatin.[1] The technology of biometrics scanners in general is still being perfected and until the errors are worked out there will be a risk that they will be able to be bypassed by allowing false-positives or not allowing authorized users by generating a false-negative.

One other area of biometrics that is worth mentioning is a category called dynamic biometrics. This is a technology that attempts to use the action of doing something to identify a person. The two most prevalent are signature biometrics, which measures the pressure and dynamics of someone signing his or her name, and keyboard dynamics, which uses the speed, length of key presses, and rhythm of a user typing at a keyboard. This technology is in the very early stages of development and it has not had very many implementations so very little data is available about its effectiveness.

One growing trend in the area of authentication is to use more then one shared secret factor (something you know) to authenticate an individual. This is done by requiring not only a password but also, in some cases, answers to predetermined questions. Another example may be the need to supply a password and select a previously agreed upon picture from a group of pictures to authenticate. This is done to try to provide additional authentication information that may not be in the possession of a potential attacker. In some of these implementations, this multiple authentication is done when something out of the ordinary occurs. This may be when the users log in from a workstation that they usually do not log in from or if they request to perform an unusual action like transferring an entire balance out of a bank account.

All in all, good authentication is important as the basis for access control to systems and applications. Authentication using shared secrets is coming under constant attack through the use of keyboard loggers and network monitoring that can record the information and make it available to a third party. Biometric authentication is becoming more widely available but still faces some usability hurdles and cannot be readily adapted to most current applications. Authentication using a token device that produces dynamic passwords is readily adaptable to most existing system that accept a password, it is cheaper than most biometrics systems and can be implemented with a PIN to provide two factors of authentication. Of the current methods available for authentication, tokens that are used to implement two-factor authentication seem the best solution for providing strong authentication, reducing the risk of compromise through interception.

Types of Tokens and How They Work

Devices or tokens that can be used to implement two-factor authentication can be grouped into a couple of different types or classes. These types are time-synced devices that produce authentication codes at predetermined intervals, on-demand or asynchronous devices that produce codes when needed, and cryptographic devices.[2] These tokens use different methods to provide dynamic authentication information. Each of these types of tokens has advantages and disadvantages in the methods that they employ.

The first type is a time-synced token. These tokens use synchronized clocks between the token device and the authenticating server to generate codes that can be used to authenticate. The token uses the time on the clock as part of the algorithm to generate a code that changes periodically. This code is then displayed to the user and is either used as the authentication code or combined with a PIN to form the authentication code that authenticates the user. In some implementations the PIN is entered into the device and is used as part of the algorithm to generate the authentication code. This method has the advantage that it will work with most applications with minimal change as the authentication code just replaces the password that would have been supplied by the user. One drawback that these types of tokens have is that the clocks will drift over time and will eventually become out of sync between the servers and the device. This may require that the tokens be resynced periodically with the servers if the drift becomes too large. It is important that the server maintain accurate time as well. Usually, this is done by using the network time protocol that uses a consistent time server to ensure that it keeps accurate time. The authentication process on the server will also attempt to measure the time drift between its clock and the token clock and adjust its authentication process accordingly. In some implementations the authentication process will use an authentication window, which will accept a range of authentication codes that are good over a predefined time period. This will prevent an excess of rejected authentications due to clock drift between the authentication server and the token but also increase the number of valid authentication codes that will be accepted. Depending on how large a window is used, this may increase the risk that an attacker may be able to guess an authentication code, but the quantity of possible codes is usually so large that this risk is pretty low. These tokens may also present some usability challenges as the code will be displayed for only a short time and may change while the user is reading it, requiring the user to start over.

The next type of token is one that generates authentication codes on demand. These devices use a counter that is incremented every time a code is generated and is used as an input into the algorithm that is used to generate the code. This counter is synchronized with the authentication server, which enables it to verify that the correct code has been presented. The authentication codes are onetime passwords and cannot be reused as the server will reject them. If the end user skips over a code without using it, the server will accept it as valid as long as it falls within a predetermined window of valid codes. The server does this by computing all of the valid codes starting with the current value it has of the counter up to the size of the window and comparing them to the presented code. If the code matches any of the computed codes in the window, the user will be authenticated and the server will resync the counter to the value used for that code and then increment it to match the value on the token. This allows the users to authenticate even if they inadvertently request a new code without using the current one. As with the time-synced tokens, this does increase the risk of an attacker guessing the password depending on the window size but the quantity of possible codes is usually so large that this risk is pretty low. One advantage of this type of device is that they are generally lower cost and last for a longer period of time than time-synced tokens because they are not always producing codes. They also do not experience any of the clock drift issues as they do not utilize clocks as part of their process. One drawback of using this type of device is that authenticating codes can be pregenerated and written down, and as long as they are used in order they will be valid. This would negate the need to have the token present while authenticating. This is a serious risk and can be prevented only through end-user awareness so that the codes are kept secure.

A third type of token device is a cryptographic smart card. This is generally implemented as a card about the size and thickness of a credit card that holds a small amount of secure storage and a processor that is capable of some cryptographic functions. The card is inserted into a reader that powers the card and provides the interface to the system. Smart-card tokens have also been implemented using devices that utilize USB connectors that are available on most newer computers. This is an advantage over the card implementation as a separate reader is not needed to be connected to the system. These devices perform authentication by relying on a type of cryptographic algorithm called public or private key. These algorithms use two different keys, a private key, which is kept secret and stored on the device, and a public key. To ensure that the correct public key is associated with a user, the key and the identifier of the user are stored together in an object called a certificate. The certificate will then be verified cryptographically by a trusted certificate authority to ensure that it is not altered. This certificate is then stored in a directory as part of a public key infrastructure (PKI). The public or private key algorithm has the property that data encrypted using the private key is able to be decrypted only using the public key and that data encrypted by the public key can be decrypted only by the private key. The most widely used public or private key algorithm is the RSA algorithm, which is named for its creators—Rivest, Shamir, and Adleman. This algorithm is used by the devices to authenticate a user by having the device encrypt a challenge string that has been supplied by the system the user is trying to authenticate to. This data is then decrypted with the user's public key by the authenticating server to verify that it has been encrypted by that user's private key. Most implementations of these devices will use a PIN to unlock the card before it will perform any functions. The use of smart cards and public or private key authentication will also require the use of a PKI and associated certificate authorities to manage and verify the public and private keys used in the authentication.

All physical tokens possess some safeguards to prevent physical attacks. If a token can be physically compromised and then reverse-engineered or if the appropriate secret information can be copied from it, then it can be duplicated without the user's knowledge. This would compromise the token as it would no longer be unique to the individual who possessed it. Tokens are usually in form factors that are difficult to break into without damaging the token to the point that it will not function and any secret key information cannot be read. There have been some attacks against smart cards that involve manipulating data that is input into the card to be encrypted and timing the amount of time it takes to encrypt it to reveal information about the secret private key. These attacks are time consuming in nature and require special equipment to enact. There have also been adjustments made on the smart-card architectures and processing to thwart these types of attacks. These kinds of attacks continue to be an area of ongoing concern as token device use becomes more widespread.

Token Management

Regardless of the type of token that is employed, there needs to be a process to manage it over its lifetime. This would include the initial distribution of tokens, replacing lost or expired tokens, and collecting tokens from employees who are leaving the enterprise. These processes generally make use of a database to manage the tokens during their life cycle. It is also important that the distribution and replacement processes use appropriate authentication methods to verify that the correct person is receiving the token. If these processes can be subverted then any subsequent authentications will be compromised, as someone other than the appropriate person may be able to obtain a token in his or her name. These processes may use trusted security officers to verify an identity or may be tied into the methods used to issue credentials for physical access to the enterprise. As a part of the procedure for issuing the token an alternate method of identification can and should be established. One method is to set up a series of challenge-and-response questions that can be used over the phone or through a self-service Web site to request actions like replacements or resets. It is important that these questions do not ask for easily obtainable information and are diverse enough not to be easily guessed. In general three to five questions chosen out of a pool of twenty are sufficient for this purpose. These questions should be used only for this purpose and should not be used for day-to-day authentication. This will reduce the likelihood that they could be intercepted.

The distribution and management of tokens can add a lot of overhead to the total cost of ownership of the token. This is especially true if tokens need to be shipped individually to end users. If they are handled via a centralized process, people would need to be paid to assign the tokens and actually pack them individually for shipping. The method of shipping would also need to give reasonable assurance that the token is delivered only to the person to whom it is assigned. This can add cost to the process especially if the enterprise is at multiple geographic sites. This cost can be reduced by using automation that will assign tokens from a pool of unassigned tokens that is kept at various sites within the enterprise and distributed as needed. A Web portal can be used by individuals to assign themselves a token, provided that they can be authenticated in a satisfactory manner. In enterprises that require more assurance that tokens are assigned to the appropriate individuals, on-site security officers or other trusted individuals can verify the identity of a person before assigning him or her a token. In all cases, detailed audit trails should be kept to document the process in case there is any question in the future about who was assigned the token.

There is also the potential to combine the physical access control of an employee badge with that of the smart card by using the same form factor. This is done by printing the badge information, usually a name, photograph, and, possibly, some other enterprise information, on the smart card itself. This gives the enterprise the option of using the smart card authentication information to control building access. This also makes it easier to remove access; when an employee leaves an organization and the badge or smart card is turned in, it will not only prevent them from entering the building but also prevent them from accessing any electronic systems or applications utilizing the smart card.

Conclusion

Authentication schemes that use static passwords are increasingly being compromised by attackers using network monitoring, viruses that install keyloggers on workstations, password guessing, and phishing that spoofs the end user into supplying the credentials to a third party. These attacks are becoming more and more common. Other methods of authentication need to be implemented to reduce the ability of attackers to compromise those systems and applications that use static passwords. Biometric schemes that implement the authentication factor "what you are" would also be effective but solutions are still somewhat immature and remain difficult to implement, especially with legacy systems. Token authentication schemes that implement two of the three factors of authentication, "something you know" (a PIN) and "something you have" (the token device), seem to be the best solution to prevent these types of attacks. Token authentication would be easier for an enterprise to implement and would greatly reduce the risk of the authentication scheme being compromised within the enterprise.

References

1. Schuckers, S. (2002). *Spoofing and Anti-Spoofing Measures*, Clarkson and West Virginia University. http://citer.wvu.edu/members/publications/files/15-SSchuckers-Elsevior02.pdf
2. Tipton, H. F., and Krause, M. (2004). *Information Security Handbook*, Fifth Edition, Boca Raton, FL, CRC Press LLC.

Access Control Administration

Chapter 12

Accountability

Dean R. Bushmiller

Contents

Introduction

What is accountability and why is no one willing to implement sound accountability measures? Accountability is neither popular with business nor is attractive enough for technologists to implement, and finally, security professionals can barely keep up with audit. You heard it here first: Accountability will be the next version of audit, identity management, and systems administration.

Accountability is about as opposite to "set it and forget it" as you can get. Everyone is looking for a silver bullet to kill the specter of compliance and regulation. But no silver bullet exists. The strength of our audit holy water gets dangerously diluted by the "turn it on when the auditor comes" attitude. It is time for the technical and business process of accountability.

Assumptions

To have a clear discussion on accountability, this chapter will be limited to the access control domain. In the access control domain, unique identification is assumed; without it, none of this concept or any access control methodology will be successful.

Discretionary access control (DAC) system failures are a reason for the need for accountability; therefore, DAC is the second assumption of this chapter. It is possible to adjust accountability concepts to fit role-based and mandatory access control systems.

Keep in mind, the author comes from a Windows background. The second section of this chapter discusses Windows file systems and tools to address logging "Windows style." Technologies discussed in this chapter can be abstracted to fit other situations such as implementations and relational database (UNIX-like) systems.

The information security management domain overlaps this topic specifically in the area of policy. Policy on consent to monitor, escalation procedures, and audit are assumed for the success of any level of accountability. Physical security is assumed to be robust.

The basic assumptions of unique identification, DAC, and Windows will help narrow the scope of this topic into a chapter instead of an entire book.

Definition and Need

The formal definition of accountability is as follows: The principle that individuals, organizations, and the community are responsible for their actions and may be required to explain those actions to others. In CISSP® terms, the organization will expect its constituents to conform to the policy or rules and, if there is a failure in compliance, the governing body will have knowledge of the infraction(s) and take action. Each of these components requires scrutiny for a CISSP to apply them to its business.

Who governs actions? What are the repercussions? The individual is a constituent of many groups or sets. For example: you are a member of a family, a community, an organization, and a business. If you do something wrong at the family holiday celebration (yes, everyone saw what you did), one or more family members will call you the next day and let you have it. If you do something wrong as a CISSP (not again?), the (ISC)²® Ethics Review Board will be sending you a nasty e-mail and perhaps revoking your membership. If you do something unacceptable on the file server at work, you should get an automated message explaining the policy violation, and your organization's counselor will expect you to set up a meeting to discuss the situation. This perfect world of repercussions for improper actions can be achieved via a mix of technical and administrative controls focused on accountability.

In the perfect world, everyone would understand the intent of the rules and follow them. With an approach that people are basically good, training would be the answer to setting clear expectations and preventing inappropriate interpretations of the rules. However, in an imperfect world, people are in a continuous state of change. In most cases, the way information is presented will have a bearing on how well it is received and acted upon. For example, the chief executive officer (CEO) of a health club says, "We are instituting a new system of accountability. Drug testing will be done every day. We will know what you are drinking, eating, and doing the night before. If you do anything wrong, you are fired!" What will the staff be feeling at this point?

Let us start over. The CEO believes they want to improve the health of the staff by showing them how to improve diet, exercise, and vitamin balance. What would be the feeling now? The same implementation of accountability can be perceived differently. Successful implementation of accountability strategies requires a smooth delivery of expectations and an accurate technology.

Regrettably, organizations break regulations, people break laws and policies; the ones who get caught get punished. So when does this happen? Auditors schedule appointments with organizations to review their activity either because of a complaint or as a part of a periodic inspection. It is rare that a surprise or random inspection occurs without some warning. Before the auditor arrives, everyone scurries around turning on the controls. The auditor checks the policy against the controls, looking for gaps. Auditors will dig until they have a finding and then submit the report to the governing body. The governing body hands out fines or, in most cases, warnings. After the auditor leaves, the controls are turned off, life goes on.

What should have happened? When the controls were turned off, the governing body and the responsible party at the organization should have been notified automatically, the summons should have arrived in the mail, and the controls would then be turned back on or the fine would be paid. The next time you drive down the road and you see a police car pulling someone over, will you slow down? The next time a red light camera catches you, will you pay the fine or go to court? The next time you see the camera, will you stop? How about following the law all the time?

That is what accountability is all about; it is a business and technical process that changes everyone's behavior to follow policy at all times.

For example, suppose you do something unacceptable. You would then get an e-mail from the system and a copy would go to your boss. You would be required to show up at his or her desk ready to explain. As a responsible member of the organization and a mature adult, you would not make excuses: you would apologize and not do it again. It would not be a fun part of the day. If employees know that inappropriate actions have repercussions, they learn quickly not to do those actions.

We need an accountability system that addresses the world we live in. We need a business process and a technical tool set that report all inappropriate activity so that self-corrective measures are applied.

Requirements Overview

Accountability requires a balance between the implementation and the business process. Relying on either one too much will reduce the accountability. If we have a poorly automated way to deliver the data, the business process cannot apply the rules and remediation equally. Once we have inequitable application of policy, it will lead to decision reversals either by human resources or, worse yet, by a court of law. We have all heard stories of courts ordering organizations to reinstate employees.

Administratively there must be clear, accurate policy and a remedy for noncompliance. Technically there must be well-defined, accurate permission systems, consolidated logging, and timely e-mail communications for all parties involved.

Business Process Details

Before we address the technical processes we need to get the business processes in place. We must define the actions, and then we can define the inappropriate actions. We must choose a governing body from the population for escalation and remediation. We must define the repercussions. A well-defined business has its functions and flows documented. This data is currently in most organizations. It could be in the risk management documents, the business impact assessment, the business plan, or the management framework.

The data we need for defining the actions includes all of the job descriptions, roles, and responsibilities in the organization. This cannot be done in the vacuum of a single department. If we examine the roles and an overlap occurs we need to find out why and make adjustments, if possible. Each position or role will have a defined set of resources that is not appropriate for others to access. Further, in a mature definition the access to resources would be as granular as possible. Our goal is to answer the questions, what are the least privileges, what are the groups, and what are the resources? In a large organization this data may be in file systems, directories, or identity management systems.

If the data is present, it most likely needs consolidation. The maximum number of groups should be less than 25 for an organization or a large, segregated department. The maximum number of resources should be 25. The reason for these numbers is that the possible number of permutations of groups and resources could be so high that administrators could not diagram or conceptualize it. It is possible to exceed these maximums, but in most cases consolidation is called for. The difficulty with this step is as follows: administrative overhead changes over the life of a business, a position, and a set of resources. The output of this step will be used to define your functional policies.

Consent to monitoring, acceptable use of resources, remediation, self-governance, and escalation are the functional policies that must be defined for use in the technical implementation of accountability. As always, policy must be communicated to staff before, during, and after employment. Consent to monitoring must detail the level of activity tracking and give clear examples. Acceptable use of resources must include a statement that specifically points to not using named files or databases that are not part of the scope of that role or group; further, personnel must be warned to protect the user account as an asset of the organization. Acceptable use must reference the other three policies listed. The remediation policy must explain the following: steps to be taken in the event the acceptable use policy is broken, who will be contacted if a violation occurs, exceptions, typical punishments, and the number of violations before escalation occurs. Self-governance policy (also called ethics handbook), if present, should explain acceptable and unacceptable behavior as it pertains to accountability. The escalation policy must name or address parties such as union representation, legal counsel, employee review boards, and human resources.

Employee review boards are a group of peers who listen to exceptions and make recommendations to the violator. This group should be a mix of all departments, with a variety of tenure, and should change frequently. It may have more impact than management. Depending on the culture of the organization, review boards may even make recommendations for termination or punishment. Just the thought of disappointing peers in certain organizations will be a deterrent to further inappropriate actions.

Technical Process Details

All businesses can implement accountability; however, the technical house must be in order. The minimum requirements are unique identity; properly named resources and groups; accurate permissions; accurate, continuous, concise, logging; automated reporting of relevant logging; and good maintenance of all of the above.

Identity management strategies include consolidation or synchronization of authentication databases, grouping of functional or departmental staff, and grouping of resources. A more organized group management strategy of tying groups of owners to their named resources using a clear naming convention will increase the clarity of accountability. If the resource is clearly marked or named and organized for the users' department or function, the users will be more likely to access the correct resources. Conversely, it will be clear to the users that the inappropriate action is not a part of their security domain. The example in the implementation section of this chapter will make this easier to understand.

In most enterprise permissions systems, administrators either are confused about the effective permissions or use a "most privilege" strategy, rather than least privilege. Resource users should be in as few conflicting permissions groups as possible. Permissions should be applied as close to the resource as possible, and grouping should be abstracted on the local resource.

The "antigroup" consists of a group of all personnel that should not have access to a specific resource, that is, the antipermission group. Antigroup is a term that the author has created because the concept is paramount to successful accountability. The antigroup should specifically be denied access to the resource by technical means. If this occurs and overall group management is accurate and automated, it will be easier to implement accountability.

Accurate logging is the last key piece of the accountability puzzle. Traditionally, logging levels have been either too high or too low. Trapping all events causes poor performance, storage issues, and log consolidation errors. Trapping too few log entries misses key events. Logging all types of access (success and failure) by the antigroup communicates all that is needed for accountability. Successful access by the antigroup indicates failed permissions settings and requires immediate action by administrators. Failed access by the antigroup indicates accountability issues to be reported as directed by the policies. If group consolidation is coupled with antigroup strategies, logging can be nearly perfect.

Indirectly related to accountability is the act of tuning the logging system itself. Changes to logging facilities indicate a policy change. Technical or administrative policy change should be carefully reviewed before implemented; accountability's assurance depends on it.

Automated reporting of accountability infractions is the final step in the set of technical processes. To limit collusion, reduce tension between employees, and provide immediate feedback to transgressors, all reporting and escalation must not have human intervention until after the offender has had a chance to review his or her own actions.

Adjustments to the technical and business processes surrounding accountability are essential to business. As infractions are recorded, the metadata will indicate gaps between what is reasonable to achieve business goals and what is written in the policy. Accountability strategies will take at least three iterations to become stable and reliable.

Technical Process Implementation

The second part of this chapter is a description of an implementation of accountability. We will use the technical implementation norms for organizations of the most prevalent operating system and typical setup to build an accountability implementation. Microsoft's Active Directory for version 2000 or better with Global Groups enabled has the widest audience. With some adjustments, this system could work for other operating systems and atypical designs.

Assumptions for this implementation of accountability are as follows: a Windows domain structure under a single forest, universal groups, permissions applied to groups only, a universal naming convention for both groups and shared resources, permissions set on every accessible resource, event logging for security and system events, and Logcaster (a log consolidation tool).

Large Windows domain structures prior to Windows 2000 were typically set up as resource domains trusting accounts domains to overcome limitations in the sizes of databases. This is no longer

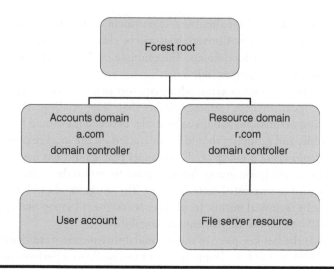

Exhibit 12.1   Example forest and domain structure.

necessary, but the concept and a diagram will help to illustrate a domain that is complex enough to be applied to most enterprises (see Exhibit 12.1). In this domain structure, the user account is located in the a.com domain, and the file server is located in a separate domain, r.com. Both domains are located in a single forest so that database replication may occur.

Universal groups are found only in a forest where the functional level has been raised to a minimum of Windows 2000 native mode for all domains in the forest. This cannot be undone unless you restore all domain controllers from backup. (A strong warning: if you raise the functional level and if you have any NT 4.0 domains, you will lose replication capability.) Raising the functional level can be accomplished in the microsoft management console (MMC) for Active Directory Domains and Trust by right-clicking each of the domain objects and choosing from the context menu.

> From Windows 2003 server Help file: The concept of enabling additional functionality in Active Directory exists in Windows 2000 with mixed and native modes. Mixed-mode domains can contain Windows NT 4.0 backup domain controllers and cannot use Universal security groups, group nesting, and security ID (SID) history capabilities. When the domain is set to native mode, Universal security groups, group nesting, and SID history capabilities are available. Domain controllers running Windows 2000 Server are not aware of domain and forest functionality.

It is possible to achieve accountability in separate forests by using a centralized logging facility, but the level of complexity increases.

Permissions need to be set on resources at the group level in a nested fashion to reduce permissions conflicts and confusion. An informal polling of hundreds of systems administrators over seven years indicates three things: There is an overwhelming attitude of confusion on how to set permissions correctly, what the effective cumulative permissions are on a share, and how to clean up the permissions creep that occurs over the life of an account.

Permissions administrators should use a practical approach to permissions systems. The practical approach from *Discretionary Access Control Knowledge, a Practical System* offers a new solution for administrators to reduce abuse of access controls and simplify permissions management.

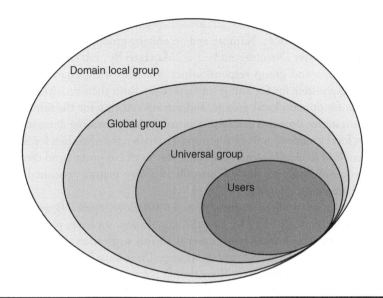

Exhibit 12.2   Nesting groups.

"If the concepts of 'THE SNAIL' and the best practices are followed, administrators will be able to reduce the confusion of calculating the effective cumulative permissions. Using THE GRID and THE FIVE RULES allow administrators to quickly identify and reduce vulnerabilities…."*

This paper also details naming conventions for groups. When inappropriate actions are logged, there needs to be a clear understanding of who did what and when. By implementing standard naming of groups, we know the "who." By implementing standard naming of resources, we know the "what." If we have time synchronization with external timeservers, we know the "when."

The organization of groups should follow "The Snail" concept of placing users only in global groups, placing global groups in universal groups, and placing universal groups in domain local groups (see Exhibit 12.2). This organization of groups allows for slow migration to a mature accountability posture. The naming conventions should support a clear path from the user account to the resource and its permissions. The following is an example naming convention:

Domain local groups
    LgDepartmentFoldernamePermission
If there is a deny permission, precede it with "x"
Universal groups
    UgDepartmentFoldernamePermission
If there is a deny permission, precede it with "x"
Global groups
    GgDepartment

The antigroup concept that is critical for accountability implementations to work is employed by assigning all global groups who do not have permission to the resource to the xUg group. This may have a high administrative cost if scripts are not employed.

---

* http://www.sans.org/reading_room/whitepapers/windows/1165.php.

This naming convention will allow for fast identification of administrative error and the ability to track down accountability issues. Naming and organizing groups will support accountability if owners are assigned in Active Directory under the "Managed By" tab of the group.

Naming conventions and group responsibilities will help with separation of duties. Server operators who are responsible for file and print servers can limit their activities to creating shares, setting permissions for domain local groups, and setting auditing for the same groups. Domain administrators for resource domains can limit their activities to creating domain local groups and assigning domain local groups to universal groups. Domain administrators for accounts domains can limit their activities to creating and assigning users to global groups and creating and assigning global groups to universal groups. It is possible in a very mature accountability structure to identify inappropriate group creation.

Permissions can be set at three levels within the Windows operating system: share, NTFS (NT File System) folder, and NTFS file. To reduce confusion, set share permissions to full control for everyone. Many administrators get upset with this suggestion. Share permissions, if left to stand alone, are never a good access control strategy. They must be supported by NTFS folder permissions that maintain least privilege. There should not be any need for NTFS file permissions. Administratively, this should be the only permissions; this can be achieved only by changing the advanced settings to remove inheritance of permissions. This is accomplished by removing the check in the "Allow inheritable permissions from parent" box.

At this point, the administrator's group still maintains full control. This group contains the local administrator account of the filer and by default contains the domain administrators of the local domain as one of its members. If administrators cannot adjust permissions, they cannot do their job. This permission should be left alone so we can see when the administrator makes changes.

When building or adjusting group membership, an organization might want to put all groups in a single active directory container to prevent domain policy inheritance from changing configuration rights. This strategy also increases the speed of searching the directory.

By executing the administrative tasks mentioned, the users are in the correct groups, nesting of group types for the organization has been achieved, effective permissions can be set, antigroups are in place, and it is possible to achieve accountability via event logging. The result should look like Exhibit 12.3. There should be two to four permissions set on the resource: local administrator with full control, antigroup with deny full control, and the one or two departments with their least privileges set.

Event logging is the core tracking mechanism for accountability. It should be configured at the domain policy level and not at the local policy level. For filers, audit should be set to success and failure for object access and success and failure for policy change. If additional auditing is turned on, extra events that do not pertain to accountability will be recorded.

Once auditing is turned on at the server and configured at the domain level, the objects or resources can be successfully tracked. The audit tab on the advanced security settings for the resource should audit for the two groups who do not need access on a regular basis: the administrators and the antigroup. Keep in mind, the antigroup is everyone who does not have permission. The antigroup was defined by the accounts domain administrator at the universal group level by adding the global groups who do not need access to the resources of the department. If the permissions administrator failed to set the deny all permission and did set the audit for both success and failure, the inappropriate access would still be logged. This is possible only for the antigroup and not the built-in "everyone group." The "everyone group" includes everyone who has access to the network, which includes the people with permissions. If everyone is audited, both inappropriate access and correct access will be logged. The goal is to log only inappropriate access.

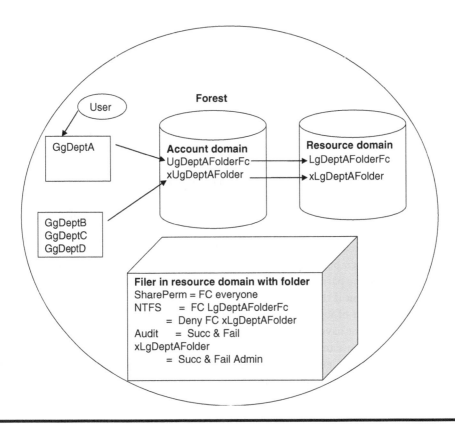

Exhibit 12.3   Complete diagram of accountability implementation.

The administrator must see both success and failure audit events at accessing resources by the antigroup. Success audit events indicate incorrectly set permissions. Failure audit events indicate inappropriate attempts. By using the antigroup as the group for logging events, the first part of accountability has been achieved.

Activity of both end-user violation and administrative maintenance must be collected, stored, and used. The use of the data for our initial purpose is accountability. Policy will need to be adjusted to fit the real working conditions, because the accountability data will indicate gaps. Because only inappropriate activity is being collected, collection and storage of logging data will be reduced to a manageable level for review. Using an event log aggregation tool such as Logcaster by Rippletech will allow us to trap critical events as they occur, rather than at the point of offline storage. Critical events such as accountability violations, policy changes, audit changes, and permissions changes should be submitted for immediate review by department managers, accountability committees, and the end user. Immediate review ties actions to consequences. Automated output allows for immediate review without judgment calls by security teams or administrators. Critical events can be done via e-mail.

Caution should be used when first implementing e-mail notification due to a potential denial of service. Summarization is the best strategy for automation until false-positives are reduced to a manageable level. Any noncritical events such as administrator access should be collected, summarized, and reviewed in a reasonable time period.

Threats

Accountability has many administrative threats. They include prerequisite failures, implementation failures, maintenance failures, and mislabeling. The prerequisites of unique identification and identity management are difficult to achieve and maintain. To hold people accountable, administrators need to be sure the account is used by one and only one person. It would be bad form to punish someone for another's actions. Shared accounts of administrators will be most troublesome if the intention is to apply accountability to technical administrative functions.

Initial implementation failures can include a high number of false-positives if the accountability systems are not installed in stages.

To address maintenance failures, keep in mind that permissions change. It is tempting to leave the past set of permissions in place and add new permissions. This violation of least privilege should be addressed by conducting regular reviews. Additional maintenance failures can be caused by staff changes on the administrative side, uncontrolled growth of staff, and lack of automation.

Organizations are likely to mislabel accountability as audit. But audit is a periodic third-party evaluation of gaps between policy and implementation. Accountability is immediate gap notification and correction by the parties involved.

There are a few technical threats, including logging costs, lack of education, and requirement of centralization. The act of logging has a dollar value. Some organizations already have logging in place; those that do not have will be starting from scratch and, therefore, spending more. Lack of education on permissions and logging consolidation cause a great deal of unnecessary overhead on accountability systems. Centralization of logging, authentication, and policy are required for most organizations to achieve accountability.

Who Needs to Be Involved?

The easy answer is everyone needs to be involved. Policy makers, technologists, employees, and auditors all need to be a part of the accountability program. Enforcement by policy makers needs to be defined and implemented by the technologists in a hands-off manner. Policy makers should make the rules and define the repercussions so that the employees take it upon themselves to self-correct. If the rules are not followed in a reasonable amount of time, human resources or an employee council should step in. Auditors should take the metadata from the accountability system and adjust policy or work habits. If everyone gets involved, accountability will change the culture of the organization for the better.

Summary

Security is not "set it and forget it"; accountability keeps this uppermost in our minds. Accountability achieves awareness by verifying every action defined in the policy. When everyone is aware, our risks to our resources decrease. Assurance is increased by an order of magnitude when security is moved from the responsibility of a few to that of the entire organization.

Do not try to go after every inappropriate action at once. Start with simple, easy-to-be-right actions. For example, only the accounting department should be in the payroll files. Work your way up to the more difficult decisions. Accountability is possible.

Methods of Attack

Chapter 13

Rootkits: The Ultimate Malware Threat

E. Eugene Schultz and Edward Ray

Contents

Introduction

Of all the things that occur in the information security arena, few are more interesting (and also more troublesome) than malicious code ("malware") incidents. Over the years we have seen malware evolve from simple viruses written in assembly language to complex programs that deliver advanced functionality that greatly facilitates the ability of perpetrators to accomplish their sordid purposes. In this chapter we have termed rootkits "the ultimate malware threat," something that is no embellishment whatsoever. When it comes to sophistication and potential for damage, loss, and destruction, few, if any, types of malware can compare to rootkits. With the constant news about viruses, worms, and Trojan horse programs, however, rootkits have somehow gotten "lost in the fog." This chapter is intended to serve as a wake-up call—it is time for information security professionals to become aware of exactly what rootkits are, what they can do, what risks they pose, and possible solutions for countering them.

Information security professionals are constantly concerned about a wide variety of security-related threats. Some of these threats pose considerably higher levels of risk than others and thus require more resources to counter. Furthermore, risks and their potential impact change over time. In the 1990s, for example, risks resulting from the activity of external attackers were some of the most serious. Attackers often launched brute-force password-guessing attacks or, if they were more sophisticated, password-cracking attacks using dictionary-based password-cracking tools that are by today's standards rather crude. During that time, damage and disruption due to virus and worm infections also comprised one of the most serious types of security risks. Things have changed considerably since then; certain types of malware other than viruses and worms have moved to the forefront of risks that organizations currently face. Rootkits in particular now represent what might safely be called the ultimate malware threat. This chapter covers the ins and outs of rootkits, the relationship between rootkits and security-related risk, how to prevent rootkits from being installed in the first place, and how to detect them and recover when rootkits have been installed in victim systems.

About Rootkits

What exactly is a rootkit? The following section defines what rootkits are, describes their characteristics, explains how rootkits and Trojan horse programs differ, and describes how rootkits work.

Definition of Rootkit

The term "rootkit" refers to a type of Trojan horse program that if installed on a victim system changes its operating system software such that: (1) evidence of the attackers' activities (including any changes to the system that have been made in installing the rootkit) is hidden and (2) the attackers can gain remote backdoor access to the system at will. Rootkits replace normal programs and system libraries that are part of the operating system on victim machines with versions that superficially appear to be normal, but that in reality subvert the security of the machine and cause malicious functions to be executed.

Characteristics of Rootkits

Rootkits almost without exception run with superuser privileges, the full set of system privileges intended only for system administrators and system programmers, so that they can readily perform virtually any task at will. In UNIX and Linux, this translates to root-level privileges; in Windows, this means Administrator- and SYSTEM-level privileges. Without superuser privileges, rootkits would not be very effective in accomplishing the malicious functions they support. It is important to realize, however, that attackers need to gain superuser-level access before installing and running rootkits. Rootkits are not exploit tools that raise the privilege level of those who install them. Attackers must thus first exploit one or more vulnerabilities independent of the functionality of any rootkit to gain superuser privileges on victim systems if they are going be able to install and run a rootkit on these systems.

Additionally, the majority of rootkits are "persistent," whereas others are not. Persistent rootkits stay installed regardless of how many times the systems on which they are installed are booted. Nonpersistent rootkits (also called "memory-resident" rootkits) reside only in memory; no file in the compromised system contains their code. They thus remain on a victim system only until the next time the system boots, at which time they are deleted.

How Rootkits Work

Rootkits work using two basic types of mechanisms, those that enable them to avoid detection and those that set up backdoors, as explained in this section.

Hiding Mechanisms

Attackers know that discovery of their unauthorized activity on a victim system almost invariably leads to investigations that result in the system being patched or rebuilt, thereby effectively forcing them to "start from scratch" in their efforts to gain unauthorized access to and control a target system or, in a worst case scenario for attackers, giving investigators clues that can be used in identifying and ultimately convicting the attackers of wrongdoing. It is to the attackers' advantage, therefore, to hide all indications of their presence on victim systems. Most rootkits incorporate one or more hiding mechanisms—as a rule, the more sophisticated the rootkit, the more of these mechanisms are part of the rootkit and the more proficient these mechanisms are.

The most basic type of hiding mechanism is one in which log data pertaining to an attacker's log-ins and log-outs on the victim system are erased so that when system administrators inspect the system's audit logs, they do not see any entries that report the attacker's having logged in or out or having done anything else on the system. Additionally, many rootkits delete any evidence of processes generated by the attacker and the rootkit itself. When system administrators enter commands or use system utilities that display the processes that are running, the names of processes started in connection with all facets of the attack (including the presence of a rootkit) are omitted from the output. Rootkits may also hide files and directories that the attacker has created in a number of ways, including changing commands used to list directory contents to have them exclude files that the attacker has created or (as explained in more detail shortly) making changes to the kernel of the operating system itself to cause it to provide false information about the presence and function of certain files and executables. To allow backdoor access by attackers, rootkits almost always open one or more network ports on the victim system. To preclude the possibility of discovering rootkits when system administrators examine open ("listening") ports, many rootkits thus also hide information about certain ports' status. Additionally, some rootkits change what happens when certain executables are invoked by legitimate users (e.g., system administrators) such that malicious executables that superficially appear to work like the original executables are run instead. Finally, some rootkits (e.g., those with keystroke logging capability) capture or change information sent to or from hardware devices that interface with victim systems.

Backdoor Mechanisms

Rootkits almost without exception also provide attackers with remote backdoor access to compromised systems. One of the most common ways of providing this kind of access is creating encrypted connections such as secure shell (SSH) connections that not only give attackers remote control over compromised systems, but also encrypt information to prevent it from being available for analysis by network-based intrusion detection systems (IDSs) and intrusion prevention systems (IPSs) as well as network monitoring tools. Additionally, SSH implementations used in connection with rootkits require entering a username and password, thereby also helping prevent individuals other than the individual or individuals who installed the rootkit from being able to use the backdoor.

Types of Rootkits

Two fundamental types of rootkits, user-mode rootkits and kernel-mode rootkits, exist. The difference is based on the levels at which they operate and the type of software they change or replace. This section describes both types and explains how each works.

User-Mode Rootkits

User-mode rootkits replace executables and system libraries that system administrators and users use. The SSH program and the C library in UNIX and Linux systems are two of the most common targets. Windows Explorer (the default shell in Windows systems) is often targeted by user-mode rootkits. Authors of user-mode rootkits take great care to hide the fact that targeted executables and system libraries have been changed. For example, if a rootkit has replaced the SSH program, both the last date of modification and the file length will be what they were when the SSH was originally installed when system administrators enter commands to query for this information. Additionally, most rootkits target only a few executables and system libraries (often only one); the fewer executables and system libraries targeted, the less likely system administrators and users are to notice that something is wrong.

Kernel-Mode Rootkits

As their name implies, kernel-mode rootkits change components within the kernel of the operating system on the victim machine or sometimes even completely replace the kernel. The kernel is the heart of an operating system; it provides fundamental services (e.g., input and output control) for every part of the operating system.

Kernel-mode rootkits hide the presence of attackers better than do user-mode rootkits. System administrators and system programmers trust kernel-level processes implicitly, but anything that has control of the kernel can cause kernel processes to produce bogus information about their status. System administrators and system programmers are not likely to have any reason to believe that this information is specious. Additionally, detecting changes in the kernel is generally very difficult, especially if kernel-mode rootkits have been developed by individuals with extremely high levels of technical expertise. Kernel-mode rootkits are thus even deadlier than user-mode rootkits.

Kernel-mode rootkits invariably change process listings to exclude processes that run in connection with the rootkits. The kernel is aware of all processes that are running, but when system administrators enter a command to list all processes, certain ones (the ones that the rootkit author wants to hide) are omitted when the kernel processes provide information to the command. Additionally, kernel-mode rootkits often redirect the execution of programs such that when system administrators and users invoke a certain program, a completely different program is run, something that is called "redirection." Redirection is an especially effective hiding technique because the original program remains intact; no changes in this program can thus be discovered.

How Rootkits and Other Types of Malware Differ

As stated in the definition at the start of this chapter, a rootkit is a type of Trojan horse program. The term "Trojan horse program" actually refers to a wide range of hidden malicious programs; rootkits are thus one kind of Trojan program. Rootkits, however, go further than conventional Trojans in that the latter are designed to go unnoticed, but do not incorporate active mechanisms that prevent them from being noticed. In general, the primary method of hiding Trojan horse programs is assigning an innocuous name (e.g., "datafile" or "misc") to them. In contrast, rootkits have mechanisms that actively hide their presence from antivirus and antispyware programs, system management utilities, and system and network administrators. Additionally, Trojan programs are generally created within systems that have been compromised, that is, they do not replace existing programs and files, but are instead new programs that are installed. As mentioned previously, in contrast, rootkits actually replace operating system programs and system libraries.

It is also important to understand that rootkits are not tools that exploit vulnerabilities. Rootkit installation instead requires that one or more vulnerabilities first be exploited. Additionally, rootkits are not viruses or worms, both of which are self-reproducing programs. If rootkits were self-reproducing, detecting and deleting them would be considerably easier; rootkit authors thus avoid incorporating self-reproducing functionality in the code they write. At the same time, however, it is important for information security professionals to realize that in some instances viruses or worms have installed rootkits in systems that they have infected.

How Rootkits Are Installed

One of the most common ways that rootkits are installed includes having someone download what appears to be a patch or legitimate freeware or shareware program, but which is in reality a rootkit. Software is sometimes modified at the source; programmers can insert malicious lines of code into programs that they write. A recent example of this is the Sony BMG Music Entertainment copy-protection scheme, which came with music compact disks (CDs) that secretly installed a rootkit on computers (see the following vignette). Additionally, malicious Web servers often install rootkits into systems by exploiting vulnerabilities in browsers such as Internet Explorer and Mozilla Firefox that allow malicious Web pages to download files of a perpetrator's choice or possibly by giving processes on the malicious Web server superuser privileges on the systems that run these browsers.

A relatively new attack vector for installing rootkits is spyware. A recent example of this is a variant of the VX2.Look2Me Spyware Trojan released in November 2005 (see http://www.f-secure.com/sw-desc/look2me.shtml). Rootkits enable spyware authors to hide configuration settings and program files, enabling the rootkits themselves to be installed in alternate data streams—features associated with files and directories in the Windows NT File System that provide compatibility with the Macintosh File System—to disguise their presence. Spyware and rootkit combinations are typically installed on victim computers via malicious Web pages or e-mail messages that exploit Web browser vulnerabilities or use "social engineering" tricks to get users to install the code unknowingly.

A final rootkit vector discussed here is viruses and worms. Although most viruses and worms usually do not install rootkits, a few of them do.

Vendor-Installed Rootkits: More Reason to Worry

The information security community in general and security vendors in particular have been slow to react to rootkit-related risks. More recently, however, a few vendors have installed monitoring software that uses stealthy, rootkit-style techniques to hide itself. Long before Mark Russinovich blew the whistle on Sony BMG's use of such software to cloak its digital rights management scheme, spyware researchers had seen traces of Sony BMG's controversial technology on personal computers without knowing what it was. As Russinovich explained, the detection of the Sony BMG rootkit was not a straightforward task. New techniques and products are emerging to make it easier for technical staff to identify rootkits on compromised machines, but identifying such machines in the first place and then removing the malicious software remain frustratingly difficult. Everyone expects the perpetrator community to write and deploy rootkits—according to McAfee, the use of stealth techniques in malware has increased by over 600 percent since 2004. At the same time, who would expect vendors to write and install rootkits in their products? Vendors such as Sony BMG have thus added another layer of complexity to the already too complex rootkit problem.

Rootkits and Security-Related Risk

Rootkits considerably raise the level of security-related risk that organizations face, namely by increasing the cost of incidents, increasing the probability of backdoor access, putting organizations' machines at risk of becoming part of a botnet, and exposing organizations to the risk of confidentiality infractions because of unauthorized capture of information, as explained in the following sections.

Escalation of Security Breach-Related Costs

Although rootkits do not break into systems per se, once they are installed on systems they are (unless they are poorly designed or written) usually extremely difficult to identify. They can reside on compromised systems for months without anyone, the most experienced system administrators included, suspecting that anything is wrong. The cost of security breaches is proportionate to their duration; anything that increases duration escalates incident-related costs.

Increased Likelihood of Backdoor Access

Because rootkits usually include backdoors, they substantially raise the probability that even if effective security measures are in place, attackers will gain unauthorized remote access to systems. Because rootkits are so difficult to discover, whoever gains such access can rummage through the contents of files within the compromised system to glean sensitive and other information. The fact that access of this nature is normally with superuser-level privileges means not only that attackers can remotely access systems any time they wish, but also that they have complete control to do anything they want with each system that they access in this manner.

Rootkits Often Run in Connection with Botnets

A bot is a malicious executable that is under the control of a master program used by an attacker to achieve a variety of malicious goals. A botnet comprises multiple bots that respond to a central source of control. Botnets may be used for numerous sordid purposes; one of the worst is distributed denial-of-service attacks. Some rootkits function as bots within massive botnets that, if not detected, can produce deleterious outcomes. If bots are discovered early enough, they can be eradicated without providing sufficient time to accomplish their goals, but rootkits are normally extremely hard to find, reducing the probability of discovering and deleting bots before they can do their sordid deeds.

Rootkits Often Include Keystroke and Terminal Loggers

Another area of risk that rootkits can introduce is having sensitive information such as credit card numbers and personal identification numbers used in banking transactions captured by keystroke and terminal loggers that are part of the rootkit. Keystroke loggers capture every character entered on a system, whereas terminal loggers (which pose even greater risk than do keystroke loggers) capture all input and output, not just keystrokes. Keystroke and terminal loggers are often used in connection with identity theft. Additionally, keystroke and terminal loggers are frequently used to steal log-on credentials, thereby enabling successful attacks on systems on which the credentials are used. Keystroke and terminal loggers can also glean encryption keys, thereby enabling successful cryptanalysis attacks that result in the ability to decrypt encrypted information.

Rootkit Prevention

Prevention is the best cure; adopting measures that prevent rootkits from being installed is far better than having to detect and eradicate them after they are installed. In a way the term "rootkit prevention" does not make sense, however, because rootkit installation is something that occurs after a system is compromised at the superuser level. The one essential element in preventing rootkits from being installed, therefore, is keeping systems from being compromised in the first place. Some measures that accomplish this goal include using prophylactic measures, running software that detects and eradicates rootkits, patch management, configuring systems appropriately, adhering to the least privilege principle, using firewalls, using strong authentication, practicing good security maintenance, and limiting compilers.

Prophylactic Measures

Prophylactic measures are measures that prevent rootkits from being installed, even if an attacker has superuser privileges. The challenge of creating prophylactic measures that work reliably despite the fact that an attacker has control of the operating system on a compromised system is great; it should thus come as no surprise that few such measures currently exist. Intrusion prevention is a promising prophylactic measure. Host-based intrusion prevention systems, IPSs that run on individual systems, can keep rootkits from being installed through policy files that allow or prohibit the execution of certain commands and prevent service requests from being processed if they potentially lead to rootkit installation as well as other undesirable outcomes. Additionally, operating system vendors are starting to incorporate prophylactic measures into their products. Microsoft, for example, has introduced a security feature called "Kernel Patch Protection," or "PatchGuard," in the 64-bit versions of its Windows operating systems. PatchGuard monitors the kernel and detects and stops attempts by code that is not part of the operating system to intercept and modify kernel code. IPSs can keep rootkits from being installed in the first place, provided, of course, that each IPS has an updated policy file that enables the system on which it resides to deny certain kinds of incoming service requests that lead to rootkit installation.

Patch Management

Applying patches that close vulnerabilities is one of the most important measures in preventing rootkits from being installed. As mentioned previously, attackers need to exploit vulnerabilities to install rootkits and run them with superuser-level privileges. If systems and network devices are up to date with respect to patches, attackers will be unable to exploit vulnerabilities and thus will not be able to install rootkits. Patch management tools that automate the patching process generally provide the most efficient way to patch systems. It is also imperative that all patches come from known, trusted sources and that the hash value for each downloaded patch matches the value provided by the developer.

Configuring Systems Appropriately and Limiting Services That Run on Systems

To prevent attackers from installing system administrator-mode rootkits on a system, the user must harden each system by configuring it in accordance with security configuration guidelines. Vendors such as Microsoft and Sun Microsystems publish such guidelines for each version of operating system that they make, and sites such as the Center for Internet Security offer guidelines as well as automated tools to "grade" a computer to see how well it is secured based on their guidelines. Many types of malware take advantage of services and software running on client or server machines. These services are sometimes turned on by default and run without the user's knowledge, or are left on because of poor security policy, or are turned on later. Organizations should have a default configuration for their clients and servers that specifies the services and software that are and are not needed and ensure not only that these services are turned off when they are not needed, but also that the executables for all unneeded services are uninstalled, if at all possible. By ensuring that machines are running only the services and software that are essential for job-related tasks, organizations can reduce the rootkit threat.

Adhering to the Least Privilege Principle

Assigning individuals the minimum level of privileges they need to get their jobs done helps reduce the likelihood that attackers will gain superuser privileges, which in turn reduces the likelihood that attackers will be able to install rootkits. For example, kernel-level rootkits almost always require drivers that run in kernel mode. In Windows operating systems, these drivers can be loaded and unloaded into memory using techniques similar to those necessary to create, enable, or terminate services. Only users with administrator or system rights (privileges) are allowed to install programs (including rootkits) that run in connection with drivers or that create services. If an attacker intent on installing a rootkit does not have at least one of these two types of privileges, therefore, the rootkit cannot start and hence cannot hide itself.

Deploying Firewalls

Firewalls can also provide some measure of proactive defense against rootkit installation. Rootkits are special applications used by perpetrators. Because firewalls are increasingly performing analysis of network traffic at the application layer (network layer 7) instead of at the network layer (network layer 3), firewalls can improve the ability to identify and intercept malicious traffic in connection with rootkits. Many perimeter-based firewalls now include application-layer signatures for known malware and scan traffic as it enters the perimeter from the edge, looking for suspicious files downloaded by users before these files are executed on the user's machines. Many proxy-based firewalls (firewalls that terminate each incoming connection and then create a new outbound connection with the same connection characteristics if the connection meets one or more security criteria) now incorporate scanning engines that increase the likelihood that content associated with rootkit traffic will be intercepted before it is downloaded and executed. At the same time, however, this added firewall functionality has the potentially deleterious effect of harming network performance. Information security professionals must thus balance the use of real-time network scanning for malicious traffic with network performance considerations.

Using Strong Authentication

The widespread use of static passwords in authentication constitutes a serious vulnerability, one that attackers and malicious code often exploit to install rootkits in systems. Strong authentication means using authentication methods that are considerably more difficult to defeat. Examples of strong authentication methods include using one time passwords, authentication tokens, and biometric authentication. The strength of authentication in both clients and servers can also be improved by requiring authentication on commonly open services and ports. Using open standards such as the IPSec protocol (which defines an authenticating header for packets sent over the network to guard against spoofing and an encapsulated security payload to help ensure confidentiality of packet contents) also substantially decreases the likelihood of compromise. IPSec is available on Windows, Linux, and UNIX platforms; multiple approaches to credential management such as shared key, Kerberos, and public key infrastructure (PKI) can be implemented. A shared-key scheme is the simplest, but the most easily compromised. Kerberos, a very strong method of network authentication, is more secure than the shared-key scheme, but is challenging to deploy in heterogeneous environments. PKI works the best in heterogeneous environments and is the most secure authentication method, but it also requires the most time and effort. The particular IPSec approach that is best depends on specific needs and business drivers within each organization.

Performing Security Maintenance on Systems

All the measures previously mentioned will do no good unless systems are kept up to date and properly maintained. A large part of system maintenance thus involves ensuring that system security does not erode over time. Patch management, discussed earlier in this section, is an important part of security maintenance, but security maintenance also requires many activities in addition to patch management. Organizations should, for example, have a centralized audit policy that mandates that system administrators regularly inspect and analyze the logs of each and every computer in their network.* Equally important is regularly inspecting systems to ensure that critical settings that affect security have not been modified without authorization and also that no new unauthorized accounts (regardless of whether they are privileged or unprivileged) have been created. It is also a good practice to perform regular security audits to see which machines are most vulnerable to attack and compromise. Additionally, for critical systems, deploying tools such as Tripwire that regularly

---

* Inspecting audit log output is essential in maintaining security, although such output is not likely to be useful in finding rootkits because hiding mechanisms in rootkits almost always delete or suppress any audit log entries that would indicate the presence of the attacker. Inspecting the output of security event management (SEM) tools that collect a wide variety of output from many sources and then apply event correlation algorithms to identify suspicious events such as rootkit-related activities is thus much more expedient.

check for possible unauthorized changes to file and directory integrity is an important piece of security maintenance. Performing vulnerability assessments, including periodic internal and external penetration testing, is yet another component of security maintenance. Regularly implementing all of these measures will substantially reduce the likelihood that rootkits will be installed.

Limiting the Availability of Compilers

Rootkits have become more complex over time. Although increased complexity has resulted in many advantages for attackers, it has also made installing rootkits considerably more complicated. Many rootkits now consist of many components that need to be compiled and installed, steps that if performed manually require considerable time and also thus increase the likelihood of detection. An increasing number of rootkits thus now contain easy-to-use installation scripts called "makefiles," instructions for compiling and installing programs. Makefiles specify program modules and libraries to be linked in and also include special directives that allow certain modules to be compiled differently should doing so be necessary. Makefiles require that compilers be installed on systems; if compilers are absent from systems that have been successfully attacked, the attackers must first install them, something that increases the time needed to install rootkits. Limiting compilers such that they are installed only on systems for which they are necessary for job-related functions is thus another effective measure against rootkit installation.

Incident Response Considerations

Responding to security-related incidents is often complicated, but the presence of a rootkit makes responding to incidents even more difficult. Incident response includes six stages: preparation, detection, containment, eradication, recovery, and follow-up [1]. Several of these stages, detection, eradication, and recovery, become particularly complex when rootkits have been installed in victim systems.

Detection

As stated previously, discovering most rootkits is difficult because so much information about the attacks that led to the deletion or suppression of their installation; considerable time, effort, and technical prowess are thus likely to be necessary. There is one comforting thought, however—no attacker or rootkit, no matter how proficient, is capable of hiding all the information about an attack, including the presence of a rootkit that has been installed. One or more clues, no matter how small, will be available if proficient investigators and suitable analysis tools are available. Among the clues that are likely to be available are subtle changes in systems, the output of rootkit detection tools, and the output of network monitoring tools.

Change Detection

Unexplained changes in systems are excellent potential indicators of the presence of rootkits. Changes in the number of bytes in files and directories from one point in time to another can, for example, indicate the presence of a rootkit. Almost every rootkit, however, tries to suppress any indication of such changes such that when a command to list directory contents is issued, the size of a file that now contains the rootkit appears to be the same. Suppose that a rootkit has changed the size of an executable in a UNIX system, but has also altered the `ls -al` command (a command used to list all files within a directory, their length, their owner, and so on) so that the output of this command falsely shows that the contents of the file containing the executable was unchanged. The solution for information security professionals is to obtain the output of hashing algorithms such as Secure Hash Algorithm version 1 (SHA1) from one point in time to another. If there is any change in file contents, the computed hash will change. With a reasonably strong hashing algorithm, there is little chance that someone could make changes in the file without the hash for the changed file being different. If a rootkit somehow masqueraded SHA1 hash-value changes that resulted from changing an executable, the change would certainly be detected by comparing the before- and after-change hash values of another hashing algorithm, such as the Message Digest algorithm version 5 (MD5). It is virtually impossible to deceive multiple hashing algorithms by changing the content of a single file, provided that the algorithms are sufficiently strong against cryptanalytic attacks. Using tools such as Tripwire that compute multiple hash values as well as several crypto checksums and other values to detect changes in files and directories is thus one of the most powerful ways to detect the presence of rootkits.

It is unlikely but not impossible for experienced system administrators and system programmers to spot rootkit-caused changes without using special tools, of which Tripwire is only one. Host-based IDSs can also spot suspicious changes that could indicate the presence of rootkits, as can system administration tools such as Tivoli and Unicenter TNG. The `lsof` command, in UNIX and Linux, and `fport`, a Windows tool, both list open ports and the processes that have opened them, although as mentioned before many rootkits change such commands to suppress information about port activity. Forensics software may also be useful in detecting changes in systems. Finally, it is essential that any detection or forensics tools and outputs from such tools be kept offline (e.g., on a CD) and in a physically secure location until they are used; if left on a system, either could be modified by attackers who have compromised the system on which they reside.

Running Tools Designed to Detect Rootkits

Running tools that are specifically designed to find and eradicate rootkits is another possible approach. Free tools such as chkrootkit (for Linux systems) and Rootkit Revealer (for Windows systems) generally use a variety of detection mechanisms to achieve their goals. These tools constantly need to be updated if they are to have a chance of being effective. It is important, however, for information security professionals to realize that these tools are far from perfect; many rootkits' hiding mechanisms are more advanced than rootkit detector and eradication tools' capabilities.

Unfortunately, antivirus and antispyware tools are currently not up to par in detecting Trojan horses, let alone rootkits, for a variety of reasons. First, rootkit writers are aware that their tools must evade detection by antivirus and antispyware software and thus include mechanisms within the rootkit code that enable them to do so. Additionally, antivirus and antispyware software largely relies on malicious code signatures, binary or character strings that distinguish one piece of malicious code from the others, for detection. Much of today's malicious code, rootkits included, uses a variety of signature detection evasion techniques, however. Additionally, signatures, even if they were to work in detecting rootkits, are invariably post hoc in nature; signatures thus cannot be used to recognize malicious code that is used in zero-day exploits. At the same time, however, a growing number of antivirus software vendors are incorporating the ability to scan kernel or user-mode memory for known rootkits. The bottom line is that currently, information security professionals should not rely on antivirus and antispyware software to detect rootkits.

If tools designed specifically for rootkit detection are not all that proficient in detecting rootkits (as mentioned previously), it should be little surprise to realize that antivirus and antispyware software does even worse.

Analyzing Output of Network Monitoring Tools

Monitoring network activity is an effective method for detecting rootkits. Finding connections that make little sense, for example, connections between a billing server of a large corporation and a machine with a domain name that ostensibly belongs to a university, can lead system and network administrators to investigate what has happened to the billing server. If an investigation of a system that has had suspicious connections leads to the discovery that information about other connections, but not the suspicious ones, is available in audit log data, the presence of a rootkit would be a very possible explanation. Activity on certain ports is another possible rootkit indicator. Although evidence of such activity is likely to be hidden on any machine on which a rootkit has been installed, network-based IDSs, IPSs, SEM tools, and firewalls will nevertheless detect port-related activity that may indicate the presence of a rootkit on such a machine. Both network- and host-based IDSs and IPSs can provide information about attempts to install rootkits as well as the presence of rootkits on systems. Aggregating the output of IDSs, IPSs, firewalls, routers, individual systems, and other sources of log data and then correlating it using event correlation software also increases the probability of detecting rootkits on systems. Effective rootkits do not leave obvious indicators of their existence, so correlated clues (no matter how obscure) about the existence of rootkits from multiple sources are in fact often the best way to discover them.

Eradication

Eradication involves eliminating the cause of any incident. If a rootkit is discovered on a system, the first impulse on the part of investigators is normally to delete the rootkit as soon as possible. Doing so is usually not the proper course of action, however. In most cases it is far better to make an image backup, a backup of virtually everything on the compromised system's hard drive (including information that is carefully hidden in places other than in files), as soon as possible. Doing this will enable forensics experts to perform a thorough forensics analysis that will enable them to: (1) preserve evidence to potentially be used in subsequent legal action, (2) analyze the mechanisms used by the rootkit and any other malicious tools that were installed, and (3) use the information to identify other machines that may be compromised on the basis of evidence within the compromised system. Remember—some rootkits are nonpersistent, so making an image backup right away is all the more critical if obtaining a copy of a rootkit is necessary.

And now the bad news—unlike viruses, worms, and most types of Trojan horse programs, rootkits often cannot be surgically deleted. Programs such as chkrootkit (see http://www.chkrootkit.org/) and Rootkit Revealer (see http://www.microsoft.com/technet/sysinternals/utilities/RootkitRevealer. mspx) may be able to delete rootkits, but considerations related to eradicating rootkits are different from those for other types of malware. Rootkits, almost without exception, run with superuser privileges. Any time a system has been compromised at the superuser level, the rootkit and the attacker who installed it could have done almost anything to that system. Discovering all the changes and software replacements is likely to be an almost impossible task, and if forensics experts overlook even one change that has been made, the attacker and the rootkit could regain control of the system shortly afterward. The best thing to do, therefore, is to take no chances—rebuild the system entirely using original installation media. Failure to do so could result in malicious code or unauthorized changes remaining in the compromised system.

Recovery

Recovery means returning compromised systems to their normal mission status. Again, if a rootkit has been installed in a compromised system, rebuilding the system is almost always the best course of action. To ensure that rootkits and other malware do not reappear once a recovered system is up and running again, the system must be rebuilt using original installation media, and data and programs must be as they were before the attack occurred. Additionally, any patches need to be installed to help make sure that the system will not succumb to the same attack(s) that was previously launched against it. Finally, before recovery can be considered complete, a vulnerability scan of the compromised system should be performed to verify that no unpatched vulnerabilities exist.

Conclusion

Rootkits pose a very high level of risk to information and information systems. Information security professionals need to learn about and analyze rootkit-related risk thoroughly and then select, implement, and test appropriate security control measures. A successful risk management strategy includes ensuring that multiple system and network-based security control measures, such as configuring systems appropriately, ensuring that systems are patched, using strong authentication, and other measures, are in place. Because rootkits are so proficient in hiding themselves, extremely strong monitoring and intrusion detection and prevention efforts also need to be implemented. Furthermore, appropriate, efficient incident response procedures and methods serve as another cornerstone in the battle to minimize the damage and disruption caused by rootkits.

In closing, information security professionals need to put the problem of rootkits in proper perspective. Rootkits were first discovered in 1994 [2]; even at that time they were remarkably proficient in hiding themselves and creating backdoor access mechanisms. Since that time, rootkits have improved immensely to the point that many of them are now almost impossible to detect. Some of them are in reality "all-in-one" malware—a complete arsenal of weapons for attackers. Additionally, many current rootkits capture sensitive information and are capable of being part of gigantic botnets that can create massive damage and disruption. The bottom line is that dealing with rootkit-related risk should be at the forefront of the proverbial radar of information security professionals.

References

1. Skoudis, E., *Malware: Fighting Malicious Code*. Upper Saddle River, NJ: Prentice Hall, 2004.
2. Van Wyk, K., Threats to DoD computer systems. Paper presented at 23rd International Information Integrity Institute Forum, Whitehouse Station, New Jersey, October, 1994.

CRYPTOGRAPHY

Chapter 14

Encryption Key Management in Large-Scale Network Deployments

Franjo Majstor and Guy Vancollie

Contents

Introduction

All corporations need to protect their business transactions, customer data, and intellectual property. At a minimum, data loss or compromise can create public relations nightmares and even seriously hurt market reputation. In the long run, it can impact customer relationships or create serious financial damage from fraud, information theft, or public disclosure of intellectual properties. This problem has presented information technology with a technological challenge because the ideal network data protection solution should require no change to network infrastructure, should not impact network performance, must work over any network topology, and must secure any type of traffic. The challenge facing information security professionals is to secure data in motion as has never been possible before. It is obvious that encryption is the solution to addressing confidentiality and integrity of the data while it transits lines that we have no control over; however, its limitations have hampered its deployment, especially on large-scale networks. Standards are normally present when interoperability among different vendor solutions should take place, and multiple good ones have been used, for example, the Internet Protocol security (IPSec) standard framework. Although IPSec delivered a portion of the solution, it also introduced its own limitations and unnecessary overlay to an existing network infrastructure, making it even more difficult to manage, maintain, and operate.

Large-Scale Network Issues

Performance

Not so long ago data network infrastructures were used only for the bulk transfer of data over slow links of various, mostly unreliable, quality. The data carried over those network infrastructures was less important and, even if stolen, modified, or lost, there were always multiple paper copies and forms in existence to replace the data when needed. Nowadays a modern high-speed network infrastructure carries the most crucial pieces of information as well as multiple crucial applications that companies depend upon for their existence. Adding encryption to the communication paths, unless assisted with specialized hardware, typically slows down the overall communication speed and, therefore, impacts the usability of the high-speed communication paths.

Redundancy

High-speed, high-performance networks are required to stay up all the time, no matter what happens with individual communication components. Therefore, modern network design includes multiple redundant devices as well as multiple available paths built into the network itself. Redundancy built into the network keeps the availability of the communication paths between multiple points in the network; however, it often causes difficulty for security mechanisms.

Load Balancing

Multiple redundant paths do not necessarily have to work in a master–slave or active–standby mode, but could be active and used simultaneously to do load balancing and share the traffic load across the multiple links. This is the preferred way for efficient networks to use multiple available links, but it also has, unfortunately, some security implications. Security relationships are typically fixed between peers and are in trouble when they lose peer relationships that have to be dynamically established when network traffic chooses another path to the same destination.

Multicast

Any kind of group communication—multicast is just one of them—requires group security member relationships as well as group member control if any of the communication peers leaves or joins the group. That makes the encrypted group communication extremely difficult, with a heavy overlay of the peer-to-peer relationships that grows exponentially with the number of peers communicating. It is a known mathematical fact that for "n" number of peers it is required to have "$n \times (n - 1)$" peer-to-peer relationships and that times 2 if each direction has to be secured separately.

Multi-Protocol Label Switching

Multi-Protocol Label Switching (MPLS) wide area networks provide most of the long-distance connectivity today and as such are replacing multiple older technologies such as Frame Relay, X.25, or leased lines. MPLS provides quite similar functionality compared to its predecessors through the creation of separate, isolated communication paths based on different labels. Traffic isolation, however, provides neither confidentiality nor authentication of the data traveling via the MPLS network and opens the data to multiple risks when traveling over a shared infrastructure, such as a possible data leakage due to configuration errors or even illegal tapping.

Encryption Options

It has been obvious throughout the history of communication protocols that protection of data while it travels over unsecured data channels could be achieved with encryption. However, encryption has proven to be a difficult task as it requires multiple other elements to be done correctly as well, so as not to impact modern data communication networks. As mentioned earlier, encryption impacts the performance, redundancy, and load balancing of modern-day networks, and also the requirement for any type of group communication makes the use of encryption problematic. Furthermore, there have been several options of where to implement encryption: on the link level, network level, or application level. Let us browse through them briefly to see the pros and cons of each.

Link-Level Encryption

Link-level encryption was one of the earliest types available and had no demand for standardization as there always was a product of the same vendor on both sides of the link. Key management protocols were often also proprietary and built-in as part of the solution. Therefore, the price of such devices was high and when a device failed in a point-to-point topology both had to be replaced. The problems for link-level encryption came with new network media connectivity options, such as mesh topologies as well as multiple different paths through the same media. This led to the option of developing encryption on other levels, such as at the application or network level.

Application-Level Encryption

Application-level encryption is, from a security standpoint, the highest level—as the application that produces the data has the best visibility on how to protect it. It would be great if each and every application had the encryption possibility built-in; however, as security was in the past often not the issue, many legacy applications remained without it and have no option to turn it on. Newer applications mostly have the option to protect the data via encryption; however, each and every one of them has its own different way of how to do it, and that makes scalability as well as intra-application data protection transfer impossible or nonscalable.

Network-Level Encryption

Owing to the limitations and drawbacks of the other earlier mentioned options and levels to encrypt the data, the network layer has ended up as the most frequent choice. Network-level encryption provides for equal protection to legacy applications as well as new applications traversing the same network protocol and requires no other application changes. As Internet Protocol (IP) has become the most dominant network communication protocol today, we will narrow our discussion on the encryption features to within IP with its security protocol framework, IPSec. The IPSec protocol got standardized in the late 1990s and through numerous interoperable implementations, IPSec-based equipment has become much more affordable than link-level encryption devices used to be, but as usual it has its advantages as well as its limitations, which we will focus on going forward.

Limitations of the IPSec Encryption

The IPSec set of request for comment (RFC) standards defined the authentication as well as the encryption of the IP packet. It also defined different modes of operation as well as the Internet key exchange (IKE) automated key-derivation protocol that helps with exchanging the keys based on a predefined time interval or amount of transferred data. Together, IKE and IPSec got wide implementation on routers, layer-three switches, and edge devices such as firewalls, as well as end nodes running on different operating systems. With wide implementation, however, IPSec and IKE have also introduced new limitations. IPSec and IKE are by definition a peer-to-peer protocol that impacts network communications if there are redundant paths or if load balancing is involved. Peer-to-peer trusted relationships also make encrypted group communication very difficult. This is illustrated in Exhibits 14.1 and 14.2. Last but not least, if not implemented in hardware, certain encryption processes also impact the performance of the communication on any higher-speed network connections.

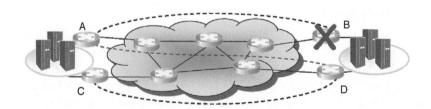

Exhibit 14.1   Redundant network architecture.

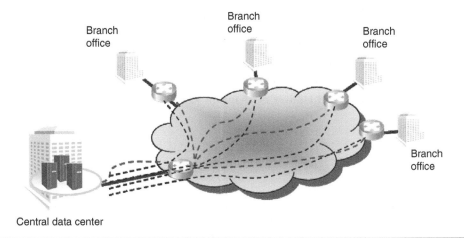

Exhibit 14.2   Group (multicast or broadcast) network architecture.

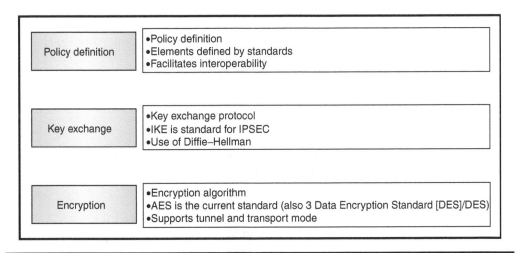

Exhibit 14.3   IPSec/IKE common architecture.

Separation of the Key Management Solution

IPSec and IKE together represent three main functions most often implemented together in the very same, single running platform. These three functions are security policy definition, key exchange, and encryption. The most common implementation for all three functions as one IPSec/IKE architecture is illustrated in Exhibit 14.3. Implementation of all three of the main encryption components on the same physical platform seems to be an obvious choice; however, it brings with it its limitations of peer-to-peer relationships and, therefore, impacts modern network communications. To be able to achieve resilient and redundant network designs, the encryption security architecture should have its components designed the same way. The three main components in essence represent three individual roles: bulk encryption, which could be done on the policy enforcement point (PEP); key management, which a key authority point could take care of; and security policies, which could be done on a management and policy server. This distributed model represented by the three individual layers, management, distribution, and encryption, is illustrated in Exhibit 14.4. Each of the main functional components could hence fulfill its job when implemented on individual platforms, thereby also bringing additional benefits such as scalability. Each of the layers in the three-tier model could be replicated up to the necessary service-scale level and support growth as required for large-scale network designs. The three-tier security architecture is illustrated in Exhibit 14.5. The key distribution layer and policy distribution layer have to be designed with redundancy and failover mechanisms as well as incorporating hardware security

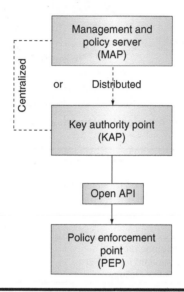

Exhibit 14.4   Distributed policy and key management architecture.

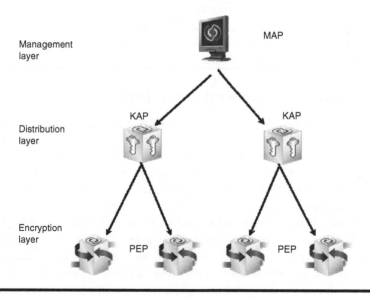

Exhibit 14.5   Three-tier encryption security architecture.

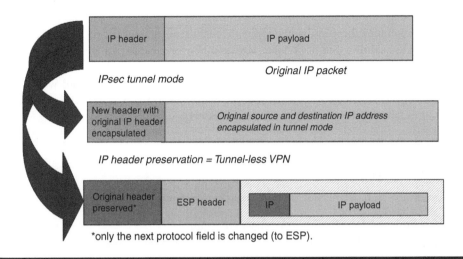

Exhibit 14.6   IPSec tunnel-mode header preservation.

modules for key generations. The key storage has to be a "hack-proof" system with no backdoor and no possible traffic-probing vulnerabilities. An additional problem to solve is security of the traffic between the layers. That could be resolved by utilizing either IKE or other secure but less heavy protocols, such as the Transport Layer Security protocol. Scaling in such a distributed model is built-in from the ground up by design. The three-layer architecture allows scalability of security policies never before possible using IPSec. Grouping networks and network device units together through group policy definitions dramatically simplifies policy generations. Therefore, the layered encryption security architecture can serve many thousands of end-node PEPs in the network and, as well, through the open application programming interface provide access to hundreds of thousands of multivendor devices, such as desktops, notebooks, cell phones, personal digital assistants, and printers.

An additional element that helps break the point-to-point relationship is that PEPs responsible for the bulk encryption doing IPSec maintain the original IP address header, as is illustrated in Exhibit 14.6.

With the original IP header preserved, there is no additional need to create any point-to-point relationships and, even more important, no need to create any overlay network on top of the existing infrastructure. That simplifies the encryption function on the existing modern networks to the maximum possible and as such only adds flexibility to enabling redundancy, load balancing, as well as group broadcast or multicast communication.

Summary

The challenge in front of the information security professional is to secure data in motion like never before. Encryption is the obvious choice for the solution but the solution must work over any network topology and must secure any type of traffic. All of that is to be done preferably without requiring changes to the network infrastructure or impacting the network performance. The IPSec protocol provides part of the solution but is also part of the problem, with its point-to-point nature as well as the network overlay model. A layered encryption security architecture brings a solution to the requirements of modern data protection through the separation of the main roles and functions of encryption into three individual layers. Such a three-tier encryption security architecture brings inherited scalability and no longer requires a network overlay for the generation and distribution of policies and encryption keys. It provides data protection but does not require any changes to network infrastructure, does not impact network performance, and works over any network topology. It is a concept that should, once widely implemented, solve the problem of data protection through encryption in large-scale network deployments.

Further Reading

1. Bauger, M., Weis, B., Hardjono, T., and Harney, H., *The Group Domain of Interpretation*, RFC 3547, IETF Standard, July 2003.
2. Davis, C. R., *IPSec: Securing VPNs*, McGraw-Hill, 2001.
3. Doraswamy, N., and Harkins, D., *IPSec: The New Security Standard for the Internet, Intranets and Virtual Private Networks*, Prentice-Hall PTR, 1999.
4. Ferguson, N., and Schneier, B., *A Cryptographic Evaluation of IPSec*, www.counterpane.com/ipsec.html, April. 1999.
5. Frankel, S., *Demystifying the IPSec Puzzle*, Artech House Inc., 2001.
6. Harkins, D., and Carrel, D., *The Internet Key Exchange (IKE)*, RFC 2409, November 1998.
7. Kent, S., and Atkinson, R., *Security Architecture for the Internet Protocol*, RFC 2401, November 1998.
8. Kent, S., and Atkinson, R., *IP Authentication Header*, RFC 2402, November 1998.
9. Kent, S., and Atkinson, R., *IP Encapsulating Security Payload (ESP)*, RFC 2406, November 1998.
10. Kosiur, D., *Building and Managing Virtual Private Networks*, Wiley Computer Publishing, 1998.
11. Maughan, D., Schertler, M., Schneider, M., and Turner, J., *Internet Security Association and Key Management Protocol (ISAKMP)*, RFC 2408, November 1998.
12. Perlman, R., and Kaufman, C., Key exchange in IPSec: Analysis of IKE, *IEEE Internet Computing*, 4(6), pp. 50–56, 2000.
13. Perlman, R., and Kaufman, C., *Analysis of the IPSec Key Exchange Standard*, WET-ICE Security Conference, MIT, sec.femto.org/wetice-2001/papers/radia-paper.pdf, 2001.
14. Weis, B., Gross, G., and Ignjatic, D., *Multicast Extensions to the Security Architecture for the Internet Protocol*, IETF draft RFC, draft-ietf-msec-ipsec-extensions-04.txt.
15. Weis, B., Hardjono, T., and Harney, H., *The Multicast Group Security Architecture*, RFC 3740, IETF Standard, July 2004.

PHYSICAL SECURITY

Elements of Physical Security

Chapter 15

Mantraps and Turnstiles

R. Scott McCoy

Contents

Introduction

The challenge with most card systems is tailgating. This is when one person unlocks a door using a security credential and three people walk into a secured room. Depending on the criticality of the secured space, this may not be acceptable.

There are many levels of access control, ranging from none to total. Total control implies that every person who enters and leaves a space is authorized, has been granted entry and exit, and that any violation of these rules is identified by an alarm condition. Most facilities focus on controlling who can enter a space through the use of one or more levels of authentication: something someone has, which could be as simple as a key or a company-issued access control token (proximity, contactless smart card, etc.); something someone knows, which could be as simple as a four-digit pin number entered into a keypad (usually integrated into the card reader); or something someone is, such as a fingerprint or retinal scan. For highly restricted areas, a combination of two or even all three may be warranted.

The level of access should correspond to the criticality of the workspace. Although these technologies can be used effectively to ensure with a high degree of confidence that only persons authorized may open a door, they do nothing to ensure that unauthorized persons do not tag along before the door shuts. Mantraps and turnstiles can be used to increase the level of control and reduce or eliminate tailgating.

Mantraps

A mantrap is used when more control on access is desired, but there is no need for total control. One reason may be that it is an entry into a clean room environment where containment is required. The mantrap is accomplished by having two sets of doors, both with access control equipment. The doors are spaced some distance apart, usually in excess of 15 ft, so that it takes the time of the first door to shut before you reach the second door. The idea is that neither door can be opened while the other door is in an open state, thereby making it impossible for someone to piggyback in or rush inside to the secured area unchecked. Mantraps usually have cameras at both the outer and the inner door and are connected by a hallway, so no one can hide their presence when they are being granted access and no one can allow more people in than authorized.

Many states have fire codes that require that free access be allowed from any secured space, usually requiring what is called "no special knowledge" to get out. This means when someone needs to get out due to a fire, they need only push on some easy-to-use latch or crash bar to exit. Because of this, most doors that use an electric strike have free egress by pushing down on a lever to retract the strike and do not require the release of the electric strike for exiting. This would not give the positive control a mantrap requires, so it is better either to keep the door hardware locked or to use a magnetic lock, which holds the door secure until activated by a touch sense bar for exit. With this form of egress, the circuit can be interrupted every time the other door is open, detected by a door contact mounted at each door. In this way, access to the other door is not allowed, thereby providing a mantrap.

If a person does tailgate an authorized worker past the first door, they can be refused entry to the secure area and would need to exit the outer door. No one is actually trapped in a mantrap, because fire codes now prohibit this, but the setup described does protect against a rush of people gaining access into a secured space by tailgating a worker through one open door directly into the restricted space.

A variation of this is used to control vehicle traffic into a secured space. The setup is similar to what is described above, but with more control, because the lanes can be broken down into entrance and exit, eliminating the chance of someone gaining entry while someone else exits. Two gates are spaced a reasonable distance apart to allow only one of whichever type of vehicle uses the site. This can be done to mandate vehicle inspections or to eliminate the possibility of tailgating. For extremely critical areas, vehicle barriers could be used in conjunction with or instead of traditional gates to ensure no vehicle could force its way in.

Turnstiles

Total control may be required for entrance into an area for audit purposes, even for data centers with Sarbanes–Oxley requirements, but usually it is not required for exit. A turnstile can be set to allow free-wheeling exit. Turnstiles are an access control product whose purpose is to ensure positive access control. Only one person per transaction is allowed entry, whether using a subway station token or a security credential to enter a building.

There are three main types of turnstiles: First is the optical turnstile, which does not offer the same level of access control as would be required in some settings and is often accompanied by a security officer (see Figure 15.1).

The second is an enhanced revolving door that is created with a mechanism that will allow only one section of the door to rotate into the secured space at a time (see Figure 15.2).

The last is the traditional type seen in most industrial settings and primarily used for outdoor applications (see Figure 15.3).

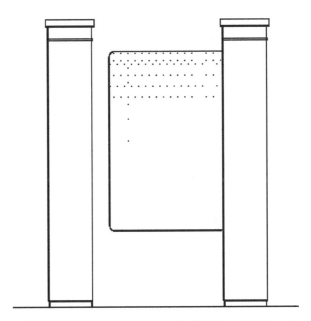

Figure 15.1   Optical turnstile with barrier.

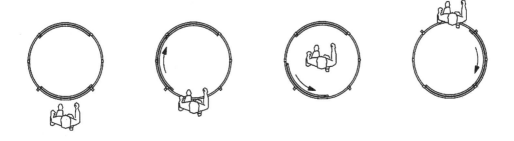

Figure 15.2   Revolving door.

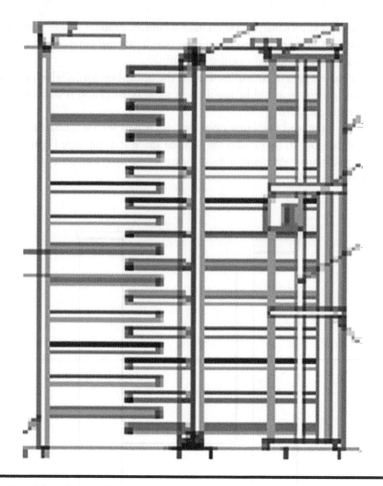

Figure 15.3 Traditional turnstile.

Optical Turnstiles

Security officers have been used for access control in many companies for years, but even if every security officer were perfect and never missed a person or mistook another card for a badge during high traffic times, there is no way for the officer to know if all of those people are still employed, only that they possess a badge and it is their face on the badge. Optical turnstiles are designed to house different types of credential or biometric readers to ensure that everyone entering is still active in the system. Of course, there is still human error, if someone forgets to turn a record inactive in the card access system, but the chance for error is less than relying on visual inspection. Practices should be in place that requires managers to submit a form to remove workers from databases when their employment ends, and emergency practices should be in place for removal of logical and physical access immediately when there is a termination for cause. Then if either the person does not have his or her badge or the manager or human resource personnel forgets to collect it, it will not register as an active card and an alarm should sound. In this way as with all alarms, security professionals should spend their time responding to exceptions and not monitoring normal or authorized transactions.

Optical turnstiles do not provide an actual barrier, with most being at the height of 36 in. and some having small wing barriers or bars to impede entry, whereas others simply alarm. They are designed for high traffic areas usually in corporate offices, where it is impractical to depend on security officers to inspect every badge visually. They are traditionally set up to alarm only when motion is detected moving in one direction for entry without a valid card read and to ignore motion when exiting, but they can be set up to require carding out if desired.

Revolving Doors

Revolving doors can also be set up for either entry only or both entry and exit control. The benefit of a revolving door is that, unlike an optical turnstile, it can be set up to allow only one person at a time entry or exit into a space and cannot be circumvented. The drawback of a revolving door is that because of the tight control, the doors move slowly and are not recommended for high traffic areas. They are best suited for highly restricted areas where tailgating is unacceptable. Exit from such an area can also be completely controlled and therefore tracked, but due to fire codes in most countries, these revolving doors are designed with a breakout feature that collapses the sections of the door to allow for emergency exit. An alarm should be connected to the door in case someone crashes out to avoid recording his or her exit.

Traditional Turnstiles

These are the turnstiles that most people envision when they hear the word. They are metal and are most commonly found in sporting arenas and parking lots. The newer models function like the revolving doors described earlier, but are designed for outdoor applications.

Because all types of turnstiles can record all entry to a controlled space, there are safety benefits that can be used when tied into most card access systems. A common feature that is mostly unused is the muster feature of card access systems. The muster feature keeps track of whoever enters and exits a specific space. For the feature to work, everyone who enters or exits must register his or her token for both entry and exit. If this does not happen, the software will think that someone is still in the space although it is actually empty or never record that they were in the space even if they are actually inside. This feature is beneficial during an evacuation for fire or chemical release, when it is critical to get a positive count of who is left inside a building or industrial complex. Fire fighters will be risking their lives entering these dangerous areas, and it is important for them to know if there are two or ten people left inside or if there are none, so there may not be a reason to enter at all.

If a muster feature is desired, then the location of exit readers is very important and may require additional readers at more remote locations to ensure a safe and speedy exit. So, for normal daily operations, there may be a row of two or three turnstiles at every main entry point with card readers on the inside and outside of a fence or perimeter wall, which require one card read per entry and exit request. For emergencies, there can be additional readers mounted at muster points a safe distance from the building, and the turnstiles can both be connected to the fire system and have a manual override to allow free-wheeling exit so as not to slow evacuation. Then at the muster point the workers can each run their card to register an exit. Most card access features run a report every so many minutes based on preference during an event, each showing fewer and fewer names until the site is empty or only the last few people left inside are listed.

If the same muster feature were used in a more limited way at, say, a lab inside a larger complex, a revolving door could be used instead of a more traditional turnstile. Normal operation can also require some form of granted access using a credential or biometric for entry and egress with a remote muster reader at a safe distance, if muster is required, or just entry if muster is not required.

Conclusion

There are many types of access control methodologies and technologies. As with most solutions related to security, a risk assessment should be done and a description of what is trying to be accomplished written. A security professional should never lose sight of the original goal, though in the quest for a solution it is easy to do so. If such an assessment indicates that there must be protection from tailgating above what a single door can provide, then a mantrap or some form of turnstile may be the answer. If positive control of entry for audit or life safety reasons is called for, then either a traditional turnstile or a revolving door (for office applications) may be required. Regardless of the access control product selected, solutions requiring this level of control should always be accompanied with video surveillance. Any camera covering higher level access control should be recorded at all times and with enough definition and number of frames so that a positive identification can be made.

Whatever level of control is required; there are a variety of access control products available to meet the need. Make sure before a solution is selected that it meets the requirements of the restricted area.

SECURITY ARCHITECTURE AND DESIGN

Principles of Computer and Network Organizations, Architectures, and Designs

Chapter 16

Service-Oriented Architecture and Web Services Security

Glenn J. Cater

Contents

The concept of service-oriented architecture (SOA) has been around in various forms for some time, but the SOA model has really become popular of late because of advances in Web technology, Web services, and standards. Although the concept of an SOA is not tied to a specific technology, in most cases SOA now refers to a distributed system using Web services for communication. Other examples of SOA architectures are primarily based upon remote procedure calls, which use binary or proprietary standards that cause challenges with interoperability. Web services solve the problems of interoperability because they are based upon eXtensible Markup Language (XML), by nature an interoperable standard. Significant effort is being put into developing security standards for Web services to provide integrity, confidentiality, authentication, trust, federated identities, and more. Those security standards will be the focus of this chapter, which will cover XML, XML encryption, XML signature, Simple Object Access Protocol (SOAP), Security Assertion Markup Language (SAML), WS-Security, and other standards within the WS-Security family.

Introduction

So what is an SOA? SOA is an architectural model based upon independent (or loosely coupled) services, with well-defined interfaces designed in such a way as to promote reuse. SOA fits extremely well with an architecture based on Web services, which by nature meet the definition of loose coupling and well-defined interfaces. For instance, as an example of a service in SOA, imagine a user directory that is accessible via Web services. In this example, the interface may specify functions, or methods, that include searching the directory (searchDirectory), password resets (resetPassword), updating user information (updateUser), and adding and removing users (addUser, removeUser). As long as the interface is adequately defined, the consumer of the service does not need to know how the service is implemented to use it. Figure 16.1 illustrates a simplified SOA.

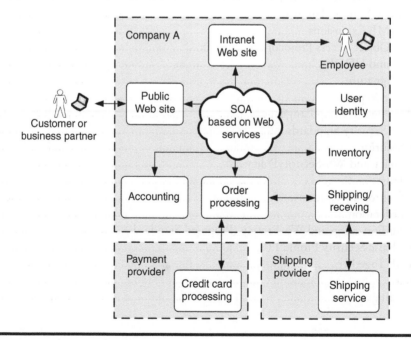

Figure 16.1   Simplified SOA example.

Figure 16.1 shows that each service is reasonably independent and has a well-defined purpose. The idea behind SOA is that, provided the services and their interfaces are designed well, they can be combined together in different ways to build different types of applications. For example, the order-processing service may be accessible from both the public Web site for placing orders and the internal Web site for sales and marketing purposes. Services expose their functionality through industry standard Web service interfaces described using the Web Services Description Language (WSDL), which is discussed later in this chapter.

In the simple example mentioned earlier, there is no security shown on Figure 16.1. To add security to this picture some of the following need to be addressed:

■ Network security, operating system security (server hardening), application security, and physical security
■ Transport security, typically via the use of Secure Sockets Layer (SSL)
■ Web service security, through the use of the Web Service-Security family (WS-*) of standards for securing Web services messages
■ Utilizing other WS-Security extensions to provide trust relationships between the company, the payment provider, and the shipping provider

Web services and Web Services Security standards make heavy use of XML. XML has revolutionized data exchange because of its simplicity and power. As a simple, human-readable, text format XML has facilitated data exchange between applications and businesses even across dissimilar systems.

The remainder of this chapter discusses Web services and the methods used to secure applications and data in an SOA environment. XML, XML encryption, XML signature, SOAP, SAML, and Web Services Security standards will also be covered as part of this chapter.

Foundations for Web Services and Web Services-Security

Web services and Web Services Security are based upon a number of standards that should be understood to some extent by a security practitioner. The idea is to provide an overview of the relevant standards here and how they fit together. Then for some of the more complex standards we will delve into more detail in later sections.

eXtensible Markup Language

XML is the basic building block upon which all the other Web services standards and Web Services Security standards are built. XML is a free, open standard recommended by the World Wide Web Consortium (W3C) as a method of exchanging data using a simple text-based format. The fact that XML is a simple, human-readable format and works across heterogeneous systems makes it perfect for Web services and SOAs for which the service and the consumer (client) may be on different platforms.

The example in Figure 16.2 is a snippet of XML describing a person. This simple example shows how XML can be easily read by a human being. The structure of the XML clearly identifies this as data related to a person (see the Person element in Figure 16.2). So in addition to exchange of data, the XML gives some understanding of what the data represents.

```
<?xml version="1.0"?>
<Person>
    <First_Name>John</First_Name>
    <Last_Name>Doe</Last_Name>
    <Eye_Color>Hazel</Eye_Color>
    <Height>5'10"</Height>
    <Date_Of_Birth>February 21, 1982</Date_Of_Birth>
</Person>
```

Figure 16.2   Simple XML example.

XML Extensions

Although not really important for the understanding of how XML relates to Web Services Security, there are some extensions to XML that should be included for completeness.

XML Schema is an important extension that allows the structure of XML to be defined similar to the way in which a SQL database schema is defined. Among other things, XML Schema specifies what the structure of the XML should be, such as the order in which elements appear, how many of each element is allowed, and the data types. XML Schema is useful for creating specifications and for automatically validating the correctness of XML.

XML also has the concept of "XML namespaces." XML namespaces provide a way to avoid naming conflicts. For example, imagine that there are two different definitions of an employee in XML; to differentiate them XML namespaces can be used. The way this is done is by prefixing the name with a namespace prefix, for example <abc:Employee>, where abc is the namespace prefix that contains a definition of the employee type.

Other extensions exist that provide powerful ways to extract and query data in an XML message. These extensions are called XPath and XQuery. XPath provides a way to reference parts of the XML structure, whereas XQuery is a powerful query language that allows queries to be written against the XML data, similar to SQL, which is the query language for relational databases.

Simple Object Access Protocol

SOAP is an important messaging protocol that forms the basis for the Web services protocol stack. SOAP messages are designed to be independent of a transport protocol, but are most often transmitted via HTTP or HTTPS when used with Web services. SOAP messages are not tied to the HTTP protocol, however, and may also be used in message queuing systems, sent through e-mail, or via other transport mechanisms.

The SOAP standard is based upon XML and defines the structure of messages that can be passed between systems. Messages defined in SOAP have an envelope, a header, and a body as shown in Figure 16.3. The SOAP header allows for the inclusion of security elements such as digital signatures and encryption within the message. Although security elements are not restricted only to the header, it is used heavily with WS-S standards to transmit security information with the message.

There are two primary messaging modes used by SOAP—"document" mode and remote procedure call (RPC) mode. Document mode is good for one-way transmission of messages, in which the sender submits the SOAP message but does not expect a response. RPC mode is more commonly used and is a request–response model in which the sender submits the SOAP request and then waits for a SOAP response.

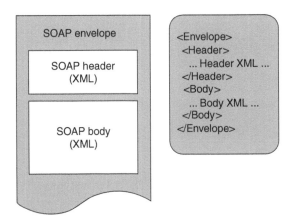

Figure 16.3   An SOAP message.

WSDL and UDDI

The Web Services Description Language (WSDL) and Universal Description, Discovery, and Integration (UDDI) standards allow a consumer of a Web service to understand how to find a Web service and how to use that service. This includes the following:

a. Discovery of basic information about the service such as the service name
b. Where to find the service, including network endpoints and protocol used
c. How to call the service (the service contract)

WSDL is essentially metadata in the form of XML that describes how to call a Web service. There is a security concern with the protection of the WSDL data, because if it falls into the wrong hands it can expose information about your network. The WSDL metadata may be stored as an XML file, but is often available via a URL on the same application server where the Web service is hosted. The WSDL should be made available only to authorized users of the service. Later in this chapter, we will discuss how security policy requirements are included in WSDL.

UDDI is different in that it defines a standard for a directory of Web services. This allows other applications or organizations to discover the WSDL for a Web service that meets their need. Businesses publish the WSDL for their Web service in the directory so that it can be easily discovered by others. UDDI directories can be hosted publicly on the Internet or internally within corporations to allow services to be discovered dynamically. Security of UDDI directories must be maintained to prevent man-in-the-middle attacks, by which a fake Web service could be published in place of a real one. UDDI builds upon other Web Services Security standards to ensure integrity and trust for the data within the directory, which is particularly important for publicly accessible directories.

XML Signature

XML signature provides for integrity and authentication of XML data through the use of digital signatures and can be applied not only to XML but to any digital content. The primary use within Web Services Security is to sign XML messages to ensure integrity and to prove the identity of

```
<Signature ID?>
  <SignedInfo>
    <CanonicalizationMethod/>
    <SignatureMethod/>
    (<Reference URI? >
      (<Transforms>)?
      <DigestMethod>
      <DigestValue>
    </Reference>)+
  </SignedInfo>
  <SignatureValue>
  (<KeyInfo>)?
  (<Object ID?>)*
</Signature>

? = Zero or One Occurrence
+ = One or More Occurrences
* = Zero or More Occurrences
```

Figure 16.4   Informal XML signature syntax.

the signer. Figure 16.4 shows an informal representation of the XML signature syntax. The details are removed to simplify explanation of the structure. Unfortunately, a more complete explanation of how digital signatures work is beyond the scope of this discussion.

XML signature is itself represented as XML, as Figure 16.4 shows. The structure contains the following elements:

- Signature is the containing element that identifies that this is a digital signature.
- SignedInfo contains the references to, and digests of, the data that is digitally signed.
- CanonicalizationMethod refers to the way the SignedInfo element is prepared before the signature is calculated. The reason for this is because different platforms may interpret data slightly differently (e.g., carriage returns <CR> versus carriage return/line feeds <CRLF>), which would cause signatures to compute differently on different platforms.
- SignatureMethod refers to the algorithm used for signature generation or validation, for example *dsa-sha1*, which refers to the use of the DSA algorithm with the SHA-1 hashing function.
- The Reference element is complex, but in a nutshell it refers to the data being signed, which is either part of the same XML data, or a uniform resource identifier (URI) that refers to external data, such as a document, Web page, or other digital content. In addition, the reference element defines transforms that will affect the content prior to being passed to the digest for computing the hash (via DigestMethod). The resultant hash value is stored as DigestValue.
- SignatureValue is the actual computed signature value. Rather than digitally signing the actual content, the signature is computed over SignedInfo so that all the references, algorithms, and digest values are digitally signed together, which ensures the integrity of the data being signed.
- KeyInfo enables the recipient to obtain the key needed to validate the signature, if necessary. This structure is fairly complex and is described in more detail under XML Encryption.
- The Object element contains arbitrary XML data that can be referenced within SignedInfo. It can also include a Manifest element, which provides an alternate list of references, where

```
<Signature Id="MySignature"
  xmlns="http://www.w3.org/2000/09/xmldsig#">
<SignedInfo>
  <CanonicalizationMethod
    Algorithm="http://www.w3.org/TR/2001/REC-xml-c14n-20010315"/>
  <SignatureMethod
    Algorithm="http://www.w3.org/2000/09/xmldsig#dsa-sha1"/>
  <Reference URI="http://www.company.com/file.doc">
    <Transforms>
      <Transform
        Algorithm="http://www.w3.org/TR/2001/REC-xml-c14n-20010315"/>
    </Transforms>
    <DigestMethod
      Algorithm="http://www.w3.org/2000/09/xmldsig#sha1"/>
    <DigestValue>j90j2fnkfew3...</DigestValue>
  </Reference>
</SignedInfo>
<SignatureValue>GFh8fw3greU...</SignatureValue>
<KeyInfo>
  <KeyValue>
    <DSAKeyValue>
      <P>...</P><Q>...</Q><G>...</G><Y>...</Y>
    </DSAKeyValue>
  </KeyValue>
</KeyInfo>
</Signature>
```

Figure 16.5   XML signature example.

the integrity of the list itself is validated, but the integrity of the actual items will not invalidate the signature. The purpose of such a list might be to include an inventory of items that should accompany the manifest. It also defines a SignatureProperties element by which other properties of the signature are stored such as the date and time the signature was created.

The XML signature standard defines three types of digital signatures, which are enveloped, enveloping, and detached. Enveloped signature refers to a signature on XML data, whereby the Signature element is contained within the body of the XML. Enveloping signatures contain the XML content that is being signed, and this is where the Object element is used to contain the data that is signed. Finally the detached signature type signs content that is external to the XML signature, defined by an URI, which may be external digital content, but can also include elements within the same XML data such as sibling elements. Figure 16.5 provides an example of a detached signature.

As discussed earlier, XML signature allows any type of digital content to be signed, and there are uses for XML signature that go beyond the scope of Web Services Security. However, this overview of XML signature is intended to provide a foundation for understanding how it relates to Web Services Security.

XML Encryption

By design, XML is a plain text format with no security built in. XML encryption provides data confidentiality through a mechanism for encrypting XML content that relies on the use of shared

```
<EncryptedData Id? Type? MimeType? Encoding?>
  <EncryptionMethod/>?
  <ds:KeyInfo>
    <EncryptedKey>?
    <AgreementMethod>?
    <ds:KeyName>?
    <ds:RetrievalMethod>?
    <ds:*>?
  </ds:KeyInfo>?
  <CipherData>
    <CipherValue>?
    <CipherReference URI?>?
  </CipherData>
  <EncryptionProperties>?
</EncryptedData>

? = Zero or One Occurrence
+ = One or More Occurrences
* = Zero or More Occurrences
```

Figure 16.6 Informal XML encryption syntax.

symmetric encryption keys. Standard key exchange techniques based on public-key cryptography provide secrecy for the shared key. Typically the shared key is included within the XML message in an encrypted form, is referenced by name or URI, or is derived from some key exchange data. Symmetric encryption keys are used to encrypt data for performance reasons because public-key encryption can be very slow in comparison.

Figure 16.6 shows an informal representation of the XML encryption syntax. The details are removed to simplify explanation of the structure.

Like XML signature, XML encryption is itself represented as XML, as Figure 16.6 shows. The structure contains the following elements:

- EncryptedData is the containing element that identifies that this is encrypted data.
- EncryptionMethod defines the encryption algorithm that is used to encrypt the data, such as Triple-DES (3DES). This is an optional element and if it is not present, then the recipient must know what algorithm to use to decrypt the data.
- ds:KeyInfo contains information about the encryption key that was used to encrypt the message. Either the actual key is embedded in encrypted form or there is some information that allows the key to be located or derived.
- EncryptedKey contains an encrypted form of the shared key. As mentioned previously this key will typically be encrypted using public-key cryptography. There may be multiple recipients of a message, each with their own encrypted key element.
- AgreementMethod is an alternate way of deriving a shared key by using a method such as Diffie–Hellman. Providing key agreement methods means that the key does not need to be previously shared or embedded within the EncryptedKey element.
- ds:KeyName provides another way of identifying the shared encryption key by name.
- ds:RetrievalMethod provides a way to retrieve the encryption key from a URI reference, either contained within the XML or external to it.
- ds:* refers to the fact that there is other key information, such as X.509v3 keys, PGP keys, and SPKI keys that can be included.

```
<EncryptedData xmlns='http://www.w3.org/2001/04/xmlenc#'
  Type='http://www.w3.org/2001/04/xmlenc#Element'/>
  <EncryptionMethod
    Algorithm='http://www.w3.org/2001/04/xmlenc#tripledes-cbc'/>
    <ds:KeyInfo xmlns:ds='http://www.w3.org/2000/09/xmldsig#'>
      <ds:KeyName>John Doe</ds:KeyName>
    </ds:KeyInfo>
  <CipherData><CipherValue>F59E7F12</CipherValue></CipherData>
</EncryptedData>
```

Figure 16.7 Example of an XML-encrypted message.

- CipherData is the element that contains the actual encrypted data, either with CypherValue as the encrypted data encoded as base64 text or by using CypherReference to refer to the location of the encrypted data, in the XML or otherwise.
- EncryptionProperties contains additional properties such as the date and time the data was encrypted.

Figure 16.7 shows an example of an XML-encrypted message. The encrypted data is clearly visible in the CipherValue element.

This basic overview of the XML encryption standard helps to give some background on how data confidentiality can be achieved with XML; however, there is much more detail than can be covered here.

The XML signature and XML encryption standards together form the basic security building blocks upon which the rest of the WSS standards rely.

Security Assertion Markup Language

SAML is a standard framework based upon XML for communicating user identity, user entitlements, and user attributes between organizations or entities in separate security domains. SAML builds upon XML signature and XML encryption to provide integrity, confidentiality, and authentication of SAML assertions.

SAML allows an entity or organization to vouch for the identity of an individual, via a SAML assertion (a portable XML authentication token). The SAML assertion can be presented as proof of identity to another entity provided a trust relationship has been established between the two parties. This can be important for SOAs for which services are located within separate companies or security domains. This concept is really the basis of federated identity, which insulates organizations from the details of authentication and identity management within other organizations.

SAML attempts to solve several problems:

- Web single sign-on—by which a user can sign into one Web site and then later sign into a second related Web site using the credentials (a SAML assertion) provided by the first site.
- Delegated identity—by which credentials supplied to an initial Web site or service can be utilized by that service to perform actions on behalf of the user. An example is a travel Web site, which can pass the user identity to other services to perform airline, hotel, and car rental reservations.

■ Brokered single sign-on—by which a third-party security service authenticates the user. The credentials provided by the third-party security service can then be used to authenticate to multiple Web sites.
■ Attribute-based authorization—by which attributes about the user are placed into the SAML assertion. These attributes are then used to make authorization decisions. For example, user "John Doe" has level "director" in the "human resources" department; based upon these attributes he is allowed certain access to the human resources systems.

Within the SAML assertion will be some information about a user's identity, such as the user's e-mail address, X.509 subject name, Kerberos principal name, or an attribute such as employee identification number. For privacy purposes, SAML 2.0 introduced the concept of pseudonyms (or pseudorandom identifiers), which can be used in place of other types of identifiers, thereby hiding personal identification information such as an e-mail address. SAML provides two main ways to confirm the subject's identity. One way is referred to as "holder of key," where the sender of the message (the subject) typically holds the key that was used to digitally sign the message. The other confirmation method is referred to as "sender vouches," which means that the digital signature on the message was created by a trusted third party.

This description of SAML is intended to provide some understanding of where it fits within SOAs. By leveraging trust relationships between service providers, SAML provides loose coupling and independence with respect to user identity. SAML is also referenced by the WS-S standards as a type of security token.

Web Services Security Standards

To gain an understanding of how all the Web Services Security protocols fit together, refer to the illustration in Figure 16.8. This diagram shows how XML signature, XML encryption, and SOAP form the foundation of the stack, with the other Web Services Security standards building upon them. Other standards, such as WSDL, UDDI, SAML, WS-Policy, and WS-PolicyAttachment

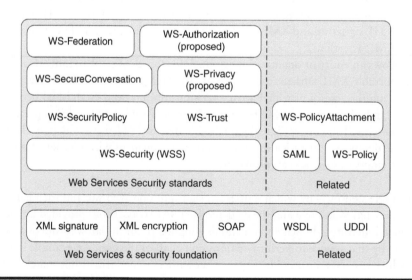

Figure 16.8   WS-S standards.

are listed down the right-hand side of the Figure 16.8 that have relationships to the security standards, but are not specifically security standards themselves.

It is clear from Figure 16.8 that the WS-Security protocol suite is complex, which can serve to discourage adoption of these standards into an SOA, particularly for application developers whose job is complicated by these security protocols. This complexity can lead to a reliance on SSL and firewall policies to provide point-to-point security for SOAP messages. Fortunately, tools are available to simplify integration of security into Web services and SOA.

WS-Security

The WS-Security standard, also referred to as WSS: SOAP Message Security, specifies extensions to SOAP that provide message integrity, message confidentiality, and message authentication. WS-Security leverages XML signature to ensure that the integrity of the message is maintained and XML encryption to provide confidentiality of the message. Security tokens are supported for authentication purposes to provide assurance that the message originated from the sender identified in the message.

There are three categories of security tokens that are defined by WS-Security: username tokens, binary security tokens, and XML tokens. Each of the security tokens supported by WS-Security fits within one of these categories. Examples of security tokens are usernames and passwords (UsernameToken), Kerberos tickets (BinarySecurityToken), X.509v3 certificates (BinarySecurityToken), and SAML (XML Token). The WS-Security header is designed to be extensible to add additional security token types.

Figure 16.9 shows where the WS-Security SOAP extensions appear within the header of the SOAP message.

```
<S11:Envelope>
  <S11:Header>
    <wsse:Security>
      (<wsse:UsernameToken>|
       <wsse:BinarySecurityToken>|
       [..XML Token..])*
      <ds:Signature>
        ...
        <ds:Reference URI="#MsgBody">
        ...
      </ds:Signature>*
      <xenc:ReferenceList>
        <xenc:DataReference URI="#MsgBody"/>
      </xenc:ReferenceList>*
    </wsse:Security>
  </S11:Header>
  <S11:Body>
    <!-- XML Encrypted Body -->
    <xenc:EncryptedData Id="MsgBody">
      ...
      <xenc:CipherData>
    </xenc:EncryptedData>
  </S11:Body>
</S11:Envelope>
```

Figure 16.9   An SOAP message with WS-S extensions.

The example in Figure 16.9 shows that the structure of a SOAP message is altered when WS-Security extensions are added. It also shows how the security tokens, XML signature, and XML encryption fit within the WS-Security (wsse) header. The receiver of a message with WS-Security extensions processes the extensions in the order they appear in the header, so in this case the signature is verified on the message body and then the message is decrypted.

The following five types of tokens are discussed in version 1.1 of the standard:

- Username token, which is the most basic type of token. A UsernameToken contains a username to identify the sender and it can also contain a password as plain text, a hashed password, a derived password, or an S/KEY password. Obviously, the use of plain-text passwords is strongly discouraged.
- X.509 token, which is a BinarySecurityToken, identifies an X.509v3 certificate that is used to digitally sign or encrypt the SOAP message through the use of XML signature or XML encryption.
- Kerberos token, which is also a BinarySecurityToken, includes a Kerberos ticket used to provide authentication. Ticket granting tickets (TGT) and service tickets (ST) are supported.
- SAML token, which is an XML token, provides a SAML assertion as part of the SOAP security header.
- Rights expression language (REL) token, which is an XML token, provides an ISO/IEC 21000 or MPEG-21 license for digital content. This type of token is used for communicating the license to access, consume, exchange, or manipulate digital content.

WS-Security allows for the inclusion of time stamps within the SOAP security header. Time stamps can be required (see WS-Policy and WS-SecurityPolicy) to determine the time of creation or expiration of SOAP messages.

In addition, WS-Security defines how to add attachments to SOAP messages in a secure manner by providing confidentiality and integrity for attachments. Support for both multipurpose Internet mail extensions (MIME) attachments and XML attachments is provided.

SOAP messages and attachments may be processed by different intermediaries along the route to the final recipient, and WS-Security allows parts of messages to be targeted to different recipients to provide true end-to-end security. There is an important distinction between point-to-point security technologies such as SSL and end-to-end security in which there are multiple intermediaries. A possible scenario is that one intermediary might need to perform some processing on a message before passing the message along; however, some parts of the message are confidential and intended only for the final recipient. SSL would not provide the necessary security in this scenario.

WS-Policy and WS-SecurityPolicy

The WS-Policy standard by itself is not directly related to security. Its purpose is to provide a framework for describing policy requirements in a machine-readable way. A policy might describe communication protocols, privacy requirements, security requirements, or any other type of requirement. WS-SecurityPolicy builds upon the WS-Policy framework to define security policies for WS-Security, WS-Trust, and WS-SecureConversation.

The following types of assertions are available within WS-SecurityPolicy:

- Protection assertions (integrity, confidentiality, and required elements), which define which portions of a message should be signed or encrypted and which header elements must be present.

- Token assertions, which specify the types of security token that must be included (or not included), such as UsernameToken, IssuedToken (third-party-issued token, e.g., SAML), X509Token, KerberosToken, SpnegoContextToken (used with WS-Trust), SecurityContext-Token (external), SecureConversationToken (used with WS-SecureConversation), SamlToken, RelToken, HttpsToken (requires use of HTTPS).
- Security-binding assertions, which define requirements for cryptographic algorithms, time stamps, and the order of signing and encrypting; whether the signature must be encrypted or protected; and whether signatures must cover the entire SOAP header and body.
- WS-Security assertions, which indicate which aspects of WS-Security must be supported within the message.
- WS-Trust assertions, which define policy assertions related to WS-Trust.

There is a related standard, called WS-PolicyAttachment, that defines attachment points within WSDL at which security policies can be defined. This provides a mechanism for describing the security policy associated with a Web service along with the Web service interface definition.

WS-Trust

WS-Trust builds upon WS-Security and WS-Policy to define mechanisms for issuing, renewing, and validating security tokens. The WS-Trust model has many similarities to Kerberos, and there are direct analogies such as delegation and forwarding of security tokens. Of course WS-Trust is designed to work over Web services and with many types of security tokens, such as X.509, Kerberos, XML tokens, and password digests. WS-Trust can also extend to trust relationships over the Internet, whereas Kerberos is more suited to providing trust within intranet-type scenarios. WS-Federation, discussed later in this chapter, builds upon these principles and adds mechanisms to provide a framework for implementing identity federation services.

In the WS-Trust model shown in Figure 16.10, the Web service has a policy that defines what security tokens are required to use the service (via WSDL). To access the Web service, the requester needs a valid security token that the Web service understands. To obtain a valid security token, the requester may directly request a token from the security token service (STS), via a RequestSecurityToken request. Assuming the requester adequately proves its claims (via digital

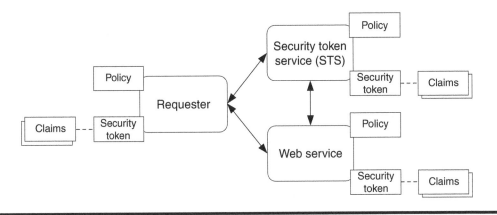

Figure 16.10 WS-Trust security model.

signatures) to the STS and meets the STS policy, the STS will respond with a RequestSecurity-TokenResponse containing a new token signed by the STS. This new token will be in a format the Web service understands, even if the client and Web service support different authentication mechanisms. For example, say the client understands X.509 certificates only and the Web service understands SAML only, then the STS can issue a SAML token for the requester to present to the Web service.

WS-Trust addresses the issue of trust in the security tokens by providing mechanisms for brokering trust relationships through the use of one or more STSs. Trust is established through relationships between the requester and an STS, between the Web service and an STS, and between STSs. So the Web service need not directly trust the requester or the STS it uses to accept security tokens, as long as there is a trust relationship between the requester's STS and the Web service's STS.

WS-SecureConversation

The WS-SecureConversation standard builds upon WS-S and WS-Trust to define the concept of a security context, or session between services. Establishing a security context aims to alleviate some of the potential security problems with WS-S, such as message replay attacks and support for challenge–response security protocols.

There are three different ways to establish the security context.

■ An STS (see WS-Trust) is used, whereby the initiator requests the STS to create a new security context token.
■ The initiator is trusted to create the security context itself and sends it along with a message.
■ A new security context is created via a negotiation between participants, typically using the WS-Trust model.

An advantage of WS-SecureConversation is that it optimizes multiple secure Web service calls between services by performing the authentication step only once for the conversation, by reducing message size with the use of a small context identifier, and by performing only fast symmetric cryptography (using the shared secret keys). WS-SecureConversation uses public-key cryptography to derive shared secret keys for use with the conversation.

WS-Federation

WS-Federation builds upon WS-Security, WS-Policy, WS-SecurityPolicy, WS-Trust, and WS-Secure Conversation to allow security identity and attributes to be shared across security boundaries. As its name suggests, WS-Federation provides a framework for implementing federated identity services.

WS-Federation defines certain entities.

■ Principal is an end user, an application, a machine, or another type of entity that can act as a requester.
■ STS, as defined in WS-Trust, issues and manages security tokens such as identity tokens and cryptographic tokens. The STS is often combined with an identity provider role as STS/IP.

- Identity provider is a special type of STS that performs authentication and makes claims about identities via security tokens.
- Attribute service provides additional information about the identity of the requester to authorize, process, or personalize a request.
- Pseudonym service allows a requester (a principal) to have different aliases for different services and optionally to have the pseudonym change per service or per log-in. Pseudonym services provide identity mapping services and can optionally provide privacy for the requester, by utilizing different identities across providers.
- Validation service is a special type of STS that uses WS-Trust mechanisms to validate provided tokens and determine the level of trust in the provided tokens.
- Trust domain or realm is an independently administered security space, such as a company or organization. Passing from one trust domain to another involves crossing a trust boundary.

These services can be arranged in different ways to meet different requirements for trust, from simple trust scenarios through to quite complex trust scenarios. The example in Figure 16.11 illustrates a fairly complex scenario in which the requester first requests a token from the STS/IP it trusts. (1) The security token is then presented to the resource's STS to request a token to access the resource. (2) Assuming the requester's token is valid, the resource's STS will issue a new token, which is then presented to the Web resource to request access. (3) The Web service resource at some point needs to perform work on behalf of the principal, so it queries another STS/IP in a separate security domain to obtain a delegated security token. (4) Assuming the Web service has the appropriate proof that it is allowed to perform delegation, the STS/IP will issue a security token. (5) This delegated security token is then presented to the resource on behalf of the principal. The chain of trust between the requester and the resource in trust domain C can be followed in the Figure 16.11.

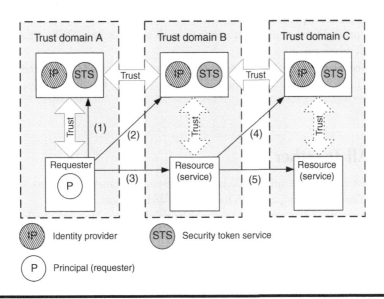

Figure 16.11   WS-Federation example.

WS-Federation introduces models for direct trust, direct brokered trust, indirect brokered trust, delegated trust, and federated trust relationships. Other services can be added to the picture, such as attribute and pseudonym services for attribute-based authorization, role-based authorization, membership, and personalization. Pseudonym services store alternate identity information, which can be used in cross-trust domain scenarios to support identity aliases and identity mapping.

WS-Federation also describes a way for participants to exchange metadata such as the capabilities, security requirements, and characteristics of the Web services that form the federation. This exchange of metadata is achieved through the use of another standard called WS-MetadataExchange, which builds primarily upon WSDL and WS-Policy.

WS-Authorization and WS-Privacy (Proposed Standards)

As these standards are not yet published, they are mentioned here just for completeness. WS-Privacy is a proposed standard language for describing privacy policies for use with Web services. The standard is intended for use by organizations to state their privacy policies and to indicate their conformance with those policies. WS-Authorization is a proposed standard for how to describe authorization policies for Web services using a flexible authorization language. The standard will describe how authorization claims may be specified in a security token and validated at the endpoint.

WS-I Basic Security Profile 1.0

With the large number of WS-* security standards, vendors are implementing them at different times, and not all of the options are common from one vendor's system to the next. WS-I Basic Security Profile 1.0 is intended to provide a baseline for WS-Security interoperability among different vendor's products. The idea is that if the products conform to the Basic Security Profile 1.0, then they should be interoperable at least to some level. This can be important when implementing SOAs with products from different vendors, such as Sun's Java J2EE, BEA Weblogic, and Microsoft's .NET platform.

The Basic Security Profile 1.0 supports a good number of security extensions, including Kerberos, SAML, X.509, and username tokens and support for SSL transport-layer security (HTTPS).

Putting It All Together

Now that we have covered the suite of Web Services Security standards, we can apply this knowledge to the problem of securing an SOA based upon Web services.

It is important to note that traditional security principles should form the basis of a secure SOA. The environment in which the systems are running should be managed appropriately to ensure that the organization's security policies are satisfied and that regulatory requirements placed upon the organization are being met. This includes attention to network security, operating system security, application security (including the Web services infrastructure), and physical security. Security risk assessments, threat analysis, vulnerability scanning, and penetration testing techniques should be used to validate the security of the SOA services, platforms, and related systems.

To perform a thorough security assessment, the following types of questions should be asked:

- What does the overall SOA look like?
- Who are the intended consumers of the service(s)?
- How are the services discovered by consumers? Is WSDL or UDDI used?
- What interactions occur between consumers and services and between services?
- Are any of the services or consumers on untrusted networks?
- What types of data are passed between consumers and services at various points?
- Is data integrity or confidentiality required at any point within the SOA?
- Does data flow through multiple intermediaries?
- Is there a need to provide end-to-end security for certain types of data?
- What are the authentication and authorization requirements for each of the services?
- Is the authorization based upon roles or attributes?
- Is data privacy a concern?
- What security technologies, such as X.509, Kerberos, or SAML, are available?
- Are multiple security domains involved? Is there a need for cross-domain trust relationships?
- Are there different Web services technologies, such as J2EE, Weblogic, or .NET, in use that might cause issues with protocol support or interoperability? If so, is the WS-I Basic Security Profile 1.0 supported?
- Threat analysis—what potential threats are there to the infrastructure, such as malicious attacks, insider threats, information disclosure, disasters, message replay attacks, or denial-of-service (DoS)?

The following summarizes the types of threats that apply to SOA and mechanisms to mitigate the threats:

- Information disclosure (confidentiality)—Use of XML encryption within WS-Security can provide data confidentiality. End-to-end message confidentiality can also be handled with XML encryption.
- Message tampering—Message tampering could be used to remove XML, add XML, or otherwise alter data or cause some unintended behavior within the application. XML signatures can be used to ensure the integrity of messages.
- Message injection—Message injection may be used to cause some unintended behavior within the application. Authentication mechanisms and input validation within the service can help to mitigate this issue.
- Message replay—WS-SecureConversation provides mechanisms to prevent this kind of attack, but otherwise, message identifiers or time stamps can be used to prevent message replay.
- Authentication—Authentication is provided by XML signatures and security tokens such as Kerberos, X.509 certificates, and SAML, or even username tokens. These methods are supported by WS-Security and WS-Trust.
- Authorization—Authorization can be role based or attribute based. The Web services platform will typically provide some form of authorization capability, but for more advanced authorization needs, the application will have to include explicit authorization checks.
- Service availability—Disasters, whether natural or human-made, need to be planned for by ensuring that an adequate disaster recovery strategy is in place. Other malicious attacks such

as DoS can affect the network, operating system, or application. Dealing with DoS attacks is beyond the scope of this chapter, however.

■ Token substitution—Attempts to substitute one security token for another can be prevented by ensuring that digital signatures provide integrity over all the security critical portions of the message, including security tokens.

Once a risk assessment is completed, and the security requirements are understood, decisions need to be made about how to secure the SOA environment. Risks are normally rated in terms of impact and likelihood and should be prioritized—for example into high-risk, medium-risk, and low-risk categories. Security measures can then be chosen to mitigate the risks and meet security requirements, based on a cost–benefit analysis.

General security principles should be followed when choosing security measures, such as:

■ Ensuring the confidentiality, integrity, and availability of data and services
■ Defense in depth
■ Principle of least privilege
■ Minimizing the attack surface
■ Promoting simplicity rather than complexity

At the network level, firewall policies can be applied to limit access to Web services, because SOAP messages are transmitted via HTTP, typically on Transmission Control Protocol (TCP) port 80, or via HTTPS on TCP port 443. Internet-facing servers should have access restricted just to the port that the service is listening on. Firewall policies can form the first line of defense by reducing the available attack surface. Other standard techniques, including DMZ architecture, security zones, and intrusion detection/prevention, can reduce risk at the network level and provide defense in depth.

At the transport level, Web services are often secured through the use of SSL, via the HTTPS protocol, and policies can be applied through WSDL to ensure that Web services are secured with SSL. The use of SSL should definitely be considered, particularly because it is a well-understood protocol, although it is important to understand that SSL provides only point-to-point encryption and that other techniques need to be applied if the security of the SOAP messages is to be maintained beyond the SSL session.

At the message level, XML is by nature a text-based standard, so data confidentiality and integrity are not built in. SOAP messages and attachments may be processed by different intermediaries along the route to the final recipient, and WS-Security allows parts of messages to be targeted to different recipients. This is an important distinction between point-to-point security technologies, such as SSL, and end-to-end security, which WS-Security supports. XML encryption can provide end-to-end data confidentiality via public-key cryptography and shared symmetric-key cryptography, whereas XML signature can meet data integrity and message authentication needs.

Other issues exist when dealing with trust relationships and cross-domain authentication. The WS-Trust and WS-Federation standards provide a technical foundation for establishing trust for SOAs. Organizational security policies and regulatory requirements should define the security requirements that need to be placed on interactions with customers and business partners. These security requirements can be used as a basis for determining the security mechanisms that need to be used to provide an appropriate level of trust, such as encryption strength or method of authentication (X.509 digital certificates, SAML, Kerberos, etc.). However, trust between organizations goes beyond technical implementation details and also needs to be addressed by contractual obligations and business discussions.

Conclusion

The WS-S family provides an essential set of standards for securing SOAs; however, the number and complexity of the standards is a definite problem. This complexity can serve to discourage the adoption of these standards into an SOA, particularly for application developers, whose job is complicated by security needs. These standards are also evolving and new security standards are being developed, so expect the SOA security landscape to evolve over time.

Fortunately vendors are providing new tools to simplify integration of WS-Security standards into Web services. These tools can help by hiding many of the lower-level details from security practitioners and architects. Expect these tools to evolve over time as SOA and Web services become more mature. At this time, however, it is still not an easy task to integrate WS-Security standards into Web services.

For the security practitioner, standard security principles can be leveraged to assist in guiding architects and developers in selecting appropriate mechanisms to secure SOAs.

Further Readings

IBM developerWorks Web Services Standards Documentation, http://www.ibm.com/developerworks/webservices/standards.

Microsoft MSDN Documentation on WSE Security and WCF Security, http://msdn2.microsoft.com/en-us/library/default.aspx.

OASIS Standards for WS-Security, WS-Trust, WS-SecureConversation, WS-Federation, UDDI and SAML, http://www.oasisopen.org/specs/index.php.

Security in a Web Services World: A Proposed Architecture and Roadmap, http://msdn2.microsoft.com/enus/library/ms977312.aspx.

W3C Standards for XML, XML Encryption, XML Signature, SOAP, WSDL, WS-Policy and WS-PolicyAttachment, http://www.w3.org/.

Chapter 17

Analysis of Covert Channels

Ralph Spencer Poore

Contents

> Technology—sufficiently advanced—is indistinguishable from magic.
>
> **attributed to Arthur C. Clarke**

Complex systems often have paths for information that were not intended by their designers. These paths or channels may exist at any layer within the open systems interconnection (OSI) model and may cross layers. Through these channels information may escape to unauthorized recipients. To the unwary, these covert channels transport information as if by magic.

What Is a Covert Channel?

The security and academic literature define the term "covert channel" in several ways. The notion of covert communication was introduced in a paper by Lampson (1973), in which he defined the term by stating that "A communication channel is covert if it is neither designed nor intended to transfer information at all." Other definitions tend to focus on the different means that result in such a communication channel (the references for this chapter include a wealth of publications discussing this). However, a covert channel becomes especially important when it can result in the leakage of sensitive information either from a more-sensitive process (e.g., one that is classified as top secret) to a less-sensitive process (e.g., one that is classified as confidential) or from one compartment (e.g., medical records) to another (e.g., office equipment inventory). This unintended path moves data from access by authorized users to access by unauthorized users. Because the covert channel is neither designed nor intended to transfer data, access control mechanisms generally cannot address the leakage.

A covert channel exists when two (or more) processes operating at different levels of sensitivity share a resource, whereby the less-sensitive process cannot read the information written to it by the more highly sensitive process, but can measure the effect on its own performance of the resource's use by the more-sensitive process. For example, if a nonsensitive file, such as a zip codes file, were accessible to both a highly sensitive process (e.g., a human immunodeficiency virus research program) and a less sensitive process (e.g., a general market mailing program), a path for information leakage (i.e., a covert channel) would exist if, by analyzing the performance of the less-sensitive process as it opens, reads, and closes the zip codes file, information could be obtained about the highly sensitive process that also opens, reads, and closes the zip codes file.

In practice, when covert channel use scenarios are constructed, a distinction between covert storage channels and covert timing channels is made, even though theoretically no fundamental distinction exists between them. A potential covert channel is a storage channel if its use scenario "involves the direct or indirect writing of a storage location by one process and the direct or indirect reading of the storage location by another process" (National Computer Security Center, 1985). A potential covert channel is a timing channel if its use scenario involves a process that "signals information to another by modulating its own use of system resources (e.g., CPU time) in such a way that this manipulation affects the real response time observed by the second process" (National Computer Security Center, 1985).

How Is a Covert Channel Exploited?

To exploit a covert channel, the perpetrators need to identify it and need to capture the performance data of the less-sensitive process to which they presumably have access. The required analysis is not trivial. However, if the sensitive information is of sufficient value and alternative means effectively prevented, then even the difficult analysis may become attractive.

Once the perpetrators have identified the covert channel, they may be able to exploit it more directly if they can create and execute a process of his or her own. An even worse situation is one in which an authorized user with access to highly sensitive data conspires with someone who does not have access to such data. The authorized user cannot just copy the data to a lower classification (as this violates access control policy). Instead, the authorized user (whom we will call "Adam") creates a program that will signal the information via a covert channel to a program created by the unauthorized user (whom we will call "Ulysses"). In this scenario,* Ulysses creates three files: synch, bit_1, and bit_0. Ulysses opens synch for writing, writes "Begin" in the file, and then closes it. Adam opens synch for reading, reads it, and closes it; this he repeats

---

* This scenario is based on a widely followed security policy of allowing high-security processes to read low-security files, but preventing low-security processes from reading high-security files. In the Bell-La Padula Model, this is the star (*) property, sometimes called the "write up, read down" policy.

until he reads "Begin" in the file. At this point, Adam and Ulysses may begin exploiting the covert channel through the following loop of steps:

1. Adam opens `bit_1` for reading when he intends to send a "1"; he opens `bit_0` for reading when he intends to send a "0".
2. Adam also continues to open `synch` for reading, reads it, and closes it, repeating this until he reads "Next" in the file.
3. Ulysses repeatedly attempts to open both `bit_1` and `bit_0` for writing. If this succeeds for both, they are closed, and this step is repeated. If Ulysses succeeds for one but not for the other, than a bit has been sent (i.e., a "1" if he failed to open `bit_1` and a "0" if he failed to open `bit_0`).
4. Adam closes the open file `bit_1` or `bit_0`.
5. Ulysses repeatedly attempts to open the file he failed to get in step 3 until he succeeds.
6. Ulysses then signals his success (indicating receiving of the bit) by writing a message (i.e., "Next") to the `synch` file.
7. This loop continues until all the bits are transferred from Adam to Ulysses.

Given machine speeds, this prearranged exploitation of a covert channel could have a very high bandwidth.

How Much Information Can Flow over a Covert Channel?

The amount of information communicated over a covert channel in a given period is called its bandwidth or capacity. Very low bandwidths, for example, 1 bit per hour, may make exploitation impractical and alleviate the need for remediation (but not always). High bandwidths, however, invite discovery and exploitation. Information theory as described by Shannon and Weaver (1964) provides a mathematical basis for determining bandwidth. The interested reader with extensive background in advanced mathematics is invited to review their paper. An additional source with somewhat simplified mathematics (but still requiring more than college algebra) is well presented in Section 4.0 of *A Guide to Understanding Covert Channel Analysis of Trusted Systems* (NCSC-TG-30). The information security practitioner, however, may need only a general understanding. To that end, here is a substantial oversimplification: the bandwidth is a function of the number of possible states available to the channel and the speed at which the states can be changed by one process and evaluated by another. For example, if the high-sensitivity process can cause four detectable independent events each millisecond, that would be equivalent to passing a 4-bit value every millisecond for a bandwidth of 4000 bps. The *Handbook for the Computer Security Certification of Trusted Systems* * contains in Chapter 8, "Covert Channel Analysis," a discussion of channel capacity that concludes that the trend toward faster systems in shared memory multiprocessors makes fast covert channels much more likely. This conforms to Moore's Law,[†] which portends serious consequences if we ignore covert channel analysis.

---

* Prepared by the University of North Carolina for the Naval Research Laboratory under contract N00014-91-K-2032 (NRL Technical Memorandum 5540:062A, February 12, 1996).

† The term Moore's Law was coined by Carver Mead (ca. 1970) and is named after Gordon E. Moore (a cofounder of Intel). He determined that the number of transistor counts for the same component costs doubled every two years. This proportional "law" has been generalized to information processing advances. Although such doubling cannot continue indefinitely, it has largely held to date.

Although much of the literature focuses on covert channels in software, the electronics of an information processing device may provide unintended communication paths that result in the leakage of sensitive data. A simple discrete circuit used to illuminate a status lamp, for example, might be manipulated to provide information to an unauthorized person through Morse code. It may also be possible to determine critical bits of information by examining power fluctuations, changes in temperature, or acoustic vibrations depending on the nature of the information processing device. Because the unintended communication paths were neither clearly designed nor intended to be information communication paths, when they exist, they qualify as covert channels.

Example of a Covert Channel

For this example, we define three domains of differing sensitivity classifications: Red, Green, and Blue. Red will be the most sensitive and act as a security gateway between Green and Blue. By security policy, no Green data should ever get to Blue. The Red process transforms Green data to Blue data (or blocks it entirely depending on security policy). Blue data may freely flow through Red to Green, that is, the Green domain may read Blue domain data, but the Blue domain may never read Green domain data. With this simple example, we have a security policy and a design that makes any channel that can transfer Green domain data to the Blue domain a covert channel. Because the Red domain is effectively a shared resource, we may have the potential for a process in the Blue domain to detect a performance impact by a process in the Green domain by its interaction with the Red domain. This could allow a covert timing channel through Red manipulated by Green. Blue can easily establish a semaphore for synchronization because the security policy allows Blue to send to Green.

If Green can signal Red to set a condition that should prevent Red from processing something sent by Blue, then Green can establish a covert storage channel with Blue through which Blue continuously queries Red and checks for a response. This would be analogous to Green setting a flag in storage, which Blue could check. The bandwidth or capacity of this covert channel would depend on machine speeds and the number of possible distinguishable states. However, even a simple binary, if it could be tested every 100 ms (a rather slow machine rate), would transfer 100 bps. If those were eight-character passwords, this would expose more than 90 passwords per minute. Or, if this were a banking system relying on cryptographic keys (e.g., two-key Triple-Data Encryption Standard, which would be 112 bits of key plus 16 bits of parity for a total of 128 bits), the key would be compromised in less than two seconds.

If Green, Red, and Blue shared a power supply, a display, or error-handling processes, additional covert channels may exist. As previously suggested, the criticality of the information potentially released determines what may constitute a sufficiently stringent constraint on information leakage. If only the compromise of gigabytes of data is of concern, then a 100-bps covert channel might not warrant countermeasures. However, if national security, life safety, or billions of dollars are at stake over the loss of a password or cryptographic key, then even 1 bps may demand remediation.

Overview of the Analysis Process

Before the investigators can identify covert channels, they must have an understanding of the overt, that is, intended or legal, channels and their associated information flow security policies. These channels may support a covert channel if an information flow contrary to policy is possible. Otherwise, the investigator documents these for use later in the analysis. Next, the investigator documents all shared resources, including storage locations, devices, CPU, power supplies, and system resources (e.g., error routines, common libraries, and system calls). These are all potential covert channels. Developing a matrix for this analysis is one practical approach (see Kemmerer, 2002).

The investigator must then determine whether each shared resource qualifies for further analysis as a potential covert channel. Any of the following three situations would be documented, but would end the analysis for a candidate covert channel.

1. If another channel already exists between the processes that share the resource and if that channel is one that would permit the same communication without violating the information flow security policies (i.e., it is a legal or overt channel), then the potential covert channel is not of consequence. This may be determined by comparing the potentially illicit information flow with the ones previously documented as legal. Where a legal channel accomplishes the same result as the potentially illicit one, then the covert channel is discounted and no further analysis is needed for that channel.
2. If the potential covert channel cannot be controlled sufficiently to signal useful information, than it is also of no consequence. For example, a state variable that is changed by the trusted computing base but does not identify the process that caused the change and can be changed by any arbitrary process may be useless as a signal to another process because it is too unreliable.
3. If the shared resource can signal to each process only information the respective process would already know, then it is, again, not worthy of further analysis. An example of this is a file attribute that states who locked a file. If it can be read only by the process that locked the file—a process that already knows it did so—then no useful information via that attribute is sent.

The remaining candidates for covert channels require more detailed analysis. Although additional analysis techniques exist, including covert flow trees (see Kemmerer and Porra, 1991) and noninterference modeling (see Goguen and Meseguer, 1982), the final determination remains one based on the experience and skill of the investigator.

For each channel identified as a covert channel, an assessment of its bandwidth or capacity is needed. This information is important in determining the risk–benefit associated with making the changes necessary to eliminate or limit the effectiveness of the covert channel. In many commercial situations, a qualitative approach using "high, medium, and low" may prove sufficient. In more formal situations, quantitative measurements or mathematical modeling may be required (some of which we discussed earlier). Once the investigators have assessed the potential capacity, they then need to identify any existing countermeasures that would further limit either the capacity or the utility of the covert channel. For example, an error condition discrete has the potential of sending one bit of information each time it is set and reset. If the processor can do this at machine speed, gigabits of information could flow within minutes—an enormous capacity. However, if a change in this register results in an interruption that shuts the system down, then the capacity is, at most, one bit. Documenting this is an important step in the analysis of covert channels.

At the end of the analysis, the investigator will probably have covert channels for which additional remediation is warranted. The next section provides some insight into protecting against covert channels. The investigator has, however, not completed the work. At each stage in the development or remediation process, additional analysis will be needed.

Protecting against Covert Channels

Good architecture and design practices that clearly identify the intended security policies for the system form the foundation for any countermeasures. The system designer can include specific countermeasures in the design, including the use of "fuzzy time" (see Hu), heuristic measure of regularity (see Cabuk et al., 2004a, b), and formal information flows. In addition, the developer can run tools against the formal design (or in some instances against the source code). Tools include the following:

1. Buffer Overrun Detection (BOON) (refer to http://www.cs.berkeley.edu/~daw/boon/)
2. Cqual (refer to http://www.cs.umd.edu/~jfoster/cqual/)
3. Flawfinder (open source; refer to http://www.dwheeler.com/flawfinder/)
4. Modelchecking Programs for Security Properties (MOPS) (refer to http://www.cs.berkeley.edu/~daw/mops/)
5. Rough Auditing Tool for Security (RATS) (open source; refer to http://www.fortifysoftware.com/security-resources/rats.jsp)
6. ITS4 (open source [but not supported]; refer to http://www.cigital.com/its4/)
7. Secure Programming Lint (SPLINT) (refer to http://www.splint.org/)
8. Stanford Checker (now known as "MC") (refer to http://metacomp.stanford.edu/)

Although each tool can provide valuable assistance in identifying problems in the design or source code, each tool has its limitations. Using more than one increases the likelihood of discovering potential problems that could support covert channels. Even with the use of tools, formal analysis by a computer scientist or engineer with experience in covert channel analysis is recommended.

Steganography as a Special Case

Steganography, from the Greek meaning covered writing, covertly encodes a message in benign data. Steganographic techniques consist of altering bytes in predominantly lossy protocols, that is, protocols that use a compression technique that does not decompress data back to 100 percent of the original (e.g., AAC, JPEG, MP3, and Motion Picture Experts Group [MPEG]) and that does not lead to a perceivable change in data quality but does allow information to be embedded without being identified. Although steganography has ancient roots, its widespread use in information processing is primarily a result of the Internet and laws against the transmission of pornographic materials. The information is encoded into a benign data stream or object and transmitted. Persons with the proper decoding software can then retrieve the original materials.

Although modern researchers often include this special case in papers that discuss covert channel analysis (see, e.g., Van Horenbeeck), this illicit information flow has not become a common component of traditional covert channel analysis. First, processes in systems that prevent higher-sensitivity processes from writing to lower-sensitivity processes—a rather standard security policy in systems that process multiple levels of sensitive information—cannot exploit this, as the overt message from the higher-sensitivity category would not be transported to the lower-sensitivity category. Second, any otherwise covert channel that might subvert the security policy would have a higher capacity for illicit information flows without recourse to steganography. Nonetheless, systems that rely on object labeling programmatically assigned by a process (as opposed to labels assigned by the trusted computing base) may need to address this threat. This situation exists when a higher-sensitivity process can label its outputs at lower levels of sensitivity either by design or by a process that does not conform to data labeling, for example, messages to a system operator and error or diagnostic messages.

Recommendations

Systems that use high-security components or warrant high-assurance application development should include an analysis of covert channels. Such an analysis should follow a formal process, for example, as described in NCSC-TG-30 or in *A Foundation for Covert Channel Analysis* (see References). The Common Criteria* requires a formal covert channel analysis only for Evaluation Assurance Level (EAL) 7—the highest level of assurance. However, as early as EAL 3, covert channels (aka "illicit information flows") must be addressed.

As systems become more complex and processing becomes faster, the potential for covert channels with dangerously high bandwidths increases. Although it may seem counterintuitive, improvements in application and system security may increase the risk of covert channel exploitation. When a simple password hack gains access, a perpetrator need not invest in more sophisticated attacks. As security improves, the more easily exploited holes close. Covert channels are generally not easily exploited, but when other doors close, they may prove to be the window that remains open.

Further Readings

Fine, T. A Foundation for Covert Channel Analysis, *Proceedings of the 15th National Computer Security Conference*, 1992, pp. 204–212, Baltimore, Maryland.

Gligor, V. D., Millen, J. K., Goldston, J. K., and Muysenberg, J. A. A Guide to Understanding Covert Channel Analysis of Trusted Systems (NCSC-TG-30), *National Computer Security Center (NCSC)*, November 1993 (available at stinet.dtic.mil).

Gray, J. W., III. On Introducing Noise into the Bus-Contention Channel, *Proceedings of the IEEE Symposium on Security and Privacy*, 1993, pp. 90–98. Oakland: IEEE.

Haigh, J. T., Kemmerer, R. A., McHugh, J., and Young, D. W. An Experience Using Two Covert Channel Analysis Techniques on a Real System Design, *Proceedings of the IEEE Symposium on Security and Privacy*, 1986, pp. 14–24. Oakland: IEEE.

International Standard ISO/IEC 15408:2005—The Common Criteria for Information Technology Security Evaluation (available from www.niap-ccevs.org/cc-scheme/cc_docs/).

Karger, P. A., and Wray, J. C. Storage Channels in Disk Arm Optimization, *Proceedings of the 1991 IEEE Computer Society Symposium on Research in Security and Privacy*, 1991, pp. 52–61. Oakland: IEEE.

Kemmerer, R. A. Shared Resource Matrix Methodology: An Approach to Identifying Storage and Timing Channels, *ACM Transactions on Computer Systems*, Vol. 1, No. 3, August 1983, pp. 256–277, Washington: ACM Press.

Levin T., Tao, A., and Padilla, S. J. Covert Storage Channel Analysis: A Worked Example, *Proceedings of the 13th National Computer Security Conference*, 1990, pp. 10–19, Washington, D.C.

Melliar-Smith, P. M., and Moser, L. E. Protection against Covert Storage and Timing Channels, 1991, *Proceedings of the 4th IEEE Computer Security Foundations Workshop—CSFW'91*, Franconia, N H, June 18–20, 1991, pp. 209–214, IEEE Computer Society, 1991.

Millen, J. K. 20 Years of Covert Channel Modeling and Analysis, *Proceedings of the 1999 IEEE Symposium on Security and Privacy*, 1999, pp. 113–114. Oakland: IEEE.

Millen, J. K. Covert Channel Capacity, *1987 IEEE Symposium on Security and Privacy*, 1987, *sp*, p. 60. Oakland: IEEE.

Minutes of the First Workshop on Covert Channel Analysis, Cipher, Newsletter of the Technical Committee on Security and Privacy, IEEE Computer Society, Special Issue, July 1990.

Moskowitz, I. S., and Miller, A. R. The Influence of Delay upon an Idealized Channel's Bandwidth, *Proceedings of the IEEE Symposium on Security and Privacy*, 1992, pp. 62–67. Oakland: IEEE.

---

* ISO/IEC15408:1999.

Moskowitz, I. S., and Miller, A. R. Simple Timing Channels, *IEEE Symposium on Research in Security and Privacy*, 1994, pp. 56–64. Oakland: IEEE.

National Computer Security Center, Department of Defense Trusted Computer System Evaluation Criteria, DoD 5200.28-STD, December 1985.

Oblitey, W., Wolfe, J. L., and Ezekiel, S. *Covert Channels: The State of the Practice*. Department of Computer Science, Indiana University of Pennsylvania, Indiana, PA, August 24, 2005.

Proctor, N. E., and Neumann, P. G. Architectural Implications of Covert Channels, *Proceedings of the 15th National Computer Security Conference*, 1992, pp. 28–43.

Siponen, M. T., and Oinas-Kukkonen, H. A Review of Information Security Issues and Respective Research Contributions, *The DATABASE for Advances in Information Systems*, Vol. 38, No. 1, February 2007. Washington: ACM Press.

Tsai, C.-R., and Gligor, V. D. A Bandwidth Computation Model for Covert Storage Channels and its Applications, *Proceedings of the IEEE Symposium on Security and Privacy*, 1988, pp. 108–121. Oakland: IEEE.

Tsai, C.-R., Gligor, V. D., and Chandersekaran, C. S. A Formal Method for the Identification of Covert Storage Channels in Source Code, *Proceedings of the IEEE Symposium on Security and Privacy*, 1987, pp. 74–86. Oakland: IEEE.

Willcox, D. A., and Bunch, S. R. A Tool for Covert Storage Channel Analysis of the UNIX Kernel, *Proceedings of the 15th National Computer Security Conference*, 1992, pp. 697–706, Baltimore, Maryland.

Wray, J. C. An Analysis of Covert Timing Channels, *Proceedings of the 1991 IEEE Computer Society Symposium on Research in Security and Privacy*, May 20–22, 1991, pp. 2–7. Oakland: IEEE.

Chapter 18

Security Architecture of Biological Cells: An Example of Defense in Depth*

Kenneth J. Knapp and R. Franklin Morris, Jr.

Contents

* The idea for this chapter came from a reading of Peter Checkland's book, *Systems Thinking, Systems Practice* (Wiley, 1999). An academic version of this chapter with full references appeared in *Communications of the Association for Information Systems*, volume 12 (December 2003), titled, "Defense Mechanisms of Biological Cells: A Framework for Network Security Thinking," by Knapp, Morris, Rainer, and Byrd. Opinions, conclusions, and recommendations expressed or implied within are solely those of the authors and do not necessarily represent the views of the USAF Academy, The Citadel, the USAF, the Department of Defense, or any other government agency.

Examining the similarities between biological cells and networked computer systems reveals valuable lessons for the security professional. In summary, the security approach in cells is consistent with the defense-in-depth notion that multiple techniques and layers help to mitigate the risk of one layer being compromised.

Today, networks are essential tools for business survival. Typically, the more employees use a network, the more valuable it becomes. The challenge is daunting: security must protect business information while allowing for open communication and commerce. Looking to nature for security approaches can yield insights into how we can better meet this challenge. In this regard, biological cells offer a security strategy that is interesting and worth emulating.

After studying security mechanisms in cells, we found that security mechanisms are present in nearly every cell component. Cells follow a multilayered, defense-in-depth approach to security. In this chapter, we offer a framework that examines the similarities between cell security and network security. In today's high-technology environment, in which security is increasingly important, this framework can help us by stimulating thinking about security while offering a model about how to design secure systems.

Before we discuss the various analogies between cells and networks, we will briefly mention what biologists call "cell theory." Understanding the basics of cell theory helps explain why cells are useful to study as a security framework. The premise of cell theory states that all living things are made up of cells—it is the fundamental unit of structure in all life. A single cell can be a complete organism in itself or cells can work together to become the building blocks of large multicellular organisms such as a human being. Although differences exist between plant and animal cells or blood and skin cells, the similarities are substantial. Because cells are considered the fundamental structure of life, we argue that it is worth examining cells because they highlight important principles valuable to today's security professional.

Figure 18.1 illustrates the fundamental architecture of a cell. For each identified cell component in the figure, we name an analogous computer network counterpart. In the following section, we will briefly examine the key aspects of this figure while providing four analogies that highlight similarities between cells and networks. As a conclusion, we offer five valuable principles based on cell security that are useful to the information security professional.

Four Analogies

Table 18.1 provides a framework of the four analogies by comparing cell biology and computer networks. The left column lists a phrase that accurately describes the functions common to both. The center column provides the computer network term with the analogous cell biology term to the right. We discuss each analogy in the following paragraphs.

Barrier Defense

After studying cells, we quickly noticed just how essential perimeter defenses are to cell security. The first line of defense is the plasma membrane, which encloses and protects the cell. The membrane

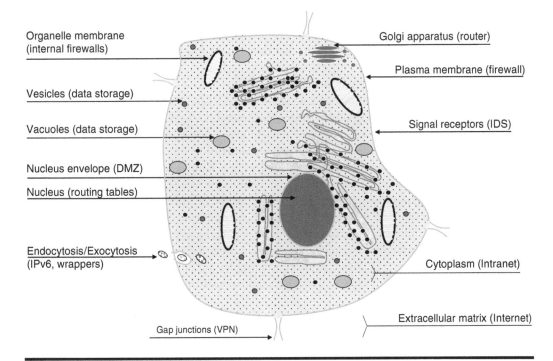

Organelle membrane (internal firewalls)

Vesicles (data storage)

Vacuoles (data storage)

Nucleus envelope (DMZ)

Nucleus (routing tables)

Endocytosis/Exocytosis (IPv6, wrappers)

Golgi apparatus (router)

Plasma membrane (firewall)

Signal receptors (IDS)

Cytoplasm (Intranet)

Extracellular matrix (Internet)

Gap junctions (VPN)

Figure 18.1 Cell components and computer network counterparts.

Table 18.1 Computer Network and Biological Cell Comparison

Analogous Function	Computer Network Examples	Cell Biology Examples
Barrier defense	Exterior router Firewall Intrusion detection system (IDS)	Plasma membrane/cell wall oligosaccharides
Barrier transmission and communication	Tunneling protocols Secure Sockets Layer (SSL) Virtual private networks (VPNs) Network ports	Variety of membrane channels Gap junctions Facilitated diffusion Extracellular matrix signaling (e.g., receptors)
Internal organization	Internal firewalls Network demilitarized zone (DMZ)	Membrane-bound organelles Nucleolus double-membrane envelope
Internal routing and communication	E-mail Instant messaging Routers Internet Protocol version 6 (IPv6) Routing tables	Endocytosis Exocytosis Golgi apparatus Cell nucleus

forms a selective barrier allowing nutrients to enter and waste products to leave. This membrane is the primary divider between the cell and its external environment. Some plant cells have a rigid cell wall in addition to the plasma membrane. For this chapter, however, we discuss cells in general without distinguishing between the different types of cells. In sum, cell membranes allow the entry of wanted elements while filtering out unwanted elements.

In comparison, network perimeters include routers, IDSs, and firewalls. Together, these devices demark an internal network from the public Internet. Like cell membranes, firewalls filter out unwanted data while permitting wanted data to enter. Furthermore, threat analogies exist between firewalls and cell membranes. A transport channel that circumvents the cell membrane can endanger the cell just as an unauthorized modem or a faulty firewall rule can endanger an entire network.

In general, membranes provide perimeter defense for the cell through three main functions: (1) mechanical protection and a chemically buffered environment, (2) a porous medium for the distribution of water and other small molecules, and (3) a storage site of regulatory molecules that sense the presence of pathogenic threats. Interestingly, devices such as a firewall and IDS together provide similar functions: (1) electronic protection through a buffered environment, (2) a "porous" medium for the distribution of packets, and (3) a regulatory listing to detect the presence of electronic intrusions.

One of the more versatile cell barrier defenses involves oligosaccharins. These fragments in the cell wall become active in an attack against the cell. Among their multiple roles, oligosaccharides perform an important signaling function that can initiate when a pathogen that threatens a cell is detected. An attack can then trigger an "oxidative burst" near the cell membrane that serves two functions relating to cell defense. First, this burst releases hydrogen peroxide, superoxide, and other active oxygen types that directly attack the pathogen in an attempt to destroy it. Second, the burst prompts a hardening of the cell membrane, making it harder for the pathogen to penetrate the membrane.

A desired quality of networks is an active defense against attacks rather than a passive, reactive one. The multiple roles of oligosaccharides serve as a model of how cells provide an "active defense." For example, the hardening of the cell membrane upon detection of a threat is like switching a firewall's rule base to a stricter configuration, thus making the firewall more difficult to penetrate under high threat conditions.

Barrier Transmission and Communication

Today, numerous cyber and privacy threats force businesses to use secure network communications. To meet this need, numerous services such as VPNs, SSL, and other tunneling protocols have emerged. Comparatively, cells have a very rich variety of specialized communication mechanisms. Intriguingly, these mechanisms all inherently incorporate security. In this section, we limit our discussion to three such cell mechanisms: membrane channels, gap junctions, and communication via the extracellular matrix.

Membrane Channels

Firewalls and routers manage communications by opening and closing thousands of ports that allow or block data. At the biological level, a similar structure exists. Cells can communicate with other cells via electrical current flowing across the cell's membrane. This current appears as bursts traveling through open channels, or holes, formed by proteins built into the membrane. If no hole is open, no significant current flows.

Signals from external substances such as calcium wanting to enter the cell can cause the opening of membrane channels. Like some network firewalls that can restrict the passage of certain protocols, cell membrane channels permit passage of selected substances while denying others.

Gap Junctions

The cytoplasm is the material that fills the inside of a cell between the plasma membrane and the membrane of the nucleus. In this sense, the cytoplasm is like an internal network within the cell. Connecting the cytoplasm between cells, channels called gap junctions allow the secure passage of molecules through the cell's membrane. Gap junctions provide a secure tunnel to allow the passage of molecules and ions between cells. In essence, gap junctions are similar to VPNs that safely link outside users (or external organizations) to an organization's internal network.

Cell-to-Cell Communications via the Extracellular Matrix

One way that cells communicate with other cells is by employing receptors that detect outside elements friendly to the cell. Receptors recognize foreign objects and then convey the message to the nucleus to induce a response. Receptors also have an important security function.

In multicellular organisms, communications that occur outside the cell do so in extracellular space, which consists of a gel material known as the extracellular matrix. The gel is composed of sugar molecules in a water-based solution filled with salts, proteins, other nutrients, and waste products.

Receptors that are associated with the cell's membrane provide communication links from the cell to this extracellular matrix. These receptors interact with protein fibers that influence cell behaviors, often leading to changes in cell shape, movement, and development.

In networks, an IDS protects a network from intrusions by flagging suspicious communications. Cells take a proactive approach to intrusion detection by deploying an array of different receptors that respond to extracellular signals in a type of signal detection system. Once detected by an associated receptor, an "approved" chemical signal triggers an event that changes a cell's behavior. Depending on the type of cell with which it is communicating, a particular chemical signal can cause different cellular reactions. In one example, a receptor will trigger the opening of a membrane channel, allowing a flow of ions into the cell, which can affect the electrical properties of the cell's membrane or cytoplasm.

Internal Organization

In recent years, some network devices have integrated firewall functionality into their services. One example is a firewall switch. In addition to these hybrid devices, organizations are making more frequent use of internal or application firewalls for use inside an organization's network. Internal firewalls can electronically segment departmental networks within an organization. They also can provide dedicated protection for high-value resources such as a financial data store. Internal firewalls not only provide a layer of protection from external cyber threats, but also can protect from internal threats.

Comparatively, cells are segmented into organelles. A dedicated protective membrane surrounds these specialized compartments. The internal membranes act as an additional layer of cellular defense for the organelle. Each organelle membrane has its own distinct composition. Like the external plasma membrane, internal membranes contain barrier transmission mechanisms that facilitate communication between organelles.

The most prominent organelle, the nucleus, is a highly protected resource. A double-membrane envelope separated by a perinuclear space encloses the nucleus. The perinuclear space is like a buffer zone or network DMZ, which forms nuclear pores through which the nucleus and cytoplasm communicate. Protein granules often guard these pores to help regulate the passage of small ions and larger macromolecules into the nucleus.

Other organelles called mitochondria are responsible for the energy transactions necessary for cell survival. Like the nucleus, mitochondria are a high-value resource and have a double membrane. Other organelles include membrane-protected vacuoles, which are sacs within the cell that store food particles, water, and other substances. Vesicles are simply very small vacuoles.

Cells teach that security is a multilayered process. Whereas the plasma membrane provides the initial protection, the organelles provide their own protection with specialized membranes. The more valuable the organelle is to the cell, the more robust its membrane seems to be.

Similarly, based on the increased use of hybrid and internal firewalls, it appears that network security is beginning to resemble cell security. The defense-in-depth approach stipulates that security should be multilayered and that processes should penetrate deep into an organization. For example, defense in depth has been a key element of the U.S. Nuclear Commission's safety philosophy. It employs a framework of successive and redundant measures to prevent accidents at nuclear facilities. This philosophy has served the nuclear power industry well and is being used as an effective architectural model for securing industry cyber defenses. Defense in depth is receiving greater acceptance as a model for information technology security. It is also consistent with the multilayered approach of biological cells.

Internal Routing and Communication

Organizations today use a variety of communication systems such as e-mail, instant messaging, and Web conferencing. Cells too have what we can call communication systems. Endo- and exocytosis is one such system. This "full service" system facilitates cell transport, communication, and routing between organelles. It is also inherently secure.

In the process of endocytosis, cells—and even some organelles—engulf material by forming an inward depression in their outer plasma membrane. The depression continues to bulge further into the cell's cytoplasm until it finally pinches off as a vesicle. Later, a transport process called exocytosis discharges unwanted materials by performing endocytosis in reverse. Together, the endo- and exocytosis mechanisms serve as reliable security escorts. They direct material to the place it needs to go within the cell while safely escorting waste out of the cell.

Some of the newer Internet standards appear to integrate security and routing like those found in endo- and exocytosis. The IPv6 adds values into a packet's header field to help ensure security and privacy. IPv6 also requires the use of certain security protocols in the IP Security framework that enhance security at the packet level. Wrappers are another network technology with similarities to endo- and exocytosis. Various wrappers exist, but generally, wrappers can be placed in front of or around a data transmission and can encapsulate it from view to anyone other than the intended recipient. Such technologies can make the Internet inherently more secure if its core functionality has security designed into it.

Like large networks, cells have an extensive routing system that moves macromolecules to their destination organelle. These "routers" are systems devoted to keeping intracellular order by delivering newly synthesized macromolecules to their proper home. These routers also have built-in security in that they are membrane-protected. Although not well understood, the Golgi apparatus is one such system. It handles many of these operations as the primary router of protein traffic in the cell.

The internal "routing tables" in a cell are contained in the nucleus. As the highly protected information hub of the cell, the nucleus provides details about the transportation of proteins into different compartments. It contains most of the cell's genetic information and houses the DNA molecules, which contain the information a cell needs to retain its unique character.

Routing and sorting in cells is not unlike that in computer networks. Although developments such as IPv6 and hybrid firewalls are improving security, the advanced level of encapsulated protection demonstrated in cell processes such as endo- and exocytosis serves as a model for network security. Beyond the scope of this chapter, a more detailed study of the advanced cell function of endo- and exocytosis may yield insight and ideas for improved network security.

Five Valuable Lessons from Cells

After a study of cell security, five principles emerged. Each of these represents a stratagem that is applicable to information security.

1. Seamless integration of communication and security functionality. Security functionality is highly integrated into cellular mechanisms. That is, security is not separate from the communication mechanism, but is rather an integral part of the system itself. In general, we do not see dedicated security mechanisms or organelles in cells. For example, we do not see any single or dedicated cell organelle in charge of cell security. What we do see is security as a shared responsibility built directly into the various mechanisms and organelles. Examples include membrane channels and gap junctions, all of which are inherently secure communication mechanisms.

2. Proactive approach to membrane defense and crossing. Cells take a proactive approach to the passage of items through the outer cell membrane. Instead of taking the approach of identifying unwanted elements, which is a common IDS method, cells generally take the opposite approach. By focusing on the "friendly" chemical or electrical signals provided by a visitor at the outer membrane, cells provide an active defense. Hence, cells identify desired elements prior to allowing their passage through the external membrane. Undesired or unidentified elements are blocked.

3. High level of specialization of communication methods. Cells have a rich variety of highly specialized mechanisms for moving molecules through the outer membrane. There seems to be a tailored communication mechanism for each type of molecule that a cell needs to cross its membrane. The cell perimeter is not a simple wall blocking out unwanted or dangerous elements. Instead, the cell perimeter works as a complex system containing numerous transporters and channels, each designed to allow specific molecules to pass.

4. Standard use of internal membrane protection for high-value resources. Cells make liberal use of internal membranes. Mitochondria, vacuoles, and the nucleus, for example, all have their own protective membrane—or multiple membranes—in addition to the cell's outer membrane. The more important the organelle's function, the more robust the internal membrane seems to be.

5. Overall, security is integrated, ubiquitous, and continuous. Considering the full range of mechanisms that inherently provide cellular security, we conclude that cells maintain a

high-security orientation. Defensive measures are present at the membrane, within organelles, during internal routing, and throughout the entire cell. In addition, the security mechanisms of a cell are not intermittently active, but rather are continuously active, or always on. Overall, we recognize that cell security is integrated, ubiquitous, and continuous. That is, in biological cells, security is a part of everything, security is everywhere, and security is always functioning.

These five principles also suggest general implications for network security design. Although such detailed recommendations are beyond the scope of this chapter, we trust that enough detail has been provided to gain a practical understanding of the general security architecture of biological cells and how such an understanding can potentially benefit thinking about network security design.

Summary

The analogies in this chapter suggest similarities between cellular functions that defend an organism compared to network systems that defend an organization. In summary, the security approach in cells is consistent with the defense-in-depth notion that multiple techniques and layers help to mitigate the risk of one layer of defense being compromised. Although we just scratched the surface of the cell analogy, we hope this discussion stimulates one's thinking about network security. Such thinking can generate ideas and insights, which, in turn, lead to security improvements.

Chapter 19

ISO Standards Draft Content

Scott Erkonen

Contents

Introduction

The development of information security standards on an international level involves the International Organization for Standardization (ISO) and the International Electronics Consortium (IEC). Although other bodies provide sector-specific standards, they are often derived from or refer to the "ISO" standards (commonly referred to as ISO/IEC). In the United States, this work is managed through the American National Standards Institute and the International Committee for Information Technology Standards (INCITS). The group directly responsible for developing, contributing to, and managing this work is INCITS CS/1, cyber security. This group, CS/1, is also responsible for standards work in the areas of information technology (IT) security, privacy, identity management, and biometric security. One major area of focus for CS/1 involves the information security standards known as ISO/IEC 27001: 2005 (information security–information security management system (ISMS) requirements) and ISO/IEC 17799: 2005 (specification for information security management). For the sake of keeping things simplified as much as possible, these will be referred to as "ISO 17799" and "ISO 27001," respectively. It is also important to note that effective April 2007, ISO 17799 has undergone a numbering change and is renumbered to ISO 27002.

ISO 27001, ISO 27002, and the ISO 27000 Series

So what are these standards, and what are the differences between them? ISO 27001 is the standard for ISMS. Most people are more familiar with ISO 17799 (now ISO 27002), which is the code of practice for information security. Although it may seem confusing at first, the relationship is not difficult to understand. Many people confuse ISO 27001 and ISO 27002 with British Standard (BS) 7799, but although they are similar, they are not 100 percent equal. It is important to acknowledge that much of the work in this area was initiated by, and developed from, BS 7799 prior to it being modified and approved as an ISO standard, ISO 17799. What we have today is the result of that initial work combined with the input and participation of multiple nations. This chapter is not designed to serve as implementation guidance, but to educate you on the topic of ISMS, specifically as it pertains to ISO 27001. Implementation guidance is best left where it belongs, in ISO 27003.

ISO/IEC 27001 is the international standard that provides requirements for the creation, structure, and management of an ISMS. It contains five major areas, often referred to as "Sections 4 through 8." These areas are ISMS, management responsibility, internal ISMS audits, management review of the ISMS, and ISMS improvement. These four sections are what allow an organization to create a program structure, or ISMS. Most information security practitioners are familiar with or have heard of ISO 9001, which deals with quality management systems. Think of ISO 27001 as having similar structure, but dealing with this in the context of information security. One way to visualize this is as an umbrella. ISO 27001 provides the top layer defining how you document, organize, empower, audit, manage, and improve your information security program. In other words, an ISMS is an organization's structure for managing its people, processes, and technology. This chapter will provide you with information about the standards, but will not go into line-by-line descriptions or list the control objectives. It is highly recommended, if you are considering going down this path or would like to learn more, that you pick up a copy of the ISO standards.

ISO/IEC 17799 provides the control objectives, along with the legal, regulatory, or business requirements, that are relevant to an information security practitioner's organization. There are ten different areas that are covered in ISO 17799. These should look familiar as you are reading this book:

1. Security policy
2. Security organization
3. Asset classification and control
4. Personnel security
5. Physical and environmental security
6. Communications and operations management
7. Access control
8. Systems development and maintenance
9. Business continuity management
10. Compliance

Together with an organization's legal, regulatory, and business requirements, these control objectives provide the foundation of an ISO 27001 ISMS. Examine Annex A of ISO 27001, and you will notice that the control objectives in ISO 17799 are replicated there. When a security manager or practitioner wants to certify his or her organization's program as conforming to ISO 17799, it is actually done through certifying against the criteria defined in ISO 27001. This could seem confusing, but understand that the objective is to prove implementation of applicable controls from ISO 17799 (also Annex A of ISO 27001), and the ISMS developed from ISO 27001 (general requirements) provides the method by which this is accomplished.

So what are the requirements of ISO 27001? Sections 4 through 8 are often referred to as "general requirements."

Section 4 covers the requirements for development, implementation, management, and improvement of an ISMS. One of the first steps in the development of an ISMS is to define the scope. This scope can be based upon physical location, function, organizational culture, environment, or logical boundaries. Many organizations use physical or logical boundaries to simplify things. A scope includes physical, technical, information, and program elements and human assets. We will go a little deeper than normal regarding the concept of scoping, as it is a critical concept in information security and audit.

When you are developing an information security program based on ISO 27001, without the goal of certification, your scope would be where you have determined that your information security program is applicable. For example, you may work for a company with multiple divisions. Your scope may include the division that you are responsible for, but not the others or the overlying corporate structure. Think of scope in terms of span of control, which is critical for any program to be successful. You may choose to leverage building a program based upon ISO 27001 to expand span of control to drive consistency or manage risk.

If creating a scope for certification purposes, there are several important things to consider.

1. What is the value of the contents of the domain defined by the scope of the organization?
2. Do you have span of control over the domain?
3. What roles and responsibilities are performed by the people associated with the domain?
4. What are the logical or physical boundaries that can be used to define the domain?
5. What exceptions exist?
6. Is the desired scope reasonable for a certification effort?

When determining the value of the contents, there are many formulas that are available for you to use. Some are based on tangible values such as the dollar value of equipment. Others are based upon risk or business impact (potential for major disruption to the business caused by lack of availability, etc.). Oftentimes, a combination of these approaches proves to be the most successful. This chapter does not go into risk-management approaches, but will discuss the ISO risk requirements later.

Span of control is a critical concept in regard to successful scoping. You need to analyze what you have direct control over, can influence, or have no say in. Certification scopes typically deal with these areas of no control or limited influence through service-level agreements, memorandums of understanding, responsibility documents, or other methods. Trying to create a scope with little or no span of control may not be a wise idea and may end in the frustration of an ineffective program or failed certification attempt.

Roles and responsibilities exist within the scope and should be defined and understood so as to eliminate overlap and duplication. Responsibility for the management of the ISMS needs to be defined as well as the responsibility for those activities that make up the day-to-day operations of the system. A great way to keep all this information straight is through the use of RACI diagrams (in which tasks are split into four types of roles: Responsible, Accountable, Consulted, Informed), or responsibility matrices.

Physical and logical boundaries can be used to help define where a scope exists and can also help clarify span of control. These boundaries can be walls, floors, fences, etc., for the physical and virtual local area networks, segments, or even filtered ports for the logical boundaries. This is particularly valuable when preparing a scope for a data center, for example. Ingress and egress points, both physical and logical, can be identified and should be examined and documented.

Another important step in creating a scope is documenting exceptions. Exceptions are anything that is not applicable from the control objectives in Annex A. The requirements in Sections 4 through 8 are just that, required. You cannot document exceptions to those areas. One way to handle this is to create a list as you go or utilize a process that keeps these exceptions organized. You may need to defend your rationale for exceptions during an audit.

OK, so we have covered most of the items to be considered (granted, at a high level) when creating a scope. The most important question that needs to be answered is the last question that was asked earlier. Is the scope reasonable for attempting a certification audit? Many organizations, when first deciding whether to go down this road, choose to certify an entire organization (often referred to by consultants as "boiling the ocean"). Although this may be successful in smaller organizations with strong span of control, it may not be reasonable for most. Experience has shown that successful certification is based upon a program that is designed and implemented enterprisewide, but in which certification specifics are applied to the assets that are of the highest value to the organization. What you end up with is a situation in which the organization is able to benefit from the information security program that you developed (your ISMS) and from a certification that is internationally recognized and applied to your highest-value assets or services. My advice to you would be not to try to boil the ocean, but to look at a certification scope that makes sense for you. Are you a service provider? Consider certifying the portions of your organization that provide those services for your customers. Are you a financial institution? Consider certifying the services or centers where your customer information is stored, used, and retained. If you have a desire for enterprisewide certification, break your efforts up into manageable domains and apply the same scoping process to those domains.

Getting back to the rest of this section, defining an ISMS policy is just what it sounds like, writing a policy. Policy templates are popular starting points, but beware trying to use a canned document if you are going for certification or trying to build a truly effective program. Any good policy should be well thought out and be exactly that—a policy. Too often people put components of specifications (i.e., 128-bit encryption minimums) into policy. This prevents you from exercising span of control. Who wants to go to the board of directors every time you need to update a technical setting? The best advice to give here is to make sure that your "policy" fits the culture and environment of your organization. Take the time to be sure that you are not setting yourself up for failure by creating an unrealistic policy that you cannot live up to.

Risk management means different things to different people, but anyone should like the flexibility and business-friendly approach that the ISO standards take. If you are looking for a "how to" document, you will be disappointed. From the ISO standard perspective, they are more concerned that you have an organizational approach to risk, criteria or thresholds, and a repeatable methodology.

Informative references (optional, informational) exist that are directly applicable. Two of them are the following:

■ *ISO/IEC 27005 Information Technology—Security Techniques—Information Security Risk Management.*
■ *ISO/IEC TR 13335-3, Information Technology—Guidelines for the Management of IT Security—Techniques for the Management of IT Security.*

I strongly recommend using these documents as resources. At the end of performing a solid risk assessment, you should have a very good idea where your risks exist, what controls are there, and what your residual risk is. Remember, acceptance or transference are also approved methods for dealing with risk.

Monitoring and reviewing the ISMS—these requirements ensure that you are actively "managing" the ISMS. You not only have to understand what you have, but you need to be reviewing for errors or security events, reviewing effectiveness, and checking to see if you are still on track with your objectives. Time should be spent on looking forward to improve the ISMS, while making sure that any identified problems or observations are acted upon.

Documents and records need to be maintained, as the remainder of the Section 4 requirements discuss. For this, certain types of documents and document control requirements are outlined. Keep all the applicable documentation in an environment that is easy to access and work with and that maintains the integrity of this information. Oftentimes, people have a content management system, portal, or Web server that can serve this purpose. However, there is no requirement that says these records need to be electronic. Pay attention to Section 4.3.1 if you are going for certification, as you will need to have those items on hand and ready for the auditors. These are the core categories of the actual documents that make up an ISMS.

Section 5 is the area of the ISMS requirements that talks about management involvement and responsibility. The support of management is critical to any program, not just an ISMS. Proof of this commitment comes in many ways, including documented responsibilities, approval of policy, funding, and active involvement with the appropriate levels of ISMS activities. Other examples of management's commitment are the hiring, training, and empowerment of staff.

Internal audits are another required function, and the requirements are described in Section 6. Internal audit is the function that reviews whether your ISMS is meeting your requirements and functioning properly. What is covered here is what you would expect regarding audit considerations, including scheduling, performance, and remediation requirements. Internal audit is an important process, as it allows for identification and resolution of issues between registrar audit cycles. If you find a problem, you can fix it—but be aware that major problems or "nonconformities" must be reported.

Management review is the subject of Section 7. This section correlates directly with the PDCA (Plan, Do, Check, Act) model, which is a foundation for all the ISO ISMS standards. Here, you review your actions, changes in the environment, and measurements among other things. There are two parts, one that deals with "inputs" and one that deals with "outputs." The "outputs" portion helps you document your actions, considerations, and outcomes. These types of records are important to show the active management of the ISMS.

The last section, Section 8, deals with ISMS improvement. This is often compared to continuous process improvement, which, in effect, it is. Section 8 can be simplified in the following manner: "corrective" actions, which focus on problems that have been identified, and "preventative" actions taken to avoid negative events and impacts. Oftentimes, these preventative actions are the result of a review of corrective actions.

That should give you a basic understanding of what is covered in the general requirements of ISO 27001. As you can see, there are various other standards and documents that work together to make an ISMS effective.

The 27000 Series of ISO Standards

Currently under development are various other documents in the 27000 series. The main purpose of these developing standards is to support organizations in their efforts to implement an ISMS based on ISO 27001.

- ISO 27000 is a standard designed to educate and inform people of what the 27000 series of documents is and how they interrelate. It will also contain vocabulary and concepts that are not specifically contained in the other 27000 series of documents.

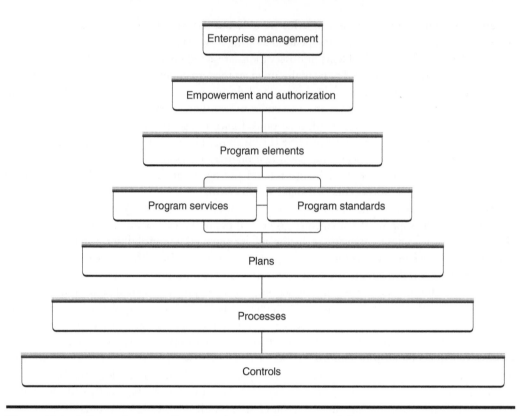

Figure 19.1   Information security management reference model.

- ISO 27002 (effective April 2007) is what is currently known as ISO 17799.
- ISO 27003 is implementation guidance for ISO 27001, focusing on the general requirements (Sections 4 through 8).
- ISO 27004 deals with how to gather measurements and metrics from an ISMS.
- ISO 27005 covers risk management in regard to ISO 27001 and ISMS.
- ISO 27006 deals with the requirements for accreditation bodies (the people who actually perform the registration audits).

Additional standards in the 27000 series will be added as needed, in support of the overall ISMS standards.

Figure 19.1 explains the relationships and functions of these standards.

Relationships to Other Standards

Although these standards focus on information security, they do not exist in a vacuum. There are various other standards, such as ISO 20000 (IT service management) that complement and interface with ISO 27001 and ISO 17799. Consider ISO 20000 as the mechanism to deal with the IT infrastructure and ISO 27001 as the mechanism to deal with the information security program and requirements. IT service management can help organizations define how to deal with areas such as change management and release management, which are both important from an information security standpoint as well.

Security managers often ask how standards such as COBIT (Control Objectives for Information and related Technology) and the National Institute of Standards and Technology standards relate to ISO standards. Although ISO 27001 will not direct someone to block a certain port on a firewall, it will require an understanding of the risk environment and the application of what is determined to be an appropriate control—that is, blocking that port. The important thing to understand is that where other standards are more operational, ISO standards deal with the issues of how security managers actually manage information security. This assists at a tactical and strategic level, while forming the processes for "informed decision," which impacts the operational level. These operational requirements are derived from legal, regulatory, or business requirements. When these elements are combined correctly, the result is a comprehensive information security program.

Why Do People Look to Implement an ISO 27001 ISMS?

There are many reasons information security practitioners and organizations are looking to implement or have implemented ISO 27001 ISMS. These reasons include looking for a way to provide proof of activities, due care, due diligence, and regulatory compliance. An ISO 27001 ISMS clearly meets the rigors of the Sarbanes-Oxley Act and other similar legislation in the United States or worldwide through the process of identifying and meeting requirements. Others see this as a road map into the future, understanding where future requirements may be met more easily by having a proven, flexible structure in place. Clear demonstration of industry leadership drives some, such as Fujitsu, PREMIER Bankcard, and the Federal Reserve Bank of New York, who were among the first worldwide to certify to ISO 27001 when it was published in November of 2005. Various organizations have leveraged ISMS efforts to accelerate maturity in their organization while maintaining flexibility.

One differentiator with the ISO 27001 standard is that it is risk based and, therefore, "business friendly." Security managers get to choose which control objectives apply to them based on their risk, legal, regulatory, and business requirements. There are many additional benefits that have been experienced firsthand, but to list them all here would be too lengthy.

How Does One Become Certified?

One potential advantage of building an information security program based on ISO 27001 is that you can achieve certification. Although there are many industry- or technology-specific certification schemes, none offer the level of international recognition that the ISO ISMS certification does. The actual certification audit is performed by an accredited registrar, working with a certification body (CB). Several of the best-known registrars include British Standards Institution (BSI) and Bureau Veritas Certification (BVQI), but recently American-based companies such as SRI Quality System Registrar and Cotecna are now beginning to offer services in this area. Globally, there are many CBs (also known as accreditation services). Several have been very active in ISMS activities. The best known of these is the United Kingdom Accreditation Service. In America, the American National Accreditation Body has expanded its existing quality management systems offerings to include ISO 27001. This is an important step toward increased adoption of the ISO standards in the United States. If someone is looking to become certified, or is interested, a program analysis is a good way to start. These can either be performed internally or with the help of an experienced partner. Following this, you should be able to have a good feel for where you sit, and what it will take to achieve your goal. Even if you are not interested in certification, the ISO standards provide a sound, accepted measuring stick against which you can examine your information security program. One last word of assistance to those who seek certification—train and educate those involved with the process. There are lead auditor and implementer courses available that should be considered. These can shorten your learning curve and bring better results in the long run.

What Is the Future?

The use of the ISO standards continues to grow in the United States. Many private and public sector organizations have information security programs built on components of ISO 17799. Although there were under 25 organizations certified to BS 7799 (in the United States), this number has already nearly doubled since the publication of ISO 27001. As awareness of the standards and the benefits of implementing ISMS continues to grow, it is estimated that the United States will begin to surpass many countries and become more on the level of the United Kingdom, Japan, and India, countries with registrations numbering in the hundreds. Security managers should take the time to explore ISO 27001 and the ISO 27000 series as important tools that can help strengthen their ability to manage information security.

Chapter 20

Security Frameworks

Robert M. Slade

Contents

Introduction

The term "security framework" has been used in a variety of ways in the security literature over the years, but in 2006 it came to be used as an aggregate term for various documents (and some pieces of software), from a variety of sources, that give advice on topics related to information systems security, with particular regard to the planning, managing, or auditing of overall information security practices for a given institution.

Some of these texts are guidelines specifically addressed toward information security such as British Standard (BS) 7799 and its descendants, particularly the International Standards Organization (ISO) 27000 family of standards. In this category are also items such as the (free, regarding both charge and access) "self-assessment questionnaire" prepared by the U.S. National Institute of Standards and Technology (NIST) (identified among their publications as 800-26). There have been a number of projects that attempted to produce similar sets of standards or practice lists, such as the now-moribund Commonly Accepted Security Practices and Recommendations and two versions of Generally Accepted System Security Principles: these listed undertakings have been amalgamated into Generally Accepted Information Security Principles. Other frameworks are peripherally related, but have come to be seen as having a bearing on system security. Probably the most widely known are the auditing standards and outlines such as Control Objectives for Information and Related Technology (COBIT) and the variety of supporting documents and processes that have grown up around the U.S. Federal Information Systems Management Act (FISMA). Others are more distantly associated, such as the Common Criteria (CC) on specifications and evaluation. Still others are even more tenuously connected, such as the advice on fraudulent financial reporting from the Committee of Sponsoring Organizations of the Treadway Commission (COSO). (The various financial instructions are generally concerned with the accuracy and reliability of reported earnings and the financial health of a company: this is felt to have implications for the management and controls on information systems, which are the primary source of all corporate data, including that related to finance.)

General Types and Differences

As can be seen, security frameworks come from a variety of sources and are intended to address a number of different ends. How relevant a specific framework will be to your operations and situation will partly depend upon the aim and objective of the framework.

This is not to say that a specific framework may not have relevance to your enterprise. All frameworks will give you different pieces of information about your systems, and all information can be valuable. In some cases, the initial intent of the framework may be irrelevant. For example, most of the financial frameworks and instructions are expected to address the issue of fraudulent reporting of the financial status of the company. To this end, they generally concentrate on requiring the disclosure of the availability of internal controls within the company. Internal controls are part and parcel of information system security, and so these frameworks can provide useful guidance, although their original purpose is outside the information security (InfoSec) realm. (It is rather ironic to note that if corporate officers are willing to lie about their finances, they would probably have no compunction in regard to lying about the state of internal controls. Therefore, financial frameworks may have more relevance to information security than to their original aim.)

Nevertheless, there are certain characteristics that tend to be consistent across frameworks from similar backgrounds.

Governance

There is frequent confusion in regard to the term governance and what differentiates it from management. Some note that management might be said to increase direct performance, whereas governance may, through analysis, redirect activities to greater effect. (In a sense this only moves the question back one level: this simply seems to be the distinction between strategic and operational management.) Some texts also note that five basic classes of decisions must be made in information technology (IT), over principles, architecture, infrastructure, business application needs, and the prioritizing of investment, and that these constitute the areas of governance.

Again, this outline does not get us much closer to a useful or functional definition. Architecture, to take a closer look at one aspect, is stated to be a level of abstraction above design, but this definition is not very helpful. A more functional description may be that architecture involves integration and standardization, but even this does not give us an awful lot of help in deciding what an IT architecture is, nor what the governance of it may be.

Security frameworks that stress "governance" tend to a management and overview perspective. Frequently they provide only a very generic structure for examining the macro levels of a very large enterprise, leaving the details to be dealt with elsewhere. Such tools are valuable for ensuring that security is assessed in a holistic manner, and that large areas are not missed in the pursuit of small details, but they will not be of much use to those who need to start on the securing of particular systems.

Breakdown Framework

A number of the governance-related security frameworks are primarily sets of divisions of activities and functions. These types of security frameworks are, in fact, the most likely to use the word "framework" in the title or description of the process. The entities provide structures that provide for the breaking down of the overall organization and operations of an institution into smaller areas that may aid in the analysis of specific risks, security requirements, and weaknesses.

Checklist

A significant number of security frameworks are presented in checklist form. This preference for the checklist format is hardly surprising: security is not a single function, but a compilation of a number of functions. Indeed, it is frequently pointed out that tremendous expenditures on security may be entirely obviated by the lack of a single control, and, therefore, a checklist of functions to be covered makes a great deal of sense.

Checklists, however, can vary in both content and intent. One checklist may be based on functional security, another may deal with audit and assurance mechanisms, whereas yet a third proceeds from an examination of business functions. The level of detail can also fluctuate from framework to framework.

When using checklist-type frameworks it is probably best to use more than one and to choose complementary documents that approach security from different perspectives. The use of multiple resources is probably more important with checklist frameworks than with other types, because there would be a psychological expectation of being "finished" once one had completed such a list.

Controls

Most security workers would probably see checklists in terms of lists of controls, but few formal security frameworks deal with specific controls. A great number of security frameworks, particularly those from the financial industry, stress "internal controls." This term is basically identical to the meaning of controls in security: it simply refers to the controls that a company implements on its own, rather than those that are required from external sources such as legislation or regulations.

Controls may be administrative, physical, or technical/logical. In planning for and considering the types of controls that we have, their effectiveness, and new ones we may need, it may be helpful to categorize controls into these different types, developed from the normal divisions of responsibility in business: management, physical plant, and operations. We divide controls into other classes as well. Corrective controls are applied when others have failed, directive controls provide guidance, deterrent controls use social pressures to reduce threats from human attackers, detective controls determine that a breach has taken place, preventive controls reduce our vulnerability to threats, recovery controls assist us to resume operations after an incident, and compensating controls provide coverage where others have been insufficient. This partition of security actions has its roots in military and law enforcement studies.

The finer the grading and codifying of controls that we can do, the better our analysis of our total security posture, and the two classifications are orthogonal. Therefore, the two divisions can be used as the basis for a matrix of controls, which can be used to assess the completeness of protection for a given system. Details of the process may be found in volume 3 of the fifth edition of *Information Security Management Handbook* (pp. 179–182).

For any given system, a wide variety of controls can be used. Indeed, a conglomeration of safeguards may be needed for a single process or structure. At some point it may become difficult to see the forest for the trees: having established a number of countermeasures, the practitioner may wonder at the necessity for ensuring against further vulnerabilities.

There are, of course, a number of tools for establishing the completeness of a risk management strategy, primarily involved with identifying specific risks, threats, or vulnerabilities. The controls matrix offers a slightly different kind of assessment of overall protections, noting broad classes of coverage and potential blind spots. The controls matrix is, therefore, a kind of breakdown framework (as noted earlier) directed at controls themselves.

Risk Management and Assessment

There are numerous products, procedures, outlines, and systems dedicated to the assessment, analysis, and management of risks. These tend to fall into three categories: those specific to information systems and security, those dealing with general business risk, and those from the financial (and particularly banking) community. Systems for information security and business risks tend to be similar in structure and general outline, with some minor variations in terms of specifics to be addressed. The banking world looks at risk management in a very different way: there is a great emphasis on the single issue of solvency and capital reserves, with everything else (pretty much what information systems and business people would know as the entire field of risk management) being relegated to a separate category of operational risk.

Risk management frameworks are very much process-oriented. Structures of committees, information gathering, and documentation are major aspects of these entities. If you are aware of deficiencies in regard to management structures and reporting in your own security environment, using a risk management framework will likely be of benefit.

Audit and Assurance

A significant number of frameworks are concerned with audit measures. These documents stress points that can be measured and demonstrated and may have little to do with the actual security environment or situation. Most of the emphasis in these frameworks is on what can be proven to others or documented. It is always a good idea to pay attention to what can be measured and documented. It is very easy to say that you know you are secure but just have not bothered to write it down. If you cannot document it, you really do not have a good idea of your situation.

At the same time, be careful of systems that require a lot of documentation that may not be relevant to your situation. You may commit a lot of resources to proving rather than doing. This is currently the situation with the Sarbanes–Oxley law in the United States: a number of smaller companies are noting that the cost of documenting internal controls is draining budgets for security operations.

Taxonomy

It would be handy to have a taxonomy of different types of security frameworks. Unfortunately, despite the proliferation of frameworks documents, there are so many different approaches and categories that it is questionable how useful such an exercise would be. In attempting to structure this chapter, and the list of frameworks to be covered, I attempted a structure of security, management, and financial orientation, as well as divisions along the lines of the characteristics noted earlier. There were, unfortunately, still a number of exceptions that did not fit well under any category, and the categories tended to group frameworks together in artificial ways. (I finally decided just to list the frameworks in alphabetical order and even that did not work too well.)

In a sense, this points out the value that using a variety of frameworks can have for you. There are a great many different viewpoints and perspectives, and the more positions you bring to a security plan, the better the result will be.

Weaknesses

Unfortunately, although security frameworks can provide some help and value, all of them do have weaknesses, and the weaknesses tend to be the same across all the systems and processes.

Content Limitations

One weakness that is very common across all the security frameworks is a narrow focus on a particular area, topic, or approach. Security should be a holistic practice, with input from a variety of fields and a wide-ranging overview of the problem, as well as details suitable to the situation or environment. Some frameworks focus on the details and do not care about an overview. Some take a management view and neglect the specifics. Some focus on functional security, others on the assurance mechanisms. Everyone has a field of expertise, and that is emphasized to the exclusion of some other aspects.

Define Secure

As Eugene Spafford has famously said, a secure system is one that does what it is supposed to. Therefore, it is impossible to define a state of security that is applicable to all computers, because not all computers are, in the minds of the users, supposed to do the same thing. In fact, security conflicts with itself. Factors promoting availability generally work against confidentiality. Controls enhancing confidentiality do not always support integrity. If we want to take the time to ensure that we can confirm integrity, that delays availability.

It should, therefore, come as no surprise that one size does not fit all when it comes to security. It is inherently impossible to create a checklist of items that, when implemented, will guarantee "security."

Best Practice

In the security field and industry, we are extremely fond of the term "best practice." It sounds quite reasonable: it does not imply that something is perfect, but it does support the idea that we are doing the finest job we can in a real (and, therefore, flawed) world. Unfortunately, we do not stop to think what that really means.

Does best practice mean something that will work for everyone in all situations? We have already determined that there is very little (possibly nothing) that will be "secure" in any and every environment. Does best practice mean a minimum level of security required by all? Does it mean an optimal balance? We do not know. There is no agreed-upon definition of "best practice." Although it sounds great, the term is close to meaningless. Probably the closest we can come to defining the term in any useful way is to say that it refers to activities or processes that a number of experienced people agree are useful or helpful in improving security in most common situations.

Description of Frameworks

As noted earlier, there is no particular taxonomy to this list. The items are generally in alphabetical order, although some entities (particularly those with limited relation to security as such) will be included with more general or derivative frameworks.

BS 7799 and ISO 27000 Family

Starting with BS 7799, a number of different security frameworks have been created. These have also become ISO standards and have created a family that is being expanded into specialty areas.

BS 7799-1, ISO 17799, and ISO 27002

BS 7799 Part 1 is one of the earliest frameworks specifically addressing information security and is currently probably the most important and widely used. Subsequent to its adoption as BS 7799-1 it became of significant interest to the information security community worldwide. The ISO used BS 7799-1 as a model for developing multiple versions of ISO 17799: the current standard is ISO 17799:2005. To promote consistency of numbering in the 27000 family of security standards, ISO 17799 is being redeveloped as ISO 27002.

This framework does not provide technical or implementation details, nor does it give a methodology or a complete list of controls or safeguards. In its ISO 17799 version, it structures a bit of a taxonomy (eleven "clauses" that are surprisingly similar to the ten domains of the (ISC)²® Common Body of Knowledge), some policy (30 "objectives"), and a number of controls (133 "controls" and more than 500 "detailed controls").

---

135 Items

There seems to be something magical about 135 in relation to security. An astounding number of the security frameworks have roughly 135 controls, or objectives, or questions. Of course, an intriguing count of the security frameworks also seems to gravitate to 150. Not as a number of items of any kind, though. When you go to purchase the various documents, U.S. $150 seems to have become a very common price point, regardless of the size or complexity of the guideline in question.

BS 7799-1 is essentially a code of practice, and it is the closest, of all the frameworks, to a list of specific security activities to perform. In the new ISO 27000 family, the updated version is to be ISO 27002.

BS 7799-2 and ISO 27001

BS 7799 seems to have promoted the use of the phrase "Information Security Management System" and the use of the acronym "ISMS" is an indicator of a BS 7799 influence. BS 7799-2 deals with ISMS requirements and is used within companies to create security requirements and objectives. This framework provides a process for implementation and management of controls and safeguards, ensuring that they meet specific security goals. Enterprises can define new (and document existing) information security management processes and determine the status of InfoSec management activities.

ISO 27000

As noted, the ISO standards related to security are being renumbered (as they are updated) and new standards are being added in the 27000 range. ISO 27000 itself will be about ISMS fundamentals and vocabulary and will essentially be the introduction to (and umbrella for) the whole group of standards. ISO 27003 will be ISMS implementation guidance, 27004 talks about Info-Sec management measurements and metrics, 27005 is InfoSec risk management, 27006 is for accreditation of certification agencies, and 27007 will deal with audit guidelines.

Control Objectives for Information and Related Technology

Widely used and, until the rise of BS 7799-1, probably the most recognized of the security frameworks, COBIT is directed at information security. However, it should be noted that COBIT was created by a specific group and intended for a specific purpose.

COBIT was created by ISACA (which used to be known as the Information Systems Audit and Control Association). Auditability is key to the COBIT, and the accounting and management background definitely shows in the choice of items in the COBIT list. Much of the activity suggested relates to measurement, performance, and reporting. Thus, in a sense, most of COBIT concentrates on what can be counted and demonstrated, sometimes disregarding what might actually be effective.

You will find all kinds of variations on the capitalization of COBIT. There are references to COBiT, CObIT, and CobiT in the security literature, and ISACA prefers to print it out with the C and T in large capital letters and the OBI in small caps. In fact, you will find variations on the expansion of the acronym. In the same way that the parent organization now prefers to be known by its initials and the original name has been discarded, COBIT itself was originally Control Objectives for Information Technology, and has now been expanded to include "and related," and ISACA's literature seldom spells out the expansion at all.

COBIT breaks the list of suggested controls into four phases or domains, dealing with "planning and organization," "acquisition and implementation," "delivery and support," and "monitoring." (It is not too much of a stretch to see the Deming Plan/Do/Check/Act (PDCA) cycle in this structure. In fact, a great many process-based frameworks demonstrate the influence of Deming's PDCA.) The checklist of controls is extensive, and it is a valuable tool to ensure that no major area is neglected. COBIT also fits very well for organizations that are primarily concerned about issues of compliance (e.g., in terms of the U.S. Sarbanes–Oxley law): the emphasis on audit provides a good utility for demonstrating the existence of controls of many types.

COBIT is not, however, confined to information security and addresses a large number of other areas. Therefore, basing a security review on COBIT may require extensive resources and will definitely demand activity from areas of the enterprise outside of the information security department.

Common Criteria

Contrary to much mistaken opinion, the CC (more properly the Common Criteria for information technology security evaluation, and also ISO 15408) is not a security framework or standard of practice. It is not even a standard for evaluating security products or systems. The CC is a structure for specifying product and product evaluation standards.

The basic result of following the CC structure is the production of a protection profile (PP). A PP outlines a general class of security devices or products, describing the environment within which such an entity is expected to work and the security functions that should be implemented. The part of the PP that can be used to evaluate a specific device is known as the security target (ST). Evaluations are done on the basis of seven levels of increasing confidence in the assessment, the evaluation assurance levels (EALs).

It is not enough to know that a product has "passed" the CC. To understand what that might imply, the details of the PP, ST, and EAL must be known as well. As those who have dealt with ISO 9000, the standard on quality, are aware, it is perfectly possible to document your quality standards and procedures in a manner consistent with the ISO 9000 requirements and still have them say no more than "we make lousy products, and we do not care." In the same way, it is possible to be CC "compliant" with a certification that says "the product provides almost no protection, and we are only judging that based on hearsay."

Sources of information about the CC have tended to bounce around. For a while you could go to www.commoncriteria.org, then that disappeared, and the best place to get an idea of how it worked was at the NIST Web site. At the moment the site http://www.commoncriteriaportal.org/public/expert/index.php?menu=2 seems to be working.

There are generally three parts, or documents, related to the CC overall. Part 1 is a general introduction, outlining the basic ideas and major terminology used. The Part 1 document is not hard to read, and probably every security professional should have read through it at least once. Part 2 addresses functional security, the aspects that we normally consider to be security technologies and activities. This document stipulates how to express the requirements for functional security for a particular device. Outside of developers or evaluators working with or toward an evaluation, Part 2 is not something you will want to plow through, unless you have serious problems with insomnia. Part 3 deals with assurance: the question of how we know that the functional security is actually providing the protection that we want it to provide. Like Part 2, it sets forth the language and format for requirements and specifications, and the document is even longer. However, this part also contains an overview of the seven EALs. Although the text is not easy to work through, this section of the CC is one with which more security professionals should be familiar.

Federal Information Systems Management Act

The U.S. FISMA mandates certain standards of information security and controls for U.S. federal agencies. It extends to contractors and other sources that support the assets of federal government departments. However, it may have wider application yet, because it provides a solid basis for security management, assessment, and assurance for large corporations as well.

Specifics on the implementation of FISMA vary somewhat. The legislation states that standards must be applied, but the standards are different for different agencies and applications. Detailed instructions can be found in directives for the military (Defense Information Technology Systems Certification and Accreditation Process), the intelligence community (Director of Central Intelligence Directive 6/3), and more generally the National Information Assurance Certification and Accreditation Process. The NIST also has outlines (see National Institute of Standards and Technology for details of this and other documents).

Information Security Forum

The Information Security Forum (ISF) Standard of Good Practice for information security is a guideline forming a checklist of policies (or even attitudes) that the company or employees should have. It is structured in five "aspects" of security management: critical business applications, computer installations, networks, systems, and development. These aspects are broken out into 30 "areas" and the areas into 135 "sections."

The areas of security management are high-level direction, security organization, security requirements, secure environment, malicious attack, special topics, and management review. For critical business applications there are security requirements, application management, user environment, system management, local security management, and special topics. Computer installations involve installation management, live environment, system operation, access control, local security management, and service continuity. Networks require network management, traffic management, network operations, local security management, and voice networks. For systems development pay attention to development management, local security management, business requirements, design and build, testing, and implementation. Not all the 135 sections do have equal levels of detail. Management, for example, gets much more attention and material. The first section (of three) from "high-level direction" (section SM1.1) deals with management commitment. It sets out the principle that senior management's direction on information security should be established and commitment demonstrated. The objective is to establish top management's direction on, and commitment to, information security. It goes on to note that board-level executives or the equivalent should have a high level of commitment to achieving high standards of corporate governance, such as those required by various national standards, treating information security as a critical business issue, creating a security-positive environment, and demonstrating to third parties that the enterprise deals with information security in a professional manner. Top management should have a high level of commitment to applying fundamental principles, for example, assuming ultimate responsibility for the internal controls of the enterprise; ensuring that controls over information and systems are proportional to risk assessed; assigning responsibility for identifying, classifying, and safeguarding information and systems to system owners; and granting access to information and systems in accordance with explicit criteria (policy). Management should demonstrate their commitment to information security by setting direction for information security (in policy), assigning overall responsibility for information security to a top-level director or equivalent, chairing key information security working groups, monitoring the security condition of the enterprise, and allocating sufficient resources to information security.

Unfortunately, a later section on malicious mobile code simply states that there should be a means of dealing with it and lists some risk factors.

The ISF standard is, however, one of the few frameworks available without charge. The 247-page document (currently the 2005 version) does provide useful advice in a number of areas (although the early material is primarily promotional in nature). It can be downloaded from the ISF Web site at www.securityforum.org or http://www.isfsecuritystandard.com/pdf/standard.pdf.

Information Technology Infrastructure Library

The Information Technology Infrastructure Library (ITIL®) is a massive (and expensive) set of documentation aimed at improving IT service management. Although ITIL does not address security specifically (any more: an original security section has been removed to be dealt with separately), proper management generally leads to better security, so it fairly naturally follows that this library of practices would be of interest to information security.

The areas addressed by the library include incident response, problems, change, release, configuration, service desk, service levels, availability, capacity, service continuity, IT financials, and the IT workforce.

A standard for IT service management, closely following the principles and activities described in ITIL, will shortly be available as ISO 20000 (and the related BS 15000).

Management Frameworks

Although some of the entities noted earlier have a definite background in the management arena, there are some additional frameworks that tend to be used in security planning.

Zachman Framework

The Zachman Framework is a two-dimensional model used to analyze an organization or process by breaking it down into smaller characteristics or considerations. Instead of trying to look at the entire enterprise at once, you break it down into a grid of perspectives and viewpoints. The "columns" of the framework are the standard W5 "five good serving men" (plus one) of "what" (entities or data), "how" (function), "where" (network), "who" (people or organization) "when" (time or schedule), and "why" (motivation). The rows of the model structure differing levels of scope and detail for various viewpoints: overall scope and context (or ballpark view), business unit (system or process owner's view), system level (architect's view), technology level (designer's view), and detail level (subcontractor or implementer's view) (Figure 20.1).

The Zachman Framework is presented as a tool for analyzing architectural conditions and operations in business. However, the original intent was to address issues in regard to sharing data and the structuring of relationships in data warehouses. Therefore, although the tool would likely identify a number of important factors in regard to information flow, direct application to security will likely require some application on the part of the analyst.

Calder–Moir IT Governance Framework

Supposedly to help you get the various security frameworks to work together harmoniously, the Calder–Moir IT Governance Framework is really only a graphical classification of the various frameworks in terms of whether they address the topics of business strategy, business and risk environment, IT strategy, operations, capabilities, and change management. You can see it at http://www.itgovernance.co.uk/calder_moir.aspx (Figure 20.2).

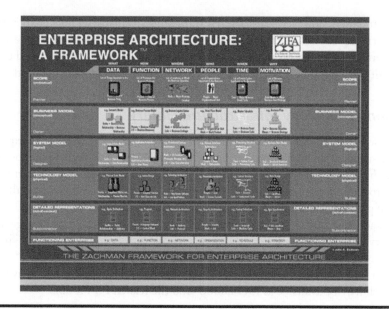

Figure 20.1 Graphical display of the Zachman Framework. (From http://www.zifa.com/ framework.html. With permission).

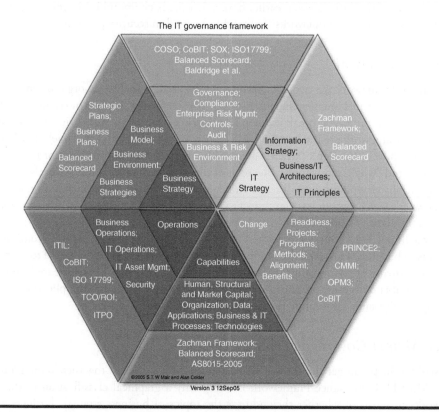

Figure 20.2 Graphical display of the Calder–Moir IT Governance Framework. (From http:// www.itgovernance.co.uk/page.framework. With permission).

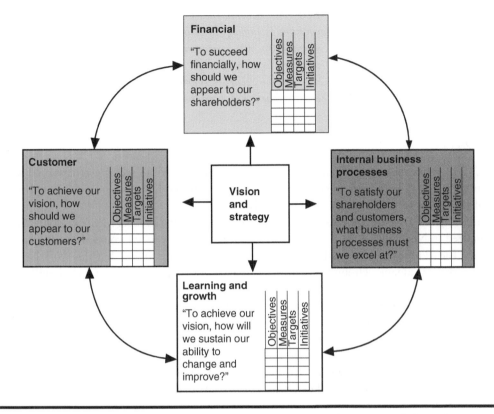

Figure 20.3 Graphical display of the balanced scorecard. (From http://www.balancedscorecard. org/basics/bsc1.html. With permission).

Balanced Scorecard

The "balanced" part of balanced scorecard is a reminder to view business processes from multiple perspectives and not to neglect any. Specifically, the process recommends setting objectives, and measuring performance, for the learning and growth (employee training), (internal) business processes, customer (satisfaction), and financial perspectives. It is very concerned with metrics and measurement-based management.

The balanced scorecard is a good approach to take when there is a concern for the establishment of security metrics. Generally, this would mitigate some of the risks of creating biased and unrealistic measurement baselines (Figure 20.3).

National Institute of Standards and Technology

It really is not fair to compare the Computer Security Resource Center of the U.S. NIST with the security frameworks we have been discussing. The center (which, although it is only one office of the institute, is generally known simply as NIST in the security community) provides a wealth of security information and resources, which are freely available from their Web site at http://csrc.nist. gov. The publications section is particularly useful, with a constantly updated stream of guidelines and aids, particularly the 800-series documents. Notable among these are the *Information Security*

Handbook: A Guide for Managers (800-100), *Recommended Security Controls for Federal Information Systems* (800-53), *Guide to Information Technology Security Services* (800-35), *Risk Management Guide for Information Technology Systems* (800-30), *Engineering Principles for Information Technology Security* (800-27), *Guide for Developing Security Plans for Federal Information Systems* (800-18), *Generally Accepted Principles and Practices for Securing Information Technology Systems* (800-14), and *An Introduction to Computer Security: The NIST Handbook* (800-12).

800-26

The NIST publications provide an embarrassment of riches, and no security professional worth his or her salt has a bookmark file that does not contain this site. However, to avoid extending the number of pages in this chapter I shall note only one.

The original *Security Self-Assessment Guide for Information Technology Systems* (800-26) was formalized in November 2001. It is a checklist of 137 questions to ask yourself about your own system. The significance and analysis of your answers are left up to you, but this work has been a tremendously valuable self-audit resource. More recently a version has been revised with NIST SP 800-53 (*Recommended Security Controls for Federal Information Systems*) references and mappings for the associated security controls, although this is, of course, more directly useful for the running the U.S. government systems. 800-26 is undergoing another revision, and this will involve a change of format to the *Guide for Information Security Program Assessments and System Reporting Form*. This new guide will be broader, and will deal with more extensive aspects of systems and protection, but it will also be more demanding of the user. Those dealing with small systems may wish to ensure that they have a copy of the original version of 800-26 before it is withdrawn in favor of the update.

Operationally Critical Threat, Asset, and Vulnerability Evaluation

The Operationally Critical Threat, Asset, and Vulnerability Evaluation (OCTAVE) process is a risk management method from Carnegie Mellon University. It is a formal and detailed set of processes and will assist in ensuring that risks are identified and properly analyzed, following the standard techniques used in most risk analysis procedures. However, due to the level of activity and overhead involved in OCTAVE, it is probably best suited to large organizations or projects.

Securities and Financial Industry Frameworks

As should be clear to everyone in both fields, the financial securities industry has very little to do with computer or information security, despite a heavy reliance on the technology. However, recent concerns in that community have concentrated on the area of internal controls, which have application in reviewing controls and safeguards, particularly in regard to insider attacks.

Basel II

This reference is shorthand for the Second Report from the Basel Committee on Banking Supervision, Risk Management Principles for Electronic Banking. The banking community has its own ideas about what risk management entails. One of the areas they are most concerned with involves having sufficient capital reserves to weather a storm, which generally is not something information security people tend to worry much about. However, the Basel II Accord also looks at operational risk, which is more in line with the risk management that InfoSec people know and love.

Committee of Sponsoring Organizations of the Treadway Commission

This title is shorthand for the Committee of Sponsoring Organizations of the Treadway Commission, Enterprise Risk Management Integrated Framework. The Treadway Commission was established, in the United States, to address a fear (subsequent to some major financial failures) that small investors would lose faith in the stock markets and, in particular, in the financial reports from publicly traded companies. As such, COSO seeks to ensure that there are internal controls to enhance the reliability of public disclosures. Like COBIT, COSO is primarily concerned with internal controls, and with audit. (In opposition to COBIT, which concentrates on IT, COSO is concerned with business risk.)

COSO outlines a three-dimensional framework for examining controls. On one axis are four categories of objectives: strategic, operations, reporting, and compliance. A second axis lists four unit levels of an enterprise: entity level, division, business unit, and subsidiary. Finally, there are eight components of risk management: internal environment, objective setting, event identification, risk assessment, risk response, control activities, information and communication, and monitoring.

Again, although COSO provides a framework for examining a number of aspects of the business, it does not provide any list of controls, practices, or methodologies.

Sarbanes–Oxley Law

The U.S. Sarbanes–Oxley law (frequently referred to as Sarbox or SOX) emphasizes that corporate management is responsible for the reliability of financial reports about publicly traded companies. It extends beyond that, touching on private companies doing business with other companies that do provide public reports and even on entities outside U.S. jurisdiction. Section 404 (and also 302, in a marvelous confusion with Web result codes) notes that the integrity of information systems supporting these financial reports must also be managed. (Note: This basically repeats the concepts established in 1977 by the Foreign Corrupt Practices Act. The big difference is in the compliance requirements.)

Security Governance

Many of the security frameworks available are in the form of a checklist, so why should not the *Security Governance* list-in-book-form for Fred Cohen's CISO Toolkit be included?

In fact, Cohen's version may be considerably easier to understand and use, particularly for those with a business, rather than a security, background. Although most security frameworks are structured according to a taxonomy of security concepts, the checklist in *Security Governance* is based on business models and concepts. For example, the four major divisions are made on the basis of business functions and modeling, oversight, business risk management, and enterprise security management. Therefore, the businessperson working through the points will start with the familiar and only later have to face items directly discussing security. (Even then, the security issues are those regarding the position and management of security within the organization.)

Regardless of other security frameworks that you may use, Cohen's checklist will be of value. Although many items will have relations to details in other indices, the articles and entities in *Security Governance* address a number of issues that are not found in most security frameworks. Let's face it: regardless of the emphasis or perspective, security frameworks tend to follow the same general outline. Cohen's work is idiosyncratic and, in this case, that is a useful characteristic.

Also, most security frameworks give you a checklist of about 135 items for roughly U.S. $150. Cohen gives you over 900 points for U.S. $49.

Systems Security Engineering-Capability Maturity Model

The Systems Security Engineering-Capability Maturity Model (SSE-CMM), more generally known as the Capability Maturity Model (CMM), is an attempt to apply standards of engineering rigor to information systems technology development. Researchers at Carnegie Mellon University noted that many technology products and applications succeed based primarily upon being the first to address a need, even if it is addressed very poorly. (Many more programs and systems fail along the way.) The model identified different levels of maturity of organizations, in terms of processes, documentation, and discipline, in an approach to development and change. The original model identified levels starting at informal or chaotic, through repeatable, documented, managed, and finally ending at continually improving. These structures and observations have been modified and applied to more specialized fields.

The SSE-CMM addresses the planning, development, and management of security and security architecture for an enterprise. The levels in security are basic, planned and verified, well-defined and coordinated, measurable and quantitatively controlled, and constantly improving. Within these levels, sublevels are identified. In general, SSE-CMM recommends determining the institution's performance level (in a number of security engineering and process areas) and then addressing individual areas to improve overall maturity.

SSE-CMM brings a good deal of discipline to management and process areas. Any large organization that has addressed basic areas of security, but wishes to formalize the process and develop a more architectural and broader outlook, can benefit from the assessment and recommended activities. However, the model does not, strictly speaking, advise on security activities and protections as such.

There is some controversy about the value of the CMM itself. Neither the "informal" nor the "continually optimizing" endpoint of the continuum is particularly well defined, and some management specialists see very little difference between them. It should also be noted that some enterprises seem to perform very well, and for a very long time, at the basic "repeatable" level, although such organizations do not tend to deal well with change. However, companies nominally at the higher "managed" level may struggle with processes that are not truly repeatable or have been improperly documented. Therefore, placing an institution on the continuum is somewhat subjective.

Most management specialists would agree that the CMM is a valuable analytical tool. It may not work as well in terms of prescriptions for action.

Summary

Although this chapter can only be the merest introduction to the security frameworks themselves, it should provide a general idea of the types of frameworks that are available and the relative areas of relevance and application for specific frameworks. It is hoped that the reader will also have noted that just as no one security framework is suitable for all situations and applications, so no single framework should be relied upon as the sole guide for any enterprise. Multiple perspectives are necessary to provide for realistic security, and multiple documents have additional viewpoints to add to the construction of a security architecture. Each folio should be considered to see if it has something to add to your security program.

TELECOMMUNI-CATIONS AND NETWORK SECURITY

Communications and Network Security

Chapter 21

Facsimile Security

Ben Rothke

Contents

Most companies do not lack for information security products. Their data centers are likely full of firewalls, virtual private networks, security appliances, and much more. Yet there is a device, hundreds of them perhaps, in many organizations, that lacks any sort of security. This is the lowly fax machine.

The fax machine poses serious potential security issues and risks to every company that uses it. The good news is that most of these risks can easily be mitigated. The issue is that most companies are oblivious to these threats and do not take the appropriate countermeasures.

Group 3 Fax Protocols

An introduction to basic fax operations is in order. The reason faxing is so seamless is that all modern fax machines operate using the same protocol, namely the Group 3 Facsimile Protocol (G3). The G3 was first published in 1980 by the ITU (International Telecommunications Union: http://www.itu.int).

The G3 standard for facsimile communications over analog telephone lines was originally approved by the Consultative Committee for International Telegraphy and Telephony (CCITT) in its T.4 and T.30 recommendations in 1980. This standard is supported by nearly every fax machine in use today and continues to be updated.

G3 is specified in two standards:

- T.4—image-transfer protocol
- T.30—session-management procedures that support the establishment of a fax transmission

T.30 allows the two endpoints to agree on such things as transmission speed and page size. Because G3 is specified for switched analog networks, and it is an all-digital procedure, it must use modems or a fax relay. They are also specified in ITU standards:

- V.21 (300 bps) for the T.30 procedures and for image transfer
- V.27ter (2400/4800 bps)
- V.29 (7.2k, 9.6k)
- V.17 (7.2k, 9.6k, 12k, 14.4k)
- Real-time Internet Protocol fax transport is specified in T.38 and replaces modems

There is a G4 standard, but this is for digital telephone networks and was approved in 1984 and updated in 1988. This standard has found greater acceptance in Europe and Japan than in the United States and is predominately used for fixed point-to-point high-volume communications.

The T.30 specification divides a call into five phases:

- Phase A—call setup
- Phase B—premessage procedures
- Phase C—image transfer
- Phase D—postmessage procedures including multipage and end of procedure signals
- Phase E—call release

These five phases are detailed in the following figure:*

---

* http://www.commetrex.com/whitepapers/FaxTech.html.

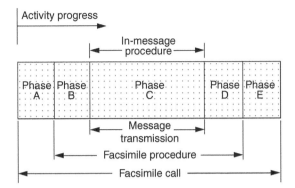

Secure Faxing

One of the important works on fax security was *Guidelines on Facsimile Transmission Security,* issued by the Information and Privacy Commissioner of Ontario, Canada, back in 1989. This document was one of the first to bring to light the need to deal with fax security. The document was updated in 2003,* and it sets out guidelines for government organizations to consider when developing systems and procedures to maintain the confidentiality and integrity of information transmitted by fax. Although the paper was written for government organizations, most of the issues and guidelines are relevant for nongovernment organizations also.

According to Ontario, Canada-based Natural Data, Inc., there are over 100 million fax machines in use worldwide today. Almost all of these fax machines are unable to connect to the Internet and as a result can send and receive faxes using only the unsecured public fax line services.

Fax Advantages and Security Issues

The fax machine, like all technologies, has security risks. The most notable fax issues are that the faxed document will sometimes not reach its intended destination. This is due to both human error (wrong number dialed) and technical issues (poor communication lines, incompatible equipment, and more).

Although there are fax security issues, one of the main benefits of a fax is that unlike an e-mail attachment, a fax document is an image file and, therefore, is inherently not an editable file. That means that no one can alter the original itself to embed another program within it, meaning a fax can never cause a computer virus or worm to invade one's network.

Secure Fax Designation

It is important to note that in a perfect world, every fax machine will be deployed with the highest levels of security. In the real world, such an approach is not practical.

---

* http://www.ipc.on.ca/index.asp?navid=46&fid1=413.

Creating a Secure Fax Infrastructure

Computer security is simply attention to detail and good design, and effective information security is built on risk management, good business practices, and project management. Creating a secure fax infrastructure is no different.

The initial step in this infrastructure is to establish policies around the use of fax machines. The ultimate level of fax security is built on this foundation of effective policies and procedures that govern their use. At the end of this chapter is a set of core policies around fax security that can be used.

Although the basic use of a fax machine is often intuitive, the secure use of a fax machine is often not so intuitive. By creating a set of standard operating procedures (SOPs) around the use of secure faxes, you can mitigate most of the threats involved.

Some of the basic procedures around fax security include ensuring that the number of pages received for the fax is the same as that being sent, reassembling the received document, distributing it appropriately, confirming receipt, and more.

Cover Sheets

As part of the SOPs, all faxes sent should have a standardized cover sheet containing the name, title, and company name of both the sender and the recipient and the total number of pages faxed.

Some organizations request that the recipient confirm successful receipt of the fax, but such a request should be used with caution, as such a request can be onerous to the receiving party.

Many companies include disclaimers on their fax cover sheets stating that the information in the fax is confidential and that the information should not be distributed, copied, or disclosed to any unauthorized persons without prior approval of the sender.

Receiving Misdirected Faxes

Just as your users will eventually and invariably send a fax to the wrong number, you will also invariably be on the receiving end of an errant fax. Your SOPs should deal with such scenarios and detail to employees what they should do when an errant fax is received.

The first thing to do is to notify the sender that a fax was received in error. It is assumed that the sender followed guidelines and used a cover sheet.

Your users should be instructed that incorrectly sent faxes should never be forwarded to the recipient. They should either be returned to the sender or shredded.

Number Confirmation

Many organizations have master lists of fax numbers. The challenge with such master lists is that fax numbers are often changed. If such lists are used, they should be audited regularly to ensure that the numbers are indeed current and accurate.

Secure Fax Locations

A key point to realize about security is that nearly every operating system, from UNIX to Linux, NetWare, Windows, and more, places the foundation of its security architecture at the physical server level. Unfortunately, physical security is often an afterthought when deciding where to place a fax machine. Such consequences can leave fax machines open to a security breach.

To create a secure fax infrastructure, fax machines must be isolated in a secure area. This area must be restricted to only authorized employees. These secure fax machines should be placed in locations that are not accessible to the general populace. Given that faxes can come in at any time, 24/7/365, this level of segregation ensures that confidential information sent during off-hours is not compromised.

Confirmation Page

Even with the advent of e-mail, one significant advantage the fax has over other forms of data exchange is that the sender immediately knows if the transmission was successful. When it comes to e-mail, it can often take hours or days for the information to actually appear on the recipient's desktop.

With that, all fax machines have the capability to print a fax confirmation sheet after each fax sent. This sheet confirms if the fax has been successfully transmitted, the destination fax number, and the number of pages transmitted. The sender of each fax should confirm the success of a transmission by checking this log after each secure fax message is sent.

Similarly, recipients should be trained to match the number of pages received against the transmitted fax cover sheet. In the event that pages are missing, the recipient should contact the sender and request a retransmission.

Secure Fax Hardware

To use fax encryption technology, both senders and recipients must have the same type of fax encrypting hardware. Most secure fax machines are identical in appearance to a typical fax machine, built on a standard commercial-based platform of product sold for general use. For secure fax machines, most of the functionality is transparent to the end user.

There are various standards for secure fax machines, including:

- MIL-STD-188-161D
- NATO STANAG 5000
- NSA NSTISSAM 1-92 TEMPEST Level 1
- NATO AMSG720B

TEMPEST models are internally shielded to prevent electromagnetic emissions from escaping, preventing interception of transmitted data signals. This is needed as anyone with the proper equipment can monitor, intercept, and reconstruct those signals, possibly while parked outside a corporate headquarters or military base. The downside is that TEMPEST capabilities can increase the price of a standard fax machine to well over $2000.

When communicating in a secure mode, a fax uses an RS-232C connection to cryptographic equipment, such as an STE (secure terminal equipment), a device that looks much like a telephone and utilizes digital signaling.

Conclusion

Creating a secure fax infrastructure does not take a lot. The function of this chapter was to raise the issue and be a starting point for companies in creating their secure fax plan.

Exhibit A: Secure Fax Hardware and Software

The following is a starters list of secure fax vendors. A Google search on secure fax will provide a much more definitive list of the various vendors.

Ricoh SecureFax
  www.ricoh-usa.com/products/category_main.asp?pCategoryId=17&pCatName=
    SecureFax
Cryptek Secure Fax
  http://www.cryptek.com/fax/default.asp
Gateway Fax Systems
  http://www.gwfs.com/JITCCertification/JITCcert.html
Venali
  http://www.venali.com/solutions/index.php
Business Security AB SecuriFax
  www.bsecurity.se
TCC CSD 3700
  http://www.tccsecure.com/products/voice-fax-data-encryption/CSD3700-summary.html

Exhibit B: Policy

Policy is critical to the effective deployment of a secure fax infrastructure. A comprehensive security policy is required to map abstract security concepts to the real world implementation of security products. It is the policy that defines the aims and goals of the business. It comes down to the fact that if you have no policies, you have no information security.

After policy comes the need for SOPs. Organizations that take the time and effort to create formal information security SOPs demonstrate their commitment to security. By creating SOPs, they drastically lower their costs (greater return on investment [ROI]) and drastically increase their level of security.

The following policies are from *Information Security Policies Made Easy*, version 10,* which is the definitive information security policy resource.

---

* https://www.informationshield.com/ispmemain.htm—Used with permission from Information Shield, Inc.

Title	Policy	Commentary
Machine repair staff confidentiality agreements	Prior to beginning their work, all external office equipment repair staff must have signed a Company X confidentiality agreement.	This policy prevents industrial or military espionage. Recent models of ordinary office equipment such as copiers and fax machines now have up to 5 MB of recent information stored in them. If repairpersons were to swap the chip that contains this information, they could walk away with significant intellectual property without detection. If there is a paper jam, some sensitive information may have been printed on that paper but it may not have been removed from the machine. The policy is written with a broad scope, and general-purpose computers, including handhelds, would be included within its purview. Some organizations refer to confidentiality agreements as nondisclosure agreements.
Maintaining classification labels	Workers in possession of any information containing a Company X data classification sensitivity label must maintain, propagate, and if need be, reestablish this same label whenever the information changes form, format, or handling technology.	This policy tells users that they must be diligent when they change the form, format, or technology used to handle sensitive information. For example, assume that information labeled as "confidential" was sent by fax to a remote location. The recipient could then extract certain details from the fax and include these details in an e-mail message. This policy would require that the "confidential" label be included in the e-mail message. Because users are in control of many of the changes in form, format, and handling technology that occur, they must be the ones to ensure that a label continues to be attached to sensitive information. This policy could be expanded to include labels and restrictions provided by third parties, such as copyright notices. The words "any information containing a Company X data classification sensitivity label" may be too stringent for some organizations; they may prefer to use the words "any information with a secret classification label" (and thus save some money).

(continued)

Title	Policy	Commentary
Equipment in secret information areas	Printers, copiers, and fax machines must not be located in the physically isolated zones within Company X offices that contain secret information.	This policy prevents people from making paper copies, from printing computer-resident information, and from otherwise removing hard-copy versions of secret information. If the devices to perform this process are not provided within a secured area no one will be able to make unauthorized copies of the information contained therein. All other avenues through which secret information could flow must also be blocked. For example, an isolated local area network could be used to prevent users from sending the secret information out over the Internet as part of an e-mail message. The very high security approach reflected in this policy works best if the movement of paper-resident secret information is strictly controlled, perhaps with sensors that detect that it has been removed from an isolated area. This policy also creates a paperless office that, when deployed in high security areas, has the potential to be more secure than any paper-based office could ever be. Diskless workstations could be employed in such an environment to increase the level of security.
Fax logs	Logs reflecting the involved phone numbers and the number of pages for all inbound and outbound fax transmissions must be retained for one year.	This policy provides a legal record of the faxes that were sent and received. This is important in business environments where contracts, purchase orders, invoices, and other legally binding promises are handled by fax. The maintenance and retention of a fax log can help resolve day-to-day operational problems. Such fax logs may additionally be useful for the preparation of expense reports and internal charge-back system reports. Many new personal computer software packages that support faxing come with their own logs, which, according to this policy, should be turned on. Fax servers also support extensive logging. Modern versions of more expensive fax machines also keep their own logs. This policy can be carried out automatically by the involved equipment as well as manually by the involved operators.

Faxing sensitive information—notification	If secret information is to be sent by fax, the recipient must have been notified of the time when it will be transmitted and also have agreed that an authorized person will be present at the destination machine when the material is sent. An exception to this policy is permitted when the destination fax machine is physically or logically restricted such that persons who are not authorized to see the material being faxed may not enter the immediate area or otherwise gain access to faxes received.	One scenario for inadvertent disclosure involves sensitive materials that have been sent by fax but not yet picked up by the intended recipient. This policy ensures that no unauthorized person examines sensitive faxed materials sitting in a fax machine. If the recipient knows a fax is coming, he or she will also be concerned if it does not arrive when expected. The policy presumes the existence of another policy that defines the term "secret." This term may be readily replaced with the comparable label used within the organization in question. Note that the policy recognizes the reality of modern fax servers that can restrict access to faxes received using recipient passwords.
Faxing sensitive information—human presence	Sensitive materials must not be faxed unless the sender has immediately beforehand confirmed that an authorized staff member is on hand to handle the materials at the receiving machine properly. When the transmission is complete, the staff member at the receiving end must confirm to the sender that a certain number of pages were received. An exception is allowed if the receiving machine is in a locked room accessible only to authorized personnel or if a password-protected fax mailbox is used to restrict unauthorized release of faxed materials.	One common scenario for inadvertent disclosure of faxed materials involves faxes that have been sent but not yet picked up by the intended recipient. This policy requires an authorized staff member to be present throughout the entire faxing process and to confirm that the faxing process was completed successfully. In addition to the exception noted in the third sentence of the policy, another exception may be permitted in those situations in which two fax machines support encryption. A higher security approach would be to prohibit the faxing of any sensitive information unless both the sending and the receiving machines employ encryption. Only with encryption can the sender and recipient be reasonably assured that a fax was not intercepted in transit. This policy assumes that the word "sensitive" has been defined elsewhere.

(continued)

Title	Policy	Commentary
Faxing sensitive information—intermediaries	Sensitive Company X information must not be faxed through untrusted intermediaries including, but not limited to, hotel staff, airport office services staff, and rented mailbox store staff.	Workers may be traveling for business, pressed for time, and not thinking about the people who may be exposed to sensitive information. The policy could be expanded to include preferred methods for sending the information, for example, by bonded courier. The use of encryption is irrelevant here because the issue is whether intermediaries can examine the information in hard-copy form. The policy requires senders to do the faxing personally to help assure that unauthorized parties are not exposed to the information in question. The word "sensitive" should have been defined in another policy.
Faxing sensitive information—cover sheet	When sensitive information must be faxed, a cover sheet must be sent and acknowledged by the recipient, after which the sensitive information may be sent through a second call.	This policy ensures that sensitive information is being faxed to the correct fax machine and that the sender is using the correct phone number. The policy prevents unauthorized call forwarding from interfering with the intended fax communication path. With so many fax machines in use these days, the chance that a wrong number would make connection with another fax machine is quite high. This policy prevents that type of error from causing unauthorized disclosure of the material on the involved fax. Another intention of this policy is to ensure that an authorized party is on hand and actually watching the destination fax machine. This prevents unauthorized parties from viewing the sensitive faxed material. Confirming that an authorized recipient is on hand is also desirable in case the second call is unsuccessful. Thus the recipient would call the sender and ask for a retransmission if some of the pages were missing, if there was a paper jam, etc. This policy could be augmented with another sentence requiring the recipient to confirm receipt of the second transmission. The policy does not specify how the destination party acknowledges receipt. This would most often occur on a separate voice line or by other means such as a pager or instant messaging.

Faxing sensitive information—unencrypted	Sensitive information may be faxed over unencrypted lines only when time is of the essence, no alternative or higher-security transmission methods are available, and voice contact with the receiving party is established immediately prior to transmission.	This policy notifies staff that sensitive information should not be faxed over unencrypted lines on a regular basis. If there is a need for regular transmission of sensitive information, then workers should request encrypting fax machines. Some international export restrictions may apply to encryption technology so check with legal counsel if establishing encrypting fax machines for international transmissions. The policy shown here may also include words requiring confirmation of receipt of a fax that includes sensitive information. Transmission to an attended stand-alone fax machine may be preferable to transmission to a fax server, if that server does not have adequate access controls and if it may be readily accessed by a number of people. This distinction may be stated explicitly in the policy. The word "sensitive" should have been defined in another policy.
Faxing sensitive information—physical security	Secret or confidential information must not be sent to an unattended fax machine unless the destination machine is in a locked room for which the keys are possessed only by people authorized to receive the information.	This policy ensures that no unauthorized person examines sensitive faxed materials. By physically restricting access, unauthorized persons are prevented from seeing secret or confidential faxes. This policy says nothing about notification of the recipient. The policy can be implemented by placing a special fax machine in a locked closet. Some organizations may wish to eliminate the reference to physical keys because there are other technologies that might be used, such as magnetic card access control systems. The policy presumes the existence of another policy that defines the terms "secret" and "confidential."

(continued)

Title	Policy	Commentary
Faxing secret information—encryption	Secret information must not be sent by fax unless the transmission is encrypted using methods approved by the Company X Information Security Department.	Encryption prevents sensitive information from being revealed to wiretappers and others who may have access to it as it travels by common carriers. At the destination, the information can be decrypted, or recovered by reversing the encryption process. Even though the transmission is encrypted, the information coming out of a destination fax machine will be readable to any person who happens to be present when the fax is received. To prevent this, other controls such as a password to print a fax will be required. This policy thwarts fax transmission wiretapping. It is relatively easy to place a wiretap, record an unencrypted fax transmission, and later play it back into another fax machine to generate readable hardcopy. If this were done, neither the sender nor the recipient would ordinarily be aware that a wiretap has taken place. This comment is equally true of the new faxing services that use the Internet rather than dial-up lines. They too can be tapped unless the transmission is encrypted. The policy presumes the existence of a policy that defines the term "secret."
Faxing confidential information—speed dial	When confidential information is sent by fax, the operator must not use preset destination telephone numbers, but must instead manually enter the destination number.	This policy prevents the misdirection of faxes because of a mistaken entry of a speed-dial number. These types of errors can result in embarrassing situations in which, for example, one important customer sees that another important customer has a different price for the same product they bought yesterday. A high-visibility case involved the misdirection of a confidential merger contract to a business newspaper.

If fax operators manually key in the phone number, they may make an error, but the error is likely to be a single digit. This will often cause the fax not to go through because a voice line or a modem line will be reached instead of another fax line. There is, however, no such automatic safety net when preset fax numbers are employed. This policy also helps to prevent the scenario in which some unauthorized person with access to the sending machine changes a previously selected speed-dial fax number, such that a sensitive fax is misdirected to an unauthorized recipient.

This policy helps to ensure that the correct fax machine has been reached. Only when a correct password is entered is this connection confirmed. There have been many reported cases in which sensitive faxes were sent to the wrong machine, and this policy helps to prevent additional problems of this nature. Two compatible machines, each supporting passwords, are likely to be required for this policy to work. This will reduce the number of machines to which secret faxes can be sent. This may also require that certain fax machines throughout an organization, machines that were manufactured by various vendors, be replaced with fax machines from a single vendor. Other passwords for printing faxes also may be required. The policy presumes the existence of a policy that defines the term "secret." The restriction of the scope of this policy to secret information means that normal (less sensitive) faxes need not bother with this process.

Faxing secret information — passwords

Secret information must not be sent by fax unless the receiving machine, prior to the initiation of a transmission, successfully receives a correct password from an authorized person at the receiving end of the transmission.

(continued)

Title	Policy	Commentary
Fax cover sheet notice	All outgoing Company X faxes must include a cover sheet that includes wording approved by the legal department.	This policy is intended to be responsive to the significant number of faxes that are mistakenly sent to the wrong number. Not only can this involve entering the wrong telephone number on the fax machine, it may also involve telephone system malfunctions, internal mail systems that incorrectly deliver faxes to the wrong person, or monitoring of transmissions by telephone company technicians. A standard cover sheet will ensure that certain legal words precede all outbound faxes. Typically such a cover sheet includes a notice that the transmission is for use only by the intended individual or entity. This notice may also state that if the reader of the fax is not the intended recipient, then the reader must not use, disseminate, distribute, or copy the information. The notice may request that the sender be notified if the fax has been sent someplace other than the intended destination. The notice can be supplemented with words requesting the destruction of a misdirected fax and that no action be taken relying on the information contained in the fax itself. The policy discussed gives the greatest flexibility in that the words on the cover can be changed without the need to change the policy itself. Changes in the words on the cover will be necessary as the legal and business status of faxes evolves over time.

Internet, Intranet, and Extranet Security

Chapter 22

Network Content Filtering and Leak Prevention

George J. Jahchan

Contents

Organizations today depend heavily on the Internet, intranets, and their network infrastructures to conduct business. Ensuring the security and integrity of data shared across networks is essential, especially in light of the various regulatory and legislative mandates they must comply with. At the same time, the enforcement challenges facing them are on the rise, and the need for effective security controls is greater than ever. Organizations strive to implement technical controls to assist in enforcing their security policies; however, under certain circumstances some organizations need to monitor the content of packets entering and leaving their network to ensure they detect leaks of confidential information.

Signature- or behavior-based detection and prevention technologies depend on the automated recognition of anomalous conditions: in the first case through signatures and in the second through exceeding a set threshold of deviation from known normal conditions (or baseline). The prevention of unauthorized disclosure of proprietary or confidential data (information leaks) through conventional technologies (such as intrusion detection or prevention) is difficult to manage. Signature-based intrusion detection and prevention relies on attack signatures (bit patterns in packet streams); extending that to include words or word patterns that are contained in application files (databases, office productivity documents, portable document files, or any of the numerous file formats in use today) that would be indicative of a leak of information is difficult.

Conventional technology solutions such as identity and access management, security information management, content management systems, and digital rights management—individually or in combination—help organizations control who has access to sensitive data; however, once authorized access is granted, they have little control over how that data is utilized.

In this chapter, we look at controls that can help organizations mitigate the risk of information leaks through networks.

Information-handling security policy should have teeth: a strong policy that clearly outlines the information-handling requirements of the organization and mandates disciplinary measures for policy violations is the first step in controlling information leaks through networks. But a policy without the means to enforce it remains ineffective.

Limiting the protocols or applications that can be utilized by network users in connections to foreign networks helps organizations reduce the vectors through which sensitive information could be leaked. Placing too many restrictions will, however, impede the business, and organizations need to compromise between security and usability.

Once this exercise is complete, and a clear picture of the traffic to be allowed is established, the attention can turn to the mitigation methods for permitted traffic. This chapter covers the most common vectors through which information can be leaked and suggests mitigating controls.

- *HTTP/FTP.* Any document types can be uploaded to a Web site that is designed to "accept" attachments (Web-based e-mail, bulletin boards, etc.). Universal resource locater (URL) filtering—which is typically part of the defense arsenal of companies—can help mitigate this risk. Free Web-based e-mail services are typically classified in the "Web mail" category of URL filtering solutions; thus access to these services can be curtailed by implementing appropriate security controls over Web access (a functionality that is available either in a stand-alone solution or as an add-on to the existing Web caching servers from several vendors). The residual risk will come from uncategorized sites. Denying access to such sites can further reduce the residual risk, but may be deemed unacceptable to the business. Either way, insofar as leak control is concerned, the URL filtering method is binary and lacks granularity.
- *HTTP/SFTP/SSH and other encrypted traffic.* The scenario is similar to the preceding one. Control is binary and lacks granularity. Once access is granted, no further control is possible over content.
- *Peer-to-peer applications.* Risk is best mitigated by preventing the use of such applications. A combination of controls at different layers can be used for maximum effectiveness.

On desktops in Active Directory (AD) environments, group policies can prevent users from installing or running unauthorized applications, including peer-to-peer.

On desktops in all Windows environments, desktop security solutions available from several vendors help organizations control desktop usage and prevent the installation or execution of peer-to-peer applications. These can be used stand-alone or in combination with AD group policies in AD environments.

At the network layer, periphery defenses can be configured to block peer-to-peer traffic, with varying degrees of effectiveness.

- *Electronic mail (corporate mail systems).* Technical solutions exist to (i) inspect the content of messages and attachments (specific file formats) or (ii) archive all or selected mailboxes. Encrypted e-mails or attachments would, however, be difficult to inspect with either of these solutions. In the first case, if the business allows it, rules can specify that unrecognized or encrypted file formats be automatically blocked.

■ *General controls.* Network forensics solutions that capture and store all (or filtered) traffic (see simplified network diagram) enable the reconstruction and replay of sessions that were previously "recorded," enabling organizations to spot security policy violations. The technology does have limitations though it is expensive and requires expertise to operate effectively. Furthermore, though encrypted traffic can be recorded "as is," its clear-text content cannot be visualized unless the organization has prior knowledge of the encryption algorithms and associated keys, which is rarely the case. HTTPs and SSH are common methods of transferring data in encrypted form.

In addition, archive tools (such as WinZip) now offer built-in strong symmetrical encryption capabilities (up to 256-bit advanced encryption standard [AES]). Any documents encrypted with a strong key that is transferred to the addressee out-of-band cannot be visualized unless the sender discloses (or is forced to disclose) the encryption method and key used. Things are even more difficult in the case of symmetrical keys that are negotiated online through an asymmetrical key exchange (such as during a Secure Sockets Layer session establishment).

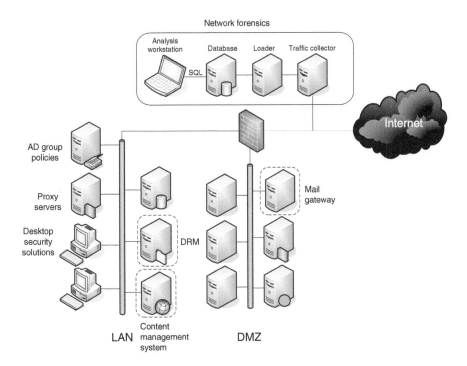

Conclusion

The technology designed to protect highly sensitive data from leaks through networks is complex and expensive in terms of acquisition and ongoing operation costs, and its effectiveness is dependent upon what type of traffic an organization allows to permeate through its periphery.

Encryption is a double-edged sword: it helps in ensuring the confidentiality of information traveling across networks, but it also prevents organizations from maintaining the visibility of what sort of information is leaving their networks.

To combat information leaks effectively through networks, organizations must follow the continuous information security plan cycle: assess, design, implement, educate, monitor, and correct. The security personnel's awareness and understanding of vectors that could be used by ill-intentioned persons to sneak sensitive or confidential information out of a network is key to mitigating its risk.

Network Attacks and
Countermeasures

Chapter 23

The Ocean Is Full of Phish

Todd Fitzgerald

Contents

It was only a little more than a decade ago when "the Internet" was not part of most individual's daily vocabulary. Today, the use of the Internet, e-mail, and text messaging is ubiquitous throughout coffee shops, cities, cell phone communications, and the workplace. This medium, despite the lack of inherent security at the network level, has become "trusted" by many to perform daily personal and business operations. As with everything that is "trusted" in our society, a criminal element is also invited to the party to penetrate that trust for personal satisfaction or financial gain. Enter the latest lucrative criminal element poised to diminish the trust that companies have built up—phishing.

Phishing Definition

Wikipedia defines phishing as "a criminal activity using social engineering techniques. Phishers attempt to fraudulently acquire sensitive information, such as usernames, passwords and credit card details, by masquerading as a trustworthy entity in an electronic communication." The Anti-Phishing Working Group (APWG) defines phishing as a form of identity theft that employs both social engineering and technical subterfuge to steal consumer's personal identity data and financial account credentials. They further define technical subterfuge as "a scheme to plant crimeware onto PCs to steal credentials directly, often using key logging systems to intercept consumers' online account user names and passwords, and to corrupt local and remote navigational infrastructures to misdirect consumers to counterfeit Web sites and to authentic Web sites through phisher-controlled proxies that can be used to monitor and intercept consumers' keystrokes."

The term "phishing" was first mentioned in the America Online (AOL) Usenet newsgroup in January 1996 and may have been used in the earlier hacker "2600" newsletter. Phishing is a variant of the word "fishing," describing the use of sophisticated techniques to "fish" for financial information by casting lures into the mouths of unsuspecting users. AOL was a large target, and many passwords, known as "phish," to AOL accounts were obtained by phishing and subsequently traded for other pieces of stolen software, such as games and copyrighted software.

Companies work very hard to protect their brand and establish trust in the presence of their brand with the consumer. When an individual goes to a McDonald's for example, he or she expects to get a consistent level of service and product and pay a price similar to that of their last experience. The transactional trust, which is built over time, causes people to have faith in obtaining products from the company. The cleanliness and safe handling of the hamburger, fries, equipment, etc., are also expected to be the same each time the consumer visits the store. All of these thoughts come to the surface when the "Golden Arches" brand is presented, and people's trust in future purchases is based upon their last interaction with the brand. Similarly, many banks have established trust over time with consumers to protect their funds and offer online banking services. When notices appear to come from the bank, complete with its logo, the individual perception of trusting the message is based upon the last interaction with the bank. Criminal phishing activity disrupts the trust model by masquerading as the "trusted brand" to gain the consumer's confidence. Consumers are left confused in many cases as to whom they should trust. This creates a very difficult problem for companies to educate the workforce as to what is and what is not a phishing attempt.

The subsequent sections describe how to identify phishing attempts, methods used to deliver phishing by the attackers, attack methods, and approaches being used to minimize the threat.

Evolution of Phishing

Originally, phishing attempts obtained passwords by tricking users into supplying the passwords in response to an e-mail request. Although this method is still prevalent today, with firms such as the major banks, EBay, and PayPal being among the largest targets, more complex and creative methods have been developed to attempt to fool the end user. These include such methods as directing users to fake Web sites that appear as if they are issued by the same company (i.e., EBay, Chase, U.S. Bank), man-in-the-middle proxies to capture data, Trojan-horse keyloggers, and screen captures. Early attempts utilized requests from individuals posing as AOL support staff asking the subscriber to "verify your account" or "confirm billing information." This resulted in AOL issuing the first statements that "no one from AOL will ask for your password or billing information." Now, these statements are prevalent across banks, online payment services, and organizations providing E-commerce activity. E-mails have been made to look like they were coming from the Internal Revenue Service (IRS) to obtain tax information to be used in identity theft criminal activities. There is typically an increase in fake IRS e-mails around April 15 filing deadline, as consumers are more vulnerable due to the short time left to file taxes. Fake job sites have been erected to entice individuals to reveal personal information. MySpace was the subject of a worm in 2006 to direct users to different Web sites to obtain their log-in credentials.

Today's Phishing Activity

Phishing activity has been increasing dramatically over the past few years. The APWG identifies itself as "an industry association focused on eliminating the identity theft and fraud that result from the growing problem of phishing and email spoofing." For the past several years they have been tracking trends in phishing activity.

■ Unique phishing attacks are defined by the APWG as unique Uniform Resource Locators (URLs) of the Web sites that the users are directed to. In January 2004, they tracked 176. Just nine months later, in October 2004, the number had risen to 1142, and by October 2005 the number was 3367. An explosion of phishing Web sites subsequently occurred, with 27,221 unique sites in January 2007.

■ The AWPG defines a phishing report as the instance of a unique e-mail sent to multiple users, directing them to a specific phishing Web site. The number of e-mails increased substantially, from 6957 in October 2004 to 15,820 in October 2005 and 29,930 in January 2007.

■ The number of brands attacked is also increasing, with 28 brands attacked in November 2003, 44 brands in October 2004, 96 brands in October 2005, and 135 brands attacked in January 2007.

■ The average time for a phishing site to be online has been steadily decreasing, making it difficult to identify and deal with the spoofed sites in a timely manner. The average time online was five and a half days in October 2005, compared with four days in January 2007. The longest time online for a site was 30 days.

■ Almost 97 percent of the ports used at the Web sites were port 80, with the other 3 percent made up of ports 84, 82, 81, and other ports.

■ The United States leads as the country hosting the most phishing sites, with 24.27 percent. The other top countries are China (17.23 percent), Republic of Korea (11 percent), and Canada, with 4.05 percent.

These statistics point out that this is a growing activity and increasingly used as a criminal activity to open an account, make an unauthorized transaction, obtain log-in credentials, or perform some other kind of identity theft. A First Data survey in 2005 revealed that over 60 percent of online users had inadvertently visited a spoofed site. A *Consumer Reports* survey indicated that 30 percent of users had reduced their overall use of the Internet and 25 percent had discontinued online shopping. Where once there was trust in the major brands, as indicated earlier, this trust is eroding with respect to online transactions, in large part due to a lack of trust in Web sites and fear of identity theft.

Phishing Delivery Mechanisms

Simple Mail Transfer Protocol (SMTP) is the primary avenue of vulnerability exploitation by phishers due to failures within the protocol. In addition to the e-mail communication channel, other methods such as Web pages, messaging services, and Internet Relay Chat (IRC) are increasingly being used to extract personal information. As vulnerabilities are plugged within SMTP over time, other methods of exploitation will emerge, because of the lucrative financial opportunity presented by phishing. Therefore, it is critical that organizations take a proactive stance to reduce consumer fears that their information may be compromised. Organizations whose primary livelihood depends upon the Internet for E-commerce and large banking institutions have been implementing proactive education for consumers and implementing tighter controls for the past several years. Obviously, with the increasing number of phishing attempts previously noted, the breadth of organizations being phished and the type of delivery are expanding.

E-Mail and Spam Delivery Method

This is the most common method of delivery, by which the end user is tricked into clicking on a link or an attachment. The e-mails are meant to look legitimate, complete with the logos of the company and an official looking e-mail address in the "Mail From:" field of the e-mail. Flaws in SMTP permit the "From" address to be spoofed, and the phisher may also put an address in the "RCPT To:" field to direct any responses to the spoofer. When the recipients of the e-mail click on the link included in the e-mail, they are directed to a fraudulent Web site set up by the phisher. Personal information is collected at the Web site to be used in further the criminal activity.

These e-mails look official and use language to sound like they could come from the company. In fact, the e-mail may be a replica of a similar notice from the organization. There is usually a sense of urgency stated in the e-mail request for a quick response to the e-mail. Some of the e-mails are Hypertext Markup Language (HTML) based to hide the target URL information using different color schemes and substituting letters, such as an I for an L, to direct the user to different sites. These e-mails are often constructed in an attempt to defeat the antispam filters by inserting random words in a color to match the background of the e-mail so that they would not appear to the end user. Open e-mail relays are also utilized to hide the real source of the e-mail. The URL may point to a different Web site through the use of an escape coded into the HTML. Nonstandard ports specified in the URL may be clues that the phisher's Web site is being hosted on a personal computer (PC) exploited by the hacker earlier.

Although most of the e-mails would direct the unsuspecting end users to a fraudulent site after clicking on the link, some may actually direct them to a real site. In this case, a JavaScript pop-up containing a fake log-in page could be used to store the credentials. Subsequently, the application could forward the credentials to the real application, and the user would be none the wiser.

Although most of the attacks have been through random e-mails sent to people that may or may not have a relationship with the company, some phishers are getting smarter and are performing spear-phishing, which is targeted phishing. In the case of spear-phishing, a group is targeted for their relationship. For example, employee names listed in a Web site directory may be sent a notice from the company's health insurance company or credit union or another firm known to provide services for the company. Additionally, as companies become larger in size and have millions of customers, there is a greater chance that their Web sites contain more information about their organizations in the name of customer service, as well as a greater likelihood that even a random e-mail will connect with someone who has a relationship with the organization.

Web-Based Delivery Method

Web sites are constructed to contain HTML links that are disguised such as in the e-mail scenarios noted earlier. Fake advertising banners with different URLs may be posted to legitimate Web sites, directing traffic to the phisher's Web site. Malicious content embedded within the Web site may then exploit a known vulnerability within the user's browser software and then be used to install a keylogger (monitors keystrokes), screen-grabber (monitors portions of the user's input screen), backdoor (to gain control of the computer for later remote or botnet access), or other Trojan program. Keyloggers may be coded to intercept specific credential information, such as the log-in information for certain banks. Phishers may establish an online account, use a fake banner pointing to a fake Web site, all with a stolen credit card and other bank information obtained to cover their tracks.

IRC and Instant Messaging Delivery Method

Communication in the instant messaging area makes it possible for the end user to fall victim to the same techniques used in other delivery methods. Embedded dynamic content is permitted in these clients, which can also point to other links that would point to fictitious Web sites.

Trojaned Host Delivery Method

PCs that have been previously compromised may act as a delivery mechanism for sending out phishing e-mails, which makes tracking the originators of the phishing scams very difficult. Although antivirus software can help with the reduction of the risk of Trojans, it is becoming increasingly difficult. Home users are often tricked into installing software as an upgrade that provides the ability for the PC to be controlled at a later date.

Phishing Attacks

Man in the Middle

In this type of attack, the attackers insert themselves in between the consumer and the real application, capturing the credentials along the way. The end user may have a false sense of security by relying on the HTTPs, as the man-in-the-middle attack could set up a secure communication path between the hacker's server and the customer and subsequently pass the information to the real Web site. While the phisher remains in the middle, all transactions can be monitored. This can be accomplished by multiple methods, including transparent proxies, Domain Name System (DNS) compromises, URL obfuscation, and changing the browser proxy configuration. Transparent proxies reside on the network segment on the way to the real Web site, such as a corporate gateway or an intermediary Internet Service Provider (ISP). Outbound traffic can then be forced through the proxies, which would deliver the information back to the consumer unnoticed. DNS caches can also be poisoned to point certain domain names to different Internet Protocol (IP) addresses controlled by the phisher. The cache within a network firewall could redirect the packets bound for the real Web site to that of the attackers. The DNS server itself could also be compromised, as well as the local host's file on the user's PC ahead of receipt of the phishing e-mail. The browser proxy can also be overridden to proxy the traffic for, say, the HTTP port, to a proxy server. This involves changes on the client side and may be noticed by the end user by reviewing the setup. Many users, however, would not be actively looking at those controls and there is a high likelihood that the controls would be named something that would sound technical, making noticing them difficult.

Man-in-the-middle attacks are particularly troublesome, as the end users think they are interacting with a trusted entity when executing transactions with a trusted bank, online shopping storefront, or service provider; meanwhile, their identity is being captured for later exploitation.

URL Obfuscation Attacks

URL obfuscation involves minor changes to the URL and directing the consumer to a different Web site. There are multiple techniques for changing the URL to make it appear as though the user is being directed to a normal Web site.

The first technique leverages bad domain names to appear like the real host, although in reality these are domain names that are registered by the phisher. For example, a firm with the name Mybrokerage.com may have a transaction site named http://onlinetrading.mybrokerage.com. The phisher could set up a fraudulent server using one of the following names:

- http://mybrokerage.onlinetrading.com
- http://onlinetrading.mybrokerage.com.ch
- http://onlinetrading.mybrokerage.securesite.com
- http://onlinetrading.mybrokerage.com
- http://onlinetrading.mybrokeráge.com

In the foregoing examples, the name was varied, extensions were added, words were misspelled, or different character sets were used. To the average user, the URL looks like a valid site.

There are also third-party services that shorten URLs to make entry easier. These sites map other URLs to their shorter ones to make entry by the user easier. These sites can also be utilized by phishers to hide the real site.

Friendly log-in URLs are another method by which the user can be deceived. URLs can include authentication information, in the format of URL://username:password@hostname/path. To trick the end user, information would be placed in the username and password fields to resemble the company Web site while directing the user to the host-name Web site, which is managed by the phisher. In the preceding example, the URL may look like http://mybrokerage.com:etransaction

@fakephishersite.com/fagephisherpage.htm. Several browsers have dropped support of this method of authentication due to the success it has had in the past with phishers.

The host name can also be obfuscated by replacing it with the IP address of the fraudulent Web site. Another technique is the use of alternate character set support, which is supported by many browsers and e-mail clients. Escape encoding, Unicode encoding, inappropriate UTF-8 (8-bit UCS/Unicode Transformation Format or variable length encoding for unicode) encoding, and multiple encoding are all techniques for representing the characters in different ways.

Other Attacks

Cross-site scripting attacks are another method by which the attacker can utilize poorly written company Web site code to insert an arbitrary URL in the returned page. Instead of returning the expected page for the application, the attacker returns a page that is under the control of their external server.

Preset session attacks make use of a preset session ID, which is delivered in the phishing e-mail. The attacker then polls the server continuously, failing as the session ID is not valid. When the end user authenticates using the session ID, the application Web server will allow any connection using the session ID to access the restricted content, including the attempts by the attacker.

Each of these methods for obfuscation can be combined with others, making it even more difficult to identify when the URL is being used to direct traffic to a fraudulent Web site.

Educating Consumers

Educating consumers about the dangers of phishing is a delicate balance. On the one hand, consumers need to be vigilant in not responding to e-mails with links to sites requesting their personal information; on the other hand, consumers should not be afraid to participate in online commerce and use e-mail wisely. Many banking and E-commerce sites have included information on phishing on their Web sites in an effort to reduce the risks. According to the National Consumers League Anti-Phishing Retreat conducted in 2006, there should be more consumer education, possibly included with new PCs, and ISP-supported pop-ups to warn users of risky URLs. They also proposed that technical staff should be made better aware of the legal and law enforcement sides of the issue, as well as law enforcement and legal staffs understanding the technical side.

Phishing has become so prevalent that the Federal Trade Commission (FTC) issued a consumer alert in late 2006 advising consumers how not to get hooked by a phishing scam. The key points from the FTC included the following:

- If you get an e-mail or pop-up message that asks for personal or financial information, do not reply. And do not click on the link in the message, either.
- Area codes can mislead (and may not be in your area due to Voice-over-IP technology).
- Use antivirus and antispyware softwares, as well as a firewall, and update them all.
- Do not e-mail personal or financial information.
- Review credit card and bank account statements as soon as you receive them.
- Be cautious about opening any attachment or downloading any file from e-mails.
- Forward spam that is phishing for information to spam@uce.gov and to the bank or company that was impersonated with the e-mail.
- If you believe you have been scammed, file a complaint at www.ftc.gov.

Technical Approaches to the Problem

Educating consumers is one avenue to combat the growing problem; however, the entire burden cannot be on the consumer. Several technical approaches are in process to address the issue.

Inbound Spam Filters

The most common method of assisting the end user is to restrict the e-mail that is coming in through the ISP or the organization through anti-phishing or antispam filters. These filters utilize IP address blacklists, Bayesian content filters (examining the semantic differences between legitimate messages and spam messages), heuristics (examining the ways that the URL may be incorporating the names of the institution), and URL list filtering. Each of these techniques needs to be consistently evaluated to determine the success rate, as the hosts are constantly changing, as are the URL specifications.

Protect the Desktop

Implementation and maintaining currency of antivirus protection, spyware detection, antispam filtering, and personal firewalls or intrusion detection systems are essential in protecting the desktop from unwanted changes. Products by the major desktop security vendors typically support one or more of these functions. Specifically, the desktop software must be able to block attempts to install malicious software; identify and quarantine spam; update the latest antivirus, antispam, and antispyware signatures and apply from the Internet; block unauthorized outbound connections from installed software; identify anomalies in network traffic; and block outbound connections to suspected fraudulent sites.

Although multiple products provide a defense-in-depth strategy for the desktop, they can also become quite expensive and complex for the typical end user. There is usually a subscription fee after the initial implementation and a reliance on the end user to renew the subscription. In organizations, the desktops are managed and this is not a consideration for internal users; however, with trust in the organization resting with the end-user experience, these costs and approaches must be understood.

Removal of HTML E-Mail

Plain-text e-mail communications could be utilized to reduce the ability to hide the actual URL the user is directed to in the e-mail. These e-mails would not look nice; however, the security would be improved.

Browser Enhancements

Enhancements have been placed into the browser software to check against a list of known phishing sites. Microsoft's Internet Explorer version 7 browser and Mozilla Firefox 2.0 contain this functionality. Users can also take further actions such as disabling window pop-up functionality, Java runtime support, ActiveX support, and multimedia and autoplay or autoexecute extensions and preventing storage of nonsecure cookies. However, these actions may increase security, but may degrade the online experience for the end user as well. Other approaches permit the user to create a label for a Web site that they recognize, so they have a reliable method of returning to the Web site (Firefox petname extension).

Stronger Password Log-Ons

Several banking Web sites have implemented the showing of a user-selected image (animal, scenery, hobby) prior to the entry of the password. In the event the end user does not recognize the image, they are not to provide the password. This is an attempt to assure the end user, by presenting them with the image they selected, that they are on the correct Web site. The phisher would not have knowledge of the appropriate image to show the consumer.

Stronger authentication may be necessary to positively identify the users to the real Web site, so that retrieval of the username or password information has limited value. Some of these solutions can be expensive, such as issuing two-factor authentication tokens to millions of consumers for an organization. This approach introduces added complexities by the fact that individuals have relationships with multiple organizations and would potentially be carrying multiple devices.

Final Thoughts

There is no silver bullet to resolve the phishing criminal activity. There is much financial gain to be made without needing to use physical force, making this an attractive option for criminals. There are multiple known delivery methods, attack vectors, and solutions to help minimize the risk. Organizations must be vigilant in their education of internal and external customers, the design of secure software, the maintenance of appropriate patch levels, and providing a phishing reporting and remediation capability and must remain continuously aware of the techniques and threats related to this type of attack. As consumer confidence decreases through personal experiences of identity theft, excessive e-mails impersonating the company, or a perceived lack of attention to the issue, they will stop doing business with the organization. The ocean is full of phish, some bite, some do not, but it only takes a few to take the bait to disrupt the ecology. Our organizations must educate and implement the technical approaches necessary to protect the ecology of our business.

Further Readings

Anti-Phishing Working Group, *Phishing Activity Trends Report for the Month of January, 2007*, http://www. antiphishing.org.

Anti-Phishing Working Group (APWG)/Messaging Anti-Abuse Working Group (MAAWG), *Anti-Phishing Best Practices for ISPs and Mailbox Providers*, July 2006, Washington, D.C.

Federal Trade Commission, *Consumer Alert: How Not to Get Hooked by a "Phishing" Scam*, October 2006, Washington, D.C.

National Consumers League, *A Call for Action—Report from the National Consumers League Anti-Phishing Retreat*, March 2006, http://www.nclnet.org.

NGS Software Security Insight Research, *The Phishing Guide, Understanding and Preventing Phishing Attacks, 2004*, http://ngsconsulting.com.

PayPal, Recognizing Phishing, http://www.paypal.com.

U.S. Department of Homeland Security/SRI International Identity Theft Technology Council/Anti-Phishing Working Group, *The Crimeware Landscape: Malware, Phishing, Identity Theft and Beyond*, October 2006, Washington, D.C.

Wikipedia, Phishing, http://en.wikipedia.org/wiki/Phishing.

APPLICATION
SECURITY

Application Issues

Chapter 24

Neural Networks and Information Assurance Uses

Sean M. Price

Contents

Introduction

Computers are wonderful tools that can be used to automate numerous manual processes. Large and complex calculations that could take an individual a lifetime to solve are trivial for a machine with sufficient memory and processing speed. In this respect, the effort of one superhuman task is easily accomplished in a reasonable amount of time by a computer. However, this vast processing capability does not easily give rise to the ability of a machine to learn, think, or reason. Human tasks involving intelligence, such as the ability to differentiate or identify complex patterns, are not easily accomplished with computers. The efforts of security practitioners could be reduced or simplified through the automation of activities that require intelligent thought. Machines with the ability to learn about simple problems and identify correct solutions could allow the security practitioner to focus on more complicated security issues. The ability of a machine to display intelligent behavior is commonly known as artificial intelligence.

A large body of research currently exists for artificial intelligence. This field has several categories that describe the specialized techniques for achieving machine intelligence. Major divisions within the field of artificial intelligence include expert systems, fuzzy logic, evolutionary algorithms, emergent behavior, and artificial neural networks. Expert systems provide users with answers or options to domain-specific problems. These systems usually contain a database of knowledge obtained from human experts. Fuzzy logic makes judgments on imprecise information to derive an appropriate solution. This type of artificial intelligence can be found in control systems and robotics. Evolutionary algorithms employ mutations within a computation to discover the best or most fit solution to a problem. These types of algorithms are typically based on concepts found in genetics and are used for optimization problems. Emergent behavior, also known as swarm intelligence, occurs when communities of autonomous entities, such as ants, bees, schools of fish, or flocks of birds, discover solutions to problems through cooperation. The application of emergent behavior is useful for solving optimization problems such as finding the shortest path between two points. Artificial neural networks (or simply neural networks) are a biologically inspired technique used to solve a host of problems. This aspect of artificial intelligence has the capability to learn, memorize, and predict patterns. Neural networks are designed, in principle, to emulate the functionality of the human brain. In this respect, neural networks have the potential to provide the security practitioner with an artificially intelligent application that could handle simplistic and recurring activities that might normally require the decision process of a human.

There are several characteristics about neural networks that make them strong candidate implementations for security practitioners. First, neural networks are adaptable. By definition neural networks have a capability to learn. This means that they can change their behavior to match an environment during the learning process. This is very helpful in a constantly changing threat environment. Second, most neural network implementations have a nonlinear analysis capability. This strength allows a neural network to find solutions to problems without reliance on a known algorithm. In essence, it can discover a solution to a problem that might require a complex algorithm. This implies that a security problem might be solved without the need to wait for a vendor update. Neural networks are also noise tolerant. They can learn or discern answers in the presence of noise. A neural network has the ability to sort through ordinary noise and find patterns related to security issues. Last, they are fault tolerant. If a portion of a neural network becomes corrupt it can still manage to perform the necessary tasks. Fault tolerance is a desirable property for distributed security implementations.

Fundamentally, neural networks are a collection of algorithms. Implementations of these specialized algorithms can be found in software packages as well as hardware (Gadea et al., 2000). Conceptually, neural networks comprise an architecture and algorithms. The architecture refers to how the input data is transformed through interconnections to derive an output. From a more simplistic viewpoint, the architecture is a map or graph of data flow through the network. A neural network is first and foremost a mathematical graph (Jordan and Bishop, 1996). The structure of the graph defines data-flow direction and transformation. There are two principle algorithms used in neural networks. First, an algorithm is used to apply weights between nodes, which are transformed by an activation function resulting in a subsequent output. The activation function is the key feature of the logical operations within the architecture. The second algorithm, called the learning algorithm, gives rise to the network's ability to adapt to the input and resolve a desired output. Whereas the activation function simply transforms an input into an output, the learning algorithm evaluates the output according to the input and makes appropriate changes to the internal weights in an effort to derive a better or more correct output. The architecture, activation function, and learning algorithms are the main features of neural networks that dictate their implementations and capabilities.

Inspiration

Neural networks are designed to mimic the structure and operations of neurons within the human brain. Scientists continue to learn new aspects about the operation and functions of the human brain. Neural networks represent an approximation of functional activity of the human brain. Some physical characteristics and theorized operational aspects of the brain are implemented in neural networks. The outer layer of the brain, known as the cortex, is made up of billions of specialized cells known as neurons. These cells form complex networks that give rise to thought, reason, and, arguably, consciousness in humans. The cells communicate with one another through biochemical reactions. The interactions and individual neuron processing of these communications occur through small.

A neural network represents a computation method. It should not be confused with an information technology (IT) network. Whereas an IT system consists of devices and applications communicating over a medium, a neural network is a method of combining discrete computations. Although a neural network might take advantage of distributed computing, it is not predicated upon it. Typically, a neural network is implemented within a single machine.

A biological neuron is composed of three principle parts known as dendrites, soma, and axon. Figure 24.1 provides a rough drawing of what a human neuron looks like. Dendrites receive chemical stimuli from the axons of hundreds or thousands of other neurons. Signals received by the dendrites are then propagated to the soma or neural cell body. The soma reacts to the level of input received by summing all the stimuli received. Insufficient stimulus causes no change in the state of the soma. However, if the stimulus received is high enough the soma will create a small electric discharge of pulses down the axon. This discharge results in a biochemical reaction between the axon and other dendrites in close proximity to it. The space between the axon and an associated dendrite is called the synapse. Essentially, dendrites act as input to a processing center, the soma, which provides an output through the axon depending on the total stimulus received. These are the basic properties of a human neuron.

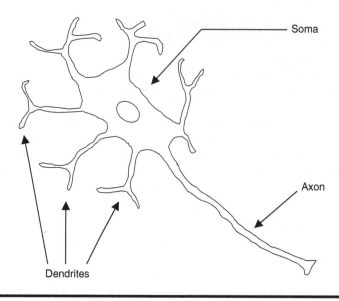

Figure 24.1   Biological neuron.

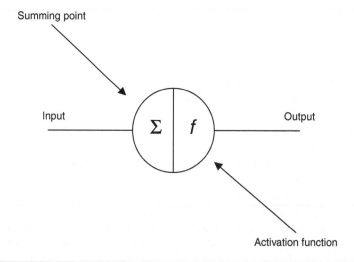

Figure 24.2   Artificial neuron.

Artificial neurons capitalize on the basic aspects of the biological neurons. The artificial neuron contains a number of inputs, a summation point, and an output. Figure 24.2 shows an example of a basic artificial neuron. From this figure we can see that a number of inputs are connected to a central node that provides an output. Each of the links between the input and the node are weighted. Individually, the weights on each link are used to identify the importance of a given input. Larger weights signify an input that is more significant in determining the output. The input values and the weights are combined at the node and fed into an activation function. This function compares the weighted input with a predetermined threshold and outputs a value according to the specifics of the function.

Typically, this value will be 0, negative 1, positive 1, or some other real number. In general a value of 0 or less indicates that the weighted input did not meet a particular threshold, whereas a value of 1 or more signifies a properly weighted input.

Architectures

The architecture of a neural network refers to the actual method by which nodes are connected. A network comprises nodes and links. Nodes can be inputs, computation points, or outputs. Usually, inputs simply introduce the data to the network. Computation points summarize the value of the input combined with any weights associated with a given link. These points also contain an activation function that determines their output. A computation point can act as the output for the network or feed the results into another layer of nodes performing computations. Output nodes can also perform some computations. Usually, they only combine the results passed to them by the computation nodes in the preceding layer. Links between nodes provide logical connectivity between nodes and also hold the weight values used for network learning. It is important to note that interconnection of nodes and links influences the function of the network and how it learns.

The artificial neuron in Figure 24.2 is also referred to as a single-layer neural network. This type of network simply connects inputs to a layer of outputs after the application of weights and the activation function (Russell and Norvig, 2003). An example of a more extensive single-layer neural network is seen in Figure 24.3. This figure also shows that a neural network can have multiple outputs. Each output could be any real number. It is important to remember that the output is a mathematical representation of the input combined with a set of weights.

Generally, neural networks are designed such that they are fully connected. This means that each node at a given layer has a link with each node at the subsequent layer. Computations propagate from one layer to the next until they reach an output. This concept is known as feedforward.

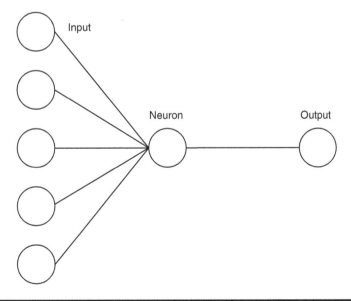

Figure 24.3   Single-layer neural network.

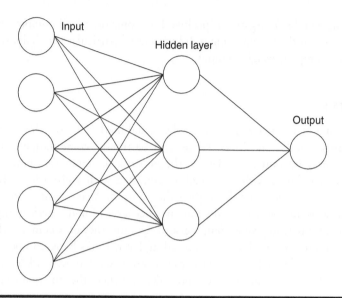

Figure 24.4   Multilayer neural network.

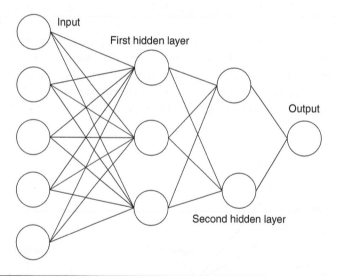

Figure 24.5   Neural network with two hidden layers.

Most neural network implementations are feedforward multilayer networks similar to the one depicted in Figure 24.4. In this configuration each layer of nodes between the input and the output is known as a hidden layer. Figure 24.4 has one hidden layer, whereas Figure 24.5 has two.

Multilayer neural networks are capable of modeling nonlinear data. Thus, they can find solutions that produce complex curves. Multilayer networks are perhaps the most common type of neural network implementations. Increasing the number of hidden layers allows the network to model more complex data. However, this also greatly increases the computation cost with respect to time. In most cases, not more than three layers are used in practice (Negnevitsky, 2005).

The number of nodes in a layer also affects the ability of the network to approximate a solution. If there are not enough nodes then the solution is likely to be too general and misclassification will occur. If there are too many nodes in a given layer then overgeneralization may occur, which can cause the network to respond strongly to test data points and too weakly to other inputs.

Some types of neural networks have the ability to reproduce patterns from a given classification. In other words, the neural network has the ability to recall a pattern as opposed to simply recognizing it. These types of neural networks are known as recurrent networks. The distinguishing feature of recurrent networks is their feedback mechanism. This requires a specialized algorithm that is different from those associated with the previous figures. Generally speaking, a recurrent network is said to possess an autoassociative memory or pattern storage capability.

Algorithms

The architectures from the earlier section provide a graphical representation of how a neural network can be connected. However, this is only half of the story. An algorithm is needed to direct how the values and weights are computed and propagated within the architecture. Some of the more common algorithms include back propagation, support vector machines, radial basis functions, and self-organizing maps.

Back propagation is perhaps the most popular neural network algorithm. The algorithm begins with initializing the weights with random values. Then training data is applied to the input. For each input node a computation is made forward through the network to each succeeding node. Once the output is reached, the difference between the computed and the desired values is computed as the error. This error is then propagated back through the network, changing the weight values according to the learning rate and momentum constants. New iterations are conducted for subsequent training data and the process continues with forward computations and backward error corrections.

Radial basis functions are limited to three layers architecturally. The hidden layer of the network utilizes a nonlinear function, but the output layer is linear. The activation function computes the Euclidean distance between input vectors as the means of learning.

In contrast to the nonlinear nature of the back-propagation algorithm, the support vector machine makes use of hyperplanes to categorize data and is, therefore, a linear machine. Essentially, a nonlinear feature space is created from the original data with multiple dimensions in which a hyperplane can be drawn to separate the data.

In a self-organized map, neurons are organized in a one- or two-dimensional architecture. Learning occurs as a competition between neurons as opposed to an assignment of weights. Neurons compete with each other to be activated. Those that are activated and their associated neighbors are ordered to create a type of topographical map, which reveals patterns in the data.

Numerous specialized algorithms exist. Many of these are simply variations of the previously mentioned algorithms. It is important to note that the algorithm is designed to support the architecture implemented. Thus, we would not see a back-propagation algorithm-supporting recurrent network because it does not support the structure. Indeed, the converse is true with respect to algorithms designed to support recurrent networks. Neural network algorithms supporting the same type of architecture are usually differentiated by their learning abilities or convergence speed.

The remainder of this chapter focuses primarily on the general multilayer feedforward architecture using the back-propagation algorithm.

Functional Characteristics

Neural networks are essentially specialized statistical models. They take a numeric input and produce a numeric output. The output will depend on the type of activation function used as well as the intended properties of the output. Many different types of activation functions have been proposed but, in practice, the most popular are the step, sign, sigmoid, and linear functions (Negnevitsky, 2005). The step, sign, and linear functions are used to find solutions to problems that can be bound by a region. Sigmoid functions are used to find nonlinear solutions.

As an example, Figure 24.6 shows a solution to a categorization problem that divides the data into two regions using a single line. This means that for any input into the neural network, the output will be within one of the two regions.

Figure 24.7 is an example of a solution to a bound-region problem. A neural network can be trained to identify a bounded region of data. It is not always possible to identify the data fully with the appropriate category. Substandard categorization or classification results in errors in the network.

In some instances the separations between data categories are not easily obtained with a straight line. In this case the neural network used must have a nonlinear capability to find the solution. Figure 24.8 shows a categorization problem with a nonlinear solution. It is important to note that a nonlinear solution is just as susceptible to errors as is a linear solution.

Each connection between the inputs, the hidden layers, and the output has an associated weight. The weight is used to indicate the importance of an individual link. Essentially, links that are the least important have smaller weights, whereas those that contribute more significantly to a desired outcome are more heavily weighted. The values of each input are multiplied by their associated weights with the results from all the inputs being summed together. This total amount is then processed by the transfer function and compared to a threshold value. Any difference between the threshold and the value computed by the transfer function produces an error value. Any error at the output node is used to adjust the internal weights in an attempt to reduce the error. The neural network algorithm implemented specifies how weights are to be adjusted to reduce this error during the learning process.

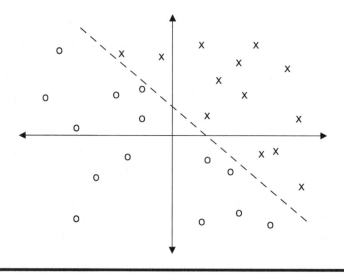

Figure 24.6 Linear categorization.

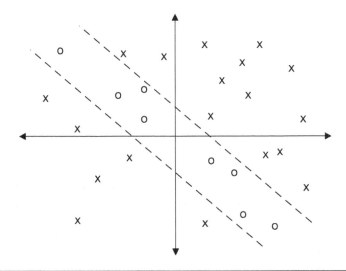

Figure 24.7 Linear bound region.

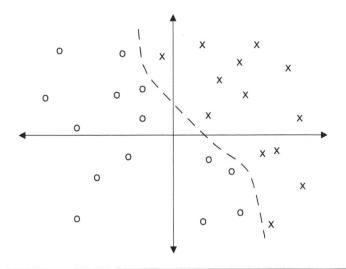

Figure 24.8 Nonlinear categorization.

The numbers of inputs, hidden layers, and outputs, as well as their connectivity, are selected to solve a specific type of problem. How these components are connected represents the architecture of the network.

The Concept of Learning

Biological organisms can learn a task or concept by observation and experimentation. Learning through observation means that an entity watches something with the explicit purpose of repeating the task or identifying with the concept. An example is a student in a class. The instructor explains a concept and the student learns by internalizing it. Young creatures learn from adults by watching them perform a task. In this way knowledge is transferred from a teacher to the learner. We can consider this form of learning as supervised learning. Learning through experimentation involves a biological entity that attempts to approach a problem or situation through trial and error. The organism tries different strategies until the solution materializes. In the human realm many of us have experienced this with the famed Rubik's cube puzzle. Aside from reading a manual, a person can learn tricks or strategies on his or her own to find the best solutions for rotating the puzzle to get the same colored blocks on the appropriate side. This form of learning is considered unsupervised. In this respect there is no teacher available to specify a strategy for solving the puzzle, as it is learned independently and based on trial and error.

Learning within a neural network is not exact. This means that the process of learning takes much iteration and yet might not result in a perfect answer or solution. Some amount of error is still likely to exist because of the statistical nature of the neural network algorithm employed. Neural networks learn by adjusting their weighted links. However, inexactness and errors are advantages for neural networks. In this sense inexactness means the network has learned a generalized answer to a problem. A network that is properly generalized will provide more consistent responses to input data than one that is over generalized or too specific.

Neural networks learn through supervised and unsupervised means. With supervised training the network learns through examples. The examples teach the network about the input and the expected output. In this respect the learning is considered to be controlled or supervised, similar to a student in a class. In contrast, with unsupervised learning the network independently attempts to discover patterns or features in the data introduced. The network looks for features in the data and then attempts to organize them, much like an individual solves a Rubik's cube. Unsupervised networks tend to learn more quickly than those that are supervised (Negnevitsky, 2005).

Supervised training specifies the input data and the desired output for the network. Under this type of training a portion of the data to be tested is set aside to train the network. The data set aside is further subdivided into two groups. One group is referred to as training data and the other is called validation data. Training data is used to teach the network about the entire data population. It should be a representative sample of all of the patterns or classes desired to be learned. Validation data is used to ensure that the error threshold is not exceeded when nontraining data is evaluated by the neural network. Validation errors exceeding an established threshold typically result in subsequent retraining of the network.

The neural network learns by adjusting the internal weights on the links between the input, the nodes, and the output until the difference between the training data values and the outputs is sufficiently low. The aggregate of the squared errors, known as the sum of the squared errors, is the criterion implemented for evaluating the learning error, especially with the back-propagation training algorithm (Negnevitsky, 2005). The network is said to have converged when the sum of the squared error for the training data is equal to or less than the predetermined threshold set by the analyst. The back-propagation algorithm is the most popular supervised training algorithm used with feedforward multilayer networks (Negnevitsky, 2005). The algorithm takes the error at the output and adjusts the weights between each node from the output back through the hidden layers to the input.

Unsupervised learning, also known as self-organized learning, utilizes rules on how to evaluate the input data to discover unique features. These features comprise the classifications that arise from the data. One of the strengths of unsupervised learning networks is the ability to learn in real time (Negnevitsky, 2005). Two examples of unsupervised learning techniques include Hebbian and competitive learning. With Hebbian, learning weights into a particular node are adjusted based on their associations with other nodes that result in the activation of the immediate node. Synchronous activations cause an increase in the weights, whereas asynchronous activities result in a decrease. In contrast, competitive learning allows only one node to be active, which is why it is referred to as the winner-takes-all neuron (Negnevitsky, 2005).

Capabilities

The central property of neural networks is their ability to learn. This capability distinguishes them from the other forms of artificial intelligence. This ability gives rise to other useful aspects due to their statistical strengths, which include pattern matching, prediction, and memory.

Pattern recognition, also known as pattern classification, is perhaps the most common implementation of neural networks. A neural network can be trained to remember multiple patterns. Pattern recognition is also called pattern matching. The true nature of a neural network with pattern-recognition capability is not to identify discrete patterns, but to make approximations of the input and produce an output classification. Each pattern learned is identified as belonging to a particular class. A neural network produces a unique output for a known pattern. A pattern-classification neural network will usually produce one of the following outputs from an input pattern:

1. The input pattern is recognized as belonging to a previously trained class.
2. The input does not match any previously known class.
3. The input is too difficult to recognize.

Consider a network that is trained to recognize circles, triangles, and squares. Each shape represents a unique class to be learned by the network. Prior to training, unique features about each shape would be selected and used to train the network. Assume that the training features selected for the network recognize each shape regardless of its size. For any input the neural network will either identify the input as belonging to one of the previously trained classes (shapes) or return an output that says it is not one of the known classes. Suppose that an oval and a rectangle are introduced to the network as input at different times. Although an oval is a type of circle and a rectangle is very similar to a square, the network might not recognize either shape as belonging to a previously trained class. Although the shapes have similarities to the known classifications, they might be too different for the neural network to recognize. If it was necessary to include either of these objects as one of the known shapes to be recognized, then a new set of features would need to be considered for training. This illustrates the point that feature selection is the first and the most important step in pattern matching (Haykin, 1999). Selecting the wrong amount or type of feature to train a network will yield less than optimal results.

Function approximation is an important capability of neural networks. Appropriately trained neural networks are capable of estimating an output based on a given input. This capability is possible due to the inherent statistical capabilities of neural networks, but is strongly influenced by the architecture and training methods employed. Function approximation is most readily seen by training a network to associate numerical input with a numerical output. In this respect the network statistically infers a formula (function) whereby a given input results in a particular output. The inferred formula represents a particular class that the neural network is trained to recognize. Feedforward neural networks are commonly used for this purpose. Given this use and capability it is easy to understand why such neural networks are recognized as universal approximators (Haykin, 1999).

Neural networks can also be used to make predictions or forecasts. Predictions can be a particular value, class, or pattern depending on the trained inputs and outputs. This capability is closely related to function approximations. A prediction is an output based on a previously untried input. To make a prediction the input data would need to fall into a previously trained classification. Approximate predictions are possible as long as the response of the neural network is well generalized. This means that the trained network should make smooth transitions from one training point to another. A neural network that is well generalized will make valid predictions within a margin of error close to the data used to train the network.

Training Considerations

Preparing for a neural network implementation requires some level of planning with respect to training. Important points of consideration include aspects of the data and the training process itself. Although selecting the right data might seem obvious, it should not be considered a trivial task. Likewise there are several aspects to actual training that also need to be considered.

Data Features

Given that neural networks are statistical models the data processed must be in a numerical form. Some software packages will transform text or other types of data automatically, but this might not be the most optimal for a given problem. The analyst must decide how best to represent the data. Arguably, if the data can be decomposed into a binary representation, that is 1's and 0's, this would potentially provide the best responses for pattern-matching problems. It is not always possible to use binary representations, in which case any real number could potentially be used to represent the input data item or feature. However, this can prove problematic. The analyst could inadvertently select numerical representations that accidentally teach the neural network something that was not intended. Therefore, nonnumeric feature substitution must be done carefully and subject to retraining to ensure that the network does not learn something unintentionally. Ideally, selecting the smallest number of features that discriminate one data class or pattern from another while allowing overall generalization and noncontradicting is the best approach (Pendharkar, 2005). A small set of features allows the network to train faster. Likewise, dissimilar features also help the neural network to recognize distinct patterns more readily. The farther apart training data points are from one class to the next, the better the network will learn the distinction between them.

Data Cleanliness and Accuracy

Only data that is known or intended to represent a particular feature for classification should be learned by the network. Neural networks possess a keen ability to discern patterns in the presence of noise (Padhy, 2005). However, too much noise in the data can unintentionally cause the network to learn aspects of the noise instead of the actual data. Therefore, it is important to reduce or remove noise from the training data where possible (Yu et al., 2006). Likewise, it is imperative in the case of pattern matching that classification identifications are valid. For instance, if a network is trained to recognize a known vulnerability as something that is allowed or valid, then the network will continually misclassify the item. Furthermore, any new vulnerabilities emerging based on the original miscategorization will probably also be identified by the neural network as valid. Therefore, it is critical that training and validation data be properly categorized and as free from noise as possible.

Over- and Undertraining

A well-trained neural network is said to generalize well. This means that for any input within a known classification an output is reproduced that closely represents a function fitting the data. The amount of training affects the generalization of the network. With too little training the output will not closely represent the desired results. In the case of overtraining, the network learns too closely training data that might cause it to not respond well to the validation or test data. Consider the example classification shown in Figure 24.9. Here we see two classes separated by a function that curves.

Suppose that an insufficient number of training epochs are conducted. This might result in an output similar to Figure 24.10. This can be easily seen by an analyst if a graphical representation of

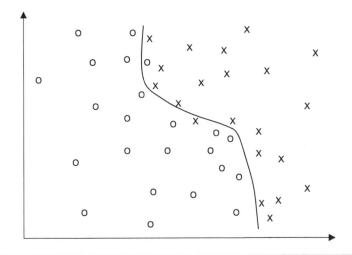

Figure 24.9   Desired output.

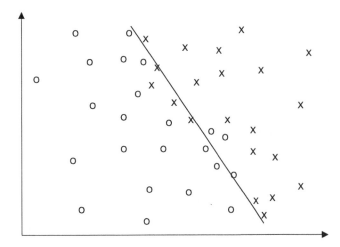

Figure 24.10   Undertraining.

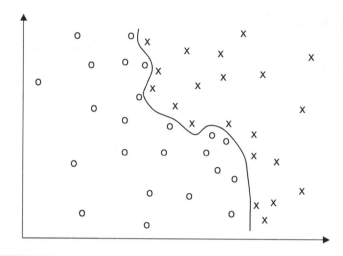

Figure 24.11 Overtraining.

the desired output is known. From the figure we can see that the shape of the function separating the two classifications is not well formed. In this case the network is too general and needs more specific training.

Sometimes a network can undergo too many training epochs. In this case the output could be similar to that seen in Figure 24.11. Note that the network has very closely matched the test points and the output is very jagged. The function output is not smooth and is not generalized.

In either case of over- or undertraining it is possible for misclassifications or poor predictions to occur. Additionally, the function represented by the output will not be a good approximation of the underlying formula. Therefore, the amount of training can significantly affect the performance of a neural network. When we consider the analyst's involvement with training neural networks, it is helpful to represent the desired output and the actual outputs graphically to ensure that under- or overtraining has not occurred.

Local Minima

The learning process for neural networks involves the determination of the best values for weights applied to the input that will most closely fit the desired output. Weights are adjusted to reduce the output error of estimating the input. The weights, individually as well as collectively, are the representative statistical functions used to reduce error. Essentially, a neural network strives to adjust the weights to find the lowest possible error. An example relationship between the output error and the weight values can be seen in Figure 24.12.

Note that relationship has low and high points. The high points are called maxima and the low points minima. The lowest point is known as the global minimum, whereas other low points are called local minima. Neural networks attempt to find the lowest point in their area of the graph. When a neural network begins to learn it will start at a random point on the graph. As learning occurs the network will move down a slope until it reaches a bottom. This bottom might be local

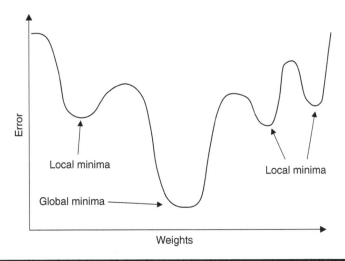

Figure 24.12   Local minima.

minima or the global minimum. Typically, the analyst will not know if the global or a local minimum is reached unless the network is retrained a number of times.

Typical Application Controls

Analysts using neural network software packages will be given a certain amount of flexibility with respect to training a network. Some of the more common controls likely to be encountered when using a back-propagation algorithm include training set specifications, learning rates, momentum, and bias.

Training Sets

This is a subset of the initial data that is used to teach the neural network. At a minimum a representative selection of each class or feature to be learned must be included. Likewise, the set should be a sufficient representation of each feature such that most of the nuances of the data can be learned.

Validation Sets

A sample of the training set is used to confirm the accuracy of the neural network. In most instances validation sets are a randomly selected small percentage of the training set. This special set is necessary to ensure that the neural network is properly learning the appropriate features or classifications about the data.

Test Sets

This is the actual data used to find the desired classifications or features.

Learning Rate

This constant is used to control the speed of change with respect to weights used. Thus, a large learning rate allows large changes in the weights, whereas a small value minimizes weight changes. This constant has a significant effect on neural network convergence.

Momentum

This necessary constant provides a level of stability in the learning process. It also affects the amount of change in weights. This constant is particularly important when the neural network encounters training data that significantly diverges from other training points learned.

Bias

This is an offset value used to affect the activation function of each neuron, which essentially adjusts the threshold value.

Learning Stop Points

Some tools allow the user to specify stop points during the learning process. Common stop points include the number of epochs, amount of time, total, and average error amounts. A well-generalized neural network will not likely be perfect, but close enough is often good enough.

Demonstrated Usage

In this section, a simple demonstration of neural network classification and prediction capabilities is presented. An inexpensive commercial neural network tool called EasyNN-Plus was used for this purpose. This tool implements a back-propagation algorithm that relies on sigmoid transfer functions. Additionally, the tool provides the user with a variety of parameters to control learning, such as learning rates, momentum, number of hidden layers, and validation parameters. The data inputs and outputs will be different for each of these scenarios. This also necessitates that two different types of networks be created. This is necessary because a neural network is created for a particular purpose.

In the classification scenario we will observe the ability of a neural network to differentiate between a sine wave, a sawtooth wave, and a Gaussian pulse pattern. All three waveform parameters can be contained in a single graph with vertical (y) values of ± 1 and horizontal (x) values from 1 to 360. Because we are interested in training the neural network to recognize a pattern it is necessary to assign a value representing each waveform type. For this exercise we assign the sine, sawtooth, and Gaussian waveforms the values of 1, 2, and 3, respectively. The input parameters for the pattern classification are the x and y coordinates associated with the pattern. The pattern value associated with the input coordinates is the output. The neural network is trained by introducing training data that states the input and output parameters.

Each pattern in our exercise consists of the integer x values from 1 to 360 and the associated y values. The training set consists of a series of coordinate values starting at 1 and then every ninth after that. So we have for our x values 1, 9, 18, 27, ..., 360. This gives us 41 elements or approximately 11 percent of the total possible coordinates in our example. These 41 coordinates represent our sample for training the neural network.

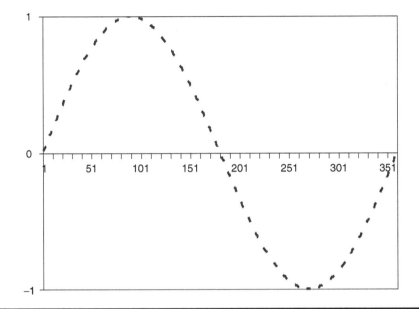

Figure 24.13 Sine waveform.

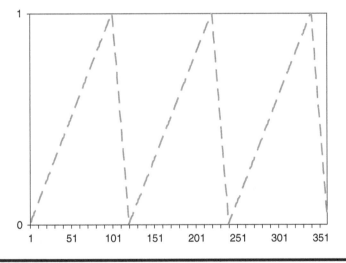

Figure 24.14 Sawtooth waveform.

Figure 24.13 shows a sine-wave plot, which is identified as classification number 1. Note that a sine wave is a nonlinear function. This necessitates the creation of a neural network that has at least one hidden layer to approximate the sine wave function.

A sawtooth waveform is shown in Figure 24.14 and is designated as classification item number 2. The sharp transitions (angles) at the top and bottom of the waveform can be a challenge for neural networks to learn. This is due in part to the transformation function used.

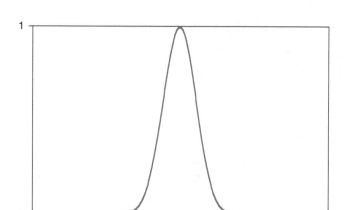

Figure 24.15 Gaussian waveform.

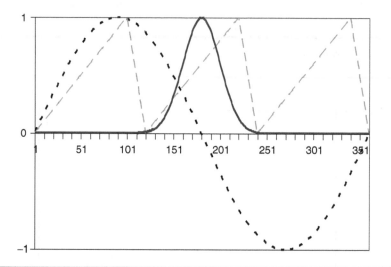

Figure 24.16 Combined waveforms.

A plot of a Gaussian waveform is seen in Figure 24.15 and represents the third classification item. This waveform should be no more challenging for the neural network to learn than the sine waveform.

An overlay of all of the waveforms is seen in Figure 24.16. Note that only the sine waveform has values less than 0.

As mentioned earlier, the first and every ninth coordinate in each waveform were used as the inputs for training the neural network. If we use each coordinate in the series as an input we would have a network with 41 inputs. Given this scenario we might not be able to train the neural network properly to generalize the waveforms. Therefore, it is prudent to introduce smaller chunks of the data to the neural network for learning purposes. It was decided that five coordinates would be used for input purposes. Now it is evident that 41 elements are not evenly divided by 5. Indeed, 41 is a prime number and is only divisible by 1 and itself. However, this is not a problem. In fact, it is irrelevant because we will use a sliding window technique to help the neural network learn each waveform. What we will do is introduce the first five coordinates as one training element. For the next element we use the last three coordinates of the prior element combined with the next two coordinates in the series. The sliding window method results in 19 elements to be used for training. Table 24.1 shows the first two and last two rows of the actual sine data used to train the network. Each row in Table 24.1 is an element used for training. The columns seen in Table 24.1 represent the input coordinates and output classification for each training element. The columns $x_1, y_1; x_2, y_2; \ldots; x_5, y_5$ are the coordinate pairs to be trained. The last column, C, is the classification or output associated with the input coordinates.

The neural network tool generates a neural network based on the training data and parameters provided by the end user. Training parameters included a momentum of 0.8 and a learning rate of 0.6. A total of 57 training elements were introduced to the neural network. From this initial amount eight were set aside for validation, whereas the remaining 49 were used to train the neural network. Figure 24.17 is a graphical representation of the neural network created by the tool.

Table 24.1 Abbreviated Training Data

x_1	y_1	x_2	y_2	x_3	y_3	x_4	y_4	x_5	y_5	C
1	0.017452	9	0.156434	18	0.309017	27	0.45399	36	0.587785	1
18	0.309017	27	0.45399	36	0.587785	45	0.707107	54	0.809017	1
...	...	...	...	...	...	...	...	...	...	...
306	−0.80902	315	−0.70711	324	−0.58779	333	−0.45399	342	−0.30902	1
324	−0.58779	333	−0.45399	342	−0.30902	351	−0.15643	360	0	1

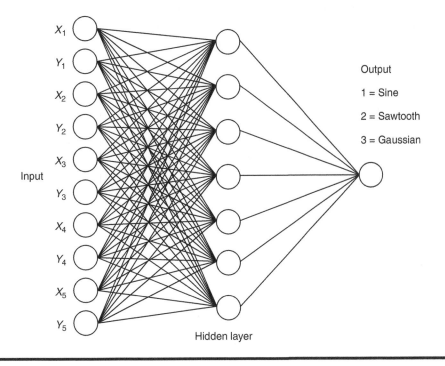

Figure 24.17 Generated neural network.

Note that the inputs match the x and y coordinates seen in Table 24.1, whereas the output is a single node. This follows the structure of the data used to train the neural network. The number of neurons in the hidden layer was generated automatically by the tool itself.

Only a few minutes of training was needed for the neural network to learn the three different classifications sufficiently. A total of 21,464 epochs were conducted prior to halting the training. At this point, the average training error was 0.16 percent, whereas the maximum error was 1.47 percent. The trained neural network was then given five elements of x and y coordinates from each of the waveforms exclusive of those elements identified in the training set. Thus, the trained network was queried to identify which waveform the element belonged to, representing the rudimentary act of classifying or categorizing the data. The element groupings were selected in series, but somewhat arbitrarily, while excluding points previously included in the training set. Some of the elements were purposely chosen across waveform transitions to determine if the neural network in fact learned the transition for a particular waveform and could correctly classify the input data.

Figure 24.18 shows the sine test sets introduced to the trained network. Most of the groupings are close together with the exception of sine 3.

In Figure 24.19, we can see that sawtooth 2 consists of points on two different slopes of the waveform, whereas sawtooth 5 was used on a steep and negative slope.

With the exception of Gaussian 4, most of the test sets seen in Figure 24.20 are kept close together. The exception element is spread out over most of the waveform.

The trained neural network successfully classified each of the input elements introduced. Although every coordinate was not tested, we might assume that in this case the neural network is sufficiently generalized to recognize a series of five consecutive coordinates as belonging to one of the previously learned classifications.

Neural networks can also be used to make predictions. This ability is demonstrated for the sine waveform. In the case for prediction we want the neural network to predict a y value given the x value. The training set consists of the x value as the input and the associated y value as the output.

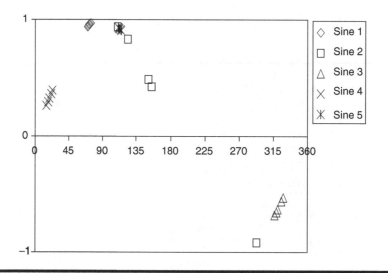

Figure 24.18 Sine test sets.

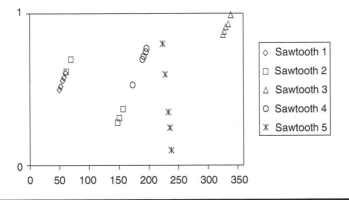

Figure 24.19   Sawtooth test sets.

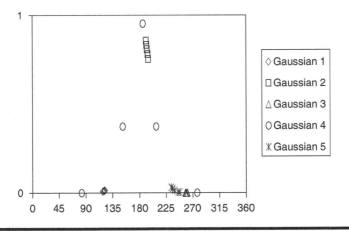

Figure 24.20   Gaussian test sets.

Each training element consists of only two values. The previously identified 41 data points for the sine waveform are used to train the neural network.

It took less than two minutes for 57,639 training epochs to be completed. Once again the learning rate and momentum were set to 0.6 and 0.8, respectively. From the 41 training examples nine were selected for validation. At the training termination, the average error was 0.0275 percent, whereas the maximum error was less than 0.095 percent. Figure 24.21 shows a representation of the generated neural network.

The neural network was queried to predict the *y* values for each *x* integer between 1 and 360, excluding those found in the training set. The prediction results can be seen in Figure 24.22. Note that the predicted results, identified as the dashed line, are very close to the actual results to be obtained. This demonstrates the ability of a neural network to generalize a function well enough to be able to predict an outcome with a fair degree of accuracy.

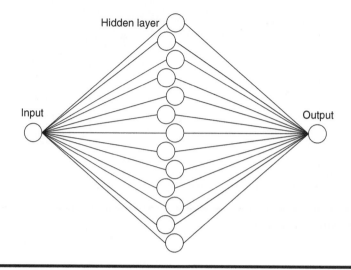

Figure 24.21 Prediction neural network.

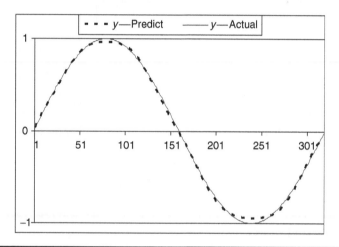

Figure 24.22 Prediction results.

Security-Relevant Applications

Perhaps the most prominent use of neural networks in security applications involves pattern classification. There exist a multitude of security technologies of which pattern classification is an essential aspect of the application. Some of the more well-known implementations are in the areas of biometrics, intrusion detection, and spam detection.

Data features form the basis by which a neural network learns a pattern. Some process is used to extract the features from the data for neural network processing. Sometimes the data features extracted are not clean. The features could be obscured, distorted, or missing. For instance, biometric data can be obscured through a variety of means. Facial recognition techniques must learn to accept different lighting situations, facial hair, and accessories such as eyeglasses that can obscure the pattern. Likewise, fingerprint recognition must be robust enough to successfully identify individuals with dirty fingers or scars that might cover up some of the minutia.

Fortunately, dirty or missing data is not always a problem for neural networks because one of their strengths is the ability to generalize. Given this characteristic, neural networks are a technology that can be very useful to the security practitioner in situations in which accurate or consistent data collection is not ensured.

A biometric is a measurable characteristic that can be used to identify an individual uniquely. Measurements can comprise angles and distances between feature points. The unique features of a biometric can be used to represent the "something a person is" aspect of an authentication scheme. Neural networks have been successfully used for pattern classification of individual physical characteristics of fingerprints (Cappelli et al., 2003), irises (Chu and Chen, 2005), faces (Zhao et al., 2003), hand geometry and palm prints (Ong et al., 2003), and voices (Quixtiano-Xicohtencatl et al., 2006) and in thermal face imaging (Bauer and Mazurkiewicz, 2005).

Other interesting types of biometrics that are not physical characteristics, but rather manifestations of an individual, for which neural networks have been used include authorship (Li et al., 2006), handwritten signatures (Al-Shoshan, 2006), and typing patterns (Peacock et al., 2005). Handwritten signatures, perhaps the most well-known form of authentication, have been evaluated with neural networks that look for unique aspects of a signature shape to classify it as belonging to a particular individual or not. Authorship is a way of identifying an individual based on their writing style. People tend to write certain ways when they conduct correspondence or formal writing, and these unique aspects can be used to identify patterns of how a person writes a message. Some of the usable feature points extracted can include grammar, punctuation, case, and word usage in a typical sentence. Likewise, the way a person types can also be considered a biometric. Aspects such as typing speed and rhythm as well as spelling can be used to actively authenticate the individual entering information into a system.

An intrusion detection system (IDS) is categorized as signature or anomaly based. A signature-based IDS, also referred to as misuse detection, relies on a database of signatures to detect attacks. In contrast, an IDS performing anomaly detection looks for abnormal activity. The generalization capabilities of neural networks make them an ideal evaluation mechanism for an anomaly-based IDS (Cannady, 1998). Neural networks have been implemented for both host- and network-based IDS applications. In network-based anomaly detectors the neural network is used to identify traffic patterns that deviate from what is considered normal (McHugh et al., 2000). Host-based anomaly detection neural networks have been used to identify abnormal events in audit logs (Endler, 1998) as well as system calls (Cha et al., 2005).

Spam filtering is another area in which neural networks are beginning to emerge. A variety of filtering techniques based on text classification are used in antispam filters. These filters range from simple keyword searches to more complex implementations of Bayesian analysis. At least one vendor has used a neural network as a means to classify an e-mail as spam or not spam (Goth, 2003). Attributes of an e-mail that can be used to identify it as spam include e-mail header information, types of words and phrases, and the existence of Hypertext Markup Language content (Clark et al., 2003). It is reasonable to assume that a human can readily classify an e-mail as spam or not spam. Given this situation it would be better for a machine to learn to handle this redundant task. In this regard neural networks are an ideal candidate for the task. Indeed, the generalization capabilities of a neural network are likely to be more effective at identifying spam than static techniques such as keyword searches given the constant change in spam content. More recently, spammers have evolved their tactics so that words that make up a spam message are embedded in a graphic image. Most spam filters are not able to cope up with this new tactic because they rely on words within the body of the e-mail to make a classification decision. However, researchers have started exploring the use of neural networks for spam image analysis (Aradhye et al., 2005).

Certainly more work is needed in this area, but neural networks appear to be an ideal tool for identifying image-based spam.

Potential Applications

Pattern classification is clearly a strength of neural networks. It is this ability that could possibly be used to further information security activities. Given this strength new applications of neural networks to security problems can be envisioned. There are many information security areas where neural networks could be used simply to differentiate between normal and abnormal activities. For example, a neural network could be used to identify system processes that are not normal for a network or user. This is closely related to the idea of secure state processing (Price, 2006), which involves knowing those processes, and their loaded libraries, that are authorized or not regarding a security policy. A neural network could be used to categorize processes by user name or group. This would result in an application that acts like a type of host-based IDS with respect to running processes. Neural networks might also be used to assist with the task of audit log reduction and analysis. Although Endler (1998) used neural networks to analyze audit logs, his approach primarily focused on IDS activities. If we consider a neural network that is trained to recognize approved patterns of activities in audit logs then it might be able to identify deviations from what is acceptable. Indeed, the neural network could potentially identify unimportant events to aid in audit reduction. Neural networks could also be used to identify attempts to steal sensitive information. This concept involves a method of tracking the flows of information on a system to identify those flows that are anomalous or not authorized. For instance, if a policy exists prohibiting users from saving sensitive information to removable media, then it may be possible to construct a neural network that could identify the occurrence of the violation. This might require that the neural network is trained to identify either information flows that are authorized or those that are not authorized. Although neural networks have been used to differentiate between possible spam-based images (Aradhye et al., 2005), more work could be done in this area. A neural network could be trained to recognize persistent aspects of an image that are common to a particular type of spam. Suppose that certain words or pictures persist in a certain type of spam. It would not be necessary for the neural network to distinguish the word or picture per se, but rather recognize that the particular aspect of an image received represents a type of spam. Thus, a neural network could be trained to identify an aspect within an image that represents spam.

Conclusion

Neural networks are an aspect of artificial intelligence that has a special ability to learn. The feed-forward neural network architecture used with the back-propagation algorithm is one the most popular neural network implementations. Security practitioners can benefit from the learning capabilities of neural networks that are taught to recognize features or patterns in data. Some of the more common neural network implementations include biometrics, intrusion detection, and spam classification. Commercial tools that exist allow the security analysts to discover new ways to use this powerful technology. Although neural networks can learn interesting things from data, it is important to ensure that applicable, clean, and accurate data features are used. Otherwise, the neural network might learn and report irrelevant results.

References

Al-Shoshan, A. I. (2006). Handwritten signature verification using image invariants and dynamic features. *Proceedings of the International Conference on Computer Graphics, Imaging, and Visualization,* 173–176.

Aradhye, H. B., Meyers, G. K., and Herson, J. A. (2005). Image analysis for efficient categorization of image-based spam. *Proceedings of the 2005 Eighth International Conference on Document Analysis and Recognition,* 914–918.

Bauer, J., and Mazurkiewicz, J. (2005). Neural network and optical correlators for infrared imaging based face recognition. *Proceedings of the 5th International Conference on Intelligent Systems Design and Applications,* 234–238.

Cannady, J. (1998). Artificial neural networks for misuse detection. *Proceedings of the 1998 National Information Systems Security Conference,* 443–456.

Cappelli, R., Maio, D., Maltoni, D., and Nanni, L. (2003). A two-stage fingerprint classification system. *Proceedings of the 2003 ACM SIGMM Workshop on Biometrics Methods and Applications,* 95–99.

Cha, B., Vaidya, B., and Han, S. (2005). Anomaly intrusion detection for system call using the soundex algorithm and neural networks. *Proceedings of the 10th IEEE Symposium on Computers and Communications,* 427–433.

Chu, C. T., and Chen, C. (2005). High performance iris recognition based on LDA and LPCC. *Proceedings of the 17th IEEE International Conference on Tools with Artificial Intelligence,* 417–421.

Clark, J., Koprinska, I., and Poon, J. (2003). A neural network based approach to automated e-mail classification. *Proceedings of the IEEE/WIC International Conference on Web Intelligence,* 702–705.

Endler, D. (1998). Intrusion detection applying machine learning to Solaris audit data. *Proceedings of the 1998 Annual Computer Security Applications Conference,* 268–279.

Gadea, R., Cerda, J., Ballester, F., and Mocholi, A. (2000). Artificial neural network implementation on a single FPGA of a pipelined on-line back propagation. *Proceedings of the 13th International Symposium on System Synthesis,* 225–230.

Goth, G. (2003). Much ado about spamming. *IEEE Internet Computing, 7*(4), 7–9.

Haykin, S. (1999). *Neural Networks: A Comprehensive Foundation* (2nd ed.). Upper Saddle River, NJ: Prentice Hall.

Jordan, M. I., and Bishop, C. M. (1996). Neural networks. *ACM Computing Surveys, 28*(1), 73–75.

Li, J., Zheng, R., and Chen, H. (2006). From fingerprint to writeprint. *Communications of the ACM, 49*(4), 76–82.

McHugh, J., Christie, A., and Allan, J. (2000). Defending yourself: the role of intrusion detection systems. *IEEE Software, 17*(5), 42–51.

Negnevitsky, M. (2005). *Artificial Intelligence: A Guide to Intelligent Systems* (2nd ed.). Essex, UK: Pearson Educational Limited.

Ong, M. G., Connie, T., Jin, A. T., and Ling, D. N. (2003). A single-sensor hand geometry and palmprint verification system. *Proceedings of the 2003 ACM SIGMM Workshop on Biometrics Methods and Applications,* 100–106.

Padhy, N. P. (2005). *Artificial Intelligence and Intelligent Systems.* Oxford, UK: Oxford University Press.

Peacock, A., Ke, X., and Wilkerson, M. (2005). Typing patterns: a key to user identification. *IEEE Security and Privacy, 2*(5), 40–47.

Pendharkar, P. C. (2005). A data envelopment analysis-based approach for data preprocessing. *IEEE Transactions on Knowledge and Data Engineering, 17*(10), 1379–1388.

Price, S. M. (2006). Secure state processing. *Proceedings of the 2006 IEEE Information Assurance Workshop,* 380–381.

Quixtiano-Xicohtencatl, R., Flores-Pulido, L., and Reyes-Galaviz, O. F. (2006). Feature selection for a fast speaker detection system with neural networks and genetic algorithms. *Proceedings of the 15th International Conference on Computing,* 126–134.

Russell, S., and Norvig, P. (2003). *Artificial Intelligence: A Modern Approach* (2nd ed.). Upper Saddle River, NJ: Pearson Education.

Yu, L., Wang, S., and Lai, K. K. (2006). An integrated data preparation scheme for neural network data analysis. *IEEE Transactions on Knowledge and Data Engineering, 18*(2), 217–230.

Zhao, W., Chellappa, R., Phillips, P. J., and Rosenfeld, A. (2003). Face recognition: a literature survey. *ACM Computing Surveys, 35*(4), 399–458.

Chapter 25

Information Technology Infrastructure Library and Security Management Overview

David McPhee

Contents

Introduction

For the purpose of this chapter, the focus will be on how information security management works within the Information Technology Infrastructure Library (ITIL®).

What Is the Information Technology Infrastructure Library?

The ITIL is a framework of best practices. The concepts within ITIL support information technology (IT) services delivery organizations with the planning of consistent, documented, and repeatable or customized processes that improve service delivery to the business. The ITIL framework consists of the following IT processes: service support (service desk, incident management, problem management, change management, configuration management, and release management) and services delivery [service-level management (SLM), capacity management, availability management, financial management, and IT service continuity management (SCM)].

History of ITIL

The ITIL concept emerged in the 1980s, when the British government determined that the level of IT service quality provided to them was not sufficient. The Central Computer and Telecommunications Agency, now called the Office of Government Commerce, was tasked with developing a framework for efficient and financially responsible use of IT resources within the British government and the private sector.

The earliest version of ITIL was called Government Information Technology Infrastructure Management. Obviously this was very different from the current ITIL, but conceptually very similar, focusing around service support and delivery.

Large companies and government agencies in Europe adopted the framework very quickly in the early 1990s. ITIL was spreading far and wide and was used in both government and nongovernmental organizations. As it grew in popularity, both in the United Kingdom and across the world, IT itself changed and evolved, and so did ITIL (http://itsm.fwtk.org/History.htm).

What Is Security Management?

Security management details the process of planning and managing a defined level of security for information and IT services, including all aspects associated with reaction to security incidents. It also includes the assessment and management of risks and vulnerabilities and the implementation of cost-justifiable countermeasures.

Security management is the process of managing a defined level of security on information and IT services. Included is managing the reaction to security incidents. The importance of information security has increased dramatically because of the move to open internal networks to customers and business partners, the move toward electronic commerce, and the increasing use of public networks like the Internet and intranets. The widespread use of information and information processing as well as the increasing dependency on information process results requires structural and organized protection of information (Figure 25.1).

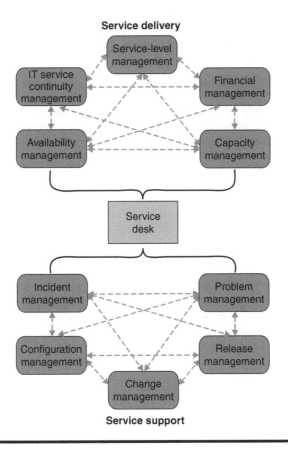

Figure 25.1   ITIL overview.

Descriptions

Service Support Overview

Service support describes the processes associated with the day-to-day support and maintenance activities associated with the provision of IT services (service desk, incident management, problem management, change management, configuration management, and release management).

Service desk. This function is the single point of contact between the end users and IT service management.

Incident management. Best practices for resolving incidents (any event that causes an interruption to, or a reduction in, the quality of an IT service) and quickly restoring IT services.

Problem management. Best practices for identifying the underlying cause(s) of IT incidents to prevent future recurrences. These practices seek to proactively prevent incidents and problems.

Change management. Best practices for standardizing and authorizing the controlled implementation of IT changes. These practices ensure that changes are implemented with minimum adverse impact on IT services and that they are traceable.

Configuration management. Best practices for controlling production configurations (for example, standardization, status monitoring, and asset identification). By identifying, controlling, maintaining, and verifying the items that make up an organization's IT infrastructure, these practices ensure that there is a logical model of the infrastructure.

Release management. Best practices for the release of hardware and software. These practices ensure that only tested and correct versions of authorized software and hardware are provided to IT customers.

Service Support Details

Service Desk

The objective of the service desk is to be a single point of contact for customers who need assistance with incidents, problems, and questions and to provide an interface for other activities related to IT and ITIL services (Figure 25.2).

Benefits of Implementing a Service Desk

- Increased first-call resolution
- Skill-based support
- Rapid restoration of service
- Improved incident response time
- Improved tracking of service quality
- Improved recognition of trends and incidents
- Improved employee satisfaction

Processes Utilized by the Service Desk

- Workflow and procedures diagrams
- Roles and responsibilities
- Training evaluation sheets and skill set assessments
- Implemented metrics and continuous improvement procedures

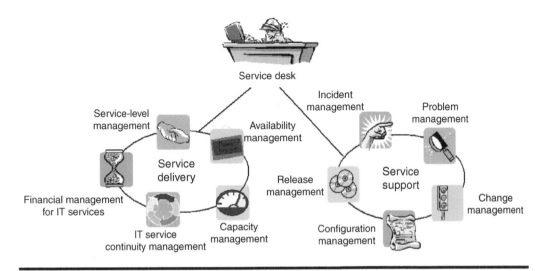

Figure 25.2   Service desk diagram (Securityfocus.com/infocus/1815).

Incident Management

The objective of incident management (http://www.itilpeople.com/) is to minimize disruption to the business by restoring service operations to agreed levels as quickly as possible and to ensure that the availability of IT services is maximized. It can also protect the integrity and confidentiality of information by identifying the root cause of a problem.

Benefits of Incident Management Process

- Incident detection and recording
- Classification and initial support
- Investigation and diagnosis
- Resolution and recovery
- Incident closure
- Incident ownership, monitoring, tracking, and communication
- Repeatable process

With a formal incident management practice, IT quality will improve through ensuring ticket quality, standardizing ticket ownership, and providing a clear understanding of ticket types while decreasing the number of unreported or misreported incidents (Figure 25.3).

Problem Management

The object of problem management (http://www.itilpeople.com/) is to resolve the root cause of incidents to minimize the adverse impact of incidents and problems on the business and, second, to prevent recurrence of incidents related to these errors. A "problem" is an unknown underlying cause of one or more incidents, and a "known error" is a problem that has been successfully diagnosed and for which a workaround has been identified. The outcome of a known error is a request for change (RFC).

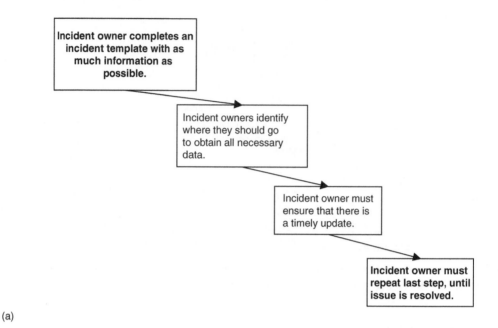

(a)

Process definition	Incident management will lead or support activities related to these steps.
Incident owner completes an incident template with as much information as possible.	• Initially, the incident owner must provide as much information as possible. The owners must also establish the initial timeframe when they will update the template next (whether negotiated or preestablished service-level agreement [SLA]).
Incident owners identify where they should go to obtain all necessary data.	• Every data point on the appended templates will have a group accountable. This means, that the incident owners must ensure the template is complete, they are not responsible for being able to complete the template on their own. Identified resources will exist which are responsible for knowing the information that should go into the template. That resource is to provide the technical data to the incident owner.
Incident owner must ensure that there is a timely update.	• Part of the update process is that the next point of contact be established with the customer. Whether this is an operational-level agreement (OLA)/SLA, or a time negotiated and agreed upon at the time of the call, that time is when the incident owners owe another update to the customer, and is when they should have a fresh update in the incident.
Incident owner must repeat last step, until issue is resolved.	• All subsequent updates in the incident must be by or prior to the agreed upon SLA/OLA.

(b)

Figure 25.3   Incident management ticket owner workflow diagram.

A problem is a condition often identified as a result of multiple incidents that exhibit common symptoms. Problems can also be identified from a single significant incident, indicative of a single error, for which the cause is unknown, but for which the impact is significant.

A known error is a condition identified by successful diagnosis of the root cause of a problem and the subsequent development of a work-around.

An RFC is a proposal to IT infrastructure for a change to the environment (Figure 25.4).

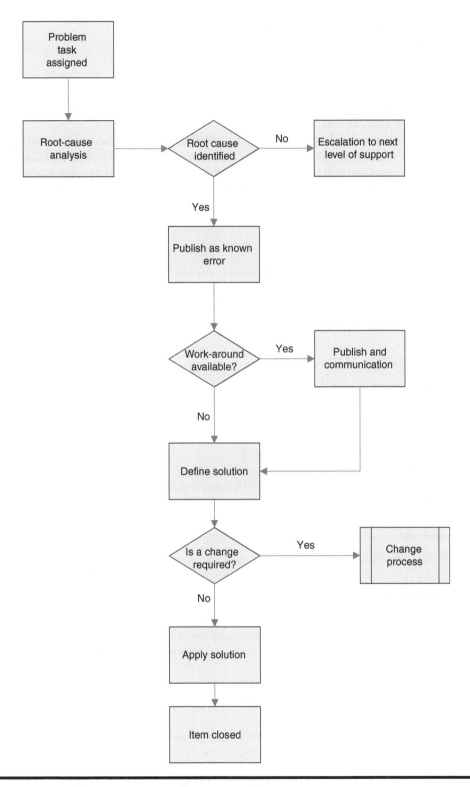

Figure 25.4 Problem management diagram overview.

Incident Management and Problem Management: What Is the Difference?

Incidents and service requests are formally managed through a staged process to conclusion. This process is referred to as the "incident management life cycle." The objective of the incident management life cycle is to restore the service as quickly as possible to meet SLAs. The process is primarily aimed at the user level.

Problem management deals with resolving the underlying cause of one or more incidents. The focus of problem management is to resolve the root cause of errors and to find permanent solutions. Although every effort will be made to resolve the problem as quickly as possible, this process is focused on the resolution of the problem rather than the speed of the resolution. This process deals at the enterprise level.

Change Management

Change management (http://www.itilpeople.com/) ensures that all areas follow a standardized process when implementing change into a production environment. Change is defined as any adjustment, enhancement, or maintenance to a production business application, system software, system hardware, communications network, or operational facility.

Benefits of Change Management

- Planning change
- Impact analysis
- Change approval
- Managing and implementing change
- Increase formalization and compliance
- Postchange review
- Better alignment of IT infrastructure to business requirements
- Efficient and prompt handling of all changes
- Fewer changes to be backed out
- Greater ability to handle a large volume of change
- Increased user productivity

Configuration Management

Configuration management is the implementation of a database (configuration management database [CMDB]) that contains details of the organization's elements that are used in the provision and management of its IT services. The main activities of configuration management are

- *Planning.* Planning and defining the scope, objectives, policy, and processes of the CMDB
- *Identification.* Selecting and identifying the configuration structures and items within the scope of your IT infrastructure
- *Configuration control.* Ensuring that only authorized and identifiable configuration items are accepted and recorded in the CMDB throughout its lifecycle.
- *Status accounting.* Keeping track of the status of components throughout the entire lifecycle of configuration items

- *Verification and audit.* Auditing after the implementation of configuration management to verify that the correct information is recorded in the CMDB, followed by scheduled audits to ensure the CMDB is kept up-to-date

Configuration Management and Information Security

Without the definition of all configuration items that are used to provide an organization's IT services, it can be very difficult to identify which items are used for which services. This could result in critical configuration items being stolen, moved, or misplaced, affecting the availability of the services dependent on them. It could also result in unauthorized items being used in the provision of IT services.

Benefits of Configuration Management

- Reduced cost to implement, manage, and support the infrastructure
- Decreased incident and problem resolution times
- Improved management of software licensing and compliance
- Consistent, automated processes for infrastructure mapping
- Increased ability to identify and comply with architecture and standards requirements
- Incident troubleshooting
- Usage trending
- Change evaluation
- Financial chargeback and asset life-cycle management
- SLA and software license negotiations

Release Management

Release management (http://www.itilpeople.com) is used for platform-independent and automated distribution of software and hardware, including license controls across the entire IT infrastructure. Proper software and hardware control ensures the availability of licensed, tested, and version-certified software and hardware, which will function correctly and respectively with the available hardware. Quality control during the development and implementation of new hardware and software is also the responsibility of release management. This guarantees that all software can be conceptually optimized to meet the demands of the business processes.

Benefits of Release Management

- Ability to plan resource requirements in advance
- Provides a structured approach, leading to an efficient and effective process
- Changes are bundled together in a release, minimizing the impact on the user
- Helps to verify correct usability and functionality before release by testing
- Controls the distribution and installation of changes to IT systems
- Designs and implements procedures for the distribution and installation of changes to IT systems
- Effectively communicates and manages expectations of the customer during the planning and rollout of new releases

The focus of release management is the protection of the live environment and its services through the use of formal procedures and checks.

Release Categories

A release consists of the new or changed software or hardware required to implement the approved change (Figure 25.5).

- Major software releases and hardware upgrades, normally containing large areas of new functionality, some of which may make intervening fixes to problems redundant. A major upgrade or release usually supersedes all preceding minor upgrades, releases, and emergency fixes.
- Minor software releases and hardware upgrades, normally containing small enhancements and fixes, some of which may have already been issued as emergency fixes. A minor upgrade or release usually supersedes all preceding emergency fixes.
- Emergency software and hardware fixes, normally containing the corrections to a small number of known problems.

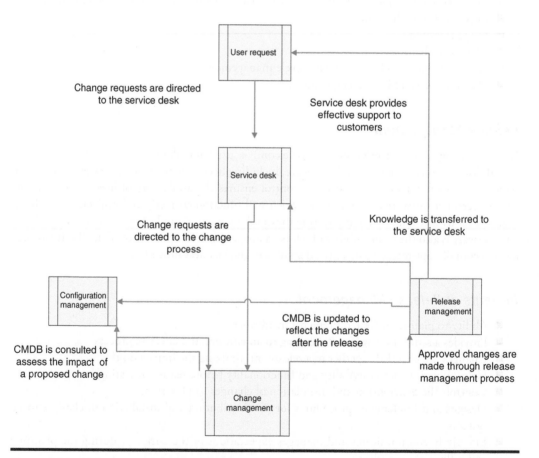

Figure 25.5   Release management overview.

Releases can be divided based on the release unit into the following:

- Delta release is a release of only that part of the software that has been changed (e.g., security patches to plug bugs in a software).
- Full release means that the entire software program will be released again (e.g., an entire version of an application).
- Packaged release is a combination of many changes (e.g., an operating system image containing the applications as well).

Service Delivery Overview

Service delivery is the discipline that ensures IT infrastructure is provided at the right time in the right volume at the right price and ensures that IT is used in the most efficient manner. This involves analysis and decisions to balance capacity at a production or service point with demand from customers; it also covers the processes required for the planning and delivery of quality IT services and looks at the longer-term processes associated with improving the quality of IT services delivered.

SLM. Service-level management is responsible for negotiating and agreeing to service requirements and expected service characteristics with the customer.

Capacity management. This is responsible for ensuring that IT processing and storage capacity provision match the evolving demands of the business in a cost-effective and timely manner.

Availability management. This is responsible for optimizing availability.

Financial management. The object of financial management for IT services is to provide cost-effective stewardship of the IT assets and the financial resources used in providing IT services.

IT SCM. Service continuity is responsible for ensuring that the available IT service continuity options are understood and the most appropriate solution is chosen in support of the business requirements.

Service Level Management

The object of SLM is to maintain and gradually improve business-aligned IT service quality, through a constant cycle of agreeing, monitoring, reporting, and reviewing IT service achievements and through instigating actions to eradicate unacceptable levels of service.

SLM is responsible for ensuring that the service targets are documented and agreed in SLAs and monitoring and reviewing the actual service levels achieved against their SLA targets. SLM should also be trying to improve all service levels proactively within the imposed cost constraints. SLM is the process that manages and improves agreed level of service between two parties, the provider and the receiver of a service.

SLM is responsible for negotiating and agreeing to service requirements and expected service characteristics with the customer, measuring and reporting service levels actually being achieved against target, resources required, and cost of service provision. SLM is also responsible for continuously improving service levels in line with business processes, with a Session Initiation Protocol; co-coordinating other service management and support functions, including third-party suppliers; reviewing SLAs to meet changed business needs; or resolving major service issues and producing, reviewing, and maintaining the service catalog.

Benefits of Implementing SLM

- Implementing the SLM process enables both the customer and the IT services provider to have a clear understanding of the expected level of delivered services and their associated costs for the organization, by documenting these goals in formal agreements.
- SLM can be used as a basis for charging for services and can demonstrate to customers the value they are receiving from the service desk.
- It also assists the service desk with managing external supplier relationships and introduces the possibility of negotiating improved services or reduced costs.

Capacity Management

Capacity management is responsible for ensuring that IT processing and storage capacity provisioning match the evolving demands of the business in a cost-effective and timely manner. The process includes monitoring the performance and the throughput of the IT services and supporting IT components, tuning activities to make efficient use of resources, understanding the current demands for IT resources and deriving forecasts for future requirements, influencing the demand for resource in conjunction with other service management processes, and producing a capacity plan predicting the IT resources needed to achieve agreed service levels.

Capacity management has three main areas of responsibility. The first of these is business continuity management (BCM), which is responsible for ensuring that the future business requirements for IT services are considered, planned, and implemented in a timely fashion. These future requirements will come from business plans outlining new services, improvements and growth in existing services, development plans, etc. This requires knowledge of existing service levels and SLAs, future service levels and service level requirements (SLRs), the business and capacity plans, modeling techniques (analytical, simulation, trending, and baselining), and application sizing methods.

The second main area of responsibility is SCM, which focuses on managing the performance of the IT services provided to the customers and is responsible for monitoring and measuring services, as detailed in SLAs, and collecting, recording, analyzing, and reporting on data. This requires knowledge of service levels and SLAs, systems, networks, service throughput and performance, monitoring, measurement, analysis, tuning, and demand management.

The third and final main area of responsibility is resource capacity management (RCM), which focuses on management of the components of the IT infrastructure and ensuring that all finite resources within the IT infrastructure are monitored and measured and that collected data is recorded, analyzed, and reported. This requires knowledge of the current technology and its utilization, future or alternative technologies, and the resilience of systems and services.

Capacity Management Processes

- Performance monitoring
- Workload monitoring
- Application sizing
- Resource forecasting
- Demand forecasting
- Modeling

From these processes come the results of capacity management, these being the capacity plan itself, forecasts, tuning data, and SLM guidelines.

Availability Management

Availability management is concerned with design, implementation, measurement, and management of IT services to ensure the stated business requirements for availability are consistently met. Availability management requires an understanding of the reasons why IT service failures occur and the time taken to resume this service. Incident management and problem management provide a key input to ensure the appropriate corrective actions are being implemented.

- *Availability management.* The ability of an IT component to perform at an agreed level over a period of time.
- *Reliability.* The ability of an IT component to perform at an agreed level under described conditions.
- *Maintainability.* The ability of an IT component to remain in, or be restored to, an operational state.
- *Serviceability.* The ability of an external supplier to maintain the availability of a component or function under a third-party contract.
- *Resilience.* A measure of freedom from operational failure and a method of keeping services reliable. One popular method of resilience is redundancy.
- *Security.* A service has associated data. Security refers to the confidentiality, integrity, and availability of that data.

Availability Management and Information Security

Security is an essential part of availability management, this being the primary focus of ensuring IT infrastructure continues to be available for the provision of IT services.

Some of the elements mentioned earlier are the products of performing risk analysis to identify how reliable elements are and how many problems have been caused as a result of system failure.

The risk analysis also recommends controls to improve availability of IT infrastructure such as development standards, testing, physical security, and the right skills in the right place at the right time.

Financial Management

Financial management (www.securityfocus.com/infocus/1815) for IT services is an integral part of service management. It provides the essential management information to ensure that services are run efficiently, economically, and cost effectively. An effective financial management system will assist in the management and reduction of overall long-term costs and identify the actual cost of services. This provisioning provides accurate and vital financial information to assist in decision making, identify the value of IT services, and enable the calculation of total cost of ownership and ROI.

The practice of financial management enables the service manager to identify the amount being spent on security countermeasures in the provision of the IT services. The amount being spent on these countermeasures needs to be balanced with the risks and the potential losses that the service could incur as identified during business impact and risk assessments. Management of these costs will ultimately reflect on the cost of providing the IT services and potentially what is charged in the recovery of those costs.

Service Continuity Management

SCM supports the overall BCM process by ensuring that the required IT technical and services facilities can be recovered within required and agreed business timescales.

IT SCM is concerned with managing an organization's ability to continue to provide a predetermined and agreed level of IT services to support the minimum business requirements following an interruption to the business. This includes ensuring business survival by reducing the impact of a disaster or major failure, reducing the vulnerability and risk to the business by effective risk analysis and risk management, preventing the loss of customer and user confidence, and producing IT recovery plans that are integrated with and fully support the organization's overall business continuity plan.

IT service continuity is responsible for ensuring that the available IT service continuity options are understood and the most appropriate solution is chosen in support of the business requirements. It is also responsible for identifying roles and responsibilities and making sure that these are endorsed and communicated from a senior level to ensure respect and commitment for the process. Finally, IT service continuity is responsible for guaranteeing that the IT recovery plans and the business continuity plans are aligned and are regularly reviewed, revised, and tested.

The Security Management Process

Security management provides a framework to capture the occurrence of security-related incidents and limit the impact of security breaches. The activities within the security management process must be revised continuously, to stay up to date and effective. Security management is a continuous process and it can be compared to the Quality Circle of Deming (Plan, Do, Check, and Act).

The inputs are the requirements formed by the clients. The requirements are translated into security services, security quality that needs to be provided in the security section of the SLAs. As you can see in Figure 25.6, there are arrows going both ways: from the client to the SLA and from

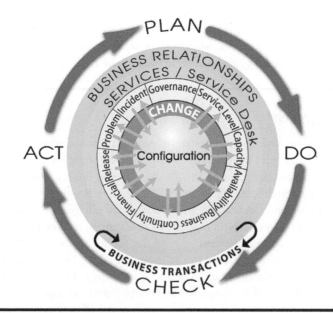

Figure 25.6   Security image diagram.

the SLA to the client, and from the SLA to the plan subprocess and from the plan subprocess to the SLA. This means that both the client and the plan subprocess have inputs to the SLA and the SLA is an input for both the client and the process. The provider then develops the security plans for their organization. These security plans contain the security policies and the OLAs. The security plans (Plan) are then implemented (Do) and the implementation is then evaluated (Check). After the evaluation both the plans and the implementation of the plan are maintained (Act).

Control

The first activity in the security management process is the "control" subprocess. The control subprocess organizes and manages the security management process itself. The control subprocess defines the processes, the allocation of responsibility, the policy statements, and the management framework.

The security management framework defines the subprocesses for the development of security plans, the implementation of the security plans, the evaluation, and how the results of the evaluations are translated into action plans.

Plan

The plan subprocess contains activities that in cooperation with the SLM lead to the information security section in the SLA. The plan subprocess contains activities that are related to the underpinning contracts, which are specific for information security.

In the plan subprocess the goals formulated in the SLA are specified in the form of OLAs. These OLAs can be defined as security plans for a specific internal organization entity of the service provider.

In addition to the input of the SLA, the plan subprocess works with the policy statements of the service provider itself. As mentioned earlier these policy statements are defined in the control subprocess.

The OLAs for information security are set up and implemented based on the ITIL process. This means that there has to be cooperation with other ITIL processes. For example, if the security management wishes to change the IT infrastructure to achieve maximum security, these changes will be done only through the change management process. The security management will deliver the input (RFC) for this change. The change manager is responsible for the change management process itself.

Implementation

The implementation subprocess makes sure that all measures, as specified in the plans, are properly implemented. During the implementation subprocess no (new) measures are defined or changed. The definition or change of measures will take place in the plan subprocess in cooperation with the change management process.

Evaluation

The evaluation of the implementation and the plans is very important. The evaluation is necessary to measure the success of the implementation and the security plans. The evaluation is also very important for the clients and possibly for third parties. The results of the evaluation subprocess are used to maintain the agreed measures and the implementation itself. Evaluation results can lead to new requirements and so lead to an RFC. The RFC is then defined and it is sent to the change management process.

Maintenance

It is necessary for security to be maintained. Because of changes in the IT infrastructure and changes in the organization itself, security risks are bound to change over time. The maintenance of security concerns the maintenance of both the security section of the SLAs and the more detailed security plans.

Maintenance is based on the results of the evaluation subprocess and insight into the changing risks. These activities will only produce proposals. The proposals serve as inputs for the plan sub-process and will go through the whole cycle, or the proposals can be taken in the maintenance of the SLAs. In both cases the proposals could lead to activities in the action plan. The actual changes will be carried out by the change management process.

The maintenance subprocess starts with the maintenance of the SLAs and the operation level arrangements (OLAs). After these activities take place, in no particular order, and when there is a request for a change, the RFC activity will take place, and after the RFC activity is concluded the reporting activity will start. If there is no request for a change then the reporting activity will start directly after the first two activities.

References

http://itsm.fwtk.org/.
http://www.itilpeople.com/.
http://www.itlibrary.org/.
ITIL—Security Management.
http://www.securityfocus.com/infocus/1815.

Chapter 26

Adaptation: A Concept for Next-Generation Security Application Development

Robby S. Fussell

Contents

Introduction

Security applications are constantly managing changes in their environment. Antivirus applications, firewall programs, network components, intrusion detection systems, and various other types of functions that are involved with security are continuously confronted with change. The next phase of security application development is to introduce adaptation mechanisms within the application. This will provide the application with the ability to adapt to changes in its environment to provide enhanced security measures. However, to provide adaptation methods, adaptation must be explained.

Adaptation is a characteristic of complex adaptive systems (CAS) that assists in causing a system's evolution. CAS have the innate ability to conform and optimize based on their current environment [20]. CAS achieve this conformity or optimization via the feedback of agents within the system [8,13,16,19]. Agents are also known as the components that comprise a system. For example, the network devices within a local area network or the people of a specific social network can be defined as agents or components. The agents within complex systems contain a set of rules [19] that instruct the agents on how to behave based on their interactions with other agents and their environment.

Therefore, complex systems that exist in unpredictable environments are constantly striving to adapt and conform to their surroundings. However, the defined rules present within the agents must also change to make the system as a whole adapt to the change in the environment [13]. This process of the agents changing their set of rules is called learning [8]. The learning process can be viewed as the central function that propels the overall complex system to adapt. Therefore, adaptation can be defined as the process by which a system changes its goals and behavior due to the alterations in its surrounding environment to survive [15]. According to Ashby, "another way to understand adaptation is to think of it as behavior by organisms in order to support the stability of their internal environment, or homeostasis" [1]. Adaptation emerges through the learning process within the complex system. The system agents constantly interact with the environment and other agents based on a rule set or stimuli–response framework as illustrated by Holland [13].

Holland [13] illustrates this in his book by describing how the immune system adapts [10]. Holland [13] states that there are "lever points" in CAS. For example, a characteristic of CAS is chaos. By adding a small change to the system, diverse results can be observed. In the immune system example, if a small amount of an antigen, such as the measles virus, is introduced into the body, the immune system will react and create antibodies for the measles virus to protect the entire body from the disease [13]. The lever point has caused the immune system to learn about the virus and produce antibodies to protect the body. The immune system adapted to its new environment, the measles-induced environment, by producing antibodies to preserve the system.

Background of Complex Adaptive Systems

Cybernetics [5] is focused on how systems change in response to their current environment. Cybernetics is demonstrated by an entity outside a target system, which controls the target system based on changes in the surrounding environment. A concern with this theory is that it prevents the system from adapting spontaneously due to fluctuations in the environment. The outside mediator provides the input for the system it change based on which or adapts; therefore, cybernetics can also be defined as a self-regulating system. An example of cybernetics is climate control inside a building. Based on the comfort of an individual, the climate fluctuates. The thermostat is a contained system and can adapt only by the predetermination of an agent outside the system, which is the individual. There is another type of adaptation, which involves complex systems that perform adaptation within the system itself, without an outside controlling agent. This theory of adaptation is the focus of this chapter.

CAS are structured to adapt to their changing environment. They perform this function without a fixation on control. The complex system is not controlled or modified by an objective observer outside the system. The agents who comprise the structure are responsible for its change [13,19]. Therefore, for adaptation to occur, the following two elements are required:

- The complex system must be placed in a state of diversity [16] or constant fluctuation for adaptation to emerge.
- Agents within the system must modify the way they interact and process feedback information, known as learning [8], which includes the use of embodied internal models.

Examining these two elements, which cause adaptation to occur, prompts the question, why does a system adapt? Complex systems adapt to optimize the system as a whole to the current environmental conditions, and because the environment is always changing, open complex systems never cease adapting. If they do cease adapting, they will become extinct. A main element of CAS is the property of diversity.

Diversity and Mimicry

Holland [13] illustrates this diversity property by explaining that if an agent within the system is removed, the system will respond with a surge of adaptations that will fill the role of the removed agent, also known as convergence [5]. One system that explains this diversity property is the biological phenomenon called mimicry [13]. Mimicry is the process of one species adapting the behavior or "likeness" of another species to obtain the other species' benefits [25]. An example illustrated in Ref. [13] is that of the monarch and viceroy butterflies. The monarch butterfly digests the milkweed plant for food, which produces an alkaloid chemical inside the butterfly. Birds that have eaten the monarch butterfly over time continually regurgitated the ingested butterfly. Birds now recognize the patterns of the monarch butterfly and avoid it as a potential prey. This could possibly be explained as an adaptation process within the bird society, through which birds have learned not to prey on the monarch butterfly by recognizing the monarch's wing markings. This learning process, called "learned avoidance" [13], is also explained as a tagging mechanism [13], in which a tag is used by the bird to identify the wing pattern on the monarch butterfly.

Back to the monarch butterfly: there is another butterfly called the viceroy butterfly that has used mimicry to imitate the monarch butterfly. The viceroy butterfly is considered a prey to birds; however, because the viceroy butterfly has adapted a wing pattern similar to that of the monarch butterfly, birds using their tagging mechanism decline to consume the viceroy due to the possible negative outcomes. Mimicry can be viewed as a type of adaptation and diversity can be seen as a result of progressive adaptations. This mimicry is also seen in other species, like lizards and the chameleon that change their skin color to resemble that of the environment on which they currently reside to avoid being prey.

In the computer network environment, honeypots and honeynets can be seen as a means of mimicry. Some companies utilize honeypots and honeynets to mimic an attractive hacking environment for potential malicious behavior to deter this behavior from the company's legitimate computer infrastructure. In addition, routing protocols have adopted the diversity principle. For example, when a router is removed from the network, the routing protocol becomes aware of this removal and will send routing table updates to neighboring routers to route traffic correctly. By observing CAS, these systems contain another property element termed flows [13].

The flows property can be visualized as resources that are transferred between agents within a system. Based on these resources and the agent's set of rules, feedback is produced. However, Holland [13] explains that flows contain a property called the recycling effect. The recycling effect is based on the reuse of resource inputs in a system. This recycling effect is explained by the rainforest example, in which continuous rainfalls wash the resources out of the soil and into the river system quickly, providing poor soil. However, the trees in the rainforest have adapted and they reuse the input resources from the soil that is retained to support over 10,000 possible distinct species of insects per tree [13]. According to Holland [13], systems like these that recycle their resources to exploit new niches for new agents will continue to thrive while other systems become extinct. Holland [13] states, "It is a process that leads to increasing diversity through increasing recycling …" also known in general as natural selection.

Learning through Embodied Internal Models

The next element in the study of adaptation is the process of learning [5]. For complex systems to adapt to their environment, the system must learn the optimal pattern of change to implement. To facilitate learning, the complex system's agents must have a model in which anticipation and prediction can be generated. The internal model has two types:

- Tacit—recommends a current action based on understood predictions of a desired future state [13].
- Overt—a "look-ahead" process in which the model is used as a basis for explicit searching of options [13].

An example of prediction using a tacit internal model is that of *Escherichia coli* searching for food based on a chemical gradient [11,13]. An example of prediction utilizing an overt internal model is that of a computer chess game predicting possible case scenarios of different moves before it makes an actual move in the game. The underlying principle for the model is that it permits us to understand that which is being modeled.

The internal model is based upon the building blocks mechanism. Building blocks make models effective. Building blocks can be viewed as various components that can be arranged to create a particular environment. For example, using the chess scenario, the chess program can create an internal model comprising a chessboard and various chess pieces. Based on the current location of the chess pieces, its environment, it can use its overt internal model to predict the best next move for an optimal outcome. Playing the different scenarios with the various building blocks, chess pieces and board, the chess program can learn how different interactions result and can predict its next move based on the forecasted results. This is also observed in game theory and in the use of genetic algorithms, to be discussed in the next section. Holland [13] effectively states, "I cannot have a prepared list of rules for all possible situations, for the same reason that the immune system cannot keep a list of all possible invaders" [10]. Given our immune system, it would be impractical for it to store a blueprint of all possible viruses and process its reaction to a particular virus within a suitable amount of time.

Adaptive Agent Construction

To understand how agents within a CAS exhibit adaptation, their internal operations must be examined. Agents, as noted earlier, contain a set of rules that define how an agent behaves. This behavior output is utilized by other agents to mold the complex system into its optimal form based on its surrounding environment. Adaptive agents typically comprise the following three identifiable characteristics:

■ The performance system—a rule base that processes input information and produces an output result [13].
■ The value/credit assignment—the process of applying positive and negative values to various parts of the performance system based on its success and failure [13].
■ The discovery of rules—the process of instantiating changes to the agent's potential by replacing the negative-value parts with new alternatives [13].

Agent Rule Set: Performance System

The performance system is basically a set of rules on how the agent will respond to various inputs from the environment or other agents. Based on the processed rules for the input message, the agent will send output in the form of a message. The agent's set of rules can be illustrated by a set of IF/THEN or CONDITION/ACTION statements [6]. Whichever terminology is applied, the functions are the same. The IF/THEN statement terminology will be used in this discussion for the agent performance system. First, the agent employs various stimuli to obtain the input message from the environment [13]. An example would be the senses used by the human body, a video camera used by various robots, or a network interface card for computer network devices. Normally, the environment will produce many messages that will be observed by the complex system; therefore, the system must filter the input. The environment produces various detectors [13] that are noticed by the agent. If the agent has a rule for that detector, it will process it. Otherwise, the agent will ignore the detector.

For example, using the chess game scenario and algebraic chess notation, the opposing player's queen is moved to cell c4. Based on this movement, the artificial intelligence (AI) chess system will have an environment identifier for "move," "queen," and "position." Each one of these identifiers will have a corresponding IF/THEN statement and the agent will process the rules and provide a response. Two actions will occur within the agent. The agent will process the input from the environment and it will also process input within the system based on actions provided by other internal rules. A series of "what if" scenarios [19] will be performed. This gives the agent the ability to produce the most optimal response to an environment input. If the agent was based on a single-rule situation, it would need a rule for every possible environmental condition. This would not be feasible, as shown by the aforementioned immune system example. As noted by Holland [13], "With simultaneously active rules, the agent can combine tested rules to describe a novel situation. The rules become building blocks" [19]. These building blocks [19] contribute to the internal model of the agent. The novel situation that is created here can be obtained using the processes of mutation and crossover in genetic algorithms discussed under Crossover, Mutation, and Genetic Algorithms. The use of rules working in parallel can also be seen in behavior-based robots [21].

Value/Credit Assignment

This process will assist in providing a solution to how systems adapt. Credit assignment [13] is the process of assigning a value to various rules based on their effectiveness. Agents will assign weights or values corresponding to a rule's helpfulness or unhelpfulness [13]. This process enables an agent and the overall complex system to adapt to environmental flux. This process is based on competition. When a rule is selected, it gives its predecessor rule an increase in value. If the selected rule produces output, then its value will increase based on its future bids. Therefore, reinforcement in rule effectiveness is substantiated, with helpful rules getting higher precedence over less helpful or unhelpful rules.

The rule selection is based on competition. The more a rule is selected and outcome is produced, the higher its value will become. Therefore, higher value rules are selected in time of competition among other rules. Then, the rules that make the final direct contribution to the environment are rewarded. The overall concept of the credit assignment process is "to strengthen rules that belong to chains of action terminating into environmental rewards" [13]. Over time, default hierarchies are created as internal models. For example, a general rule that can typically satisfy any input from the environment can be executed. However, what if a more specific rule exists that can satisfy the majority of conditions inputted from the environment? The process will construct internal models that consist of hierarchies or subsets, which can otherwise be seen as nesting.

Discovery of Rules

The next process in how agents adapt is in regard to rule discovery. How agents adapt with preexisting rules has been discussed earlier. This process will examine how agents adapt by the creation of new rules to manage new environmental conditions.

There is one method by which new rules can be created and tested and that method is trial and error. Random trial and error states that what might have happened before has no effect on what happens next. This method is not a feasible approach to rule discovery. The method that is employed is one of plausibility [13]. Holland [13] explains this by stating, "a component that consistently appears in strong rules should be a likely candidate for use in new rules." By choosing a number of strong rules and extracting the components within these rules to create new rules, the agent builds new rules on tested components, which is a more efficient approach than random trial and error. Holland [13] demonstrates this by providing the example of the digital computer. The use of building blocks provided innovation that brought about the digital computer. Components such as Geiger's particle counter, cathode ray tube images, wires for electrical current, and others were combined to create the digital computer. Therefore, the agent not only processes rules based on environmental input but also constantly attempts to discover new rules that will assist it in optimizing its behavior.

Crossover, Mutation, and Genetic Algorithms

Crossover is a genetic operation by which two messages are used to generate a new message for testing [13]. The process of selecting the rules to be crossed over is based on their values or credit assigned. This process is called reproduction based on fitness [2,8,24] ranking. For example, the following are two different messages:

- M1 = 100#101
- M2 = #00####

M1 and M2 compose a message string based on a particular binary sequence used for conditional rule–based testing. The # symbol denotes either a 1 or a 0.

Example of rule:

R1 = IF (100#101) THEN (do_this_action)
R2 = IF (#00####) THEN (do_this_action)

The two rules, R1 and R2, have the highest values assigned compared to any other rule within a particular agent. The crossover process then selects a crossover point to generate a new message for implementation into a new rule for testing. For example, if the crossover point selected were position 5, with the first position being counted as 0, the new message for testing in a new rule would be the following:

■ M1^ = 100#1##
■ M2^ = #00##01

Example of rule:

R1^ = IF (100#1##) THEN (do_this_action)
R2^ = IF (#00##01) THEN (do_this_action)

The crossover process provides means for evolution through adaptation to ever-changing environmental conditions. This is an overt process that creates internal models with novel building blocks.

According to Foster, "Adaptive mutation is defined as a process that, during non-lethal selections, produces mutations that relieve the selective pressure whether or not other, non-selected mutations are also produced" [11]. Mutation is rather simple in that a 1, 0, or # in the above rules R1 and R2 is arbitrarily changed in the message rule. This mutation will yield another hypothesis for testing that includes plausibility as opposed to random trial and error. One might think, why does crossover or mutation need to be executed? If crossover or mutation does not occur, the same rules will just be copied to the next generation. Doing this only allows the existing generation to thrive; however, because CAS exist in continuously changing environments, permitting crossover and mutation allows for new hypotheses to be tested.

Last is the replacement of rules or strings in the new-generation agent over the current rules.

The process discussed here is a genetic algorithm [7,22,26] or genetic process for agents of CAS. The first step was to select the best fit set of rules and the strings or messages contained in those rules. The second step was to use the crossover and mutation procedures to generate new strings for testing. The third and final step was to replace the new strings in the next generation of the agent. The genetic algorithm is used to provide the agent with the most optimal set of rules for producing the most advantageous set of responses to environmental input, in other words, enabling the agent to adapt to changes in its environment.

Current and Future Trends

The understanding of adaptation in complex systems is essential. By attempting to discover the processes and components needed to explain adaptation, CAS can then be modeled. How can the framework of an adaptive agent as previously discussed be applied to current and future developments?

Artificial Intelligence

AI is a popular computer science discipline that scientists are continuously attempting to develop. AI has a component that is being researched constantly, which is adaptation [26]. AI is concerned with attempting to manufacture intelligence by human means. As stated by Bredeweg and Struss [4], "Reasoning about, and solving problems in, the physical world is one of the most fundamental capabilities of human intelligence and a fundamental subject for AI." An example is that of a robot that can function in an ever-changing environment. The goal sought after is to provide the machine the correct model to solve problems with fluctuating input, in other words, to exhibit intelligence [5,22]. For example, people exhibit intelligence by being able to solve problems they have never actually encountered. A person can be given an algebraic model such as:

■ $x = 2y + z$

Next, that same person can be confronted by various situations that call for solving a quantity given two distinct inputs. The inputs encountered and situations containing those inputs can always be changing; however, because the persons know the algebraic algorithm or model, they can always produce a correct solution. Simply trying to provide the person all the solutions for all possible inputs would be infeasible. This is the process of adaptation, and a framework for how agents adapt was discussed earlier. That framework is the type of model that is being applied to AI systems.

As stated by Sharkey and Ziemke [21], "Intelligence is found in the interaction of the robot with its environment." The framework discussed here is based on this statement by providing a way for an agent to learn, which provides a means for the agent to adapt. However, when dealing with AI and robots, interaction with the environment provides cognition and this cognition can be embodied using two different views: Loebian and Uexküllian (see Ref. [21]). The objective with allopoietic machines is to make them into autopoietic (living) systems. Scientists are trying to use the two different views to accomplish this; however, more research must be performed on the behavior of agent-based systems [15].

Adaptive Protocol for Streaming Video Real-Time Transmission Protocol

The Internet provides a communication structure of which many people are taking advantage. Streaming video has become a popular means of delivering information to the consumer based on human cognition studies. However, protocols developed to allow for the transmission of information across the network factored in the idea that all routers had the same amount of connections. According to Ottino [19], "it was shown recently that the real Internet has a scale-free structure, i.e., the distribution of the number of connections decays as a *power law*" [12]. It has now been shown that a few specific routers employ the most connections and this is changing how communication protocols are being developed.

There are different protocols being developed to provide an adaptive means for delivering video media data [14,23]. The Real-Time Transmission Protocol (RTP) [3] was developed to provide a quality-of-service means for streaming video data across the Internet. In this situation, the fluctuating environment is the data connection rate between the client and the server. The architecture of the RTP contains certain modules that perform certain functions such as delivery of the video data; however, the quality-adaptation module performs the calculations needed to adapt to the fluctuations in the data connection rate so that the streaming video will be delivered on a timely basis.

The quality-adaptation module receives feedback information between the client and the server regarding data rates, and adapts the server based on the information analysis calculated by the quality-adaptation module.

Other Areas of Research

There are other areas that are exploring agent-based models and the characteristic of adaptation. One area would be adaptation in computer security [9,10]. Some researchers are studying this area using the idea of having agents modeled after the immune system [10,27]. Corporations today have their own internal networks that provide internal communication among different departments and functions. This internal network also provides access for remote users and the ability for new systems to be directly attached to the internal network. Research is attempting to discover a way to permit authorized and nonintrusive systems on the network without infecting other systems or accessing restricted areas. Researchers have seen that this scenario resembles the immune system. The immune system's function is to protect the human body from any chemical intruders. The immune system, as discussed, does not keep a list of all viruses but employs an adaptive framework for detection and deletion of the virus. Researchers are striving to utilize this concept and apply it to a model for computer network systems.

Other areas in which researchers are aiming to employ agent-based models are the stock market and economic sectors. This research has been undertaken by John Holland [6,13] and some of his colleagues at the Santa Fe Institute and by Epstein and Axtell [19] in economics. Holland and his colleagues have attempted to use the agent-based framework along with genetic algorithms [7] to have their agents mimic the stock market based on a specific company's stock prices and other market indicators. One final area would be an adaptive protocol for wireless local area networks (LANs) [18] and other quality-of-service issues with network or system load [17]. Wireless LANs continuously encounter fluctuations to their environment and would benefit from the ability to adapt to those changes.

Conclusion

CAS can be termed as nonlinear structures that contain agents that interact and have the ability to adapt to a fluctuating environment. These systems can also be characterized by their ability to self-organize. CAS evolve by performing random mutation, crossover, self-organization, alteration of their internal models, and natural selection. Examples of CAS range from organisms to societies and the nervous system to the immune system. The complex systems contain agents that have internal rules of behavior to solve input conditions from the environment or other agents. The agents are diverse, evolve, and adapt by assigning fitness values to their internal rules. Those rules with the lowest fitness rating eventually die out, whereas new rules are created by evolving the stronger rules through mutation and crossover. This process of evolution demonstrates the creative ability of CAS. One of the main elements in adaptation is diversity. For CAS to be creative, the following conditions must be satisfied:

- Nonaverage behavior must be encountered
- Agents in the system must not be identical and must interact with one another in various ways
- Environmental fluctuations or "noise" must be propagated into the system

For complex systems to adapt, they must learn. This learning process is shown by the system receiving a favorable response from the environment when the system produces output pertaining to some input from the environment. According to Murray Gell-Mann, "Complex adaptive systems are pattern seekers. They interact with the environment, 'learn' from the experience, and adapt as a result." This can be seen in the operational states of various corporations across the world. By examining the corporate structure as a complex system in which the corporation has many interactions with customers, suppliers, employees, and so on, if the environment that the corporation operates in suddenly changes, the corporation must adapt or it will become extinct. If the corporation learns from the environmental changes and constructs internal models that produce favorable responses, it can survive.

Acknowledgments

I would like to thank the true complexity factor, God; Dr. Jim Cannady; the speakers; and the authors for their presentations and insights on the topics concerning CAS, AI, and adaptation.

References

1. Ashby, W.R., *Design for a Brain*. Chapman & Hall, London, 1960.
2. Boettcher, S., and Percus, A.G., Optimization with extremal dynamics. *Complexity*, 2003, 57–62.
3. Bouras, C., and Gkamas, A., Multimedia transmission with adaptive QoS based on real-time protocols. *International Journal of Communication Systems*, 2003, 16, 225–248.
4. Bredeweg, B., and Struss, P., Current topics in qualitative reasoning. *AI Magazine*, 2004, 13–16.
5. Brooks, R.A., Intelligence without reason. *Computers and Thought, IJCAI-91*, 1991, 1–28.
6. Casazza, D., The effects of violence on the evolution of a simple society. *Consortium for Computing in Small Colleges*, 2002, 243–245.
7. Chalmers, D.J., The evolution of learning: An experiment in genetic connectionism. In D.S. Touretzky, J. Elman, T.J. Sejnowski, and G.E. Hinton, editors, *Proceedings of the 1990 Connectionist Models Summer School*. Morgan Kaufmann, San Mateo, CA, 1990.
8. Chiva-Gomez, R., The facilitating factors for organizational learning: Bringing ideas from complex adaptive systems. *Knowledge and Process Management*, 2003, 99–114.
9. Dandalis, A., Prasanna, V.K., and Rolim, J.D.P., An adaptive cryptographic engine for IPSec architectures. In *Proceedings of the 2000 IEEE Symposium on Field-Programmable Custom Computing Machines*, IEEE, 2000.
10. Forrest, S., Hofmeyr, S.A., and Somayaji, A., Computer immunology. *Communications of the ACM*, 1997, 88–96.
11. Foster, P.L., Adaptive mutation: Implications for evolution. *BioEssays*, 2000, 1067–1074.
12. Gong, P., and van Leeuwen, C., Emergence of scale-free network with chaotic units. *Physica A*, 2003, 679–688.
13. Holland, J.H., *Hidden Order: How Adaptation Builds Complexity*. Perseus Books, Reading, MA, 1995.
14. Kasiolas, A., Nait-Abdesselam, F., and Makrakis, D., *Cooperative Adaptation to Quality of Service Using Distributed Agents*. IEEE, 1999, pp. 502–507.
15. Lerman, K., and Galstyan, A., Agent memory and adaptation in multi-agent systems. In *AAMAS 2003*. ACM New York Press, Melbourne, Australia, 2003, pp. 797–803.
16. Levin, S.A., Complex adaptive systems: Exploring the known, the unknown, and the unknowable. *Bulletin of the American Mathematical Society*, 2002, 3–19.

17. Michiels, S., Desmet, L., Janssens, N., Mahieu, T., and Verbaeten, P., Self-adapting concurrency: The DMonA architecture. In *WOSS '02*, ACM New York Press, Charleston, SC, 2002.

18. Obaidat, M.S., and Green, D.G., An adaptive protocol model for IEEE 802.11 wireless LANs. *Computer Communications*, 2004, 1131–1136.

19. Ottino, J.M., Complex systems. *AIChE*, 2003, 292–299.

20. Raz, O., Koopman, P., and Shaw, M., Enabling automatic adaptation in systems with under-specified elements. In *WOSS '02*, ACM New York Press, Charleston, SC, 2002, pp. 55–61.

21. Sharkey, N., and Ziemke, T., Life, mind and robots: The ins and outs of embodied cognition, 2000.

22. Sipper, M., On the origin of environments by means of natural selection. *American Association for Artificial Intelligence*, 2001, 133–142.

23. Striegel, A., and Manimaran, G., A scalable QoS adaptation scheme for media servers. In *Proceedings of the 15th International Parallel and Distributed Processing Symposium (IPDPS'01)*. IEEE, 2001.

24. Venkatasubramanian, V., Katare, S., Patkar, P.R., and Mu, F.-p., Spontaneous emergence of complex optimal networks through evolutionary adaptation. *Computers and Chemical Engineering*, 2004, 1789–1798.

25. Wagner, D., and Soto, P., Mimicry attacks on host-based intrusion detection systems. In *CCS '02*. ACM New York Press, Washington, DC, 2002.

26. Wildberger, A.M., Introduction and overview of artificial life: Evolving intelligent agents for modeling and simulation. In *Proceedings of the 1996 Winter Simulation Conference*, ACM New York Press, 1996.

27. Williams, J., Just sick about security. In *ACM New Security Paradigm Workshop*. ACM Press, New York, NY, 1996, pp. 139–146.

Chapter 27

Quantum Computing: Implications for Security

Robert M. Slade

Contents

Introduction

There have been numerous mentions of quantum computing in the security trade press over the years. Generally, these concentrate on aspects of cryptography. However, our view of quantum computing tends to be contaminated by our knowledge of, and familiarity with, traditional digital computing. Quantum computers, as they have been developed, are based on architectures that are not the same as those in digital computers. Therefore, it is probable, and even desirable, that quantum computers will not simply be "faster" versions of what we have now.

Quantum computing will probably make possible certain types of calculations and analyses that have been difficult or impossible to do with traditional digital computers. These new operations will, like every new development in information technology, have implications for security. New means of analysis and detection will be possible. At the same time, new vulnerabilities and methods of attack will be developed.

Quantum Introduction

> If someone says that he can think or talk about quantum physics without becoming dizzy, that shows only that he has not understood anything whatever about it.
>
> **Niels Bohr**

I use that section title deliberately and with two meanings attached. Yes, it is necessary to introduce some basic concepts in quantum physics and mechanics, to proceed with a discussion of the possibilities of quantum computing. However, it should also be noted that quantum physics, as most people understand it, involves very small things.

Therefore, I want to stress that quantum mechanics, and even the field of quantum computing, covers an enormous range. This introduction can be only the most cursory review of the topic, and, necessarily, not only will it lack scientific rigor, but also it cannot address the full spectrum of technologies being pursued in regard to quantum technologies that may be of use to information technology.

Quantum Concepts

Quantum theory has been developed to explain and examine the state (particularly energy states) in regard to entities at very small size ranges, typically atomic and smaller. Although it is frequently stated that quantum mechanics explains operations at small sizes and classical mechanics applies to larger sizes, quantum mechanics is necessary to explain a number of characteristics of the larger world, such as superconductivity. Because we are much more familiar with the operations of classical mechanics, many aspects of quantum mechanics contain apparent paradoxes, such as the fact that the only way to specify exact energy states of small items is with quantum mechanics, but these precise measurements can often only be expressed as probability clouds.

Superposition

One of the concepts of quantum mechanics is that of superposition. One of the aspects of superposition is that a given entity may have multiple possible states at the same time. In traditional digital computing, a bit (binary digit) has two possible states, on or off (representing data states of 1 or 0, respectively). Quantum computing is based upon qubits (pronounced cuebits), which may be in a state representing both 1 and 0 at the same time and which may, in fact, represent many more than two distinct states. Qubits can, therefore, potentially carry much more information than traditional binary digits. Computing devices built using qubits may (and, in research situations, seemingly do) process multiple pieces of data at the same time.

Single photons are frequently seen and used as carriers of single bits of information, but they are also subject to quantum effects. Recently, photons have been made to carry sufficient information as to re-create entire (if somewhat simple) images and graphics are very data-intensive entities. The capacity to carry a good deal of information in a single photon may have additional implications for superposition and quantum computing overall.

Entanglement

If two objects (such as subatomic particles or photons) are created together, or become entangled, then certain properties are related (generally as opposites). Even when the objects are spatially separated there will be correlations between certain observable physical properties. Owing to the nature of quantum mechanics, when a property of one object is observed, it becomes fixed and the measurement of the other object will show an opposite property. The properties may be in an indeterminate state until they are observed, and, therefore, the fixing of state in an entangled object may indicate observation by an outside party—however, observation of the state will also determine it. This is known as the observer effect, applicable to all quantum objects and not just those that are entangled.

Difficult Problems

Digital computers are a wonder and have allowed us to do so many things that we could not before they existed. Digital computers are getting better and faster every year. Still, there are certain types of problems that classical computer architectures solve poorly, if at all. Many of these restrictions are not simply limitations that will be overcome as computers get faster, but are inherent in the way traditional computers work.

People are very good at finding and recognizing patterns. Computers do this poorly. Given an object, a computer can be taught to recognize it—if it is the same distance from the camera, if it is placed in the same orientation, and if the background has not changed. It is very difficult to get computers to take all these factors into account, compare two objects, and reliably decide that they are the same, because "same," to a computer, means identical. It is, therefore, even more difficult to get a digital computer to look at a number of different objects and decide which two, of all of them, are closest to being the same. All kinds of calculations have to be done, and then redone, and then redone again, as each aspect of each item is compared against every other aspect of every other item. The more items are presented, the more work the computer has to do.

Some problems are just generally hard. There is, for example, the traveling salesman problem. A salesman has a territory and a number of cities to visit. What is the best route to be taken to visit them all, minimizing the distance and time to cover the circuit? If there are only two cities, the answer is obvious. Three is still obvious. Four might be harder, and you might have to calculate a couple of paths before you find the best. In fact, if the answer does not jump right out at you (and, as good pattern matchers, people generally can take a good stab at creating a reasonably good itinerary without doing much calculation), there is no algorithm for finding the very best route other than creating each possible course, calculating the distance or time, and then comparing the courses until the shortest is found. Every city that you add does not just add to the complexity of the calculation: it compounds it exponentially. Other examples of this level of difficulty are problems that are NP-complete, nonconvergent problems, and the Ising model (which is, itself, related to some quantum technologies in that it has implications for materials science and possibly superconductivity).

This "least path" problem turns up surprisingly often in all kinds of situations. It relates to staff scheduling and to efficiency studies. (Those who have had to deal with seating plans for a wedding or other special event will have encountered it: what is the best seating plan, given all the factors of who will speak to whom, which pairs cannot be seated together, and all kinds of preferences and social obligations.)

Weather forecasting and climate prediction are other applications that are extremely difficult. Simulations of all kinds require the processing of a great deal of data. With digital computers we have to break the problem up into small boxes, and then process each box, and then figure out how the change in box A affects boxes B, C, and D, and then recalculate how the change in box B caused by the change in box A affects boxes C and D. And then we have to recalculate how the change in box C caused by the change in box B caused by the change in box A will, in fact, change box A, and so forth.

It is felt that quantum computers will be able to deal more effectively with a number of these difficult problems. Superposition will allow for the processing of vast numbers of possibilities simultaneously, so that a "best" answer, of a number of potential answers, can be arrived at quickly. Entanglement may be able to allow us to impose additional conditions on calculations, beyond straightforward computation. Other aspects of quantum physics and mechanics may allow us to build computing devices that can perform calculations that are completely beyond our current capabilities and those of the projected developments in digital information technologies.

Quantum Computing and Encryption

A good deal of confusion exists about the possibility and capability of quantum computing, particularly in regard to the field of cryptography. There are those who say that quantum computers will destroy the possibility of strong encryption and others who assert that quantum computing will make decryption by an outside party impossible. Proponents of both positions will state their cases firmly and generally without ever coming to agreement.

This is because there are multiple aspects of quantum mechanics that are applicable to information processing and many possible types of quantum computing. The following are three broad categories, which, although do not exhaust the possibilities, comprise the major areas of current research into the field.

Quantum Computers

A great deal of the research into quantum computing has, in fact, been based on traditional digital architectures. The idea is intriguing: if you create a register that can hold two states at the same time, what kind of operations can you perform with it? Can you create basic logic circuits, the Boolean algebra of AND and OR? If so, can these basic logic circuits be combined into processing functions to create arithmetic or control circuits? Can those processing circuits be linked into programs? And, if you do create programs, can you process all possible initial inputs simultaneously and still come out with a meaningful answer?

You can create quantum registers. In fact, you can create them in a variety of ways. Unfortunately, the means of creating quantum registers that have been found so far tend to involve rather specialized environments. You can trap atoms using crossed beams of coherent light (lasers). You can use electrons floating on liquid helium. You can use the molecules of a liquid and process them with nuclear magnetic resonance. There are a number of other possibilities. Unfortunately, all of them demonstrate a number of problems with control, measurement of results, and noise.

With all the difficulties, why create devices that do what we already do? In part this is because the reduction in size of computing circuitry (at the chip level) is starting to reach the size at which quantum effects would become a problem. To keep Moore's Law going, and create ever-smaller circuitry (and thus more capable and faster computers), we have to start changing the structure of transistors and logic circuits at that level. This is sometimes referred to as nanometer-scale classical computing and may be seen as a branch of nanotechnology.

It is, in fact, now felt that Turing's "universal" computers are not completely universal. For one thing, the classical computer architectures are irreversible (a given process will give you a result starting from known values, but knowledge of the result and the process will not necessarily tell you what the initial values were), and the laws of thermodynamics, therefore, require that a certain minimum dissipation of energy takes place during each computation. This means that we cannot keep making computers faster and faster by cramming more and more components into a smaller and smaller space: at some point we simply will not be able to get rid of the waste heat, and the processor will start to melt. Theoretically, quantum computing can be made to be reversible, and so computations can take place with arbitrarily small heat dissipation. As well as keeping the computer from burning up, this also allows you to create computers with very small power requirements.

Owing to somewhat different restrictions of physics, it is also felt that simulations run on computers with traditional architectures can be only approximations and that as you try to make the approximation more exact, the attempt very quickly makes the processing requirements excessive. Once again, theory holds that quantum simulations are exact and that the accuracy of the results we obtain from such simulations is simply dependent upon the care used to obtain the answer. Turning back to Turing, it is also felt that we may be able to reformulate the attempt to create a universal computational device with quantum theory and that this time it will work.

However, much research is looking toward a different kind of computational device, one that is based on classical digital architecture, but processes qubits with superpositioned data in a massively parallel way. Although there are experiments that have demonstrated the operation of this type of computing at a single gate level, and with limited numbers of qubits, at present most are confined to very basic functions. In addition, most results have been concerned with single state changes and, therefore, single operations. It is not clear that operations can be strung together into a program. This may even be inherently impossible: because of the observer effect, the benefits of superposition may frequently be restricted to a single operation.

Quantum Encryption

Although there are many possibilities for the use of quantum technologies in regard to cryptography, so far the field has concentrated on quantum communication channels. Through the use of single photons as data carriers, a system may be devised so that secret keys may be derived despite communications being observable by all parties or such that the two communicating parties can determine whether any eavesdropping is taking place, or both.

Key negotiations can be determined using polarizations of photons. Single photons may be polarized in two ways and each type of polarization can result in one of two values. The values can be determined if the right detector is used, but the same detector cannot detect both types of polarization. (In fact this does not exhaust the possibilities: there can be linear and circular polarizations or polarizations at multiple angles for which the detectable values require the correct orientation of the detector. However, for the purposes of the negotiation the simplest level will suffice.) The initiator of the negotiation ("Alice," in all the crypto literature) sends a string of photons, each of which is randomly polarized using one of the two ways and to one of the two values. The receiver ("Bob") measures each photon, randomly picking one of the two detection methods and records his results. If he chooses the wrong detection method he will get the wrong answer, but, statistically, he is going to get about half of the answers correctly. Bob then publishes, publicly, the type of detector he used to measure each photon, but not what value he got. Alice can, publicly, tell him which photons he measured correctly. An eavesdropper ("Eve") can try and measure the photon stream, but, even using the publicly declared information, will obtain only about half the data necessary to determine the key being used.

If Eve is eavesdropping on the line while the key negotiation is going on, she can, like Bob, guess correctly about half of the time. But roughly half of the photons will be polarized such that she cannot measure them. For certain types of detectors, if she makes a mistake in guessing the type of polarization, her detector will randomize the value of the photon passing through. Therefore, even if Eve re-creates the photons that she did measure correctly, her eavesdropping will generate errors in about one-quarter of the data. Therefore, Alice and Bob can take a random subset of the data and publicly compare it (and discard it). The comparison will make it obvious that someone is listening in.

The previous key negotiation and eavesdropping detection measures are based on the "BB84" algorithm by Charles H. Bennett and Gilles Brassard. Artur Eckert later proposed a detection scheme using the fact of entanglement. If entangled pairs of photons are created and submitted to Alice and Bob, then Alice can make measurements and determine, with above average probability, what Bob has measured. If Eve attempts to measure the photons, her measurements will weaken the correlations and this fact can be determined by Alice and Bob.

Although these systems are strong, they are not perfect, and Eve may have some information about the key being used and, therefore, some information about the communication going on. However, using other cryptographic functions, we can create privacy amplification starting with the key that Eve knows something about and creating a key that she knows very little about. Entanglement-based cryptography can do this at the quantum level, and this shows promise for the future of quantum encryption.

All traditional forms of encryption are subject to the man-in-the-middle attack, in which a malicious observer (Eve gets a break here: this one is generally referred to as "Mallory") reads the message and modifies it to insert her own key. In the case of quantum encryption this becomes much more difficult, because Alice and Bob have so many means of detecting whether someone is listening in and so much redundant data that Mallory cannot fully determine.

At the moment, quantum encryption requires a dedicated fiber-optic connection, thus limiting its use in general communications.

The concept of superposition is one of the reasons quantum computing is so tied, in the mind of the security professional, to cryptography. The application is obvious: build a quantum computer with a thousand qubits, and you will be instantly able to decrypt an encrypted message with every possible thousand-bit key, because all possible keys can be simultaneously represented in the machine.

This idea is not only generally attractive, it has, in fact, been formalized, in an algorithm by Peter W. Shor, as far back as 1994.

And, of course, there are certain large governmental bodies with large research budgets that are very interested in any paper that mentions the possibility of using quantum computing for decryption purposes. Therefore, a great many research papers mention this possibility.

However, although the possibility exists and research has been done in this area, the technical details of creating such a computer on a usable level have not yet been completely worked out. It is likely that other applications for quantum computing hold greater promise in the near future.

Quantum Computing

We have already discussed quantum computers: why are we now talking about quantum computing? Isn't it the same thing?

There are a great many computing devices that are not traditional digital computers. In fact, we use many of these devices to assist computers. There are a number of proposals to use quantum devices to perform certain calculations as coprocessors to digital computers, rather than replacing them entirely. Quantum computing devices may not use traditional digital architectures.

Analog Computing

Aren't all computers digital? No, not by a long shot. There are a number of computers, or computing devices, that are analog.

One example is the spaghetti computer. Sorting is a rather time-consuming process in a digital computer. We have numerous sorting algorithms, and some of them are astonishingly efficient (compared to the good old Bubble Sort), but all of them require that each entry in a list be compared multiple times before everything is complete. (And the longer the list, the more times each entry gets compared.)

Take a bunch of spaghetti. Cut a piece to length for each number you want to sort. Holding the bunch of spaghetti firmly enough to keep it under control, but loosely enough that the pieces slide against each other without jamming, bring one end of the bundle down against a flat surface. Instant sorting of the whole bunch with completely parallel processing. The spaghetti computer is rather restricted to one application, and the data entry and output are somewhat tedious, but the processing itself is faster than any digital computer could accomplish: a single step.

Slightly more useful than the spaghetti computer is the slide rule. A slide rule gives completely precise calculations of certain multiplicative and logarithmic functions. Any imprecision results from our inability to be exact in either machining the device or setting the inputs and reading the output. And, once again, the processing is instant: as soon as you set the inputs, the result is available.

Analog computers have also been used in conjunction with digital computers. In the early days of digital computing, multiplication was a very time-consuming operation. Therefore, some computers had analog multipliers that used amplifiers to speed up the process.

Quantum Analog Computing

Not all quantum computers are based on a digital model. An adiabatic quantum computer looks at energy states in the system. By finding the lowest energy state we also find the best answer to a specific problem. Using superconducting adiabatic quantum computers application-specific processors can be created that are very much faster than normal digital computers and also use very little power for the processing itself. (If certain theories of information are correct, it may be possible that such computers are inherently the best at solving those specific problems: that no possible computer that obeys the law of physics could do a better job. However, we are, at the moment, a long way from being able to take full advantage of these hypotheses.)

The best answer (and lowest energy state) turns out to fit very nicely with a number of the difficult problems noted earlier. The correspondence to the minimization problem would seem to be obvious, but the ability also relates to pattern matching and to simulation.

Applications and Implications in Security

Herewith is an overview of possibilities and problems raised by quantum computing as we examine the various domains of security. In terms of applications we cannot yet be completely certain of the actual operations and power of quantum computers, but this listing and examination concentrates on the three functions that are typically seen as areas where quantum computers have a decided advantage over classical digital computers. These are calculations of selection of least path or least state, simulation, and pattern recognition.

Security Management

In security, we are all familiar with the importance of risk assessment, analysis, and management. Assessment and analysis are probably still difficult and time-consuming, but we do have software tools that help us with the management aspect.

Typically, these utilities have to be loaded with all the risk assessments and analysis that have been done, the calculations of annualized loss expectancies for each risk, the various countermeasures, factors by which the safeguards will reduce the risks, and the cost of running the countermeasures. (Among other things.) Once all of this data is loaded, the program will operate as a spreadsheet, allowing you to play "what if" games, in which you reduce or increase your expenditure on the various controls and see what impact that has on the bottom line. The intent, of course, is to try to find the greatest total cost savings given the set and (usually inadequate, but we will ignore that for now) budget that you have for security.

What these programs will not do is to tell you what that most desirable state is. To find it, you would have to create every possible combination of spending on controls, calculate the savings created by each blend, and then determine which one gives you the greatest reduction in risk. Sound familiar? It is our old least path problem. Therefore, a quantum computer may be able to do that last risk management step for us (as long as we have done the assessment and analysis properly in the first place).

Information classification is a difficult and time-consuming task and one that is hard for people to do in a consistent manner. There are very few software tools that can assist us with the classification process. A good deal of the inconsistency results from not recognizing patterns that indicate this information is of the same sensitivity as that data. Therefore, a system that can match patterns may be able to do a good deal toward helping us with this particular problem.

Quantum computing is a new technology. Any new technology will require a new risk assessment: part of the following sections of this chapter note areas where the existence of the new technology may create new vulnerabilities or require greater vigilance on our part. There is one risk assessment that management should probably be looking into: what, for our particular industry and company, is the risk of investing, or failing to invest, in quantum technologies?

Security Architecture

Computer and system architectures have security implications. Any new technology needs to be assessed in terms of the risk it may present. A completely new architecture means that there will be new vulnerabilities. We would be remiss in implementing any such novel technology without understanding potential security issues.

However, we have great difficulty in analyzing our current architectures, and security architectures, to determine whether they are effective. The standard practice tends to create and implement an architecture, using experience and shared wisdom (such as security guidelines and frameworks), and then see how effective it is (or whether it is effective at all). It would be very helpful to have a simulation of vulnerabilities and protections driven by a given architecture and to be able to evaluate different architectures in terms of which one gives the best result. Simulation is, however, very difficult and time-consuming—with traditional systems. If quantum computing allows for more effective simulation we may be able to do better than trial and error.

One aspect of a quantum architecture is in regard to integrity. Quantum devices are highly susceptible to noise of all types, thermal, electromagnetic, and radio frequency. Some have to operate at temperatures close to absolute zero, others need to be in a vacuum, most need to be shielded from radio transmitters (including wireless local area networks and cell phones) and various electrical devices. All quantum equipment needs careful handling of input and output, and an analog apparatus in particular requires input/output filtering. Even with all this care there still seems to be just a bit of indeterminacy in the results.

At the moment, and with the fairly rudimentary computing mechanisms developed, "voting" (comparison of multiple devices or multiple runs) and checking of errors against other standards is sufficient. However, as applications become more complex, these measures may no longer be sufficient.

Fortunately, quantum error correction is a recently determined general outline, which indicates that, using a concept of entanglement transfer, quantum information processing can be used to correct a wide range of noise in a properly designed quantum system. It has been demonstrated that rectification can be achieved even when the remedial operations are faulty. This may have ramifications for fault-tolerant computing.

Access Control

The posited pattern-matching capabilities of quantum computing may have a couple of different applications in access control. Biometrics would likely benefit from improved abilities to match and compare. At the moment biometric matching must be done on the basis of constructs and representations of biometric data that lose a great deal of information in the symbolization process. In addition, the stored data may be fairly arbitrary, and, therefore, real similarities between samples and stored data may not be as evident. The ability to do more direct comparisons may have implications for accuracy, as well as speed and new forms of data representation.

Intrusion detection relies on two major forms of analysis: the matching of patterns of known attacks and the noting of deviations from normal operations. In both cases the ability to identify patterns would be of benefit. Quantum computing support for anomaly-based intrusion detection would be able to picture, more accurately, the normal state of affairs, as well as determining which deviations are significant. Signature-based systems would be able to use a baseline to identify new attack signatures and also to note attacks that are similar to those already in the database.

Information flow analysis is a useful exercise for determining possibilities for improper information disclosure. It is, however, a tedious and time-consuming business. The processing involved in finding potential flow paths requires the investigation of many possibilities and is, therefore, quite similar to our least path problem. In addition, simulation-type activity is involved. Therefore, on two counts, the analysis of flow paths and determination of covert channels could likely benefit from quantum computing.

Cryptography

I have already discussed, in some detail, quantum communications and encryption, as well as key negotiation and eavesdropping detection, and have noted that parallel factorization, processing, and decryption activities have been much explored in the popular literature. There are, however, additional areas and topics to consider in regard to cryptography.

Given the feeling that current encryption algorithms may be susceptible to attack by quantum methods, work on new algorithms tractable by neither classical nor quantum computing would be indicated as a useful field of study. Indeed, although the prime factorization of large numbers is seen as a threat to the Rivest–Shamir–Adleman algorithm, it is by no means obvious that other currently used algorithms are equally at risk. The need for assessment of nonfactoring algorithms, and the development of new algorithms, is manifest.

We are all aware of the importance of randomness in using and operating cryptographic systems. Quantum devices may be of benefit to cryptography in terms of generation of randomness. As previously noted, most quantum machinery is delicate and subject to significant issues of noise. We can turn this to our advance by capturing and processing that noise. In addition, numerous quantum structures can be established with indeterminate outcomes and can be used as automated "coin-flipping" devices. (Using these structures is not always easy: care should be taken to ensure that the devices are not somehow biased because of careless construction. Even this can be used to advantage: we may be able to use a biased, but random, keystream in certain situations in which we may be either correcting for biased data or attempting to disguise the nature of the traffic or the type of encryption. We can, of course, bias pseudorandom streams, but a biased but still random stream may be an advantage.)

Implementation has always been the greatest source of problems and weaknesses in cryptographic systems. Analysis of implementation vulnerabilities is not a straightforward task. The use of quantum computing to improve simulation of a system may be able to identify these types of flaws in operation.

Physical Security

There is probably not a great deal that quantum computing can do to benefit physical security. As previously noted, biometrics may be improved and are being increasingly used for physical access control. Those charged with physical security should, however, be aware of the new demands and requirements that quantum computing will place on the plant environment.

As has also been mentioned in prior discussions, a number of proposed quantum devices are highly susceptible to radio frequency and electromagnetic interference. Specially constructed computer rooms will probably return as some of these computing systems are introduced. Faraday cages and other TEMPEST measures may also come back into prominence. These elements would not be used to preclude emanations from disclosing information, but to prevent noise from corrupting data and processing.

We have always had to pay attention to air conditioning and refrigeration requirements for computers, but quantum computers have entirely different needs in this realm. Many quantum devices require operating temperatures near absolute zero, either for superconductivity or for other physical effects. Room temperature, which is quite suitable for normal computer equipment, is about a hundred times greater than the temperature in interstellar space. Interstellar space, as cold as it is, is a thousand times too hot for the proper operation of the D-Wave Systems Orion computer, for example.

> There is some irony in the fact that these computers may have extremely small power requirements in terms of the information processing itself, but will demand huge refrigerators to keep operating near absolute zero. However, when ENIAC was built, it was famous in business and academic circles for being the largest computer constructed up to that time—and in physical plant communities for having the largest refrigeration system ever put in one place.

In the near term, as quantum devices begin to come onstream, they will be extremely expensive pieces of equipment, with special requirements that are poorly understood. (For example, the gate-level operations of these devices are poorly understood even by their designers, and undoubtedly we will discover failure modes under unusual conditions.) Initially, the advantages to a company that is running an application supported by quantum processing will make it distinctive in the marketplace. However, the failure of that device will also jeopardize the special place of the company and will create yet another possible point of failure. Therefore, special attention must be paid to the creation of definite controls and protections that will guard the devices, not only against attacks, but also against carelessness and ignorant usage.

Business Continuity Planning

As with risk analysis and management, so business impact analysis is a difficult and laborious aspect of business continuity and disaster recovery studies. The same type of least path calculation that can aid risk and safeguard analysis will assist in this area as well. Both least path and simulation analyses can be used to find functions with a high concentration of business dependence as well as single points of failure.

Simulation will also assist with the testing of business continuity plans. We already use simulation tests, but on a very limited level. Quantum simulations will be able to assess a very wide range of conditions and possibilities and to determine combinations of events and situations that may overwhelm our prepared plans.

In the medium term, quantum computing applications, along with various forms of artificial intelligence, will likely be able to guide and assist decisions about the optimal assignment of resources to address disasters. This will probably be initially used by governmental agencies in managing large-scale disasters, with capabilities and systems being made available to regional governments as the technology develops. Very soon thereafter the costs and capabilities will be within the range of large corporations (initially possibly on a contract or service basis) for the management of disaster recovery and response, and the benefits, in terms of damage mitigation and recovery speed, will probably be immediate.

For those companies using quantum computing, there will be considerations for continuity of operations for these special devices. For example, given the nature and operating environment of the equipment created to date, damage may result if the power or cooling fails. In the near term, it is probable that a mere loss of power will result in damage to, or loss of, the computing elements themselves and a requirement to re-create sections of the environment.

Applications Security

There are many applications for quantum computing in the field of application security; these examples are only a few.

Testing of software is necessary, but problematic. Although much work is being done in the field, it is still the case that testing of applications and systems is more of an art than a science. Testing involves a kind of simulation, and test inputs are generally submitted for processing based on a "best guess" of which combinations might present a potential difficulty for the program. Quantum simulations should be much more accurate in identifying problems and should be able to test a much wider range of inputs and combinations.

A great deal of security work involves database analysis, such as the pattern-matching requirement mentioned earlier in regard to biometrics. Therefore, a number of new security applications themselves are likely to result from the capability. This, of course, raises both benefits (in regard to safety) and concerns (in regard to privacy).

In terms of database security itself, two long-standing and intractable problems have been data aggregation attacks and inference attacks. Although it is unlikely that any specific protections against database aggregation will result from quantum computing, the problem analysis, using pattern matching and simulation, will be useful in determining the extent of the problem, the information classification level appropriate to a given collection, and probably the effectiveness of controls applied in a given situation.

In attempting to extract useful information out of ever-larger databases we have turned to artificial intelligence methods. Part of this research involves creating applications that learn how to find "interesting" results for themselves. This requires the ability to determine and match patterns, and we have previously noted the suitability of quantum computing in this regard. In terms of traditional computing, the most effective programs have used the neural network model, based on what we know about the formation of neurons in the brain and the strengthening of links as they are used and encountered in new situations. Quantum computing can be used to support neural net analysis with faster pattern matching. In addition, quantum computing can do direct pattern matching, finding the same patterns in different ways. Similarly, cross-supporting assistance can be applied to fuzzy logic.

Neural nets are subject to specific and systematic types of errors, known as superstitious learning. A pattern may appear randomly and, due to chance associations, become learned and then strengthened over time, even though there is no real relation. We have previously noted that noise and errors are a problem for quantum computers. However, because of the different architectures and approaches, neural net superstitious learning will result in errors that are different from the random errors generated out of quantum equipment. Therefore, the two types of processing can act as checks on each other's errors: mistakes may arise, but they will be different types of miscalculations.

The ability to assess errors will be a major consideration. A standard approach, when testing new systems, is to check results computed against those that are expected. Given the new capabilities of quantum computing technologies this becomes problematic: how do you check on the results when the question you are processing is impossible to compute by classical methods?

As previously noted in relation to intrusion detection, the pattern-matching capabilities of quantum computing can be applied to malware detection and the assessment of botnet operation, control, and ownership. These questions have become extremely complex and new approaches and tools are needed badly.

The question of malware analysis relates to an earlier point in regard to the universality of Turing machines. Fred Cohen's determination of the "undecidability" of computer viruses is based on analysis using the Turing machine model. Cohen found that there cannot be a "perfect" antivirus program: any detection program will err either by failing to find a virus or by raising a false alarm over an innocent program, or both. Given that Turing machines are not truly universal, does this result hold?

In the case of virus detection, it appears that the original result is valid. However, there are many theories in security that have been assessed based upon the initial Turing model. Academic research into security architecture models should be checked for additional implications of quantum models.

As stated earlier, these notes are the merest beginning of the implications of quantum computing for the security of applications. Quantum methods will result in completely new paradigms in programming, and the changes will be even greater than those that accompanied the introduction of object-oriented or functional programming to the original procedural archetype.

Operations Security

As if securing computer operations was not hard enough, combinations of classical and quantum devices and functions will vastly increase the complexity of the situation. Troubleshooting of problems will become even more difficult. At the same time, quantum simulations can greatly assist in troubleshooting of intricate dilemmas.

An ongoing and intractable problem in operations is the detection of insider attacks or misuse. More sophisticated pattern matching and recognition, made possible by quantum computing, may be able to assist in catching such activity in the planning or setup stages rather than long after the damage has been done.

Telecommunications and Networking

In terms of network security, it is likely that quantum technology will be more of an additional demand than an assist. As noted, quantum encryption will require special channels and those of special types. In addition, given their cost and special environmental requirements, quantum devices are likely to be remotely accessible for some years to come. Therefore, data and results of a highly sensitive nature will have to be protected during communication.

However, as with intrusion and malware detection, network attack analysis using pattern-matching capabilities may be greatly enhanced. Proper large-scale network simulation may also be able to assist with network architectures and provisioning that is more resistant to failure.

Law and Investigation

Taking advantage of quantum capabilities in pattern matching and simulation, new forensic analysis tools may be able to speed the time-consuming task of finding relevant evidence in computer systems and data. However, even our current forensic findings make presentation and acceptance of the implication problematic in court situations. The often counterintuitive nature of quantum technologies will make the educational and explanatory problems all the greater.

As noted in regard to business continuity planning, incident response will likely benefit from guidance systems based upon quantum computing and artificial intelligence. In the long term, similar systems will likely be available to guide response to even minor incidents, ensuring that covert attacks are not able to masquerade as minor glitches or annoyances and that the best combination of attack restriction and evidence collection allows for both protection and investigation, without one activity compromising the other.

Summary

Quantum computing is a field that is only just starting to move out of the arena of research and into real application. However, the implications for security indicate that attention should be paid to developments to be able to take the earliest opportunity to address a number of difficult tasks and problems.

LEGAL, REGULATIONS, COMPLIANCE, AND INVESTIGATION

Information Law

Chapter 28

Compliance Assurance: Taming the Beast

Todd Fitzgerald

Contents

As children we are taught by our parents to behave ourselves, obey their instructions, and be kind to others. As we go to school, teachers tell us to sit at our desks, follow the rules, learn the material, and prepare for the exams. As teenagers, we test the rules, bending the edges, seeing what we can "get away with" to define our own independence. Parents understand that we are "just growing up"

377

and this is part of the process of becoming an adult, so they are tolerant within reasonable limits. As children graduate high school and move on to college or other life experiences, more rules are learned, yet this time they do not come from our parents, they are society's rules and breaking them has defined civil, criminal, and societal consequences. Frequent speeding tickets, drunk driving, and large numbers of accidents equal increased insurance rates or loss of driving privilege. Studying hard and getting good grades in school equal graduation and increased job opportunities. Learning the sales techniques on that first sales job combined with hard work equals increased income.

Rules. Regulations. Policies. Standards. Just as we learn as we grow from being children to adults that there are rules that must be followed, so too have organizations "grown up" in an environment of increasing rules and regulations. The increasing number of similar but different regulations makes achieving compliance a very time-consuming activity.

What Is Compliance?

Answers.com provides a definition for compliance as "the act of complying with a wish, request, or demand; acquiescence." It further provides a definition, which may resonate with how many companies feel about the plethora of government regulations, "a disposition or tendency to yield to the will of others"! Compliance with security regulations is no trivial task; in fact, in a survey conducted by the Security Compliance Council, as much as 34 percent of information technology resources were being consumed to demonstrate compliance. These are valuable, technical resources that could be deployed to other high-value, new development efforts or to improving the efficiency of operations, but rather are being utilized to ensure that the regulations are being followed. This is a significant burden for large businesses; however, in smaller businesses the resources dedicated may be smaller in numbers, except that the hidden costs must be considered, such as burnout of the one or two information technology (IT) people who are working many hours of overtime to comply.

Compliance ensures that due diligence has been exercised within the organization to meet the government regulations for security practices. Compliance can be achieved in many ways, as many of these regulations provide a higher level definition of the requirement of "what" must be done; however, the lower level, platform-specific details of how the solution is implemented are typically not stated in the regulation itself. The regulation's primary task is to ensure that the appropriate processes are in place, people are aware of their responsibilities, and technical issues are appropriately managed. The regulations are drafted at a policy level and, as such, it would be difficult to mandate the selection of a specific platform from a particular vendor, as this would provide an undue advantage for that vendor. Furthermore, because technology changes at a pace faster than the policy-making process, by the time new legislation was enacted, the legislation would most likely be out of date. This approach would also stifle innovation by mandating the use of specific, recent technology to address security challenges.

The landscape of government regulations and security control frameworks covered in the subsequent sections is shown in Exhibit 28.1.

The Regulations Are Coming, the Regulations Are Coming!

Over the past several years, an increasing number of regulations that focus on providing adequate security have appeared. These regulations are typically focused on a vertical industry or segment of the economy, in an attempt to mitigate known issues within an industry.

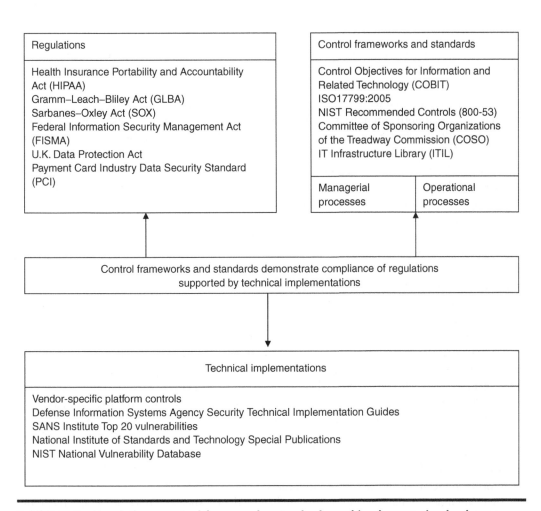

Exhibit 28.1   Regulations, control frameworks, standards, and implementation landscape.

One of the earlier U.S. government regulations that provided broad public coverage of information security issues was the Gramm–Leach–Bliley Act (GLBA) of 1999. GLBA was also known as the Financial Services Moderation Act of 1999 and was aimed at financial institutions that maintain, process, and collect financial information. The Sarbanes–Oxley Act of 2002 was enacted following the inaccurate accounting practices of organizations such as Enron/Arthur Andersen and WorldCom and to fulfill a need to have adequate internal audit controls for financial reporting. Organizations are required under this act to have the controls independently audited and attested to. In addition to these regulations targeted at financial transactions, the Payment Card Industry (PCI) Data Security Standard, first released in 2005, establishes extensive requirements for payment card security. The major credit card companies, in an effort to help ensure the implementation of consistent global security measures for payment processing, formed the PCI Data Standards Council.

The Health Insurance Portability and Accountability Act (HIPAA) was enacted in 1996; however, the Privacy Rule was not in effect until April 2003, and the compliance for the final security rule was effective April 21, 2005, following a two-year period subsequent to the publishing of the rule for implementation. The final security rule was rewritten based on many public comments and reoriented to align better with and support the privacy rule. The intent of the HIPAA final security rule is to ensure that adequate security protections are created to protect the security and privacy of healthcare information maintained by healthcare providers, health insurance plans, employers, and those handling healthcare electronic transactions. Congress recognized that as efficiencies are gained through the implementation of electronic transactions, individual privacy rights need to be protected by the application of appropriate security safeguards.

Security breach notification laws are appearing in many states (34 states had adopted legislation by late 2006), with the most noteworthy being California Senate Bill 1386, which went into effect July 1, 2003. The laws generally require the prompt notification to each individual of disclosure of their personal information. The laws vary on the definition of what is considered personal and the timeframes; however, the intent is consistent that companies have an obligation to consumers to protect their information and when these protections are compromised, there is a corporate responsibility to "make it right." Identity theft has become a front-and-center issue over the past several years, receiving increased media attention.

For those organizations involved in international business, country-specific laws and regulations need to be researched as well. The U.K. Data Protection Act of 1998 has requirements for the privacy of information with respect to what can be maintained, processed, used, and disclosed. The European Union Data Retention Laws passed in 2005 place requirements on Internet service providers and phone companies to maintain phone and electronic messages for a period of six months to two years.

The Federal Information Security Management Act (FISMA) of 2002 was formulated to ensure that adequate information security practices were being performed across the large, disparate computing infrastructures of the U.S. government. FISMA is applicable to all U.S. government agencies and their contractors, whereby the security program is evaluated in a report card style, with letters A, B, C, D, and F. The results are reported annually to Congress for each of the government agencies. For most agencies, the average was a D to D+ score (2003–2005), with these scores increasing in some government agencies to bring the total average score to a C− in 2006. There is still much to be done and the measurement is providing a barometer to gauge the improvement. FISMA represents the government's efforts to perform the due diligence necessary for information security and sets the expectations.

There are more regulations and security policy guidance, such as Office of Management and Budget Circular A-123; Homeland Security Presidential Directive HSPD-7, for critical infrastructure protection plans to protect federal critical infrastructures and key resources; IRS Publication 1075; tax information security guidelines for federal, state, and local agencies; the list goes on.

Control Frameworks and Standards

If a person wants to build a new house, he or she cannot just put the house anywhere. The land must be approved by the city for development, the appropriate building permits must be obtained, and there are certain rules for connecting to services such as water, electricity, and roads. These are the regulations, or policies, that the homeowner and builder must comply with. Once the expectations of these regulations are understood, the builder can utilize many different processes to build the house for the homeowner. Maybe he builds 10–15 homes at once, rotating the electricians, plumbers, and carpenters from one house to the next. Alternatively, he may be a small builder, doing much of the work with jack-of-all-tradesmen. The houses may have different solutions for the exterior, such as brick, wood, vinyl siding, and stone. To implement the architecture, each role has a different function and a different set of supporting procedures. The electrician's tasks are much different from the plumber's; however, they both contribute to the same big-picture goal, to build a house.

Building the "security house" starts with understanding the policies, or regulations, noted earlier. From there, control frameworks are decided upon to establish the next level of requirements or the approach to demonstrating that compliance is being achieved. In the housing example, this would provide the framework for how the electricians, plumbers, and carpenters are governed, or supervised; the identification of the tasks that must be performed; and a way of measuring and monitoring the results. The detailed procedures or specifications for how an electrician performs job are analogous to the lower-level, detailed technical, platform-specific standards that support the overall framework. For example, the secure settings for mobile code and active content controls (i.e., ActiveX, Java, and VBscript) may be defined in a technical standard, just as the electrician's procedures would specify the correct wiring required for a 220 V dryer circuit in the house. The control framework defining the requirement to identify if a dryer is needed, and to implement the circuit, would typically not contain this level of details.

Let's Name a Few Control Frameworks and Security Standards

Multiple frameworks have been created to support the auditing of the implemented security controls. These resources are valuable to assist in the design of a security program, as they define the necessary controls to provide secure information systems. The following frameworks have each gained a degree of acceptance within the auditing or information security community and add value to the information security investment delivery. Although several of the frameworks/ best practices were not specifically designed originally to support information security, many of the processes within these practices support different aspects of confidentiality, integrity, and availability.

Committee of Sponsoring Organizations of the Treadway Commission

The Committee of Sponsoring Organizations (COSO) of the Treadway Commission was formed in 1985 to sponsor the National Commission on Fraudulent Financial Reporting, which studied factors that lead to fraudulent financial reporting and produced recommendations for public companies, their auditors, the Securities Exchange Commission, and other regulators. COSO identifies five areas of internal control necessary to meet the financial reporting and disclosure objectives. These areas are (1) control environment, (2) risk assessment, (3) control activities, (4) information and communication, and (5) monitoring. The COSO internal control model has been adopted as a framework by some organizations working toward Sarbanes–Oxley Section 404 compliance.

Information Technology Infrastructure Library

The IT Infrastructure Library (ITIL) is a set of 44 books published by the British Government's Stationary Office between 1989 and 1992 to improve IT service management. The framework contains a set of best practices for IT core operational processes such as change, release, and configuration management; incident and problem management; capacity and availability management; and IT financial management. ITIL's primary contribution is showing how the controls can be implemented for the service management IT processes. These practices are useful as a starting point for tailoring to the specific needs of the organization, and the success of the practices depends upon the degree to which they are kept up to date and implemented on a daily basis. Achievement of these standards is an ongoing process, whereby the implementations need to be planned, supported by management, prioritized, and implemented in a phased approach.

Control Objectives for Information and Related Technology

Control Objectives for Information and Related Technology (COBIT) is published by the IT Governance Institute and contains a set of 34 high-level control objectives, one for each of the IT processes, such as define a strategic IT plan, define the information architecture, manage the configuration, manage facilities, and ensure systems security. Ensure systems security has been broken down further into control objectives such as manage security measures, identification, authentication and access, user account management, data classification, and firewall architectures. The COBIT framework examines the effectiveness, efficiency, confidentiality, integrity, availability, compliance, and reliability aspects of the high-level control objectives. The model defines four domains for governance, namely planning and organization, acquisition and implementation, delivery and support, and monitoring. Processes and IT activities and tasks are then defined within these domains. The framework provides an overall structure for IT control and includes control objectives, which can be utilized to determine effective security control objectives that are driven from the business needs.

International Organization for Standardization (ISO) 17799

The ISO 17799 standards can be used as a basis for developing security standards and security management practices within an organization. The U.K. Department of Trade and Industry Code of Practice (CoP) for information security, which was developed from support of industry in 1993, became British Standard (BS) 7799 in 1995. The BS 7799 standard was subsequently revised in 1999 to add certification and accreditation components, which became Part 2 of the BS 7799 standard. Part 1 of the BS 7799 standard became ISO 17799 and was published as ISO 17799:2000, the first international information security management standard by the ISO and International Electrotechnical Commission (IEC).

The ISO 17799 standard was modified in June 2005 as ISO/IEC 17799:2005 and contains 134 detailed information security controls based upon the following 11 areas:

- Information security policy
- Organizing information security
- Asset management
- Human resources security
- Physical and environmental security
- Communications and operations management

- Access control
- Information systems acquisition, development, and maintenance
- Information security incident management
- Business continuity management
- Compliance

The ISO standards are grouped together by topic areas and the ISO/IEC 27000 series has been designated as the information security management series. For example, the 27002 CoP will replace the current ISO/IEC 17799:2005 Information Technology—Security Techniques—Code of Practice for Information Security Management document. This is consistent with how ISO has named other topic areas, such as the ISO 9000 series for quality management.

ISO/IEC 27001:2005 was released in October 2005 and specifies the requirements for establishing, implementing, operating, monitoring, reviewing, maintaining, and improving a documented information security management system taking into consideration the company's business risks. This management standard was based on the BS 7799 Part 2 standard and provides information on building information security management systems and guidelines for auditing the system.

Federal Information System Controls Audit Manual

Although the Federal Information System Controls Audit Manual (FISCAM) was not designed specifically as a security control framework or standard and was created to assist auditors of federal government systems to evaluate the general and application controls over financial systems, it can be a useful guide in developing a security program. From a compliance perspective, government auditors needing to evaluate whether controls are in place for government agencies utilize the FISCAM controls. The General Accounting Office reports on the security of government agencies utilizing FISCAM as the basis.

National Institute of Standards and Technology 800-53 Controls

The National Institute of Standards and Technology (NIST) was granted $20 million to create security-related documents to support FISMA. Although these documents were created to support the federal agencies, the documents are very well written and can be utilized by private industry free of charge with no copyright restrictions. Many man-hours of government resources and public comments have gone into the construction of the control framework and supporting documents.

Special Publication 800-53, *Recommended Security Controls for Federal Information Systems,* is an excellent document, which describes 17 control families, such as access control, awareness and training, audit and accountability, risk assessment, personnel security, and contingency planning. The families are broken down into specific controls, along with supplemental guidance, which typically refers to other more detailed NIST documents, and control enhancements that designate increasing levels of control required depending upon the security level of the system (low, medium, and high). The set of controls represents the minimum assurance requirements to be compliant with the control.

Technical Control Standards

There are many sources of specific technical control standards, including vendor documentation, the SANS Institute's Top 20 vulnerability list, NIST special publications, Defense Information Systems Agency (DISA) Security Technical Implementation Guides (STIGs), National Security Agency Security Configuration Guides, and others. These standards are increasingly being utilized by auditors, as well as being integrated into or used as the basis for vendor security products to demonstrate compliance with the higher level security control frameworks. NIST was also funded by the Department of Homeland Security to create a "National Vulnerability Database," which combines the vulnerabilities from multiple sources in an effort to automate compliance assurance of the technical controls. Vendor products are starting to incorporate the database into their product sets. If the effort is successful, this could provide a standardized mechanism for reporting assurance of compliance with the FISMA requirements, which could be leveraged by private industry as a method of demonstrating compliance to a standard.

Penalties for Noncompliance

The laws have done an excellent job at creating visibility of the need for stronger information security controls. However, compliance with many of these regulations is still lagging. According to a 2006 Global Information Security survey, 35 percent of U.S. respondents indicated they were not compliant with Sarbanes–Oxley legislation, and 40 percent were not compliant with HIPAA security regulations, although they were aware the laws pertained to them and they should be compliant.

There appears to be a lack of enforcement and penalties with some of the regulations. For example, the HIPAA security rule enforcement is "complaint driven," whereby claims that damage has occurred due to a perceived lack of security are reported and addressed. The concept of proactive HIPAA enforcement monitoring does not exist, lessening the attention some organizations place on the HIPAA rule. This may help explain why 40 percent of respondents still report they are not compliant, several years after the regulation came into effect.

There is also the viewpoint that compliance with government regulations is very, very expensive and organizations may make a risk-based decision not to implement the controls. In a lawsuit-driven society, this could be a recipe for disaster, not to mention the risks that would be taken with the public perception of the brand by the consumer. In the early 1970s, Ford became aware that if the Ford Pinto automobile was hit from behind, the car would explode and cause death or injury. Ford performed a cost–benefit analysis and determined that approximately 2100 burned vehicles, 180 serious burn injuries, and 180 deaths would most likely occur. Considering jury awards of $200,000 per death and $67,000 per injury and the cost of replacing the cars, they figured the "benefit" was $49.5 million versus a cost of $137 million ($11 per car) to fix the problem. Ford seriously erred in their judgment, as they put a price on human life and inflicting pain on individuals versus "doing the right thing." As a result, juries awarded millions in compensatory damages through lawsuits.

Although security issues may or may not impact life and death, depending upon the industry and the environment, organizations need to consider whether it is worth the risk not to comply with the standards that are practiced by other organizations within the industry. Subsequent juries hearing these cases in court, whether criminal convictions, civil monetary penalties, or civil suits are at stake, may view the organization as not performing the standard of due care necessary to operate its business. Just one of these lawsuits in which someone is victimized through identity theft, a violent attack due to lack of physical security controls, or the disclosure of personal information or a conviction due to lack of compliance could pay for the implementation of many security controls.

Enter Best Practices

Today's risk and real cost from a lack of compliance assurance appears to be related more to bad publicity from the lack of security. This may be a reflection of the fact that security has only begun to receive increased attention, in large part due to the recent regulations, over the past several years. However, as leading organizations and government agencies place increased focus on their information security programs, the bar becomes higher for their peer companies. Control frameworks and detailed technical standards are being increasingly applied within organizations. The vendor tool sets to assess compliance to support this activity are becoming richer. Besides, who wants to be the lone sheep, standing in the wilderness trying to defend its own wooly hide, when the herd is somewhere else working together on protecting themselves from the big bad wolf? The herd sets the standard and it is important to pay attention to where the herd is going. The notion of "best practices" today is an elusive one; the best approach is to grab onto a framework that is suitable for the business vertical and the culture and work diligently toward implementation of the strategy.

The 11-Factor Security Compliance Assurance Manifesto

The regulations, control frameworks, standards, technical implementation guides, and penalties for noncompliance provide insight into "what" needs to be achieved to provide the organizational compliance assurance to the various security-related regulations. Now, this begs the next question, what actions need to be taken to achieve and maintain compliance with the regulations? To answer that question, the 11-Factor Security Compliance Assurance Manifesto, as shown in Exhibit 28.2, sets out the principles by which compliance assurance may be achieved.

1. Designate an individual responsible for compliance assurance oversight. Whereas many of the policy-type regulations may not appear to change on a frequent basis, the supporting documents, technical specifications, and current areas of concern do change over time. New laws are also created, such as the incident breach reporting laws mentioned, where

1. Designate an individual responsible for compliance assurance oversight
2. Establish a security management governing body
3. Select control frameworks and standards
4. Research and apply technical controls
5. Conduct awareness and training
6. Verify compliance
7. Implement formal remediation process
8. Dedicate staff, automate compliance tasks
9. Report on compliance metrics
10. Enforce penalties for noncompliance to policy
11. Collaborate and network externally

Exhibit 28.2   The 11-factor security compliance assurance manifesto.

state-by-state adoption of some form of the law is enacted. Similarly, when the HIPAA Privacy Rule was being made effective, each state had groups that were focused on creating a preemption analysis. Staying on top of these changes and ensuring that someone is directing the security compliance efforts is essential. In medium-sized organizations, this is likely to be the manager or director of security, whereas in larger organizations the chief information security officer, chief security officer, or security officer is likely to be responsible for ensuring that the security compliance assurance activities are performed. The chief information officer's organization and the other business units carry out the mitigation work as appropriate.

2. Establish a security management governing body. To achieve support for the implementation of security policies throughout the organization and to ensure that the security policies do not disrupt the business, it is advisable to establish an information security council. Councils made up of representatives from IT, business units, human resources, legal departments, physical security, internal audit, ethics and compliance, and information security can be effective in achieving compliance with the regulations. Their oversight and interaction provide feedback as to whether the security activities planned are feasible and whether there is a high probability of compliance success.

3. Select control framework and standards. The frameworks mentioned, such as COSO, ITIL, ISO 17799, COBIT, NIST, and FISCAM, offer an excellent place to map the security controls that are in place to the framework, uncover the gaps in compliance, and create action plans to increase the security assurance with these objectives. Multiple control frameworks can be selected for different levels of detail. For example, COBIT may be selected to provide a governing framework, whereas ISO 17799 controls may be mapped to the framework (already available from the IT governance institute) and then linked to the NIST control objective families and supported by the DISA STIGs. The mapping provides a mechanism to review how a set of technical controls supports the higher level statements in the other frameworks. The same controls serve multiple purposes. Comprehensive frameworks are created through this process, enabling the other compliance assurance activities.

4. Research and apply technical controls. There are many approaches at the technical level for being compliant with the control objectives. Analysis must be performed to determine the best control based upon the risk profile of the organization. For example, achieving compliance with a requirement to provide adequate off-site backups of information in the event of a disaster could be achieved in a small regional office by placing a daily tape in a fireproof safe and rotating the weekly tape off-site. Alternatively, a small office may decide to store the backup tapes remotely with a tape storage facility, transmit the backup information securely over the Internet for backups, or assign an individual to take home the backup tape nightly. Each of the scenarios has their own costs and risks inherent in the control selection.

5. Conduct awareness and training. The documented security policies and procedures are necessary; however, if individuals do not truly understand their responsibilities to comply with the security controls, the likelihood that the appropriate processes will be followed is greatly diminished.

6. Verify compliance. Vulnerability assessments, penetration testing, and internal audit reviews of the security controls ensure that the policies and procedures that were created are being followed. Implemented security on the computing platform can be tested and compared with the documented baselines, configurations, and change control records to provide assurance that the security controls are being maintained as per the requirements implemented through the control frameworks.

7. Implement a formal remediation process. When weaknesses in the security controls are discovered, through internal audits, external audits, vulnerability assessments, risk assessments, or other internal reviews, the issue must be logged and tracked to completion. Accountability should be placed at a middle management or senior management level to ensure that the appropriate attention and priority are placed on remedying the issue. Completion dates must be assigned (preferably no later than 90 days after creation of the action plan). Documentation of the remediation (evidence) must be provided when the issue has been resolved. The existence of a formal tracking of the security issues provides the assurance that security is an ongoing, management-supported process.

8. Dedicate staff, automate compliance tasks. Compliance initiatives are very time-consuming and drain the organization of resources to collect evidence, provide explanations, participate in interviews, and locate the policies and procedures that support the regulations. Without an organized automated process, this activity becomes even more challenging and time is wasted on inefficiencies. The same information may be requested multiple times to answer similar questions, where one report may have provided a reasonable answer. Initially, more staff should be allocated to the compliance efforts to provide a focus to the activity. When the compliance tasks are added to the regular jobs of predominant IT staff, they may be given lower priority and resources. As automation increases, the staff required to support the compliance efforts should either remain constant or decrease. A constant staff may be needed to ensure that the new regulations and changes are adequately addressed.

9. Report on compliance metrics. Dashboards of red, yellow, and green or heat maps are useful tools to demonstrate where security is weak within the organization and where more focus should be placed. These metrics should be reported in a manner that is meaningful to the business, such as unavailability issues, which could impact major, mission critical applications, or confidentiality concerns that may affect the consumer trust in the brand.

10. Enforce penalties for noncompliance to policy. Does one grin and bear it when the security control objectives are not followed or grit one's teeth? This is one area that needs ... teeth! There must be sanctions in place for those that do not follow the security policies. Associates must also be trained that compliance with the security controls is part of their job responsibilities. The individual responsible for compliance assurance must ensure that the guidelines are established for sanctions and that the appropriate parties follow through with the sanction (who may be the manager and legal and human resources representatives).

11. Collaborate and network externally. Many organizations must comply with the same regulations, why not leverage that experience? Working with peers, within the industry vertical for dealing with industry-specific regulations, and across industries for understanding various methods to implement the control frameworks, standards, and technical controls can be invaluable. For example, nonprofit organizations such as the HIPAA Collaborative of Wisconsin were formed to bring together healthcare providers, payers, and clearinghouses to discuss approaches to implementing HIPAA. The presentations, network contacts, and information sharing that happen are phenomenal. Attending conferences and industry associations such as the Information Systems Security Association and Information Systems Audit and Control Association helps to gain a common understanding of the regulation and implementation approaches. This also provides input as to what the "herd" is doing to be compliant with the regulation.

Final Thoughts

Compliance assurance seeks to demonstrate that the organization has implemented adequate security controls to satisfy the many government regulations. Control frameworks, standards, and technical implementation guides are selected to provide more detailed frameworks to assess and implement the controls necessary. Ongoing monitoring of the frameworks increases the probability that security controls are in operation and that unnecessary risks to availability, confidentiality, and integrity are not being taken. Compliance assurance can have a positive impact on business by being more proactive versus reactive, providing better, more thought-out strategies to mitigate threats and risks, increase visibility of senior management, and align the security program better with the rest of the organization. Compliance assurance should be regarded as more than a paperwork exercise and viewed as a method by which the overall security of the environment can be improved. Owing to the criticality of the need to establish due diligence required for the function, it should be recognized as an ongoing, funded, integral business activity and provided the necessary ongoing business support, time allocation, and resources.

Further Readings

1. Federal Information Security Management Act of 2002, November 27, 2002, http://csrc.nist.gov/policies/FISMA-final.pdf.
2. GAO/AIMB-12.19.6, Federal Information Systems Controls Audit Manual, January 1999, http://gao.gov/special.pubs/ai12.19.6.pdf.
3. Cobit 4.0, IT Governance Institute, http://www.itgi.org.
4. The CSO's Security Compliance Agenda: Benchmark Research Report, *CSI Computer Security Journal*, XXII, November, 2006.
5. Wikipedia, http://www.wikipedia.com.
6. Answers.com, http://www.answers.com.
7. National Institute of Standards and Technology, Special Publications, http://csrc.nist.gov/publications/nistpubs.
8. Defense Information Systems Agency Security Technical Implementation Guides, http://iase.disa.mil/stigs/stig.
9. National Security Agency, Security Configuration Guides, http://www.nsa.gov/snac.
10. ISO/IEC 17799:2005 Information Technology Security Techniques—Code of Practice for Information Security Management, International Standards Organization, http://www.iso.org/iso/en/prods-services/popstds/informationsecurity.html.
11. HIPAA Collaborative of Wisconsin, www.hipaacow.org.
12. The Global State of Information Security 2006, PricewaterhouseCooper, CIO, CSO Magazine, www.pwc.com.
13. SANS Institute Top 20, www.sans.org/top20.
14. NIST National Vulnerability Database, http://nvd.nist.gov.
15. Seventh Report Card on Computer Security, http://republicans.oversight.house.gov/media/pdfs/FY06FISMA.PDF.

Incident Handling

Chapter 29

Enterprise Incident Response and Digital Evidence Management and Handling

Marcus K. Rogers

Contents

Introduction

Terms like "incident response" (IR) and "computer forensics" have become all too familiar in our modern technology-dependent society. Few if any organizations can claim immunity from the possible negative side effects of this dependence, namely misuse and abuse and other criminal behavior. Organizations today are paying more attention to protecting their information technology (IT) assets and the sensitive information that may be contained therein. The attention is directly translated into increased budgets, reallocation of resources (both personnel and equipment), and in some cases increased complexity of the enterprise-computing environment.

Regardless of the industry, there seems to be increasing statutory and regulatory compliance issues related to financial reporting controls (e.g., Sarbanes–Oxley, United States; CEO/CFO Certification, Canada), private information (e.g., Health Insurance Portability and Accountability Act), and financial information (e.g., Gramm–Leach–Bliley Act), to name just a few. The common element with these requirements is the ability to detect when a problem has occurred and the ability to respond in an effective and efficient manner. The consequence of not having these abilities is not only the danger of being in noncompliance and suffering financial or criminal consequences, but also includes the very real danger of never recovering and going out of business in less than a noble fashion. The risks faced today, other than regulatory compliance, stem from the increased frequency and prevalence of external and internal criminal activities. For various reasons that are beyond the scope of this chapter, deviant computer behavior is on the rise and shows no sign of abating. Reported losses due to insider misuse and abuse have been estimated annually to be millions of dollar. Errors and omissions also account for a significant financial drain on organizations; these events can prove more costly than intentional abuse and misuse and often much harder to deal with, as the root cause can be difficult to ascertain. Wrongly configured systems can also endanger our personal safety (e.g., air traffic control systems and power grids) or create a very large national security risk.

There are other business considerations apart from the traditional information assurance and security risks. As the corporate world becomes increasingly more litigious, there is a corresponding increase in responding to requests for discovery for electronically stored information (ESI). An organization may have its house in order regarding compliance, information assurance, errors, and omissions and still be required to investigate, collect evidence, and provide reports in response to a request for discovery by another party who has or is anticipating filing a legal action against the organization (Rowlingson, 2004). The flip side is applicable as well. An organization may be in a position to initiate an action against another party and thereby be making the request for ESI in support of that action.

Those of us who have been in the information assurance and security field for a while recognize that incident management and response is the primary control strategy that organizations implement to meet the various risks that they face on a daily basis. However, what might not be readily apparent is the fact that the IR has evolved into a fairly mature systemic (enterprisewide) process. Owing to increased demand, organizations are becoming more comfortable in dealing with IT-related security incidents and the need to investigate negative events. The corollary to this increased need to respond to incidents in a formal manner is the requirement to collect digital evidence during the course of these incidents and investigations. Unfortunately the management and handling of digital evidence are not a process that most organizations are knowledgeable about or necessarily comfortable in dealing with. Digital evidence and how to deal with it appropriately is an extremely immature concept or process in most organizations.

The purpose of this chapter is to assist with the understanding and comfort in dealing with digital evidence in the context of dealing with an incident. We begin by discussing some of the misperceptions surrounding the collection of digital evidence during an IR situation and then continue on by exploring the IR model. We will then look at the digital evidence management and handling methodology and focus on the similarities and differences between the two models. The chapter concludes with an examination of how to combine the two process models to accentuate the strengths and reduce the inherent weaknesses and shortcomings of both.

Misperceptions

Most discussions on digital evidence and IR ultimately touch on the perceived issues in combining these two models. Many business managers are very concerned with the possible negative impact that collecting evidence will have on the pressing need for business resumption (Rowlingson, 2004). Recall that one of the primary goals of IR is the timely resumption of business to minimize the economic impact of the event. In some industries, every minute that an organization is unable to use its information system translates into hundreds if not thousands of dollars of lost revenue (e.g., stock exchanges and e-commerce) or penalties (e.g., application service providers and telecommunications). Obviously, the loss of consumer or shareholder confidence has an economic impact as well.

The proper handling and management of digital evidence are commonly thought of as a process that interferes with or at the very least slows down the recovery and resumption of business operations. This is not necessarily the case. Even if it were, the failure to act in a reasonable manner that demonstrates due diligence may result in a larger impact than the cost of losing an hour or two. Businesses operating in an industry that falls under the various regulatory compliance requirements may face criminal or civil sanctions for failing to conduct a proper investigation that includes the proper handling of digital evidence.

A properly implemented and planned-out approach to combining digital evidence and IR should function in a manner that allows the two activities to occur in parallel, thus resulting in a minimal slowdown in time needed to recover (see Forensic Readiness). It also ensures that the resumption of business (recovery phase) is handled in a manner that does not place the organization in a more vulnerable position by rushing the recovery and placing the systems back online without being properly secured. Looking at the digital evidence allows the investigators and IR personnel to understand the full impact of the event and conduct a proper root-cause analysis. There are several documented cases in which businesses rushed the process and came back online only to be attacked again in the same or a similar manner. These businesses learned the hard way that patience really is a virtue.

Incident Response Process Model

The term "IR" can be defined in many ways. Several authors have focused on the incident handling aspect of the process, whereas others have dealt with the management and response capability (Rogers, 2007). Regardless of how we formally define the process, the ultimate goal is to respond in a manner that reduces the impact of the incident and allows the organization to recover appropriately so as not to be vulnerable to the same incident in the future. Specific goals of IR can be summed up as follows:

■ Provide an effective and efficient means of dealing with the situation in a manner that reduces the potential impact to the organization.
■ Provide management with sufficient information to decide on an appropriate course of action.
■ Maintain or restore business continuity.
■ Defend against future attacks.
■ Deter attacks through investigation and prosecution.

The process assumes that prior planning has occurred, in the form of policies and procedures specific to IR management and handling, and that proactive (e.g., intrusion detection systems and intrusion prevention systems) as well as reactive controls (e.g., logs and monitoring) are in place.

The actual model used to conduct or implement an enterprisewide IR capability may vary from organization to organization in regard to minute details. However, at the conceptual level, the framework is usually based on a multiphase formal/methodical approach (Rogers, 2007; Rowlingson, 2004) (see Figure 29.1).

Limitations on the size of this chapter prohibit a detailed discussion of each phase, but readers interested in more details can refer to Schultz and Shumway (2002) or Rogers (2007).

It should be recognized that IR is a vital component of any organization's IT security posture. With the move toward a systemic or enterprise approach to information assurance and security, IR has now become part of the information security life cycle (Schultz and Shumway, 2002) (see Figure 29.2). The information security life cycle begins with the detection of an event (incident) and encompasses the response to the incident and any countermeasures that are identified and implemented. The life cycle is dynamic and is a circular process that feeds back into itself.

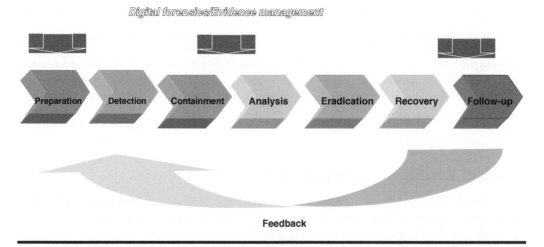

Figure 29.1   Incident response process model.

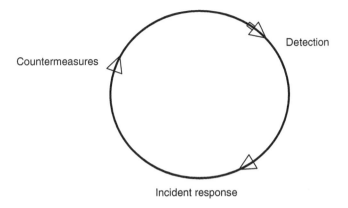

Figure 29.2 Information security life cycle.

This approach also places IR into the system development life cycle and thus IR considerations should be part of every project undertaken. The inclusion of IR in the system development life cycle allows IR to become a systemwide or enterprise-level event. Although there are numerous usages for the term "enterprise," for this discussion enterprise will refer to large-scale implementation across all business units and inclusive of all IT assets. It is important to have as broad a coverage as possible given that systemwide (enterprise) vulnerabilities and threats are a very real occurrence, thus risk must be dealt with at the enterprise level as opposed to the more "siloed" approach of dealing with business units as unrelated entities. The days of IT risk management being purely a technology or an IT business unit problem are long gone.

Cyber-Forensics Process Model

Let us turn our attention to cyber-forensics and digital evidence and examine a common approach or model. Before we jump into the model it is important that we properly define what is meant by "cyber-forensics" or "computer forensics." Cyber-forensics can be defined as follows (from Mandia and Prosise, 2001; Rogers, 2007):

> The scientific examination and analysis of digital data in such a way that the information can be used as evidence in a court of law.

At first glance this definition appears somewhat simplistic, but upon deeper examination it becomes clear that by focusing on the modality of the evidence (digital), the definition overcomes the tendency to have multiple different terms depending upon the location of the evidence. In the past there have been many a heated debate regarding network forensics versus computer forensics, or small-scale versus large-scale device forensics. The common element in all these is in fact the nature of the evidence—it is digital.*

---

* One could argue for the inclusion of an electronic evidence as well as a digital, but most electronic or analog materials are converted to digital for the analysis phase, so the argument is considered moot.

Although it is apparent that currently there are only emerging standards and protocols related to cyber-forensics, the underlying framework is rather generic and is derived from the fundamentals of forensic science or criminalistics. The framework focuses on the investigative nature of the activity and can be broken down into the following phases or steps (Rogers, 2007; Rowlingson, 2004; Taylor et al., 2006):

- Identification
- Collection
- Preservation
- Examination
- Analysis
- Documentation and report

Like the IR process model the cyber-forensics process model is an iterative process that follows a logical approach to dealing with both the crime scene and the durative evidence that is digital in nature.

Incident Response versus Cyber-Forensics

There have been numerous discussions and articles published on the topic of IR and cyber-forensics. Some authors take the view that these two terms are analogous, but this is incorrect. Granted, both IR and cyber-forensics are investigative in nature and both tend to deal with incidents in a reactive manner. However, the major difference lies in the standard of proof that is required. Cyber-forensics is a forensic science and by definition the admissibility of evidence is a major consideration with every task or phase. However, IR is concerned with the resumption of business and the return to a steady state—which, it is hoped, will be less vulnerable than before. IR does not by definition or convention deal with admissibility of evidence concerns, nor does it treat each event as having the potential to end in litigation (Kent et al., 2006; Mandia and Prosise, 2001).

Although the objectives and standards of proof for IR and cyber-forensics are somewhat different, they are not mutually exclusive or contradictory activities; they are very complementary. In fact, exemplary IR programs integrate cyber-forensics into their response capacity. When an event triggers the IR process, care is taken to ensure that the admissibility of evidence, chain of custody of evidence, and ability to reproduce the "scene" are taken into consideration. In most cases, the IR and the cyber-forensics teams work in parallel and each team coordinates its actions with those of the other to ensure that nothing is overlooked. This symbiotic relationship has been recognized by the courts in many countries (e.g., United States, Canada), with the passing of guidelines for determining the cost to the victim of the attack in criminal and civil cases. Here the value of the information and the cost to the organization to recover from and investigate the attack (e.g., prorated system administrator and IR team salary costs) are combined to arrive at an aggregate total loss for the victim (exceeding, it is hoped, the magic $5000 mark that has been established for some jurisdictions).

As indicated in Figure 29.1, the introduction of cyber-forensics and the collection and preservation of digital evidence logically occur during different phases of the IR process model. What is very important to understand is that with digital evidence and cyber-forensics, once the evidence or scene has been contaminated, it cannot be decontaminated; there is no "do over" or "undo" button. Digital evidence and digital scenes are extremely fragile and volatile, and in some cases the evidence has a very short life span.

Digital Evidence

As was stated previously, when dealing with forensic investigations the primary concern is with evidence. Although the focus of this chapter is on digital evidence, we cannot ignore physical evidence or physical crime scenes. In most instances, the digital evidence exists within a physical crime scene. Although we might be looking for spreadsheets, log files, pictures, etc. that are stored on a device, these devices exist in a physical space. The location of the system in a room, how the system or device was physically connected to the network, and what physical access points there were to the room may all be crucial to determining the context of what happened or who had or did not have exclusive opportunity. Although a majority of the incidents investigated are assumed to be the result of external attackers, the reality is that internal attacks are still the most predominant and costly events. With internal attacks, proving unauthorized access or exceeding account privileges may hinge on the physical evidence (e.g., closed-circuit TV and building access logs).

To truly integrate IR and cyber-forensics, it is necessary to reduce the process to its most basic element(s). In our case it is really all about digital evidence management and handling. If we assume that the IR process is fairly well understood and make an even larger assumption that the IR process is reasonably implemented and supported across the organization (i.e., enterprisewide), then the focus needs to be on the digital evidence.

Before moving on to a more detailed discussion of digital evidence management and handling, let us quickly discuss what digital evidence really is and place it within the context of the business environment. So what is really meant by the term digital evidence? One would think that defining digital evidence would be fairly straightforward, yet here again there has been some debate. Rather than getting caught up in semantics, let us turn to the physical domain and criminalistics, which has profited from its history of case law. Saferstein (2004) defines physical evidence as follows:

> Physical objects that establish that a crime has been committed, can provide a link between a crime and its victim, or can provide a link between a crime and the perpetrator (p. 34).

Using this well-established and accepted definition as a foundation, Carrier and Spafford (2003) define digital evidence as follows:

> Digital data that establish that a crime has been committed, can provide a link between a crime and its victim, or can provide a link between a crime and the perpetrator (p. 6).

Within a business environment the digital evidence can encompass the actual data itself, contraband images, rootkits, log files, e-mails, etc. It is obvious that to list all possible examples or sources of digital evidence would be extremely time consuming. However, one of the most common sources or types of digital evidence is based on the concept of records (Ghosh, 2004). As a quick aside, businesses now produce more electronic records than paper records. Records in our context can be subclassified into (a) computer stored, (b) computer generated, and (c) computer generated and stored (Ghosh, 2004).

a. Computer stored pertains to such items as documents, e-mails, chat logs, and other "records" that capture or record what has been created by a person. Here the technology is not an active entity in the creation of the content but is merely a passive receptacle.
b. Computer generated refers to records created without human intervention (nonhuman generated). These records rely on an automated process (this category is important when addressing the business exception to the hearsay problem). Examples here include output from computer programs, log files, event logs, and transaction records.
c. Computer generated and stored covers records that combine automated process and program outputs with human-generated input. Spreadsheets that contain calculations and formulas (computer) and manually entered data (human) are a good example.

Evidence Management and Handling

Regardless of whether the evidence is record based or not, there are some special considerations that one must be aware of when dealing with digital-based evidence. One of the most important considerations is the legal authority to actually collect the evidence. A number of countries are struggling with the balance between protecting the privacy of the individual, while at the same time allowing private organization and government entities to conduct investigations. Cyberspace has drastically changed the notion of what constitutes a reasonable expectation of privacy (REP); when does one's private space overlap with the public domain?

Reasonable Expectation of Privacy

The concept of REP is fundamental to most countries when defining what is an acceptable or unacceptable search and seizure of information/evidence. Businesses are not immune from these issues, as several jurisdictions have codified rules relating to the monitoring of employees and their activities, even when these individuals are using the technology belonging to the business. Investigators must be extremely careful to ensure that they both have a policy-based authority to take action and are legally allowed to. Corporate counsel should be consulted before taking any action. As a rule of thumb it is usually not a good idea to run afoul of the law when conducting an investigation! Even the most noble of intentions is not an excuse here and places the organization in the uncomfortable position of being open to criminal or civil redress.

Volatility

Digital evidence is very fragile (volatile) and in some cases has a very short life span (e.g., data in cache memory and random-access memory [RAM]). Digital evidence can easily be modified or overwritten either as part of the normal system operation or during the identification and collection phase. Care must be taken to ensure that the evidence is handled in such a manner that any modifications are avoided or at least minimized. In the event that modifications occur (e.g., running programs for live memory analysis), detailed documentation must be made to explain the changes in the state of the scene or the evidence from its original state (state at which it was found by the investigator) and what impact this might have on evidence (Casey, 2006; Mandia and Prosise, 2001; Rogers, 2007).

Volume and Commingling

Given the sheer volume of data these days it should come as no surprise that often the data we are interested in (evidence) is commingled with other data that is of no evidentiary value or, in some cases, mixed in with information that is protected (e.g., lawyer–client and trade secret). Most desktop workstations these days have hard drives in excess of 300 GB and some are now being bundled with 1 terabyte (TB) of storage capacity. Business-class server farms routinely exceed 1 TB of data spread across several drives that may or may not reside in the same geographical location (e.g., grid computing). It is vital that an investigator be sensitive to potential commingling and be aware that it is functionally infeasible to expect to search every possible sector of storage for potential evidence. In response to these issues several jurisdictions have defined specific criteria for determining the scope of "discovery" and usually require a detailed investigative plan to ensure that the investigations are conducted in an efficient and effective manner. In an IR situation in which the authority to search is based on the ownership of the technology, commingling and volume of data are no less of a problem.

Integrity

Maintaining and demonstrating the integrity of the digital evidence is one of the integral in the consideration of admissibility of the evidence. Although the ultimate decision of what is admissible and what will be suppressed is up to a judge, precedent has provided guidance on the criteria that provide for the best chance of the evidence being admissible. The main method for demonstrating or proving that the evidence is an exact copy of the original, in the case of creating forensic copies, or that the data/evidence has not been altered from the original time of collection is through hash functions. These hash functions create a digital fingerprint of the data (128 bits in the case of MD5). The hash totals are extremely sensitive to bitwise changes. Most courts have accepted that if the hash totals match, the data has sufficient integrity.

Chain of Custody

The second most important consideration for evidence in general is the chain of custody. Simply put, the chain of custody deals with the who, what, when, where, and how of the collected evidence over its entire life span, from identification and collection to final disposition. If any part of the chain is broken or is doubtful, the evidence in question may be suppressed. At the very least a break in the chain of custody creates doubt in the minds of a judge, jury, arbitrator, etc., which can have serious ramifications if the evidence or its integrity is disputed.

Digital Evidence Life Cycle

Digital evidence management has a life cycle of its own. This life cycle starts with the initial design of systems to capture evidence and ends with determining the evidentiary "weight" of the data (Ghosh, 2004). In between we have the production of records, the collection of evidence, the analysis and examination of the evidence, and the report or presentation (Ghosh, 2004). This model highlights a key component for integrating computer forensics with IR, "design evidence." Design for evidence literally means that those individuals developing and designing systems and applications must understand digital evidence, its business life cycle, and the process model. Here again digital evidence management and handling, like IR, should be part of the system and software development life cycle. Systems across the enterprise must be forensically aware or, as Rowlingson (2004) termed it, have forensic readiness. History has shown us that trying to retrofit something onto an already in production system or process is costly and usually ineffective.

Forensic Readiness

As was mentioned earlier, the forensic process needs to be conducted in parallel with any IR actions. To facilitate this, the typical approach of being reactive needs to be modified. Organizations need to be proactive and develop and implement policies, guidelines, and procedures that clearly articulate how the two processes will interact and who will be responsible for overseeing the combined approach and clearly define the so-called rules of engagement (Kent et al., 2006; Rowlingson, 2004). Waiting until one is engaged in the chaos of dealing with an incident is not a good time to start trying to institute this combined model or create policies, etc., literally on the fly; this ad hoc approach is doomed to failure for obvious reasons (numerous organizations bear witness to this fact).

Although it is beyond the scope of this chapter to go into great detail as to how to prepare properly, it is necessary to at least touch on the higher-level concepts that must be considered. Apart from having policies and procedures in place as the National Institute of Standards and Technology (NIST) (Kent et al., 2006) recommends, it is actually necessary to have personnel trained in cyber-forensics. Remember, the skill sets for cyber-forensics are similar to, yet different from, IR skills. It is acceptable to have individuals cross-trained, but do not assume someone with IR training can perform an acceptable cyber-forensics investigation and vice versa. The cyber-forensics training, education, and ongoing skill development will have costs associated with them. But, just as with the IR teams, these costs are marginal compared to the cost of properly dealing with an incident.

An excellent primer on considerations for implementing forensic readiness into the IR process is the NIST-SP800/86 Guideline (Kent et al., 2006). In a nutshell the guideline recommends that organizations:

- Have a capability to perform cyber-forensics,
- Determine a priori who is responsible for cyber-forensics,
- Have incident handling teams with robust forensics capabilities,
- Have many teams that can participate in forensics,
- Have forensic considerations clearly addressed in policies, and
- Create and maintain guidelines and procedures for performing forensic tasks.

Rowlingson (2004) also provides a framework for implementing a "forensic readiness program" that is more focused on the private sector and corporate entities. The ten tasks he lists are similar to the recommendations by NIST but predate the formal publication of the NIST document:

- Define the business scenarios that require digital evidence.
- Identify available sources and different types of potential evidence.
- Determine the evidence collection requirement.
- Establish a capability for securely gathering legally admissible evidence to meet the requirement.

- Establish a policy for secure storage and handling of potential evidence.
- Ensure monitoring is targeted to detect and deter major incidents.
- Specify circumstances in which escalation to a full formal investigation (which may use the digital evidence) should be launched.
- Train staff in incident awareness, so that all those involved understand their role in the digital evidence process and the legal sensitivities of evidence.
- Document an evidence-based case describing the incident and its impact.
- Ensure legal review to facilitate action in response to the incident.

Although policy and procedures are important to ensure that IR and the management and handling of digital evidence interact properly, there are also some technical considerations to forensic readiness (Kent et al., 2006; Mandia and Prosise, 2001; Rogers, 2007; Rowlingson, 2004). These considerations build on the technical capacity to collect meaningful and trustworthy digital evidence. Log and event files are probably the most common sources of information and evidence. But, if the system or network has been completely compromised, then how do we trust these sources of information? If proper care is not taken, then the data collected or the record is not trustworthy enough to be used as evidence, even if it can be trusted to help recover systems and resume business operations.

Given that there has not been a considerable amount of applied testing or implementation of forensic-ready technology at the enterprise network level, it is prudent to discuss this only at the research level. As NIST and Rowlingson (2004) have indicated, the actual design and development of this technology stem from a thorough understanding of IR requirements and sound digital evidence or forensic practices. The current research in the area of forensic readiness of enterprise systems shows promise in several general areas:

- Kernel-level forensic capacity
- Distributed authenticated logging
- Digitally signed and encrypted logs
- Automated live forensic imaging of all affected systems

Hooking into the actual kernel level of an operating system to obtain valid and reliable information on what is being executed and by which process is extremely important. Those working in antivirus research have recognized the need to operate at the kernel level as opposed to any of the higher layers of abstraction; the same holds for obtaining information to be used as evidence.

Logs are a vital and rich source of information and potential evidence as to what transpired and the approximate timeline of events. However, we need to be able to trust the logs from these systems. This can lead to a conundrum: how do we trust logs from systems that we assume have been compromised and thus are now untrustworthy? A possible solution is to distribute the appropriate security and event logs to other systems not part of the primary network. These systems would require proper authentication not tied to any information that may be present on the potentially compromised systems. Although not foolproof, distributed authenticated logging would definitely increase the cost of the attack to the attacker and allow for greater trust of these logs.

Tied to the notion of distributed and authenticated logs is the integrity of the logs themselves. Even if we can show that the logs are trustworthy we need to demonstrate not only that they are a true and accurate recording of the events at the time of recording, but also that they have not been altered at any time from their creation to their presentation or use as evidence in a legal proceeding. A process that automatically signs the logs with a hash total that is stored in a trusted database and then encrypts the logs that are then stored in an authenticated and distributed manner would be beneficial.*

The ability to collect and analyze live systems and running memory is becoming increasingly more important. Large enterprise systems cannot be taken offline or shut down during the investigative process for business or technical reasons. Likewise, shutting down a system with 1–16 GB of RAM results in the loss of a great deal of potential evidence. However, how to collect the evidence with a live system in a forensically sound matter is difficult. To perform the collection one must load code or execute an operation on the suspected system, thus changing the state of the system and potentially overwriting evidence that may have been in memory. This is not a comfortable situation considering that forensics is concerned about the admissibility of any derived evidence. The ability to analyze the content of memory, etc., once collected is beyond the scope of this discussion but suffice to say it is rather difficult. The reality is that live system and memory collection and analysis will soon surpass the current approach of dealing with a powered-off (in a forensically sound manner, it is hoped) or "dead" analysis.

Summary

The business environment is a seemingly constantly changing landscape. The demands placed on information security professionals is also changing to meet the new demands of business and technology. The ability to conduct effective and proper investigations is now a standard requirement for most organizations. This requirement has arisen due to various forces such as regulatory compliance, requests for discovery that include ESI, and the almost ubiquitous use of technology by businesses in general.

We are in a similar position today with cyber-forensics (digital evidence management and handling) that we were in about five years ago with IR. Organizations today are struggling with implementing digital forensic capabilities into their enterprise-level response processes and many are taking shortcuts and liberties with the management and handling of digital evidence. This is an extremely slippery slope that has some very serious and tangible consequences to businesses. Dealing with digital evidence occurs within the context of a forensic event and by its very nature carries the requirements and obligations related to the admissibility of evidence into a legal or quasi-legal arena. Criminal and civil liability considerations must be taken into account; this illustrates the fact that although cyber-forensics and IR are related processes they are not identical and must be treated as such.

Digital evidence has its unique characteristics and considerations that traditional physical evidence does not necessarily have, yet at the same time digital evidence resides in physical space. It is, therefore, important to understand the life cycle of digital evidence, its uniqueness, and where digital evidence management and handling fit into the IR process. IR and digital evidence management and handling are not mutually exclusive processes. Both models have considerable overlap and in some cases are mutually dependent upon each other. The key to combining these two investigative models or tools successfully is prior planning, such as developing policies, guidelines, and procedures that address both. IR and cyber-forensics teams as well as managers need to be

---

* One could argue that the database hash totals could be altered and thus they must be signed, etc., until we collapse under the weight of the infinite loop of signing the signer. Fortunately, the courts have recognized that at some point it is necessary to trust a person unless evidence exists to the contrary. Thus, unless proved otherwise, the database administrator could testify that nothing was altered.

properly cross-trained for everyone involved to understand the dependencies that each process has and the effect, if any, that certain actions may have on the other's primary goal.

Management needs to abandon the outdated notion that dealing with digital evidence will slow down or impair the time of recovery. With increased public and government scrutiny, speedy business resumption must be tempered with the proper mix of patience and strategic thinking. Knee-jerk reactions to incidents are no longer appropriate and are actually more costly in the long run. It seems plausible that attacks against our enterprise IT infrastructures from both external and internal sources will continue to grow before any type of plateau occurs. Thus, we must use and adapt security controls and tools to aid us in our effort to protect our systems and our information. The combining of process models and tools such as IR and digital evidence management and handling is a prime example of the synergistic activities that must continue if we are to deal effectively with the risk that we face today and will face tomorrow.

References

Carrier, B., and Spafford, E. (2003). Getting physical with the digital investigation process. *International Journal of Digital Evidence*, 2(2).

Casey, E. (2006). Investigating sophisticated security breaches. *Communications of the ACM*, 49(2), 48–54.

Ghosh, A. (2004). *Guidelines for the Management of IT Evidence*. Paper presented at the APEC Telecommunications and Information Working Group: 29th Meeting. Retrieved November 1, 2006, from http://unpan1.un.org/intradoc/groups/public/documents/APCITY/UNPAN016411.pdf.

Kent, K., Chevalier, S., Grance, T., and Dang, H. (2006). *NIST SP800-86: Guide to Integrating Forensic Techniques into Incident Response*. Retrieved January 5, 2007, from http://csrc.nist.gov/publications/nistpubs/800-86/SP800-86.pdf.

Mandia, K., and Prosise, C. (2001). *Incident Response: Investigating Computer Crime*. New York: McGraw-Hill.

Rogers, M. (2007). Law, regulations, investigations and compliance. In H. Tipton and K. Henry (Eds.), *Official (ISC)² Guide to CISSP CBK* (pp. 683–718). Boca Raton, FL: Auerbach.

Rowlingson, R. (2004). A ten step process for forensic readiness. *International Journal of Digital Evidence*, 2(3).

Saferstein, R. (2004). *Criminalistics: An Introduction to Forensic Science*. Upper Saddle River: Pearson Education.

Schultz, E., and Shumway, R. (2002). *Incident Response: A Strategic Guide to Handling System and Network Security Breaches*. Indianapolis, IN: New Riders.

Taylor, R., Caeti, T., Loper, D. K., Fritsch, E., and Leiderbach, J. (2006). *Digital Crime and Digital Terrorism*. Upper Saddle River, NJ: Pearson Prentice Hall.

Chapter 30

Security Information Management Myths and Facts

Sasan Hamidi

Contents

Introduction

In February 2007, I was part of a panel at the RSA Conference addressing the subject of security information management or SIM. The panel consisted of industry practitioners, specifically those who had implemented this somewhat new and complex technology. It was intended to serve as a "lessons learned." However, I soon realized that the one hour dedicated to this issue was not even a particle of dust in the vast space of this subject. First of all, there seems to be a great deal of confusion regarding the nomenclature itself. So, if SIM stands for security information management, then what is SEM (security event management)? Are the technologies the same? If yes, why the different acronyms, and if no, what are the similarities and differences? I was besieged after the panel by attendees and those who could not attend for the lack of space in the massive room. The questions were mostly about fundamentals and how this technology could be smoothly implemented (normally SIM is not synonymous with words such as "smooth," "easy," "eventless," etc.).

Motivation

Originally, when I was asked to write about this subject, I thought that it would be appropriate to dedicate the entire paper to the fundamentals. However, I realized that by having implemented this technology (pardon the use of the word "technology" as it is a loose fit—I will explain later) two years earlier, the experience gained was not only very relevant, but also incredibly valuable. One can Google the vast databases of the Internet and find hundreds of hits on this subject but it would be extremely difficult to find an actual implementation case, from beginning to the end (the word "end" does not really apply in this context because the implementation and operation of a SIM resemble the mathematical equivalent of the old classic "Gideon's Trumpet," where the issue at hand does not have an end or a "limit"). I should mention that I am a big advocate of the "Socrates" method of teaching and presentation, in which the subject is explained using actual "cases" and real-world examples, rather than merely defining the terms and implementation conditions. (This method of teaching is utilized by many law schools as cases are studied and adjudications analyzed to understand their relevance to laws).

Background

In the mid-1990s, it became apparent that manual analysis of logs belonging to critical systems (UNIX in particular) was not practical. Systems administrators began to write "scripts" that would search through megabytes of data for certain events. For example, if the number of unsuccessful log-in attempts exceeded a certain threshold, the script would make a note. Other searches looked for direct "root" access and guest accounts. The practice became standard mainly in the UNIX community. The problems with this method were multifold:

1. The Windows operating system did not have the flexibility of UNIX; scripts could not be easily written and did not extend to many events.
2. The strength of this method was only as good as the script including many of the common events (and even then, there were always some that were missed or overlooked).
3. The results would be dumped into a file, which would then be reviewed by an administrator or security personnel. In almost all cases, the results were not available until the next day or days later.

All of the above issues would then render the script method ineffective. It was not until a few years later that vendors used this methodology and designed software to address some of its shortcomings. However, it took a few more years before these products matured.

In addition to the obvious security advantages, the new generation of SEM tools (as they were referred to in the early 2000s) addressed another much needed issue, compliance. Section 404 of the Sarbanes–Oxley Act of 2002 required publicly held companies to review financially relevant systems' security events (in-scope systems) and document them for internal and external auditors' inspection. These "controls" (as they are referred to by the Act) required that organizations devise policies and procedures to retain and review logs of in-scope systems.

Clarification of Terms—Technology Defined

Earlier I mentioned the use of SIM and SEM. To add to the confusion, there are other terms such as "log management," "event funneling," "log aggregation," and a few others that are less common. It would not be prudent to define and analyze all these terms, as they are all so very loosely or, in some cases, tightly coupled. Instead, the clarification will consist of explaining what the technology is intended to address, and it would be up to the reader to use an appropriate term to frame it. For the purposes of this discussion and simplicity, we will refer to this "technology" as SIM. SIM also happens to be the word chosen by the information security industry today.

In a way, SIM brought together all of the areas mentioned earlier. It incorporated all of the concepts mentioned and more.

1. It made it possible to aggregate logs of many different systems with various formats (normalization of logs).
2. It centralized the management of security events (or security information), making it possible to build sophisticated and effective security operation centers (SOCs).
3. It allowed real-time analysis of events, which previously was not possible. The term "real time" is somewhat misleading, however, because network and system delays do not make alerting available instantaneously.
4. It provided correlation and intelligence; perhaps the most important and notable characteristic of SIMs. Without "C&I" these systems would be just glorified log aggregators.
5. It improved forensics analysis of events.
6. It improved incident response handling.

Log Aggregation

Linux, Solaris, Windows, Cisco IOS, mainframes, firewalls, intrusion detection and prevention systems with proprietary operating systems (IDS/IPS), and other platforms make it impossible to feed events directly to a correlation engine (CE; explained later). If all these platforms employed the UNIX "syslog" format, it would make it much easier for the SIM's CE to understand and decipher the messages; but, clearly, that is not the case. Checkpoint uses its own proprietary format, and then there are SNMP traps. In this case, "normalization" of logs is an absolute requirement. Normalization is the process of reducing the complex structure of data into a simple form without losing all its attributes and characteristics. Once the data is normalized it is then fed into the correlation engine (SIM vendors employ many different architectures; however, the underlying premise remains constant).

Centralized Management

With today's complex networks, multiple data centers, global hubs, disaster recovery sites, and many flavors of platforms, the information security well-being of organizations depends on how well the millions of events generated by these systems are collected and analyzed. Centralization of data allows the otherwise disparate and seemingly unrelated information to be gathered, analyzed, and presented as a single source. This is crucial in building a successful SOC. An organization with a well-designed and deployed SIM funnels events from everywhere in the network into a central console that is being monitored by level I or level II support personnel. The advantage is that information sharing becomes much more robust and the speed by which incidents are responded to is improved. Add this to the capability of many SIMs with built-in IPSs and one can have instantaneous shunning of attacks. Of course, a great deal more thought should be given to activating the IPS capabilities of SIMs as they can block legitimate production traffic as well.

Real-Time Analysis

Earlier I mentioned the archaic practice of writing scripts to search system logs for security events. I also wrote that it could be days before the results would be available for review by system administrators. In some cases, this delayed reaction could cost companies hundreds and even millions of dollars. A brute force attack would have bells ringing through a SIM-based solution. Alerts can be routed to the Help Desk, the SOC, the enterprise operation center (EOC), e-mail accounts, cell phones, pagers, and PDAs. The delay in response would be reduced from days to minutes practically. This improvement would have a direct impact in terms of not only reducing the risk of financial loss but also avoiding embarrassing and negative media coverage. In essence, real-time analysis closes the gap between incident and response.

Correlation of Events

There are many catchy words and phrases in today's IT world—words designed to make a technology sexy and slick. In my 20 years of experience in this industry I have heard it all; and frankly, I have never been a fan of using such terminology. From time to time, a word comes along that perfectly describes the underlying premise, theory, or technology. I believe "correlation" is one of those words. One does not have to dig deep to figure out what correlation means when it is put in the context of security events. Sure, there may be some confusion as to its true benefits, or how it actually works, but there is never a doubt as to its meaning.

In a typical network, there are routers, switches, firewalls, Web servers, Web applications, etc. Each component generates messages either because of its own internal design or as it processes data. The components communicate with one another and in doing so generate more messages. There are interactions between E-Commerce systems, Web application servers, databases (more likely placed inside the network segmented by firewalls), and other pieces of the infrastructure spread out through the entire enterprise. It would be nearly impossible for typical human resources to sift through and decipher all these messages and even more challenging to make sense of events that happen separately but almost simultaneously in different areas of the network. This is certainly a daunting task. Event correlation provides the following:

1. It reduces the amount of traffic by setting thresholds for certain alerts—for example, instead of generating thousands of alerts "root log in" the threshold is set to three messages per minute.
2. It makes sense of seemingly unrelated anomalies and tries to establish a relationship among them—for example, a Domain Name System (DNS) poisoning attack launched simultaneously in different parts of the network. The event correlator determines that the attacks have the same source IP and orders boundary routers and firewalls to modify their ACL and rule sets to block the address.
3. It translates complex data to detect whether traffic is safe.

Forensics Analysis

The term real-time forensics is new; the concept, however, is not. The technology has been on the wish list of many security personnel. In the traditional forensics world, after an incident has occurred, one would gather logs and events, collect hard drives, bring production systems to a halt, freeze applications, interview employees, call in the experts to tear apart TCP/UDP packets, and perform a slew of other dizzying tasks that could take up tremendous human and financial resources. This linear approach to forensics analysis could take days or even weeks to complete the analysis; by then, the organization may have lost valuable proprietary data and the perpetrator would have been able to clean up their footprints. The new "parallel forensics processing" is a combination of intelligence, correlation, and real-time processing of security events that do not take place sequentially. It is important to note that, even with the sophistication of SIMs today, a comprehensive and robust incident response policy is absolutely critical to the overall effectiveness of incident handling.

Correlation is an integral part of modern SIM systems. As a matter of fact, one of the most important criteria that I recommend for the evaluation of an effective SIM is how well the CE responds to disparate attacks, which can be simulated using common tools (such as Nmap).

Incident Response Handling

One of the very first tasks that I undertook as the chief information security officer of my company was to write a comprehensive and robust incident response policy (IRP). I cannot stress the importance of a well-written and practical IRP. Aside from the obvious benefits of having an IRP (I will not go into explaining the typical benefits, as it is one of the most saturated subjects of information security), it is mandated by legislative and regulatory statutes, such as Sarbanes–Oxley, Section 404. And for those organizations that process credit cards, the Payment Card Industry Data Security Standards compel them to have one as well. However, having been the author and implementer of many IRPs, I have learned that even the best documents can suffer from what I refer to as "field challenges." Field challenges consist of the following:

1. The time that it takes to collect forensics information.
    a. Determining which systems/applications have been compromised.
    b. Preserving the evidence according to the "chain of custody" rules.
    c. Traveling to multiple locations to do (a) and (b).

    d. Halting systems that may have been compromised but are not yet determined as such (sometimes infected systems do not exhibit abnormal behavior and time is needed to search through system and application logs to make this determination).

    e. Interviewing systems administrators, developers, security staff, etc.

2. Examination of information collected.

    a. Look through hard drives and system and application logs. If forensics tools and in-house expertise are not available, media and logs must be sent off-site for analysis.

    b. Look though hand-written notes collected from interviews and other observations.

3. Reporting: Place all findings in a manner understandable for management and law enforcement.

For the sake of simplicity I have kept the above to only three items; a more detailed and comprehensive list could include more than ten items. What does this all mean? All of the above efforts translate into time—time that a security officer does not have. A typical information security incident could sometimes take up to 30 days to investigate. A well-designed and configured SIM with detailed forensics capabilities, such as "deep packet inspection," could reduce the incident response time to hours, even minutes, versus days or maybe even months. In cases in which deep packet inspection is required to determine the type of attack, source or destination spoofing, and payload changes, manual examination of these packets is nearly impossible. Even if there is resource constraint, time is a factor. SIMs equipped with this type of analysis will take the examiner directly to the infected packet and by clicking through hyperlinked areas show the exact bit impacted. This is a tremendous gain in terms of time and resources. Almost all SIMs come equipped with reporting capabilities that enable the user to generate incident reports in a matter of minutes. Canned and custom reports provide flexibility and ease for security officers.

Challenges

As most technologies make certain tasks not only possible but more efficient and accurate (like sifting through gigabytes of log data), they also present unintended challenges that in some cases, at least initially, require tremendous resources and expertise to overcome. SIMs are not immune to this "side effect." In this case, however, the efforts are well worth it; the end result could be a state-of-the-art SOC with the SIM as its core component. This is an important point, because the investment in a typical SIM is so high that tearing it down and starting over would not be practical in most cases.

In the following, I have highlighted several challenges based on personal experience, although I must confess that there may be other challenges that others may have faced that are not well publicized.

Deployment

A badly deployed SIM could have grave consequences. A false sense of security is perhaps the most prevalent. I have explained in more detail deployment strategies, again, based on my personal experience. Although I had researched SIMs for years and have written extensively about them, the practical experience of deploying one is invaluable.

Configuration

There are many checks and balances to consider when configuring a SIM; for example, checking "agents" for reporting and database issues. A misconfigured SIM will not be effective.

Agent Coverage

To maximize the effectiveness of SIMs one must make sure that all platforms are covered. At the time of my evaluation (early 2004), no vendor provided support for all the platforms spelled out in my request for proposal, and only one was willing to develop one for a particular platform. For proprietary platforms and applications, one must consider SIM vendors who are willing to work with their clients to develop the right agents. Make sure that your contract includes service level agreements with regard to this issue.

Rules

Many SIMs employ a combination of behavior-based modeling and rules to catch anomalies. The systems are generally shipped with a set of canned rules, signatures designed to catch many of the common forms of attacks. Some SIMs, such as netForensics, offer a set of rich graphical tools that allow the user to devise new rules without the use of complicated script languages. As SOC personnel and security engineers become familiar with the system and the environment that it monitors, they can build custom rules targeting a set of specific events. However, even with the existence of these tools, writing effective correlation rules is very challenging. I would recommend attending the SIM's technical training (almost all SIM vendors offer extensive off-site training that includes a day or two on the subject of rules).

Event Filtering

Perhaps the most complex and challenging of all implementation tasks; as I have mentioned several times, network components generate gigabytes of data that funnel into the SIM's databases. The correlation and rules engines pour through this data attempting to make sense of them. In the process, thousands of alarms are generated that include "false positives" and "false negatives." False positives are alerts that indicate a potential issue when in fact there is none. A false negative (which happens to be an even bigger concern) is when an anomaly is missed by the SIM. Initially, after deployment, it would be safe to assume that at least 50% of the generated alerts are false positives. These could be normal chatter among various network components such as the Virtual Router Redundancy Protocol between firewalls for failover. It takes weeks, if not months, for dedicated and knowledgeable security staff to pore over these messages, identify their sources and destination, perform research, contact the SIM vendor, and work with system administrators to eliminate them.

Below are some guidelines for message filtering:

1. Stop message flow from the source—a responsible system administrator will turn off messaging for a specific event at the source.
2. Stop message flow at SIM—rules can be written to ignore the message. Action can be "drop," which eliminates the message altogether from the database, or "store," which means ignore the message but keep it in the database for future use. Future use could include forensics and compliance.
3. Examine the "canned" rules and write rules customized for your environment (please see more on this topic later).

I found that in the process of message filtering, finding systems that are misconfigured is not uncommon. During the 16 weeks of intense alert filtering, we discovered several UNIX and Windows

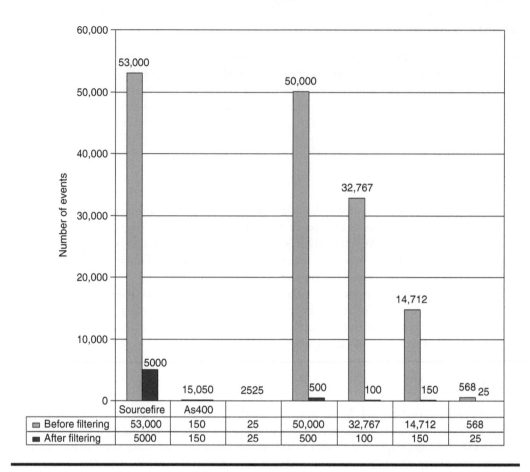

	Sourcefire	As400					
Before filtering	53,000	150	25	50,000	32,767	14,712	568
After filtering	5000	150	25	500	100	150	25

Figure 30.1 Graph indicating the number of reductions before and after even filtering. *Note*: **Operating system-specific information has been removed from this graph for security purposes.**

servers that had not been configured correctly. For example, a DNS server was generating 443 and 80 traffic, which indicated that the Internet Information Server was running and the system was functioning as a Web server as well (although the system administrator had not intended as such).

Figure 30.1 depicts a graph showing the number of alerts before and after alert filtering efforts at my organization.

Deployment Tips

1. A sound architecture is priceless. Let us not forget the fact that SIM is an expensive and complex technology. Regardless of what the vendor claims, rest assured that deployment is not going to be easy. With fragmented LANs, ensure that your SIM, whether appliance based or not, has a view into every segment of the network that you intend to monitor. Virtual LANs can obstruct the flow of information into the SIM's database. Obtain an up-to-date copy of your organization's network topology and identify all critical areas.

2. Ensure the collection of data from all sources—by correctly configuring and architecting the SIM one can ensure that all network segments are covered.

3. Devise controls and policies—how do you ensure that all your devices are pointing their logs to the database of your SIM? The first step is to write policies and procedures in support of this item. In my organization, we require two sets of documentation with every new device: one is a Change Control Form (CCF), which is part of Change Management, the other is a form called a New Device Certification Form (NDCF). The CCF is required because a change in production is about to occur; a new device is being added to the environment. This is required even if the system is a developing one, because it is not known whether it will be running production data. The purpose of an NDCF is to allow the Office of Information Security (OIS) to perform a thorough vulnerability scan of the platform and applications for the new system. It also allows the OIS to ensure that this device is properly configured to send its logs to the SIM database. The OIS logs device information into a database for future checks. Additionally, there is a control written to oversee this entire process. The control is tested monthly by the OIS and internal audit.

4. There is, of course, technology to support the procedures above. Your SIM may come equipped with technology that can detect new devices as they are plugged into the network or removed from it. This would make it easy to pinpoint such devices and alert the appropriate department. In many cases, however, this technology is supplied by a third party (Sourcefire's RNA is such an example). In either case, it is invaluable to have such a technology to support all policies, procedures, and manual audits.

5. Staff, staff, and then staff—I cannot begin to stress this point enough, that the most successful SIM deployment is not the one that is well designed and implemented, but the one that is well managed. There is no sense in deploying a technology like this if the organization does not have the human resources dedicated to its management and maintenance. SIM requires minute-by-minute attendance. Whether it is the daily update of signature files, watching critical alerts flow into the console, looking for false positives and negatives, or merely checking the overall health of the systems, it is extremely demanding and unforgiving. When planning for a SIM the budget must allow for resources in addition to EOC and Help Desk personnel.

Conclusion

It took nearly one year and the efforts of two people dedicated to the evaluation and testing of SIMs before we were ready to announce the product that best fit our environment. Choosing a SIM is not easy; but it is not magic either. There are many considerations and issues that must be well studied. I found that developing a "matrix" with our requirements seemed to work best. For example, we wanted a system that supported all of our platforms. In the end, although such a product did not exist, we found a vendor who was willing to develop an agent needed to support the platform.

This was indeed one of the most challenging deployments I had been personally involved with. But, it is never over; once you make a commitment to a SIM, your job never ends.

Index

415